Industrial Energy Systems
Handbook

RIVER PUBLISHERS SERIES IN ENERGY ENGINEERING AND SYSTEMS

Series Editors

BOBBY RAUF
Semtrain, LLC
USA

The "River Publishers Series in Energy Engineering and Systems" is a series of comprehensive academic and professional books focussing on the theory and applications behind various energy-related technologies and control systems. The series features handbooks for related technology, as well as manuals on the fundamentals and theoretical aspects of energy engineering projects.

The main aim of this series is to be a reference for academics, researchers, managers, engineers, and other professionals in related matters with energy engineering and control systems.

Topics covered in the series include, but are not limited to:

- Energy engineering;
- Machinery;
- Testing;
- HVAC;
- Electricity and electronics;
- Water systems;
- Industrial control systems;
- Web based systems;
- Automation;
- Lighting controls.
- Difference between AC and DC;
- Batteries;
- Electrical Power;
- VFD's and Motors.

For a list of other books in this series, visit www.riverpublishers.com

Industrial Energy Systems Handbook

Albert Williams

Institute of Energy Professionals Africa, South Africa

LONDON AND NEW YORK

Published 2022 by River Publishers
River Publishers
Alsbjergvej 10, 9260 Gistrup, Denmark
www.riverpublishers.com

Distributed exclusively by Routledge
4 Park Square, Milton Park, Abingdon, Oxon OX14 4RN
605 Third Avenue, New York, NY 10017, USA

Industrial Energy Systems Handbook / Albert E. Williams.

Routledge is an imprint of the Taylor & Francis Group, an informa business

ISBN 978-87-7022-660-8 (print)
ISBN 978-87-7022-659-2 (online)
ISBN 978-1-003-35643-1 (ebook master)

While every effort is made to provide dependable information, the publisher, authors, and editors cannot be held responsible for any errors or omissions.

This handbook has been rewritten from the original BEAT Course which was based on the SADC Industrial Energy Efficiency Project authored originally by the Energy Training Foundation, prior to the name change to Institute of Energy Professionals Africa (IEPA).

Contributors to the corrections and updates were Louis Lagrange, Albert Williams, Eustace Njeru, and Yolanda de Lange.

Contents

Chapter 2
Fundamental Principles of Energy   25
Louis Lagrange

Chapter 3
Energy Conversion and Efficiency   43
Louis Lagrange

Chapter 5
Fundamentals of Thermal Energy   119
Albert Williams

Chapter 6

Energy Management Systems and Industrial Energy Audits   **139**
Albert Williams & Yolanda de Lange

Chapter 7

Instrumentation and Control   **159**
Albert Williams

Chapter 8
Energy Investigation Support Tools   179
Albert Williams

Chapter 9
Fuels, Furnaces, and Fired Equipment   195
Albert Williams

Chapter 12

Motors and Drives   **301**

Albert Williams & Eustace Njeru

List of Contributors

de Lange, Yolanda, *Institute of Energy Professionals Africa, South Africa*

Lagrange, Louis Francois, *University of the Free State, South Africa*

Njeru, Eustace Murithi, *Energy and Petroleum Regulatory Authority, Kenya*

Williams, Albert Edward, *Institute of Energy Professionals Africa, South Africa*

List of Figures

List of Tables

Chapter 1

Global Energy Situation on Climate Change

Albert Williams

Institute of Energy Professionals Africa, South Africa

Increasing levels of heat-trapping greenhouse gases – i.e. carbon dioxide (CO_2), methane, and nitrous oxide – in the atmosphere are causing global average temperatures to rise. Surface temperatures in each of the last three decades have been successively warmer than in any preceding decade since 1850.

Between 1880 and 2012, global average temperatures (land and sea temperatures combined) rose 0.85°C. Ocean warming accounts for more than 90% of the energy accumulated between 1971 and 2010. This is in contrast to only about 1% stored in the atmosphere.

Globally, the ocean has warmed the most in the water closest to the surface, with the upper 75 m warming 0.11°C per decade from 1971–2010. Scientists expect global mean surface temperatures to increase an additional 0.3–0.7°C from 2016–2035. Scientists also expect that global surface temperature change will likely exceed 1.5°C between 2081–2100 in all but the most conservative projections. 2020 was the 44th consecutive year with a global temperature above the 20th century average.

1.1 The Negative Impacts and Forecasts of Climate Change

1.1.1 Sea levels

Today, on average, seas are rising 25% faster than in the late twentieth century. Researchers conclude that even if the strictest global emissions standards are met, sea levels would still rise from 0.7 to 1.2 m within the next two centuries. Dozens of countries are exposed to the risk of coastal flooding caused by rising seas. Nearly one-third of the world's population, or 2.4 billion people, live within 100 kilometers of a coastline and vulnerable to seas rising even faster.

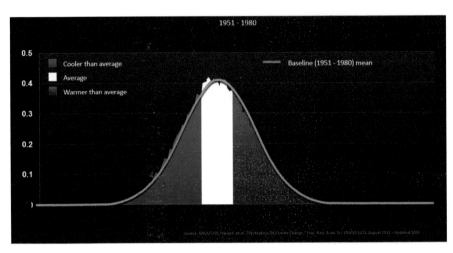

Figure 1.1 Standard deviation graph of the frequency of cool, average, and warm summer temperatures in the Northern Hemisphere, 1951–1980.

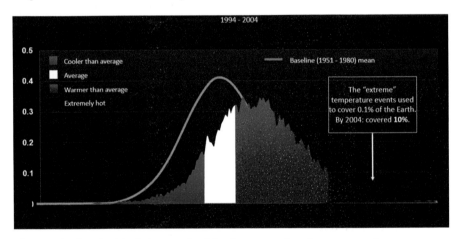

Figure 1.2 Standard deviation graph of the frequency of cool, average, and warm summer temperatures in the Northern Hemisphere, 1994–2004 (compared to a 1951–1980 base period).

Winter seasons are also becoming shorter, with more warm days perpetuating ice melt and increasing sea-level rise. Melting glaciers and ice sheets in Greenland and Antarctica are major contributors to rising seas. Between 2011 and 2014, satellite and modeling data found that the Greenland ice sheet lost an approximated 269 billion tons of snow and ice annually, raising sea levels about 0.74 millimeters (mm) each year. Ice melting into water in glaciers, together with the plant and microbial life it fosters, darken the ice and increase absorption of solar energy, which leads to even more melting.

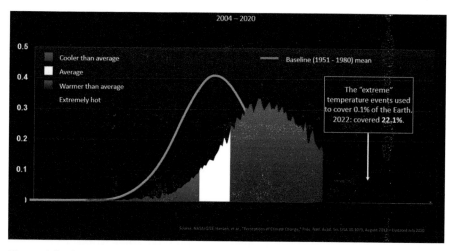

Figure 1.3 Standard deviation graph of the frequency of cool, average, and warm summer temperatures in the Northern Hemisphere, 2005–2015 (compared to a 1951–1980 base period).

In addition, scientists are researching the impact of melting ice streams, which are located inside and under ice sheets, lubricating them and causing them to move more quickly into the sea. Nearly half of the past century's sea-level rise comes from thermal expansion, the phenomenon where water expands when heated. Increased ocean heat means oceans are literally occupying more space. Thermal expansion is responsible for about 1.6 mm per year of sea-level rise.

Projections show global sea-level rise could range from 0.2 to 2.5 m by 2100. Experts estimate that by the end of the century, 48 islands may disappear due to rising seas worldwide. The melting has been accelerating quite dramatically; four times faster than originally thought. By 2050, flooding is projected to inundate coastal cities an average of 40 times more often than present day. The risk of extreme floods – such as those caused by Hurricane Sandy in 2012 – will likely increase to about once per year after 2100.

1.1.2 Ocean currents

Oceans circulate heat around the world through massive surface and deep-water currents – one of the largest of which is the Atlantic Meridional Overturning Circulation (AMOC) – which help regulate global climate and weather. Warmer, less dense water can slow down ocean heat circulation, as can salinity changes (a notable consequence of runoff from melting land-based freshwater ice). According to the IPCC (Intergovernmental Panel on Climate Change), it is very likely (90–100% confidence) that the AMOC will weaken between 11 and 34%, on average, over the twenty-first century.

This slowdown could mean cooling across the entire Northern Hemisphere while parts of the Southern Hemisphere become hotter. While cooler temperatures might sound good in the face of global warming, it could mean massive sea-level rise in eastern North America and shifting rainfall patterns that could dry up Europe's rivers.

1.1.3 Coral reefs

Coral reefs are the most biodiverse habitats on the planet, home to nearly one-quarter of all ocean species, yet occur in less than 1% of the world's oceans. Prolonged high water temperatures (among other factors) can cause coral polyps to expel their symbiotic algae partners (zooxanthellae) that help them produce food. The result is coral bleaching, which puts the health of the whole reef system at risk. The world's largest reef, the Great Barrier off the Australian coast, frequently suffers from catastrophic bleaching events in response to regular heat stress.

1.1.4 Ocean acidity

Climate change is making oceans increasingly acidic, disrupting natural processes and entire ecosystems. The ocean plays a critical role in the storage of carbon, as it holds about 50 times more carbon than the atmosphere. The ocean absorbs this carbon largely through a chemical reaction at its surface: CO_2 combines with sea water to form carbonic acid which results in increased ocean acidity.

Since the Industrial Revolution, global oceans have absorbed about 28% of the CO_2 from burning fossil fuels. Ocean acidification makes it more difficult for creatures – like plankton, corals, and shellfish – to produce calcium carbonate, the main ingredient in their hard skeletons or shells. This can lead to broader changes in the overall structure of ocean and costal ecosystems, which can affect fish populations and the people that depend on them. Increased ocean temperature combined with excessive nutrients like phosphorous and nitrogen (often from agricultural fertilizer runoff that comes with increased precipitation) are conducive to rapid algae growth known as algal blooms.

Algal blooms can produce extremely dangerous toxins that can cause eye and lung irritation and worsen asthma, or kill people and animals. The growth of the algae depletes oxygen content necessary for marine organisms to live, forcing species to flee or perish. Over the past 50 years, the area of oxygen-starved waters grew by 4.5 million square kilometers, more than one-third the size of India.

1.1.5 Wildlife

According to a 2015 report by the World Wildlife Fund (WWF), human activity has severely damaged almost every single aspect of our global oceans. The study found that marine populations have declined 49% on average between 1970 and 2012. The WWF's Living Planet Index database, maintained and analyzed by the Zoological Society of London, tracked 5,829 populations of 1,234 species ranging from sea birds to sharks to leatherback turtles to coral reefs. WWF's report found that human activity is the primary driver of this decline: from over-exploiting fisheries and damaging marine habitats to climate change. Experts predict that if the current rate of warming persists, by 2050, one-half of all plant and animal species will be threatened with extinction.

The sex of sea turtles is determined when they're born by the water temperature. When they're born in the Northern part of the Great Barrier Reef closest to the equator, 99% of the young green sea turtles are now being born female.

The complexity of plant-pollinator relationships relies on stable climatic cues for precise timing and synchrony. About 35% of crop species worldwide depend on or benefit from pollinators, like honey bees.

Climate change is shifting where species live much faster than previously thought. According to a study of the changing ranges of different species, climate change is pushing land-based plant and animal species to higher elevations and toward the poles.

1.1.6 Hurricanes

Since 1995, more than 90% of the excess heat retained by Earth has been absorbed by the oceans. Warmer ocean temperatures – which are like fuel for tropical storms – can result in more intense storms, rapid intensification of storms, and higher wind speeds. Trends indicating an increasing number of rapidly intensifying tropical cyclones have already been observed, including in the Atlantic basin. Research suggests an increased likelihood of rapidly intensifying tropical cyclones and an increasing number of major tropical cyclones over time.

1.1.7 Floods

Warmer oceans and warmer air above the oceans results in more water evaporating from the ocean's surface into the atmosphere. There is already 4% more water vapor over the oceans than there was only 35 years ago. For every 1°C that the atmosphere warms, it can hold about 7% more water vapor. In turn, this extra water vapor can lead to heavier downpours and subsequent flooding.

Warmer water also takes up more space. This, along with melting land ice, has caused global sea levels to rise, yielding storm surges that are higher and can move further inland than they otherwise would.

1.1.8 Fires

The fires in Australia in 2019/20 captured the world's attention because of the many tragedies caused by those fires. And a lot of people also noticed the harsh impact on wildlife; more than a billion animals were killed. Climate change is creating hot, dry conditions that increase the risk of fire activity.

Wildfires are not only getting bigger and fiercer but also burning hotter and longer. Fire seasons are also lasting longer. Wildfires already burn millions of hectares and force hundreds of thousands to evacuate each year, threatening both their immediate safety and long-term health.

Experts project that wildfires and related damages will increase globally this century, thanks to warmer temperatures and drier conditions. The area burned by boreal fires is expected to increase 130–350% by mid-century, threatening to turn boreal forests into net carbon emitters

1.1.9 Forests

When managed sustainably, forests increase resilience and provide economic services like food, wood energy, and materials. They also provide a range of environmental services, such as cleaning our water and air, and employment opportunities, both in the protection and utilization of forest resources. In addition, forests absorb and store carbon dioxide and provide habitats for a large number of species. In 2015, the world's forests stored about 296 Gigatonnes of carbon.

In a healthy rainforest ecosystem, when rain falls, it's absorbed by the soil and surrounding trees. This water is returned to the atmosphere through transpiration - the release of water from plants' leaves during photosynthesis.

This water contributes to the formation of rain clouds that return the water back to the surrounding forest.

When trees are removed from the ecosystem, less water goes into the atmosphere and less rain falls on the surrounding area. Deforestation, together with warming temperatures and an altered water cycle, can lead to desertification, or the transformation of fertile lands into desert.

Climate change can increase the frequency of droughts, which make forests more susceptible to fires and make forest fires more likely to be intense and longer burning. Changing temperatures will likely also shift the range of suitable habitats for tree species while simultaneously expanding habitat ranges for pests and invasive species, which will alter entire ecosystems and potentially lead to die-offs.

Human-caused deforestation, mainly from cutting down trees for agriculture or development, is one of the biggest threats to global forests. In the Amazon, forests are cleared with fire to make way for other uses like cattle-ranching, which can conflict with the land rights of indigenous populations. In addition, the impact of these fires is made worse by drought.

Compared to May 2020, deforestation of the Amazon Rainforest rose 67% in May 2021. Widespread drought conditions in the Amazon Rainforest have dramatically increased in 2021, which makes the forest more susceptible to fires. Major drivers of human-led deforestation in the Amazon include legal and illegal logging, cattle ranching, farmland, and mining.

1.1.10 Droughts

Increased evaporation from soils affects plant life and can both reduce rainfall and increase other risks. When rainfall does come to drought-stricken areas, the drier soils it hits are less able to absorb the water, increasing the likelihood of flooding.

Nearly 40% of the world – 1.3 billion people – relies on agriculture as the main source of income. The result: water shortages put the health and wellbeing not only of animals and crops at risk, but also of the farmers and communities that depend on them. Under future projections, soil moisture is expected to decrease globally with real and dangerous consequences.

Short-term droughts (four-to-six-month duration) are expected to increase in frequency throughout the twenty-first century. Projections show that even in an optimistic scenario of only 1.5°C warming, more than 3.3 billion people will be exposed to water stress, and almost 500 million people will be exposed and vulnerable to water stress.

1.1.11 Human health

Vector-borne diseases, heat stress, air pollution, and waterborne diseases are all influenced by a changing climate. Two major climate impacts influencing human health worldwide are higher average temperatures and changing rainfall patterns. Both factors affect the food we eat, the water we drink, the air we breathe, and the weather we experience.

In 2003, for example, Europe was hit by a major heatwave that caused an estimated 70,000 deaths. In June 2015, more than 800 people died during an extreme heatwave in southern Pakistan. In the US, extreme heat events cause more deaths annually than hurricanes, lightning, tornadoes, floods, and earthquakes combined. Warming can allow for vectors – small organisms such as mosquitos or ticks that can carry diseases – to expand their habitat ranges.

Zoonotic diseases, or diseases spread from animals to humans, are estimated to make up 75% of new infectious diseases. E.g. Covid-19. Experts believe these diseases are associated with an increase in human and animal contact as humans continue to trespass into animal habitats to cut down trees. According to EcoHealthAlliance, deforestation is linked to 31% of outbreaks for diseases such as Ebola, Zika, and Nipah.

Burning fossil fuels not only drives global warming – it also pollutes the air. Worldwide, air pollution kills approximately an average of 6.5 million people annually. The average expected lifespan in Northern China declined by 5.5 years in 2013.

Warmer air holds more water, which is increasing the number of heavy downpours in many places around the world. Increasing downpours together with rising temperatures can create more favorable environmental conditions for the growth, survival, and spread of waterborne diseases. Waterborne diseases can be deadly: contaminated drinking water causes an estimated 502,000 diarrheal deaths each year. In the US, waterborne pathogens are estimated to cause acute gastrointestinal illness cases affecting between 12 and 19 million people annually. By 2040, pollen levels are projected to increase, which will cause some people's allergies to become more severe.

1.1.12 Social cost

Mining, drilling, and burning fossil fuels like coal, oil, and natural gas are harming our environment and our health. We see the cost of carbon clearly in devastating impacts from extreme weather events like flooding and deadly storms to fast-spreading diseases to rising seas to ecosystem loss. What we don't always see are the costs of the lingering aftermath and recovery from these disasters, such as increased health care expenses, destruction of property, increased food prices, and more. The current estimate of the social cost of carbon is roughly $50 per ton, which many experts argue is far lower than the true cost of carbon pollution.

1.2 The Positive Global Trends to meet the Goals of the Paris Agreement

Wind and solar are the cheapest sources of electricity generation for people across more than two-thirds of the world as of 2019. In 2020, Europe generated more electricity from renewables (38%) than from fossil fuels (37%) for the first time, driven by rapid growth of wind and solar in recent years. The highest shares were recorded in Denmark (61%), Ireland (35%), Germany (33%), and Spain (29%).

While renewables nearly doubled since 2015, coal-fired power generation has halved. In the US in 2019, 70% of all the new electricity generation was from solar and wind.

1.2.1 Coal

To meet the goals of the Paris Agreement, approximately half of gas reserves and more than 80% of proven coal reserves must stay in the ground.

Global coal demand continued to decrease in the first quarter of 2020 as the world grappled with COVID-19. In 2020, the world invested over $501 billion in the low-carbon energy transition – a new record, despite COVID-related setbacks. Coal demand is faltering across much of Asia as economic growth stalls, electricity demand drops, and comparatively cheaper renewables crowd the market.

Over 110 global financial institutions have announced that they will stop financing new coal-fired power plants. Investors have committed to divesting more than $14.15 trillion from fossil fuels, led by faith-based organizations, philanthropic foundations, educational institutions, and governments. As of mid-2020, over 1,240 institutions are divesting from coal.

In January 2020, the world's largest asset management fund, BlackRock, announced it would divest from coal. The news came less than a year after a report estimated it had lost inventors over $90 billion during the previous decade, largely due to ignoring global climate risk.

Globally, coal is responsible for over 800,000 premature deaths per year and many millions more serious and minor illnesses. In China alone, around 670,000 people die prematurely per year as a result of coal-related air pollution. In India, coal contributes to between 80,000–115,000 premature deaths annually. In the US, coal kills around 13,000 people annually. In Europe, it kills about 23,300 each year. Eastern Europe, Russia, and India still have many older power plants equipped with insufficient flue gas treatment. As a result, these power plants only remove a fraction of the pollutants in coal emissions – while also often burning coal of inferior quality.

US coal generation was cut in half from 2010 to 2019. In 2019, US coal use fell 18% – to its lowest level since 1975 – and coal-fired emissions fell by 190 million metric tons. In spite of offsets from increased natural gas generation, the decline in coal reduced overall power sector emissions by almost 10% in 2019.

Economics have flipped India's energy equation – new renewable energy is now cheaper to build than running most existing coal-fired power plants. The tipping point may have been 2016-2017, when renewable energy installations surpassed coal for the first time, adding twice the capacity. Coal plants nation-wide already only run around half of the time, nearly every Indian coal plant violates the country's new air pollution standard, and India's Central Electricity Authority has proposed closing nearly 50 GW of coal capacity by 2027.

1.2.2 Wind

Wind energy has the potential to supply the world's electricity needs 40 times over.

In 2000, the IEA (International Energy Agency) projected global wind capacity would only reach 30 GW by 2010. Instead in 2010, it reached 200 GW, overshooting projections by over 660%. Global wind capacity reached almost 650 GW in 2019. Wind capacity is expected to quadruple by 2040, relative to 2017, with $3.3 trillion in investments.

Global offshore wind is expected to grow dramatically, with projections showing the potential for up to a 15-fold increase in capacity and around $1 trillion of cumulative investment by 2040.

Offshore turbines are experiencing an arms race, with individual turbines getting larger. One rotation of a Vestas 8.8 MW wind turbine is enough to power the average home in the United Kingdom for an entire day and next generation turbines are expected to be even larger at 12–15 MW.

1.2.3 Solar

Solar technology has been around since the 1970s but its capacity has grown significantly in recent years, with more solar installation in 2017 than coal, gas, and nuclear combined. The increase is driven by falling solar costs, continued government support, and technological innovation.

Major greenhouse gas emitters like China and India are taking the lead in installing large-scale solar PV. It is estimated that India will have installed 100,000 MW of solar power by the year 2030, and further to 200,000 MW by the year 2050.

The cost of solar has dropped 99% in the last four decades globally. In 2017, the average solar panel converted only 17% of all solar energy to usable electricity. By 2027, experts project that number will to grow to roughly 25%.

1.2.4 Employment

The renewable energy sector provides a large source for employment opportunity, and as the sector continues to grow, more people will need to be hired to satisfy demand. The renewable energy industry employed 11 million people worldwide in 2018, up from 10.3 million in 2017. China, Brazil, the USA, India, Japan, and Germany were the leading job markets during that year.

1.2.5 Industrial energy efficiency

Aggressively increasing renewable energy sources by 2050 are required to meet the terms of the Paris agreement. However, energy efficiency is at least

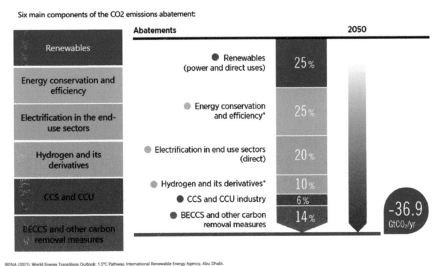

IRENA (2021), World Energy Transitions Outlook: 1.5°C Pathway, International Renewable Energy Agency, Abu Dhabi.

Figure 1.4 Six main components of the CO_2 emissions abatement.

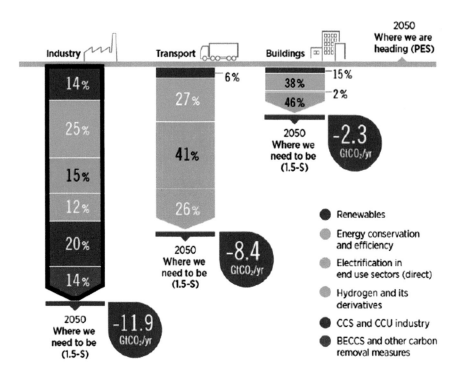

Figure 1.5 CO_2 emissions abatement options between the 1.5°C Scenario and PES in the industry, transport and buildings sectors.

an equally critical component in terms of the potential for CO_2 abatement. Although previous studies have alluded to the fact that energy efficiency is the abatement component with the largest potential, the world energy outlook report of 2021 have given equal weight to renewables and energy efficiency. Irrespective of this, these two components are the two most critical components with a total of 50% of the emissions abatement shared between them.

In the CO2 abatement comparison of industry, buildings, and transport, between the Planned Energy Scenario (PES) which reflects the current energy plans of governments, and the 1.5°C scenario, industry will have the largest responsibility to reduce emission by 11.9 $GtCO_2$ per year, in addition to the current PES where we are currently heading. In addition to this, energy efficiency (25%) is the largest of the six main abatement components, as is shown below.

Therefore, this handbook will focus on Industrial Energy Efficiency.

1.3 International Protocols and Conventions

The environmental and climate change international protocols and conventions that will briefly be discussed are:

- Paris Agreement

- Kyoto Protocol

- Montreal

- Basel convention

- Stockholm convention

1.3.1 Paris agreement

The Paris Agreement took place at the United Nations Convention on Climate Change's (UNFCCC) 21st Conference of Parties (COP21) in Paris on 12 December 2015. This is a landmark environmental accord that was adopted by nearly every nation in 2015 to address climate change and its negative impacts.

The deal aims to substantially reduce global greenhouse gas emissions in an effort to limit the global temperature increase in this century to two degrees Celsius (2°C) above preindustrial levels, while pursuing means to limit the increase to one and half degrees Celsius (1.5°C). The agreement includes commitments from all major emitting countries to cut their climate-altering pollution and to strengthen those commitments over time.

The pact provides a pathway for developed nations to assist developing nations in their climate mitigation and adaptation efforts, and it creates a framework for the transparent monitoring, reporting, and ratcheting up of countries' individual and collective climate goals.

The pathway towards limiting the global temperature increase to 1.5°C above preindustrial levels, are given below, with the required reduction for the different sectors shown. This is according to the 2021 World Energy Transitions Outlook report that was published by the International Energy Agency.

In 2018, the global Total Final Energy Consumption (TEFC) was 378 EJ. The 1.5°C scenario pathway requires the decoupling of economic growth from Carbon emissions, in order to limit the TEFC to 348 EJ. Figure 1.8 below depicts the current share in global energy consumption, with renewables of 25% of electricity consumption, and the envisaged share of global energy consumption by 2050, with a renewable share of 90% of electricity consumption.

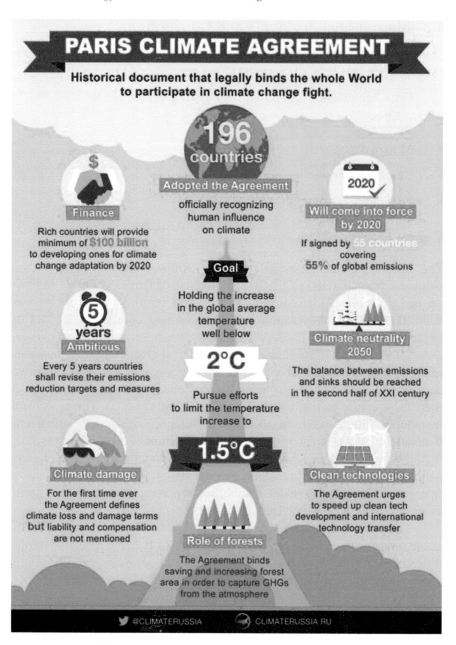

Figure 1.6   The aims of the Paris Climate Agreement.

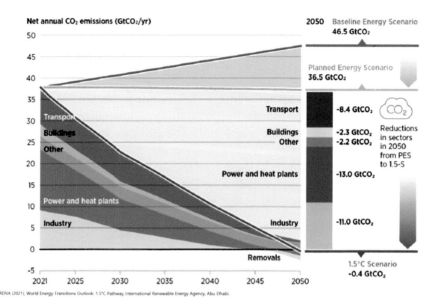

Figure 1.7   Sectoral reductions required for the 1.5°C scenario - IEA report.

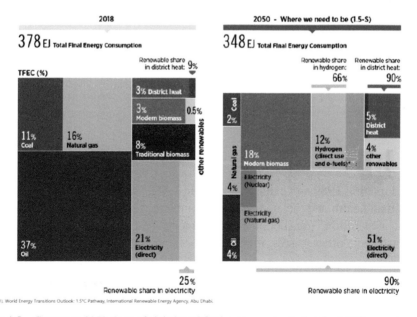

Figure 1.8   Current vs 2050 share of global total final energy consumption for 1.5°C scenario.

1.3.2 Kyoto protocol

The Kyoto Protocol was adopted on 11 December 1997. Owing to a complex ratification process, it entered into force on 16 February 2005. Currently, there are 192 Parties to the Kyoto Protocol.

Kyoto Protocol operationalizes the United Nations Framework Convention on Climate Change by committing industrialized countries to limit and reduce greenhouse gases (GHG) emissions in accordance with agreed individual targets.

The Convention only asks those countries to adopt policies and measures on mitigation and to report periodically. The targets for the first commitment period of the Kyoto Protocol cover emissions of the six main greenhouse gases, namely:

- Carbon dioxide (CO_2);

- Methane (CH_4);

- Nitrous oxide (N_2O);

- Hydrofluorocarbons (HFCs);

- Perfluorocarbons (PFCs); and

- Sulphur hexafluoride (SF_6)

The maximum amount of emissions (measured as the equivalent in carbon dioxide) that a Party may emit over a commitment period in order to comply with its emissions target is known as a Party's assigned amount.

1.3.3 Bessel convention

Adopted in 1989 and came into force in 1992, the convention aims to protect human health and the environment against the adverse effects resulting from the generation, transboundary movements and management of hazardous wastes and other wastes. It covers:

- Sets to control Transboundary Movements of Hazardous Wastes and their Disposal

- By 2011, 175 countries and parties and adopted Bessel convention making it nearly a universal convention

- Energy wastes, especially nuclear, are one of the major targets of Bessel convention.

1.3.4 Montreal protocol

The 1987 Montreal Protocol on Substances that Deplete the Ozone Layer is a landmark agreement that has successfully reduced the global production, consumption, and emissions of Ozone-Depleting Substances (ODS's). These are substances like:

- Chlorofluorocarbons (CFCs) used in refrigeration systems

- Methyl Bromide

- Carbon tetrachloride

1.3.5 Stockholm convention

Stockholm Convention on Persistent Organic Pollutants is an international environmental treaty, signed in 2001 and effective from May 2004, that aims to eliminate or restrict the production and use of Persistent Organic Pollutants (POPs). Some persistent organic pollutants are:

- Aldrin – used as an insecticide

- Chlordane – used as pesticide

- Dichlorodiphenyltrichloroethane, popularly known as DDT

*"**Energy security:** In countries with economies based on exported oil and gas, the larger concern is security of demand, a demand with little changes*

***Industrial competitiveness:** Different industries competing with one another relating to the supply and demand of the same product. In this case competing in terms of energy efficiency mechanisms."*

1.4 Resources for this Chapter

The following resources were used in this chapter:

- Bloomberg New Energy Finance, "Energy Transition Investment Trends: Tracking global investment in the low-carbon energy transition," January 19, 2021. https://assets.bbhub.io/professional/sites/24/Energy-Transition-Investment-Trends_Free-Summary_Jan2021.pdf

- Rajendra K. Pachauri et al., "Climate Change 2014: Synthesis Report," Contribution to the Fifth Assessment Report of the Intergovernmental

Panel on Climate Change, Cambridge University Press, Topics 1 and 2 (November 2, 2014): 40-62. https://www.ipcc.ch/site/assets/uploads/2018/05/SYR_AR5_FINAL_full_wcover.pdf

- The Maritime Executive, "Sea Level Rising Faster This Century," April 26, 2017. https://www.maritime-executive.com/article/sea-level-rising-faster-this-century

- Josh Gabbatiss, "Global sea level to rise by up to 1.2 m despite Paris agreement, say scientists," Independent, February 20, 2018. https://www.independent.co.uk/environment/sea-level-rise-climate-change-paris-agreement-global-warming-greenhouse-gas-a8219681.html

- National Aeronautics and Space Administration (NASA), "Living Ocean," last updated July 2020. https://science.nasa.gov/earth-science/oceanography/living-ocean

- National Oceanic Atmospheric Administration, "Is sea level rising?," last accessed February 2020. https://oceanservice.noaa.gov/facts/sea-level.html

- Christina Nunez, "Sea level rise, explained," February 19, 2019. https://www.nationalgeographic.com/environment/global-warming/sea-level-rise/

- Eli Kintisch, "The great Greenland meltdown," Science Magazine, February 23, 2017. http://www.sciencemag.org/news/2017/02/great-greenland-meltdown

- Rebecca Lindsey, "Climate Change: Global Sea Level," National Oceanic and Atmospheric Administration, last updated January 25, 2021. https://www.climate.gov/news-features/understanding-climate/climate-change-global-sea-level

- John Podesta, "The climate crisis, migration, and refugees," Brookings, July 25, 2019. https://www.brookings.edu/research/the-climate-crisis-migration-and-refugees/

- Center For Climate And Energy Solutions, "Wildfires and Climate Change," last accessed April, 2021. https://www.c2es.org/content/wildfires-and-climate-change/

- Jason Daley, "Study Shows 84% Of Wildfires Caused By Humans," Smithsonian Magazine, February 28, 2017. https://www.smithsonianmag.com/smart-news/study-shows-84-wildfires-caused-humans-180962315/

- R. Sari Kovats et al., "Climate Change 2014: Impacts, Adaptation, and Vulnerability. Part B: Regional Aspects," Contribution of Working Group II to the Fifth Assessment Report of the Intergovernmental Panel on Climate Change, Cambridge University Press, Section 23.4.4 (March 31, 2014): Pages 1267-1326. https://www.ipcc.ch/site/assets/uploads/2018/02/WGIIAR5-PartB_FINAL.pdf

- John Balbus, et al., "Climate and Health Assessment Chapter 1: Climate Change and Human Health," (The US Global Change Research Program, 2016). https://health2016.globalchange.gov/climate-change-and-human-health

- Physicians for Social Responsibility, "Heat's Deadly Effects," last updated October 8, 2013. https://www.psr.org/wp-content/uploads/2018/05/heats-deadly-effects.pdf

- Adil Jawad, "Heat wave subsides in Pakistan as death toll reaches 860," Phys.org (blog), June 25, 2015. http://phys.org/news/2015-06-subsides-pakistan-death-toll.html

- Climate Communication, "Heat Waves: The Details," last accessed March, 2018. https://www.climatecommunication.org/new/features/heat-waves-and-climate-change/heat-waves-the-details/

- World Energy Outlook, "Energy and Air Pollution" International Energy Agency (2016). http://www.iea.org/publications/freepublications/publication/WorldEnergyOutlookSpecialReport2016EnergyandAirPollution.pdf

- Adam Taylor, "The Most Polluted City in the World isn't Beijing or Delhi," The Washington Post, May 13, 2016. https://www.washingtonpost.com/news/worldviews/wp/2016/05/13/the-most-polluted-city-in-the-world-isnt-beijing-or-delhi/

- John Platt, "Pollen counts — and allergies — expected to double by 2040," Mother Nature Network (blog), March 25, 2013. http://www.mnn.com/health/allergies/stories/pollen-counts-and-allergies-expected-to-double-by-2040

- Juli M. Trtanj, et al., "Climate and Health Assessment Chapter 6: Water-Related Illness," (US Global Change Research Program, 2016). https://health2016.globalchange.gov/water-related-illness

- World Health Organization, "Drinking Water," last updated July, 2017. http://www.who.int/mediacentre/factsheets/fs391/en/

- Food and Agriculture Organization of the United Nations, "Forests and Climate Change," (2016). http://www.fao.org/3/a-i6374c.pdf

- Rhett A. Butler, "Rainforests help maintain the water cycle," Mongabay, last updated July 16, 2020. https://kids.mongabay.com/elementary/404.html

- Robert McSweeny, "Explainer: Desertification And The Role Of Climate Change," Carbon Brief, August 6, 2019. https://www.carbon-brief.org/explainer-desertification-and-the-role-of-climate-change

- Union of Concerned Scientists, "The Connection Between Climate Change and Wildfires," last updated March 2020. https://www.ucsusa.org/global-warming/science-and-impacts/impacts/global-warming-and-wildfire.html#.Wuc83dPwbBI

- US Environmental Protection Agency, "Climate Impacts on Forests," last updated December 22, 2016. https://19january2017snapshot.epa.gov/climate-impacts/climate-impacts-forests_.html

- Shannon Sims, "The Land Battle Behind the Fires in the Amazon," August 27, 2019. https://www.theatlantic.com/science/archive/2019/08/amazon-fires-indigenous-lands/596908/

- Sandrine Boukerche & Rianna Mohammed-Roberts, "Fighting infectious diseases: The connection to climate change," World Bank Blogs, May 19, 2020. https://blogs.worldbank.org/climatechange/fighting-infectious-diseases-connection-climate-change

- Andrew Kann, "Extreme drought and deforestation are priming the Amazon rainforest for a terrible fire season," CNN, June 22, 2021. https://www.cnn.com/2021/06/22/weather/brazil-drought-amazon-rainforest-fires/index.html

- The Climate Reality Project, "The Facts About Climate Change and Drought," June 15, 2016. https://www.climaterealityproject.org/blog/facts-about-climate-change-and-drought

- Justin Sheffield and Eric F. Wood, "Projected changes in drought occurrence under future global warming from multi-model, multi-scenario, IPCC AR4 simulations" (2008): 31-79. https://www.ipcc.ch/report/ar4/wg2/

- Ove Hoegh-Guldberg et al., "Impacts of 1.5°C global warming on natural and human systems," Contribution to the Special Report: Global

Warming of 1.5°C, Chapter 3 (October 8, 2018): 175-311. https://www.ipcc.ch/sr15/chapter/chapter-3/

- Nicola Jones, "How Climate Changes Could Jam the World's Ocean Circulation," Yale Environment 360, September 6, 2016. https://e360.yale.edu/features/will_climate_change_jam_the_global_ocean_conveyor_belt

- NOAA Fisheries, "Shallow Coral Reef Habitat," National Oceanic and Atmospheric Administration, last updated February 6, 2018. https://www.fisheries.noaa.gov/national/habitat-conservation/shallow-coral-reef-habitat

- Ben Smee, "Great Barrier Reef: 30% of coral died in 'catastrophic' 2016 heatwave," The Guardian, April 18, 2018. https://www.theguardian.com/environment/2018/apr/19/great-barrier-reef-30-of-coral-died-in-catastrophic-2016-heatwave

- National Oceanic and Atmospheric Administration, "Carbon Cycle," last updated February 2011. http://www.noaa.gov/resource-collections/carbon-cycle

- US Environmental Protection Agency, "Climate Change Indicators: Ocean Acidity," last updated August 2016. https://www.epa.gov/climate-indicators/climate-change-indicators-ocean-acidity

- Climate Central, "Algae Blooms and Climate Change," August 23, 2017. http://www.climatecentral.org/gallery/graphics/algae-blooms-and-climate-change

- OMZ Microbes, "How oxygen minimum zones form," The Scientific Committee on Oceanic Research, last accessed June 2018. http://omz.microbiology.ubc.ca/page2/index.html; US Central Intelligence Agency, "The World Facbook: India," last updated June 4, 2018. https://www.cia.gov/library/publications/the-world-factbook/geos/in.html

- Tim Wallace, "Oceans Are Absorbing Almost All of the Globe's Excess Heat," The New York Times, September 12, 2016. https://www.nytimes.com/interactive/2016/09/12/science/earth/ocean-warming-climate-change.html

- Jeff Masters, "Climate change is causing more rapid intensification of Atlantic hurricane," Yale Climate Connections, August 27, 2020. https://yaleclimateconnections.org/2020/08/climate-change-is-causing-more-rapid-intensification-of-atlantic-hurricanes/

- Climate Signals, "Atmospheric Moisture Increase," December 4, 2018. https://www.climatesignals.org/climate-signals/atmospheric-moisture-increase

- Climate Central, "Hurricanes and Climate Change: What We Know," September 6, 2017. https://medialibrary.climatecentral.org/resources/hurricanes-climate-change-2017

- Jess Colarossi, "Climate Change and Overfishing are Driving the World's Oceans to the 'Brink of Collapse'," ThinkProgress, September 18, 2015. http://thinkprogress.org/climate/2015/09/18/3702590/ocean-collapsing-worse-thought/

- Amy E Boyd, "Timing, Pollinators, and the Impact of Climate Change," Union of Concerned Scientists, July 7, 2017. https://blog.ucsusa.org/science-blogger/timing-pollinators-and-the-impact-of-climate-change

- I-Ching Chen et al., "Rapid Range Shifts of Species Associated with High Levels of Climate Warming," Science 333, no. 6045 (August 19, 2011): 1024-1026. http://science.sciencemag.org/content/333/6045/1024

- Agora Energiewende, "Renewables overtake gas and coal in EU electricity generation," January 25, 2021. https://www.agora-energiewende.de/en/press/news-archive/renewables-overtake-gas-and-coal-and-coal-in-eu-electricity-generation-1/

- International Energy Agency, "Global Energy Review 2020 – Coal," (April 2020).

- firesInstitute for Energy Economics and Financial Analysis, "Over 100 and counting," last accessed June 2020. https://ieefa.org/finance-exiting-coal/

- Fossil Free, "1000+ divestment commitments," last accessed July 2020 https://gofossilfree.org/divestment/commitments/

- Ann Pettifor, "BlackRock gets praise for coal divestment. What it really needs is regulation," The Guardian, January 16, 2020. https://www.theguardian.com/commentisfree/2020/jan/16/blackrock-coal-divestment-regulation-fund-manager

- Tim Buckley, Tom Sanzillo, and Kashish Shah, "Inaction is BlackRock's Biggest Risk During the Energy Transition," Institute for Energy Economics and Financial Analysis (August 2019). https://ieefa.org/wp-content/uploads/2019/07/

Inaction-BlackRocks-Biggest-Risk-During-the-Energy-Transition_
August-2019.pdf

- End Coal, "Health," last accessed July 2020. https://endcoal.org/health

- The Economic Times, "India's powerplants 'unhealthiest' in the world: study," February 21, 2019. https://economictimes.indiatimes.com/ news/environment/pollution/indias-coal-power-plants-unhealthiest-in-world-study/articleshow/68092635.cms?from=mdr

- Trevor Houser and Hannah Pitt, "Preliminary US Emissions Estimates for 2019," Rhodium Group, January 7, 2020. https://rhg.com/research/ preliminary-us-emissions-2019/

- US Energy Information Administration, "More U.S. coal-fired power plants are decommissioning as retirements continue," July 26, 2019. https://www.eia.gov/todayinenergy/detail.php?id=40212

- Xi Lua, Michael B. McElroy, and Juha Kiviluoma, "Global Potential for Wind-Generated Electricity," Proceedings of the National Academy of Sciences of the United States of America 106, No. 27 (July 7, 2009): 10933-10938. http://www.pnas.org/content/106/27/10933.full.pdf

- World Wind Energy Association, "World wind capacity at 650,8 GW, Corona crisis will slow down markets in 2020, renewables to be core of economic stimulus programs," April 16, 2020. https://wwindea.org/ blog/2020/04/16/world-wind-capacity-at-650-gw/

- Bloomberg New Energy Finance, "Global wind and solar costs to fall even faster, while coal fades even in China and India," June 15, 2017. https:// about.bnef.com/blog/global-wind-solar-costs-fall-even-faster-coal-fades-even-china-india/

- Bloomberg New Energy Finance, "New Energy Outlook 2019," (2019). https://bnef.turtl.co/story/neo2019?teaser=true

- David Roberts, "Why do 'experts' always lowball clean energy projections?," Grist, July 9, 2012. http://grist.org/renewable-energy/ experts-in-2000-lowballed-the-crap-out-of-renewable-energy-growth/

- International Renewable Energy Agency, "Offshore wind to become a \$1 trillion industry," October 25, 2019. https://www.iea.org/news/ offshore-wind-to-become-a-1-trillion-industry

- Jason Deign, "Global Wind Market to Add 65 GW per Year to 2027," GreenTechMedia, January 1, 2019. https://www.greentechmedia.com/ articles/read/global-wind-market#gs.wtl6fv

- Silvio Marcacci, "India Coal Power Is About to Crash: 65% of Existing Coal Costs More Than New Wind and Solar," Forbes, January 30, 2018. https://www.forbes.com/sites/energyinnovation/2018/01/30/india-coal-power-is-about-to-crash-65-of-existing-coal-costs-more-than-new-wind-and-solar/#59576be34c0f

- Reliable Plant, "India seeks 20,000 MW of solar power capacity by 2020," last accessed March 1, 2019. https://www.reliableplant.com/Read/18150/india-seeks-20,000-mw-of-solar-power-capacity-by-2020

- Renewable Energy Policy Network for the 21st Century, "Renewables 2018 Global Status Report (2018)". http://www.ren21.net/gsr-2018/

- National Renewable Energy Laboratory, "Renewable Energy Technical Potential," last accessed June 2019. https://www.nrel.gov/gis/re-potential.html

- St. John, Jeff, "Global Energy Storage to Hit 158 Gigawatts-Hours by 2024, Led by US and China," Greentech Media, April 10, 2019. https://www.greentechmedia.com/articles/read/global-energy-storage-to-hit-158-gigawatt-hours-by-2024-with-u-s-and-china#gs.pqfxhk

- Joel Makower, "The growing concern over stranded assets," GreenBiz, September 10, 2019. https://www.greenbiz.com/article/growing-concern-over-stranded-assets

- Arcadia Power, "Renewable energy's job market continues to grow – with no end in sight," last accessed July 23, 2019. https://www.arcadia-power.com/energy-101/energy-efficiency/renewable-energy-s-job-market-continues-to-grow-with-no-end-in-sight/

Chapter 2

Fundamental Principles of Energy

Louis Lagrange

University of the Free State, South Africa

Introduction

As an energy auditor, you need to be aware of the different forms of energy, the effective conversion between forms and the units used to measure energy.

2.1 Forms of Energy

2.1.1 Definition of energy

Energy forms an important part of most aspects of our everyday life, our life depends on the availability of energy. The concept of energy can be viewed as the ability to cause changes and to do work.

Thermodynamics can be defined as the science of energy. The word stems from the Greek words therme (heat) and dynamis (power). It includes all aspects like the sources and forms of energy, the interaction and transformation of energy from one form to another and the results from these conversions. We know that energy exists because we can observe (and measure) its effects on the surrounding environment.

Some observations of energy can be made, namely:

- All systems possess energy (system property).

- Energy may enter or leave a system.

- Energy is always conserved (accounted for).

- Energy may be accumulated in a system.

- Energy in a closed system remains constant.

- Sum of energy in various parts = total system energy.

2.1.2 Different forms of energy and energy flow important to energy audits

Energy exists in numerous forms such as thermal, mechanical electric chemical and nuclear energy and the sum of all the different forms constitutes total energy. Even mass can be considered a form of energy but is mostly not considered as it constitutes a very small amount.

In thermodynamics we define the terms system (what we consider), system boundary (delineate the selection we want to consider) and the surroundings. This will help us to determine through either measuring or calculation from known characteristics the amount of energy that is inherently contained in the system we are considering. It also serves to understand the interactions and relationship(s) between the system and the surrounding environment and specifically the amount of energy that is transferred over the defined boundary. A very important point is that we measure energy when it crosses the selected boundary. This forms the basis of any energy measurements and is used in an energy audit. See Figure 2.1. Energy is thus measured when it crosses the selected boundary, and it is measured as either Heat (Q) or Work (W).

Thermodynamics always a defined point of reference and the relative change of energy in a system and between systems is calculated. The reference point is usually selected to suit the measurement and to be convenient for completing the calculations.

The total energy of a system can be seen as falling into two distinct groups, macroscopic energy and microscopic energy.

The macroscopic forms of energy are those a system possesses in relation to some outside reference frame, and can be subdivided into:

a) <u>kinetic energy</u> – energy of motion/movement where all particles in the system move in the same direction,

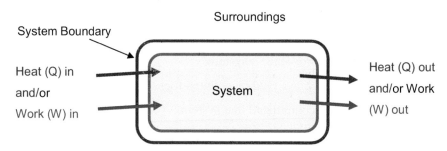

Figure 2.1   Thermodynamic system, boundary and surroundings.

b) <u>potential energy</u> – "stored" energy waiting to be released by some inter-action, e.g., a force or elevation (in a gravitational field) above a ref-erence point, a potential difference (in a battery), or energy in food or chemical bonds "waiting" to be released, and

c) <u>magnetism, and surface tension</u> – these are for special cases and are not considered in this course.

"A coal fired power station transforms one form of energy (energy imbedded in coal) into another form, electricity. Coal plants use the potential chemical energy stored in fossil fuels and transform it into electricity which in turn act as a transporter of the energy in the form of electrons moving through conductors."

The microscopic forms of energy are related to the molecular structure of a system and the degree of molecular activity and structure of a sys-tem. It can be considered as the internal energy which a system possesses and can be considered as the sum of the kinetic and potential energies of the molecules themselves on a microscopic level. They are independent of the outside reference frames of external potential and kinetic energies. The sum of all the microscopic forms of energy is referred to as the internal energy of a system (U). Two separate distinct forms of internal energy can be observed:

a) <u>sensible energy</u> - energy associated with activity/random motion of molecules and atoms (kinetic). The measured temperature of the sys-tems provides an accurate indication of the average velocity of move-ment and degree of activity., and

b) <u>latent energy</u> - energy associated with the binding forces (poten-tial) between molecules (structural arrangement), between atoms and between particles and the nucleus. This change in relative position and distance between the molecules is called a phase change

Figure 2.2 represents the concept of the structural arrangement and distances between molecules of a substance (e.g., water) diagrammatically. From the solid phase to liquid phase the molecular bindings are broken, and the mol-ecules are still nearly the same distance from each other but can move ran-domly (for most substances this distance is slightly larger, but for water the solid phases expand slightly). With a phase change from liquid to gas the distances between the molecules increase significantly, with a similar large increase in energy required for this process.

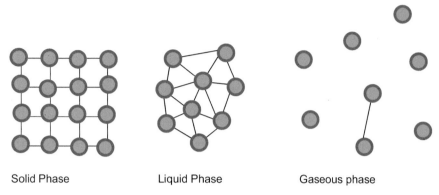

Solid Phase   Liquid Phase   Gaseous phase

Figure 2.2   Conceptual differences in molecule arrangement between substance phases.

The sum of all the energies in a system is shown in Figure 2.1. When energy is added to a system, typically through the addition of heat, either the pressure changes and the volume stays the same, or the volume changes for the pressure to stay the same. We now introduce a new and very useful term, enthalpy (H), to describe the total internal energy change of system including the change in either pressure or volume during energy the conversion process.

Enthalpy is defined as the sum of a system's internal energy (U) plus the mathematical product of the related pressure (P) and volume (V) changes

$$H = U + (\Delta).$$

The internal energy is one of the thermodynamic properties of a system as the sum of the kinetic and potential energies of the particles that form the system energy.

Enthalpy values for specific substances cannot be measured directly; only enthalpy *changes* for chemical or physical processes can be determined. For processes that take place at constant pressure (a common condition for many chemical and physical changes), the **enthalpy change (ΔH)** is:

$$\Delta H = \Delta U + P\Delta V$$

The mathematical product $P\Delta V$ represents work (w) is also referred to as workflow. It can be in the form of either expansion work or pressure-volume work. By their definitions, the arithmetic signs of ΔV and w (work) will always be opposite:

$P\Delta V = -w$. If a chemical or physical process is carried out at constant pressure with the only work done caused by expansion or contraction, then the heat flow (q_p) and enthalpy change (ΔH) for the process are equal.

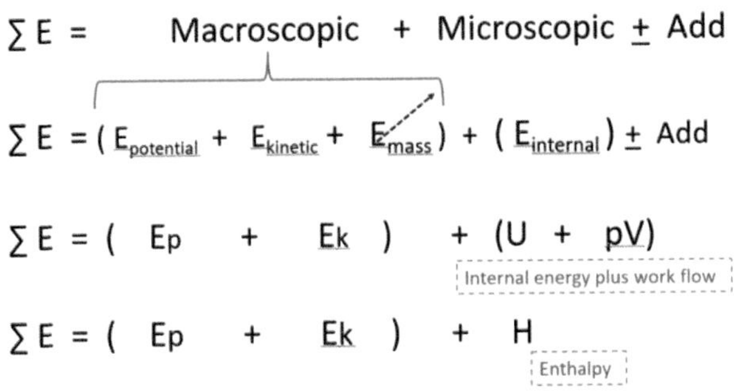

$$\sum E = \quad \text{Macroscopic} + \text{Microscopic} \pm \text{Add}$$

$$\sum E = (E_{potential} + E_{kinetic} + E_{mass}) + (E_{internal}) \pm \text{Add}$$

$$\sum E = (\quad Ep \quad + \quad Ek \quad) \quad + (U + pV)$$
Internal energy plus work flow

$$\sum E = (\quad Ep \quad + \quad Ek \quad) \quad + \quad H$$
Enthalpy

Figure 2.3 Distinctive parts of energy of a system.

The energy due to mass flow can be discarded as it is an insignificant amount for the type of systems encountered in this course.

The inherent internal energy contained or "stored" in a system is labelled as the static energy, while the energy not stored in a system which can be recognised as it crosses a selected boundary is known as dynamic energy. The forms of energy interactions associated with a closed system (a fixed mass) are:

a) Heat (Q) - an energy transfer (flow crossing a boundary) to or from a closed system if a temperature difference is causing it.

b) Work (W) – when caused or equated to a force acting through a distance.

c) Mass transfer (disregarded in this course due to its insignificant effect).

Heat (Q) and work (W) are the two main forms of energy interactions to be considered in this course. We use the lower case of Q and W to denote energy per unit.

The macroscopic kinetic energy of an object or system (orderly motion of all parts in a direction) is an <u>organised</u> form of energy while the microscopic kinetic energy is random and <u>disorganised</u>. Organised forms of energy are generally more useable/valuable than disorganised forms, an important concept which will be utilised in energy audits, calculations, and determination of both the effectiveness of using the specific energy source as well as the efficiency of the energy transformation.

Energy transfer through heat (Q) can take place in three different formats. All three modes of heat transfer require the existence of a temperature difference and takes place from high temperature region to a low temperature region.

- Conduction

- Convection

- Radiation

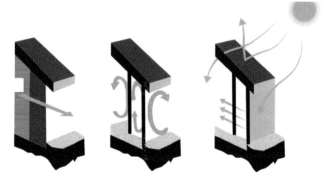

Figure 2.4   Three mechanisms of heat transfer.

The three mechanisms are:

a) conduction,

b) convection, and

c) radiation.

Conduction is the transfer of energy from the more energetic particles of a substance to adjacent less energetic particles due to the interactions between particles, i.e., the collisions of the molecules due to their random motion. Molecules of good conductors are close to each other, allowing good agitation e.g., metals. Low density leads to poor conductors, called insulators. Gas temperature differences causes a flow of energy from higher temperature to colder temperature. Conduction can take place in solids, liquids and gases.
A general formula for heat transfer through conduction is:

$$Q = U * A * \Delta T$$

Where:
   Q = energy passing through the material (Watt)
   U = heat transfer coefficient (m°C/W)
   A = surface area (m²)
   ΔT = Temperature difference across the material surfaces (°C)

Convection is the transfer of energy which occurs on the surface of the material, i.e., between a solid surface and the adjacent fluid or gas which is commonly in in motion. This energy transfer is the result of the combined effects of conduction as well as fluid motion. The faster the fluid motion through the rising motion of groups of particles where groups of particles move together

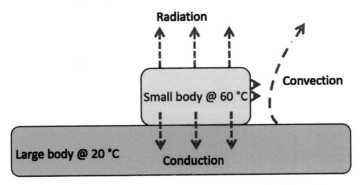

Figure 2.5 The three general modes of energy transfer through heat.

and form "currents", the greater the heat transfer through convection. Several factors such as the type of and roughness of the surface, the way the fluid moves and the speed of the movement, etc. determines the actual amount of energy transfer.

Forced convection is when the fluid is forced to flow in a tube or over a surface using external means of propulsion like a fan, pump, or the wind. Natural convection is when the fluid motion is caused by the buoyancy forces induced by density differences of the fluid because of the resulting temperature difference of the fluid. A higher temperature results in an increase in the distances between the molecules, which causes lower density which in turn results in a rise of the fluid vertically upwards, which creates a lower pressure underneath it and this process becomes the flowing motion of the fluid. Radiation is the transfer of energy due to the emission of electromagnetic waves or photons, both visible & invisible e.g., sunrays. No contact between bodies is required (can be in a vacuum) and energy is transferred when waves striking the body transfers energy, it then agitates the molecules and normally it heats up. Figure 2.5 provides a schematic of the three general modes of energy transfer through heat.

2.2 Definition of Energy Efficiency

The term efficiency refers to how well an energy conversion process is accomplished and is also referred to as performance. In general terms efficiency can be considered as the ratio of the output (useful energy) to the input (amount of energy procured) to provide a metric of how effective or ineffective the procured energy is used.

An energy auditor must also be aware when energy is converted from one form to another, it is often associated with some effect(s) on the environment which may be adverse and should thus be taken into consideration as well.

The broad definition of energy efficiency is the ratio of the amount of useful energy which exits a system to the amount of procured energy which enters the system (which is the amount you pay for), expressed as a percentage or decimal.

$$Efficiency, n = \frac{Useful\ energy\ out}{Procured\ energy\ in\ \left(you\ pay\ for\ this\right)}$$

Figure 2.5 depicts the energy conversion from coal (potential energy, Q) which when burned, releases the energy as heat, a "disorganised" form of energy, and converts it through several processes into work (W) in the form of electricity which is a "highly organised" form of energy. It is worth noting that the conversion from disorganised energy into a more organised form of energy is usually lower than 50%, and because electricity is a highly organised form of energy, the efficiency in this example is in the order of 30%.

Figure 2.5 depicts the path of energy transmission and conversion until it results with water flowing from a pipe. Typical related individual efficiencies of components in the system are also shown. An example of the energy used in a pump system can be calculated are as follows:

$$\eta_p = \frac{P_{out}}{P_{in}}$$

Where:

η_p = *pump efficiency*
P_{out} = *shaft power out (Watt, W)*
P_{in} = *electric power into pump (Watt, W)*

A Sankey diagram (added on top of Figure 2.6) is a handy and visual method to show the flow of energy through the system up to where the useful energy manifests in the form of moving water.

It is important to understand that energy conversion in a system consists of discrete separate components and each separate energy conversion will be unique to the specific component. It is furthermore of cardinal importance that the **stated <u>theoretical</u> efficiency as provided on the component nameplate is altered to the <u>actual</u> efficiency** due to the operational circumstances before any calculations on actual energy use is conducted.

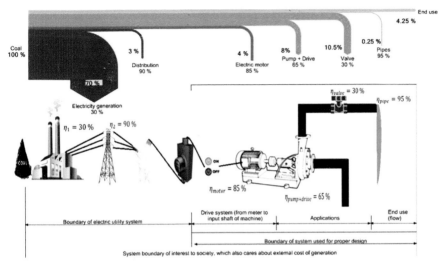

Figure 2.6   Energy conversion through a typical energy value chain.

Table 2.1   Common efficiencies of different electrical equipment.

Equipment	Input - output	Typical efficiency range
Electrical resistance heater	Electrical - heat	97 – 100 %
Incandescent lightbulb	Electrical - light	5 – 10 %
Electrical motor (Small)	Electrical - Mechanical energy (Torque)	50 – 95 %
Electrical Motor (Large)	Electrical - Mechanical energy (Torque)	65 – 97%
Centrifugal pump/fan	Electrical - Pressure resulting on flow	30 – 65%
Compressed air compressor	Electrical - Pressurised air	5 – 10%

By multiplying the individual efficiencies of each component together the **overall system efficiency** is obtained. Coherent **sub-systems can also be selected** with their related thermodynamic boundaries to provide the efficiency of such a delineated section. Examples include the sub-system inside the factory, the sub-system of pump and belt efficiency, the sub-system of water transport efficiency, etc. This will be addressed in more detail with supporting calculations in section 4.

Some common efficiencies of different electrical and electrical drive equipment are provided in Table 2.1

2.3 Definition of Energy Density

Energy density, also known as specific energy, is the amount of energy that a given system or space contains per unit volume or per unit mass. This includes magnetic and electric fields which can store energy. The SI unit of measurement is thus J/volume or J/mass. The unit of Joule is very small, so kJ or J or GJ is commonly used.

The concept of energy density is a very handy tool for the energy auditor. It provides an instant quantity of the amount of energy contained ("stored") and available for use in the specific type of fuel. This can be used to determine the amount of fuel to be procured to obtain a certain energy output, which can then be compared to the actual amount of fuel purchased. The answer to this leads to the identification of possible Energy Management Opportunities (EMOs) which forms the core of energy audits.

Table 2.2 lists several common sources of energy with their "typical" energy densities.

Some observations on energy can now be made, namely:

Table 2.2   Specific energy CONTAINED in different fuels (Higher Heating Value).

Natural Gas	37.6	MJ/m³
Fuel oil nr 2 (Diesel)	45.3	MJ/kg
Fuel oil nr 2 (Diesel)	38.7	MJ/l
Fuel oil nr 2 (Diesel)	38.7	GJ/m³
Gasoline (petrol)	35	MJ/l
Propane (LPG)	25.3	MJ/l
Propane (LPG)	25.3	GJ/m³
Propane (LPG)	45.65	MJ/kg
Bunker C oil	42.7	MJ/kg
Bunker C oil	40.5	MJ/l
Wood (Average)	19.9	MJ/kg
Natural Gas	37.6	MJ/m³
Electricity	3600	kJ/kWh
Electricity	3.6	MJ/kWh
Electricity	0.0036	GJ/kWh
Coal Anthracite	32	MJ/kg
Coal Grade A	29	MJ/kg
Coal Grade B	27	MJ/kg
Coal Grade C	24	MJ/kg

a) Energy is the ability to do work and energy exist in useful and not useful forms.

b) Energy can be converted several times between different forms of energy.

c) Energy conversion always increases the remaining non-useful amount of energy (also known as entropy) thus the amount of entropy increases.

d) Energy has a quantity, but also a quality, which is an indication of the usefulness of the energy to do specific work.

e) Energy consists of macroscopic energy (potential and kinetic) and microscopic (internal) energy, and the total energy of both need to be considered.

f) Energy crosses a thermodynamic boundary in two forms:

- Organised, macroscopic - work or mechanical energy (includes electrical energy) (W), or

- Disorganised, microscopic - heat or thermal energy transfer (Q).

2.4 Units of Energy

The measurement of energy and the metrics used to describe the energy is vitally important to determine the quantity as well as the quality of energy in order to predict (calculate) the changes in the quantity and quality of the energy through conversion processes. Any physical quantity can be characterized by dimensions and the magnitudes assigned to dimensions are called units.

Despite efforts to unify the world with a single unit system, there are still two sets of units in use today, the English system known as the United States Customary System (USCS) and the metric Le Systeme International d'Unites (SI) system. The SI systems will be used in this book, with some reference to the English system to enable the reader to convert between the two should the necessity arise. Normally all unit names are written without capitalization if it was derived from a proper name, but the abbreviation of a unit is capitalized, and the full name of a unit may be pluralised, but its abbreviation cannot. Table 1.3 lists the seven fundamental dimensions and their units.

The following units are primarily used as metrics to determine the quantity of energy contained in a system, as well as to quantify the rate at which

Table 2.3   Fundamental dimensions and their SI units.

Dimension	Unit
Length	meter (m)
Mass	kilogram (kg)
Time	second (s)
Temperature	kelvin (K)
Electric current	ampere (A)
Amount of light	candela (cd)
Amount of matter	mole (Mol)

energy crosses the system boundary from when it enters and exits the system. Multiplying the rate with the duration of the process provides the quantity of energy which crossed the boundary.

2.4.1 Calorie

The term calorie(s) refers to the nutritional energy (heat) present in food. The term calorie or more accurately thermodynamic Calorie refers to the **amount of heat energy** [Q] required to raise the temperature of 1 gram of water at sea level pressure (101.325 kPa) from 14.5°C to 15.5°C. One calorie is equal to 4.184 Joule [J] of energy.

The term British thermal unit [Btu] is the amount of energy required to raise the temperature of 1 pound of water from 63°F (17.22°C) to 64°F (17.78°C). One Btu is equal to 1055.1 J

2.4.2 Joule

The joule is a metric to determine a quantity of energy required, or work done, to exert a force of 1 newton [N] over a distance of 1 meter [m].

One newton equals a force that produces an acceleration of one meter per second on a one kilogram [kg] mass. Therefore, one joule equals one newton-meter [Nm].

In energy audits and energy management the unit joule is very small, therefore the terms kilojoule [kJ], megajoule [MJ] and gigajoule [GJ] are commonly used. The term joule refers to the quantity of energy contained in a system under consideration and does not indicate the quality or usefulness of the energy to be converted into another form.

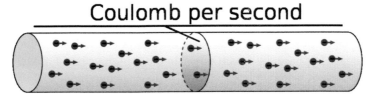

Figure 2.7   One ampere flow.

2.4.3 Pascal

The pascal is the measurement of a pressure, 1 pascal [Pa] is the pressure of the force of 1 newton exerted over an area of 1 square meter [m²], or, in SI base units, one kilogram per metre per second squared [kgm⁻¹s⁻²]. One pascal is the force which 1 kg of substance (e.g. butter), evenly spread over an area of 1 m² (e.g. a very large slice of bread), exerts on the unit area. As this unit is inconveniently small for many purposes kilopascal [kPa] and megapascal [MPa] are more commonly used.

2.4.4 Ampere

One ampere is defined as the current which flows when an electric charge of one coulomb [C] (=6.25 * 10¹⁸ electrons) per second pass a point in a conductor, see Figure 2.7.

2.4.5 Ampere-hour

An ampere-hour (amp-hour or Ah) is the measure of the flow of current past a certain point in a conductor over time. One ampere-hour (or amp-hour [Ah]) is a current of one ampere flowing for a duration of one hour. The amount of charge transferred during that hour is 3,600 coulombs (ampere-seconds). Abbreviations used are: Ah, a.h., amp-hr, amp. hr.

2.4.6 Volt-Ampere

The volt-ampere is an electric measurement unit, equal to the product of one volt and one ampere which is equivalent to one watt of power for direct current systems, also known as real or active power.

For alternating current systems with an inductive load, it is the unit of apparent power. The symbols used are dimensionally equivalent to the watt $[1 \text{ V·A} = 1 \text{ N·m·A}^{-1}\text{·s}^{-1}\text{·A} = 1 \text{ N·m·s}^{-1} = 1 \text{ J·s}^{-1} = 1 \text{ W}]$.

With a purely resistive load, the apparent power is equal to the real power. Where a reactive (capacitive or inductive) component is present in the load, the apparent power is greater than the real power as voltage and current are no longer in phase with each other. In the limiting case of a purely reactive load, current is drawn but no power is dissipated in the load.

For single phase resistive systems, the relationship for power is derived from Ohm's law

$$\text{Ohm's law: Voltage [V]} = \text{Current [A] * Resistance [Ohm } \Omega]$$
$$\text{Power [Watt]} \quad = \text{Voltage [V] * Current [A]}$$
$$= I * R * I$$
$$= I^2R$$

For three phase resistive systems the relationship for power is derived from in Ohm's law

$$\text{Power [Watt]} \quad = \sqrt{3}\ V * I$$

The relationship between power, voltage and current for an alternating current single-phase system with resistance is shown in Figure 2.8.

If the load on the system is not purely resistive, but inductive (as found in most cases) the immediate on phase following of the current flow due to the existence of a voltage is delayed, also known as lagging (behind the voltage). As the value of the current drops, the value of the calculated power also diminishes. This relationship is called the power factor, and is depicted by the term cos Ø.

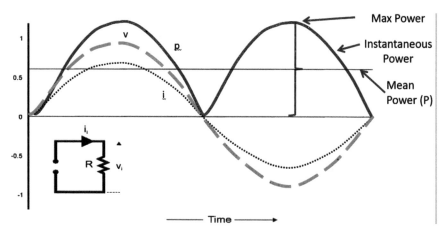

Figure 2.8   Relationship between power, voltage and current for an alternating current SINGLE-PHASE system with RESISTANCE only.

For single phase inductive systems, the formula to calculate power changes to:

$$\text{Power [Watt]} = \text{Voltage [V]} * \text{Current [A]} * \cos Ø$$
$$= VI * \cos Ø$$

For three phase inductive systems the formula to calculate power changes to:

$$\text{Power [Watt]} = \sqrt{3} * \text{Voltage [V]} * \text{Current [A]} * \cos Ø$$
$$= \sqrt{3} * VI * \cos Ø$$

The relationship between power, voltage and current for an alternating current single-phase system with inductance is shown in Figure 2.9. The lagging of the current is depicted as shifting to the right, and the magnitude of shifting is represented by the value of cos Ø.

One of the consequences of an inductive load on a circuit is that the utility need to increase the power it produces and delivers to a client in order to counter the lagging effect, thus increasing the cost of generation. This cost is then passed on to the customer and is known as Apparent Power [VA], normally measured in kilovolt-ampere ([kVA].

Some devices, including uninterruptible power supplies (UPS), have ratings both for maximum Apparent Power [VA] and maximum Power [W]. The VA rating is limited by the maximum permissible current [A], and the power [W] rating by the power-handling capacity of the device. When a UPS

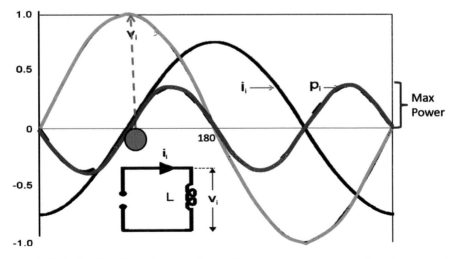

Figure 2.9 Relationship between power, voltage and current for an alternating current SINGLE-PHASE system with INDUCTANCE.

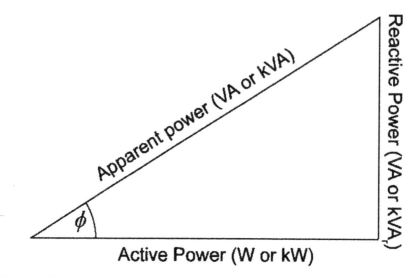

Figure 2.10 Diagrammatic representation of the electrical relationship between apparent, active and reactive power.

powers equipment which presents a reactive load with a low power factor, neither limit may safely be exceeded.

VA ratings are also often used for transformers; maximum output current is then VA rating divided by nominal output voltage. Transformers with the same sized core usually have the same VA rating.

2.4.7 kiloVolt-Ampere reactive

The relationship between apparent power [kVA], active or real power [kW] and reactive power [kVAr] is shown diagrammatically in Figure 2.10.

The correct symbol is lower-case "var", although the spellings "Var" and "VAr" are commonly used, and "VAR" is widely used throughout the power industry. Due to the relatively small size of the var, the industry normally uses kilovolt-ampere [kVAr].

Power factor = Cos Ø   (phase displacement between the supply voltage and the current)

$$= \frac{\text{Active power [kW] (real power which you get)}}{\text{Apparent power [kVA] (power you pay for)}}$$

To increase the power factor nearer to 1, also called unity, the lagging current must be more aligned with the voltage. When the value of cos Ø increases

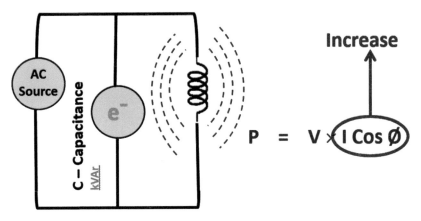

Figure 2.11 Addition of a capacitor in parallel with an inductive load to reduce the power factor.

it means that the real active power and the apparent power values are nearer to each other. On the electrical triangle in Figure 3.9 the top line [kVA] will swivel downwards towards the horizontal line [kW] and the angle between the lines will reduce, which means the power factor cos Ø will approach the value of 1. One of the most practical and used methods to obtain this change is to add a capacitor in parallel with the load, as shown in Figure 2.11 Figure 2.3: Distinctive parts of energy of a system

For the energy engineer/auditor a simple economic calculation can take the initial cost of the capacitor and compare it to the monthly savings in demand charges.

2.4.8 Watt

The watt [W] is a unit of power and is used to indicate the <u>rate of energy transfer</u>, the amount of energy per time duration (normally one second) (how "fast") which crosses a thermodynamic boundary. In the International System of Units (SI) it is defined as a derived unit of 1 joule per second [J/s]. The symbol is [W] and more commonly the kW, MW, and GW are used. It is also discussed under the heading volt-ampere.

2.4.9 Watt-hour

The watt-hour [Wh] is a measurement of the <u>quantity of energy</u> that was transferred past a measuring point by multiplying the rate [W] with the duration of the event, in this case 1 hour (3600 seconds). The term kilowatt-hour [kWh] is normally used.

2.4.10 kiloWatt and gigaWatt

The watt [W] is a relatively small unit, and 1 kiloWatt [kW] = 1000 W or 1 megaWatt [MW] = 1000 000 W or 1 GW = 1000 000 000 W is commonly used in industry.

Chapter 3

Energy Conversion and Efficiency

Louis Lagrange

University of the Free State, South Africa

The main focus of the learning in this knowledge module is to build an understanding of energy conversion and the efficiency of the conversion process.

3.1 Energy Conversion, Electricity and Energy Efficiency

Energy as such cannot be created or destroyed but can be converted into other forms of energy. Not all the final forms of energy are necessarily available as useful energy. This section explains the energy conversion process(es).

3.1.1 Total energy, useful and not useful energy

The total amount of energy as such cannot be created or destroyed, but the forms of energy in each of the sub-sections of the total quantity of energy change with each conversion process. The total amount of energy can be divided into an:

- available (useful) part that we can convert through a process to another form, and

- non-available (thus also not useful) part that remains not useful for further processes after any conversion.

Figure 3.1 depicts schematically the useful and non-useful parts of energy relative to total energy. Scientists and engineers refer to the non-available/not useful energy as Entropy (S). The amount of entropy changes during any process where energy is converted from one form to another, it normally increases. This also means that the entropy section of all energy in the entire

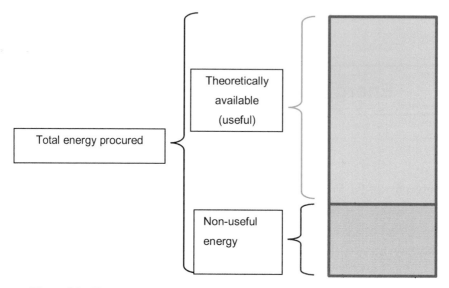

Figure 3.1   Total energy, available (useful) and non-available (non-useful) energy.

world increases all the time as all conversion processes ends with less useful energy and more not useful energy.

The available (useful) part of energy has, however, another aspect which the energy manager/auditor need to be aware of. The available energy can also be subdivided into two parts, namely:

• Total theoretical available energy, and

• Real practically available energy.

Inherent aspects like inertia and friction that is part of conversion processes reduces the real practical amount of energy that can be converted. This real/actual practical available energy, known as exergy, is depicted in Figure 3.2

An energy conversion process can thus be seen as <u>taking the available exergy</u> and <u>converting as much as possible of the exergy into the end-use energy form</u> and continuing with this process until all the exergy has been depleted. We can now state that the maximum possible amount of practical energy to "get" out of a process is the amount of exergy available, and when all the exergy is depleted, we have a 100% conversion or "efficiency" through the process. Such a process will have achieved full exergy depletion as all available energy has been extracted/converted. The aim of the energy engineer is to achieve complete full exergy depletion.

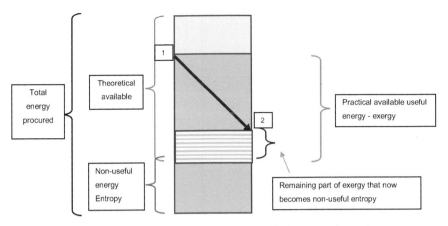

Figure 3.2 Theoretical and practical available energy (exergy).

Unfortunately, there are no processes that can achieved this due to the inherent inefficiencies of any conversion process. It is, however, a useful concept for the energy manager/auditor to understand as it indicates the maximum amount of useful energy that can be expected from any process.

The exergy depletion which takes place during a conversion process is indicated graphically with an arrow from start (point 1) to the end (point 2) on Figure 3.2. It also shows that a process can rarely deplete all the exergy, and the remaining not-depleted exergy now becomes part of the non-available energy, or entropy. This confirms the statement that the entropy increases after each process. This remaining part of the Exergy which was not converted to useful output forms the maximum amount of process efficiency which can be attained if full 100 % exergy depletion was achieved.

We can now use the definition of energy efficiency introduced earlier of how well an energy conversion process is accomplished to graphically depict the ratio of the output to the input in Figure 3.3

The importance of the term <u>exergy depletion</u> now becomes clear when we consider that we need to pay for all energy procured and measure the real practical and useful output attained to determine understand the actual efficiency of any conversion process. The <u>efficiency of any system cannot be greater than the amount of exergy available to energy procured</u> and this determines a limit to the maximum amount of possible savings that we can expect from any process where energy is converted. This is of particular importance to the energy auditor when quantifying possible Energy Management Opportunities (EMOs).

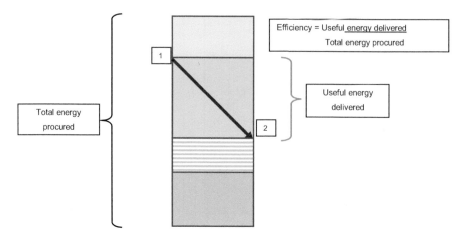

Figure 3.3   Schematic representation of the definition of energy efficiency.

The sequential approach of understanding energy conversion can be summarised as:

i. determine the type and quantity of energy procured

To measure efficiency, we need to determine the position **where** we measure the procured energy input relative to **where** we measure the output. For this we need to establish the earlier discussed thermodynamic system boundary, namely what do we want to include is situated inside the chosen system boundary, and where to measure the actual movement of energy which crosses the selected boundary, normally in the form of Heat (Q). or Work (W).

We choose the related system boundaries relative to questions we need to solve, for instance:

a) If we measure input at the initial conversion (coal to electricity) and output at the final process (inside a factory) we obtain a view of the entire system of interest to society.

b) If we measure the input at the factory inlet and the output at the final process, we obtain a view of the efficiency of conversion for the factory only. This can broadly be an indication of the possible amount of EMO's that could be available.

c) If we measure a selected combination of steps in the system, we obtain a view of the energy conversion for the specific selected process, e.g., the pumping of a fluid/water which considers the electric motor, drive, and pump.

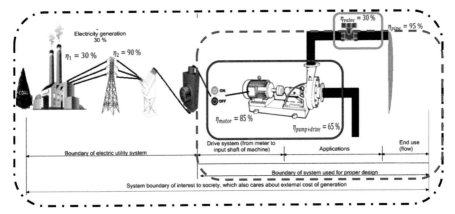

Figure 3.4 Four different boundaries to consider for energy efficiency audits.

d) If we measure a single step, e.g., a valve, we can obtain a <u>view of each step/component</u> in the process.

Figure 3.4 show examples of the 4 possible boundaries schematically.

Boundary a for entire system = black

Boundary b for factory = blue

Boundary c for a selected process = red (e.g. Motor, drive and pump)

Boundary d for a single step/component = green

Once the boundary position has been selected, the energy auditor must compile a list of the identified EMO's within the boundary and the exact positions where energy cross (enter and exit) the system boundary to enable the appropriate measures required for decision making. This list should include any organization specific required information. The list could contain the following, but should not be limited to:

a) Current efficiency of each EMO (step/component).

b) Expected monetary savings value of each EMO.

c) Expected effect on energy usage of the system.

d) Estimated cost of implementation.

e) Estimated ease of implementation.

f) Financial metrics like Simple Payback Period (SPP) and where required by the institution add additional metrics like Net Present Value (NPV) and Internal Rate of Return (IRR).

To obtain the efficiencies of the entire system, process, or combination of steps the efficiency of each separate step is multiplied by each other.

From Figure 3.4, the following efficiencies can be determined:

i. Efficiency of entire value chain

$$= \eta_{\text{Generation}} \; 0.3 * \eta_{\text{Transmission}} \; 0.9 * \eta_{\text{Motor}} \; 0.85 * \eta_{\text{Pump \& drive}} \; 0.65 *$$
$$\eta_{\text{Valve}} \; 0.3 * \eta_{\text{Pipe}} \; 0.95 = \underline{\mathbf{4.25 \%}}$$

ii. Efficiency of the factory (wrt water pumping)

$$= \eta_{\text{Motor}} \; 0.85 * \eta_{\text{Pump \& drive}} \; 0.65 * \eta_{\text{Valve}} \; 0.3 * \eta_{\text{Pipe}} \; 0.95 = \underline{\mathbf{15.7 \%}}$$

iii. Efficiency of the process consisting of the electric motor, drive and water pump

$$= \eta_{\text{Motor}} \; 0.85 * \eta_{\text{Pump \& drive}} \; 0.65 = \underline{\mathbf{55.25 \%}}$$

iv. Efficiency of the valve

$$= \eta_{\text{Valve}} \; 0.3 = \underline{\mathbf{30 \%}}$$

These values are then included into a <u>list of possible EMO's</u>. This energy audit list should be compiled to consider the:

i. Components,

ii. Processes,

iii. Sub-systems, and

iv. Systems.

The energy auditor should approach the above in a sequential manner. It is important that the energy auditor, as a first step, <u>consider and interrogate the individual components/equipment</u> with the lowest efficiencies to determine the <u>possibility of single component interventions affecting efficiency increases</u>. This should be <u>followed by quantifying each EMO</u> on the list, again following the individual components to processes and systems sequence. This information can then be prioritised according to the company requirements for effective managerial energy related decisions.

3.2 The Four Thermodynamic Laws

3.2.1 Definition and interpretation of thermodynamic law nr 0

The interpretation of this law for this course is as follows: Energy tend to flow in a specific direction, in terms of temperature energy flows from a region of higher temperature to a lower temperature, and when it crosses a selected thermodynamic boundary, it is known as heat (Q).

3.2.2 Definition and interpretation of thermodynamic law nr 1

The first law of thermodynamics, also known as the Law of Conservation of Energy, states that energy cannot be created or destroyed in an isolated system, energy can only be transferred or changed from one form to another, with no regard to its quality.

This is depicted in Figure 3.5 and can be summarised as:

Sum of all energy in = sum of all energy out + sum of energy retained in the system.

Energy has a measurable quantity and through using accounting principles all streams of energy flow over a thermodynamic border are accounted for. As <u>energy is conserved it means the total amount of energy remains constant</u> and any change in the internal energy (ΔE) of a system is given by the sum of the heat (Q) that flows across its boundaries and the work (W) done on the system by the surroundings.

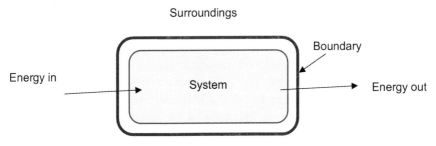

Figure 3.5 Thermodynamic law 1: sum of energy in = sum of energy out if no retention in system.

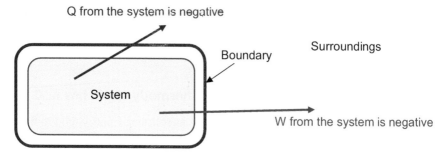

Figure 3.6   Sign convention for energy flow across a thermodynamic border.

Since both heat and work can be measured and quantified, this is the same as saying that any change in the energy of a system must result in a corresponding change in the energy of the surroundings outside the system (in other words, energy cannot be created or destroyed). If heat flows into a system or the surroundings do work on it, the internal energy increase and the signs of Q and W will be positive. Conversely, heat flow out of the system or work done by the system (on the surroundings) will be at the expense of the internal energy, and the signs of Q and W will therefore be negative. This is diagrammatically depicted in Figure 3.6.

3.2.3 Definition and interpretation of thermodynamic law nr 2

The second law of thermodynamics states that energy has quality as well as quantity. This is a very important statement for the energy auditor because if available energy is not of the required correct quality for a specific process, it is in reality not available to be utilised to do work.

The second law states that actual processes occur in the direction of decreasing quality of energy, and not in the reverse direction. An example is a cup of hot tea in a room cools down to eventually reach the room temperature and cannot heat up again by itself. The high temperature of the tea (quality) is lowered (entropy increase). This implies that "disorder" is taking place in one direction in an isolated system and supports the statement that the non-useful energy (entropy) as a result of a conversion process always increases.

When isolated systems are considered, they spontaneously evolve towards thermal equilibrium where the temperature of the system and the surroundings are the same, as indicated in the preceding paragraphs. This is also the state of maximum entropy of the system. More simply put: the entropy of the universe (the ultimate isolated system) only increases and never decreases.

A simple way to think of the second law of thermodynamics is that a room, if not cleaned and tidied, will invariably become messier and more disorderly with time. When the room is cleaned, its entropy decreases, but the effort to clean it has resulted in an increase in entropy outside the room that exceeds the entropy lost.

The <u>second law thus identify the direction of processes</u> and consider the <u>energy quality</u> as well as <u>quantity</u>. It is important for the energy auditor to consider the quality, as well as the amount of degradation, of useful energy during processes. The second law of thermodynamics is used by engineers to predict the degree of completion of processes (amount of exergy depleted) and to identify the areas where inefficiencies can be addressed, and the upper limit of efficiency increase which can possibly be attained.

3.2.4 Definition and interpretation of thermodynamic law nr 3

The third law of thermodynamics states that the entropy of a system approaches a constant value as the temperature approaches absolute zero, with absolute zero the lowest temperature that is theoretically possible. This will be the state where a system will have the minimum possible energy. The third law of thermodynamics will not be used in this book.

Entropy is a thermodynamic property that is the measure of a system's thermal energy per unit of temperature that is non-available for doing useful work. This law is applicable under specific extreme conditions and is not applicable to the typical everyday processes that is covered by this course.

General observations from the laws of thermodynamics that is practically applicable to this course are as follows:

a) Processes occur in a certain direction, and the direction can be predicted.

b) Energy has quality as well as quantity, and processes reduces both the quality as well as quantity of the available energy.

c) A process cannot take place unless it satisfies both the first and second laws of thermodynamics.

d) A process which satisfies the first law alone does not necessarily ensure that the process will actually take place.

e) In other words, it defines the theoretical maximum level of conversion efficiency that can be achieved for thermo-processes, and for the energy auditor assist to point out the direction to possibly eliminate or reduce inefficiencies (losses).

f) Predicts the degree of completion of chemical reactions.

3.3 Energy Performance Criteria

Energy Management Systems (EnMS) is a means for organisations to implement **systems and procedures** necessary to monitor, manage and control the effective and efficient use of energy, as well as to establish long-term energy efficiency improvement processes and mechanisms. EnMS use the whole systems approach to provide the framework and means (not an end) towards assisting a company to build capacity and to focus on continuous improvement. As it establishes system and procedures for improvement, it and does not measure or guarantee energy savings or reductions on its own.

The International Standard of Energy Management System (ISO50001) was promulgated in 2011. Among the EnMS components, energy performance evaluation and the related criteria to use plays a fundamental supporting role in determining if improvement has taken place and quantifying the improvement. This is achieved through specific measuring and evaluating of the improvement of energy performance using the prior discussed thermodynamic boundary methodology. Therefore, developing a mature and practical energy performance evaluation methodology becomes a key point to promote and implement an EnMS.

One of the fundamental aspects is to sequentially determine the performance of the energy use systems and operations using Energy Performance Indicators (EnPIs). The evaluation indicator, or metric, uses a specific common unit to enable the energy engineer/auditor to compare levels of efficient operation.

A variety of energy performance criteria, and subsequent different metrics, are available for use in an EnMS and it provides management information from an overarching high-level view of the energy value chain down to specific processes and individual components. This is the opposite sequence of the earlier discussed energy audit efficiency percentages. It is also used for continuous improvement of energy use.

Additional metrics which can be derived from primary energy performance data through using general unit conversion factors include greenhouse gas emissions, CO_2 reduction, and other related environmental metrics.

Energy performance evaluation forms an important role in an energy management system to provide insight into the organizational level efficiencies and can also fulfil the following additional roles:

- Understand the current level of operation of the system or components depending on the chosen thermodynamic boundary.

- Identify the areas and/or intervention opportunities to carry out energy efficiency measures for the next step and improve energy efficiency on a continuous basis.

- Prioritise the systems and/or components for interventions, including the possible ease of implementation, savings, cost and payback of each EMO.

- Evaluate whether the interventions function as planned and quantify to what extent the goal has been achieved.

- Indicate when a system is moving away from accepted performance ranges and thus indicate possible problems or (eminent) future equipment failure.

- Serve as basis of reward (or punishment) for energy efficiency policies, standards, interventions.

- Link energy performance with personnel management and ensure both accountability and responsibilities are clear and well understood. It can also rouse enthusiasm for energy efficiency improvement(s).

A typical process flow of how management systems promote continuous improvement through organisational practise and processes, including the development of teams to execute planning, evaluation, measurement and tracking is shown in Figure 3.7.

The evaluation of energy performance on a high level is normally associated with energy efficiency policies and standards. This metric is normally

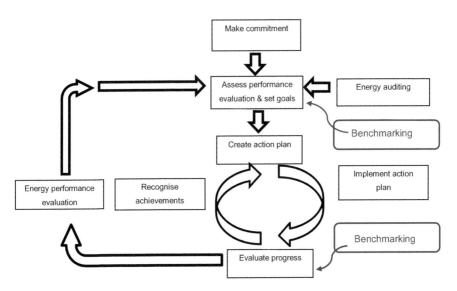

Figure 3.7   Energy performance in an Energy Management system (EnMS) (after APEC 2012).

referred to as <u>Energy Performance Benchmarking</u>. It may even be mandated by government and may require buildings to publicly display their bench-marking certificates.

<u>Benchmarking refers to relative performance</u>, and because high level averages are used, care must be taken with the interpretation and subsequent understanding of possible inaccuracies. Checks for commonalities like occu-pancies, climates, sizes, operational parameters and so forth should be built into the metrics.

Benchmarking is one of the fundamental practices EnMS as it provides confirmation of the final effect of executed interventions, and quantifies the effect on a high level. It is normally based on the comparison of management practices or on selected energy data. Two types of benchmarking are normal used, namely:

- Practice benchmarking. Identify opportunities by comparing best energy management practices, This is a qualitative process comparing actions.

- Energy Benchmarking. Identify how well an entity perform, track improvement over time, and position the entity relative to other simi-lar entities in terms of energy performance. It is a quantitative process which is data driven and compares numbers.

Furthermore, benchmarking can also be used for the following relative comparisons:

- Internal. Performance is compared against an <u>internal baseline,</u> e.g., other similar buildings within the organisation.

- External. Performance is compared against a metric <u>outside of the organisation</u>, e.g., best in class.

- Best available practices. Performance is compared to the <u>best of avail-able practices</u> in the market outside of the organisation.

Generally, the steps involved in energy best practices benchmarking include:

- Identify areas for improvement that will benefit most from the benchmarking.

- Research and identify key factors and variables used to measure the improvement.

- Determine if the data is already available, how to obtain it and the data accuracy and validity.

- Analyse the data and identify the best practice/performance by selecting the best-in-class category (e.g., companies that perform each function at the lowest cost with the highest energy efficiency).

- Determine the conditions under which the best practices can be achieved and specify the action(s) that must be taken to achieve the desired results.

Set specific improvement targets and deadlines for implementation. Develop a continuous procedure to monitor, review and update the data and analyse it over time. This will provide a basis for the monitoring, revision and recalibration of the measurements for further benchmarking studies.

The positioning of energy performance metrics to be used is provided within context of performing energy audits. Note that the determination of metrics is only finalised when the pre-assessment or preliminary audit has been completed and the audit mandate confirmed.

In summary: energy performance evaluation means applying scientific criteria, methods and procedures, using correct metrics for the correct reason and in the correct way to ensure correct evaluations on energy performance achieved by organizations. The establishment of a practical energy performance evaluation methodology and continuous management is necessary to implement plans and to realise savings.

3.4 Calculation of Energy Efficiency Performance

Energy Performance Indicators (EnPI) can be used as a simple but relevant metric for benchmarking the energy performance of systems or processes against a known value for similar systems, either inside the company or outside of the company, or against best practices in the market. Energy Performance Benchmarking focusses on a comparative analysis of energy use per unit of physical production, a terminology also known as energy intensity.

Best benchmarking involves comparing the energy operation status of whole facilities, systems and/or processes with the best-in-class operations in the market. The EnPI's for benchmarking energy efficiency can be grouped as follows:

i. High level Metrics

    a) Energy Use Index (EUI)

    b) Energy Cost Index ECI)

    c) Several models exist and some are available free of charge, e.g., Retscreen, EnergyStar, etc

  ii. Productivity Metrics

    a) kJ/person, kWh/person

    b) kJ/kg product, kWh / kg product

    c) kJ/item manufactured; kWh/item manufactured

    d) Energy Efficiency Ratio (EER) and Seasonal Energy Efficiency Ratio (SEER)

  iii. System Performance Metrics

    a) $kW_{electrical} / kW_{cooling}$

    b) $kW_{electrical}$ / litre of water pumped

    c) $kW_{electrical}$ / lumen produced (efficacy of lights)

    d) Window energy rating

The Energy Use Index (EUI) is calculated as the total energy consumed in a building over a year divided by total built up area in kWh/m²/year or MJ/m²/year. Take note the square meters [m²] refer specifically to conditioned space, and areas like parking garages and verandas needs to be left out. It is a simple and convenient high-level indicator for comparing a building to a norm as energy efficient or not.

Although it provides an answer to the overall efficiency of energy use, it is at too high a measurement level to indicate specific energy management opportunity areas, processes or equipment.

3.4.1 High level benchmarking metrics

The ability to accurately measure current and forecast future energy consumption is an important strategy in achieving the objective of managing and reducing energy demand and cost, with the additional benefit of tracking and improving energy performance. This strategy requires several different methods and metrics of energy performance, widely referred to as indexes. Some of the more common indexes are presented here.

3.4.2 Energy use index

The Energy Use Index (EUI) is also known as the Energy Performance Indicator (EPI) for buildings is considered the simplest and most relevant high-level indicator for buildings.

Table 3.1 Typical EUI figures for buildings in the northern hemisphere.

Type of building	Typical annual energy use per m²
EUI Entertainment and public assembly	400 kWh m^{-2}a^{-1}
Theatrical and Indoor Sport	400 kWh m^{-2}a^{-1}
Places of Worship	110 kWh m^{-2}a^{-1}
Places of Instruction	400 kWh m^{-2}a^{-1}
Large shop (incl. shopping malls)	240 kWh m^{-2}a^{-1}
Offices	190 kWh m^{-2}a^{-1}
(average USA office = 293 kWh m^{-2}a^{-1})	
Warehouses	120 kWh m^{-2}a^{-1}
Hotel	600 kWh m^{-2}a^{-1}

Process to determine the EUI

- Formula: Energy Use Index (EUI) - kWh / annum / m² of conditioned space

- Convert the different fuels into kWh through the specific energy content of each

- Determine the area of conditioned space

- Calculate the EUI

- Compare the EUI with industry averages

3.4.3 Energy cost index

The Energy Cost Index (ECI) adds up the energy costs for all different types of energy used. It accounts for the fact that MJ$_{electric}$ is usually more expensive than MJ$_{natural}$ gas in the northern hemisphere (higher PoU cost). Beware ECI incorporates a variable that cannot be controlled, namely the variation in energy rates by location, season and/or time of use.

Process to determine the ECI

- Formula: Cost of energy [Rands] / annum / m² of conditioned space

- Use the same EUI data of the previous exercise

- Obtain typical costs for each energy source

- Calculate the ECI

3.4.4 Productivity metrics

To promote the efficient use of energy, governments worldwide have mandated minimum standards of energy preforming equipment.

The metric compares the energy used to produce a unit number of deliverables (per unit of product) or unit number of people using the energy (per person). Indexes like kJ/person, kWh/person, kJ/kg product, kWh/kg product are common.

Productivity Indexes provide a relative high-level metric to compare the efficiency of a system/group of operations for comparison reasons, and from this metric more detailed audits of selected equipment can follow.

3.4.5 Energy efficiency rating, seasonal and integrated

The performance of air-conditioners and heat pumps can be expressed as the Energy Efficiency Ratio (EER) or Seasonal Energy Efficiency Ratio (SEER), based on certain test standards. This metric is commonly used for products from the European Union.

EER is the measure of <u>instantaneous energy efficiency</u>, the ratio of the rate of heat removed from a cooled space by the equipment to the <u>rate of electricity consumption</u> in a steady operation, with the units British thermal unit per Watthour [Btu/Wh]

SEER is the ratio of the <u>total amount of heat removed by the equipment during a normal cooling season</u> to the <u>total amount of electricity consumed,</u> with the units Btu/Wh.

Using the relationship of 1 kWh = 3412 BTU, thus 1 Wh = 3.412 BtU, the relationship EER = 3.412 COP_r can thus be derived.

For refrigerators, air-conditioning systems and heat pumps the EER and SEER ratings are commonly used. Many air-conditioners and heat pumps have a SEER rating of between 13 and 21, which correspond to COP values of between 3.8 and 6.2. The EER or COP of a refrigerator decreases with decreasing temperature, with the effect that it is not economical to refrigerate at a lower temperature than required, and important aspect to determine during an energy audit.

The efficiency of air-conditioners and heat pumps differ through the day due to the variation in ambient temperature, with the hottest part of the day resulting in the highest COP. It also varies with the actual load on the equipment. The metric, Integrated Energy Efficiency Ratio (IEER) is used to determine the cooling EER rating based upon the weighted average of efficiencies at various loading levels.

The formula is as follows:

$$IEER = (0.02*A) + (0.617*B) + (0.238*C) + (0.125*D)$$

Where:

    A = EER at 100% net capacity at AHRI standard condition (35°C)
    B = EER at 75% net capacity and reduced ambient (27.5°C)
    C = EER at 50% net capacity and reduced ambient (20°C)
    D = EER at 25% net capacity and reduced ambient (18.3°C)

3.4.6 System performance metrics

System performance indexes uses a more detailed level of energy metrics, and the system boundaries can be carefully chosen to reflect the performance of systems, sub-systems and even individual equipment. It is still used as benchmark for comparison.

3.4.7 Typical system performance indexes

Typical system performance indexes in include kWelectrical / kWcooling, kWelectrical / litre of water pumped, kWelectrical / lumen produced (efficacy of lights), and window energy rating.

    The Energy Rating (ER) measures a window's overall performance, i.e., how well it: delivers solar heat gain in winter; prevents heat loss through the frame, the space between the panes of glass, and the glass itself; and. helps control heat loss due to air leakage.

3.5 Calculation of Point of Use (PoU) costs

The term "Point of Use" (PoU) cost refers to the nett cost to deliver a certain amount of energy where it is finally converted into its end use. It is crucial for the energy engineer/auditor to determine PoU costs as this enables the direct comparison between different types of fuels where the individual efficiencies of each type is already taken into account, converted to a common basis in kJ, GJ or kWh. Practically this means that PoU cost depends on the:

  i. Purchase price of the procured energy,

  ii. Specific energy contained in the type of fuel (also called energy intensity), and

  iii. Conversion efficiency of the type of equipment used.

  iv. $PoU\ cost = \dfrac{Procured\ cost\left[R\right]of\ energy\ per\ common\ unit\left[Gj\ or\ kWh\right]}{Effiency\ of\ conversion}$

The sequential steps to determine the PoU is indicated in Table 3.2, with some actual figures for applications where the fuel is used for heating purposes.

Table 3.2   Examples of PoU calculations.

Energy type	Cost (Rand)	Unit	Heating Value (energy intensity)	Unit	Cost (R/GJ)	Cost (R/kWh)	Heating Efficiency	PoU Cost (R/kWh)
Coal (B grade)	855.25	R/ton	27	MJ/kg	31.66	0.114	30 %	0.38
Gas (LPG)	30.35	R/kg	45.7	MJ/kg	664.11	2.39	72 %	3.32
Diesel	18.50	R/liter	39	MJ/liter	474.36	1.71	68 %	2.51
Electricity	2.00	R/kWh	3600	kJ/kWh	555.55	2.00	92 %	2.17

- Step 1: Convert to cost per energy unit GJ, using the energy intensity of the energy source.

- Step 2: Convert the cost per GJ to cost per kWh, using the relationship of 1 kWh = 0.0036 GJ (step 1 answer * 0.0036GJ/kWh).

- Step 3: Take the inefficiency of the energy conversion process into account by multiplying with 1/efficiency (Step 2 answer /decimal efficiency of the process).

The Point of Use costs of the different sources of energy can now be compared to each other in terms of actual cost per unit of energy. It is important for the energy auditor to realise that additional aspects may require consideration as well, namely: regular availability from a risk point of view, special storage requirements, safety requirements, environmental aspects, etc. Determining the actual PoU cost is always the first step for the energy auditor to complete, and, depending on the company some additional aspects will be added before a final decision can be made.

It is also important to remember that the price of an energy source could be linked to it geographical position, for instance for Liquified Petroleum Gas (LPG) there are 25 different zones and the price differs for each zone. Equally important is to obtain the actual energy intensity of the fuel used from the supplier, instead of using the average values in the table provided.

3.5.1 Energy conservation and energy conversion (energy flow)

Energy cannot be created or destroyed, this implies that the total amount of energy is fixed (already conserved), so what does the term energy **conservation** mean? The term energy conservation can refer to:

- The conservation of the quality of the energy, not the quantity.

- The <u>conservation of the useful quantity</u>, in other words full use of the available exergy.

The performance of how well an <u>energy conversion</u> or transfer/flow process happens is measured by the term efficiency, i.e., the ratio of the desired over the required input when energy is converted from one form to another.

3.5.2 Heat flow and heat loss

Energy can be transferred from a system in three forms, heat, work, and mass flow. <u>These energy interactions are recognised at the system boundary when they cross it</u>.

When energy crosses a thermodynamic boundary due to a difference in temperature, it is known as heat. Heat transfer to a system which increases the internal energy of the molecules, and thus the internal energy of the system, is heat gain. Heat transfer from a system transfers energy out of the system and is known as heat loss.

3.5.3 Mass- and energy-balance

To enable the study of energy and energy transfer it is advisable to identify and set apart a specific system or group of systems. We have previously seen that it is very handy to delineate the selected system with a boundary and then study, measure and account for all energy that crosses this boundary. Whatever changes happen within the system are known as the process.

It is also important to note that a system is defined to be closed when there can be no exchange of matter with its surroundings and open when an exchange over the boundary does occur.

Material and energy balances are based on the law of conservation of mass and energy which states:

The mass of material/energy entering a system in a steady state

equals

the mass of material/energy leaving the system.

This has applications in any process and a typical mass balance normally takes the following form:

$$\text{Inflow} = \text{outflow} + \text{accumulation} + \text{losses}$$

Mass of raw materials in = mass of products and waste out + mass of material stored in system + losses.

Two types of material balances prevail. One can <u>consider the plant as a whole or consider only a sub-system or process</u>. It is important to determine exactly which components affects the system or are being affected by the system. A mass balance is a very efficient way of determining unknown quantities in a process or stream.

The second type of material balance is the <u>theoretical one that treats what is often a small part of the process</u> such as a length of pipe or the tray of a distillation column in order to establish general design equations. This type of balance is the basis of much of the theory of fluid flow and other unit operations.

By tracing and accounting for the inflow and outflow of material in a process, the quantities of various materials in each process stream can be established. It is important that the boundary of the system under consideration be chosen carefully to simplify calculations. There are two fundamental initial steps involved in the solution of material balances, namely:

• Select the *system*

• Select a *basis* (as a point of reference from which to calculate material or energy changes)

After these initial steps, equations for each stream of mass are formed and solved simultaneously.

The selection of a system requires arbitrarily locating boundary lines. Everything outside these boundaries is considered outside of the system, the surroundings. Now, only those streams crossing boundaries, either entering or leaving the system, which was arbitrarily chosen, need to be considered as far as immediate calculations are concerned. The boundary should be selected to cross only those streams that are associated with the materials under consideration.

Figure 3.8 provides a conceptual layout of a mass and energy balance, whereas Figure 3.9 provides an example of a mass flow diagram for dehydration in a food processing facility.

Similar to the law of conservation of material, the equation on which the energy balance is founded is:

The total energy entering a system

equals

The total energy leaving the system (in steady state)

Amount of heat or work energy in = energy leaving with products and waste + stored energy + energy lost to the surroundings.

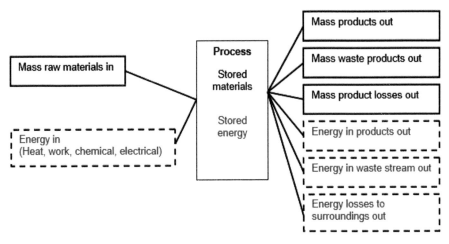

Figure 3.8 Conceptual layout of a mass and energy balance.

Mass of raw materials in = **mass of products and waste out**

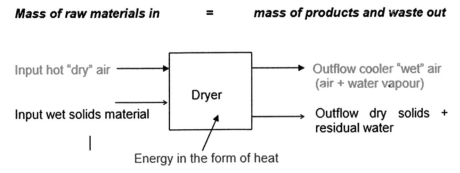

Figure 3.9 Mass flow diagram of a typical dehydration process.

In more academic terms: the net change, either increase or decrease, in the energy content of a system is equal to the difference between the energy entering (input) and the energy leaving (output) the system during a process. This relation is known as the energy balance and is applicable to any kind of system undergoing any kind of process.

The change in the total energy of a system during a process is the sum of the changes in its macroscopic (kinetic and potential) and microscopic energies as previously discussed.

If a system is stationary from a position point of view, the value of both the kinetic and potential energy is zero if the reference position is the same as the actual position, and only the microscopic energy change reflects the nett energy change on the system.

$$\Delta E_{system} = E_{in} - E_{out}$$
$$\Delta E_{system} = \Delta \text{ Kinetic energy} + \Delta \text{ Potential energy} + \Delta \text{ Internal energy}$$

There are two distinct types of energy balances. First there is the type that considers the energy requirements of an entire plant. This often takes the form of a heat balance without considering other forms of energy.

The second type is the one that considers a small sub- section of the plant to establish some design equation.

Similar to material balances, it is necessary to select both a system and a basis for energy balances. In the case of energy balances, it is usually necessary to select a temperature basis as reference - a temperature above which everything is measured. This is often, but not always, taken as 0°C.

Figure 3.10 provides an example of an energy flow diagram through a typical yoghurt production facility. The mass reference is one kg of final product. The energy is reflected in kJ of energy required for the specific component/step per kg of final processed product, in the case of this example yoghurt. The different stream of energy flow as well as the direction of flow are indicated in different colours as indicated in the legend.

3.5.4 Energy demand

The use of energy in a plant is determined by the plant operator/manager. The energy is "waiting to be deployed" by the push of a button or start of a process or equipment. Energy demand will be discussed here using electrical energy as input and thermal energy as output.

In order to understand energy demand it is necessary to

The first aspect to understand is that if the air-conditioning equipment unit has a Coefficient of Performance (COP) of 3, the 1000 $kW_{thermal}$ energy requirement in the middle of the day will translate to only one third $kW_{electrical}$, namely 333 $kW_{electrical}$ real power required from the electrical supply utility.

Figure 3.11 shows a typical daily energy usage pattern for an air-conditioned building over a 24-hour period in 2 hourly increments. As per specific tariff agreement the supply utility must generate electricity to be on standby for the full 24-hour period for whenever the customer requires to use the energy. This implies that if the customer does not necessarily utilise all of the energy on "standby", the utility which has generated it must recoup the costs from the customer some way or another.

In the example in Figure 3.11 this "standby rate of energy use" is 1000 $kW_{thermal}$ or 333 $kW_{electrical}$. The utility must thus generate a quantity of 333 $kW_{electrical}$ * 24 hours = 7992 $kWh_{electrical}$ for the 24-hour day. The corresponding $kW_{thermal}$ for the period is 1000 kW * 24 h = 24 000 $kWh_{thermal}$ while the actual $kW_{thermal}$l used is the sum of the actual usage, 14000 $kWh_{thermal}$.

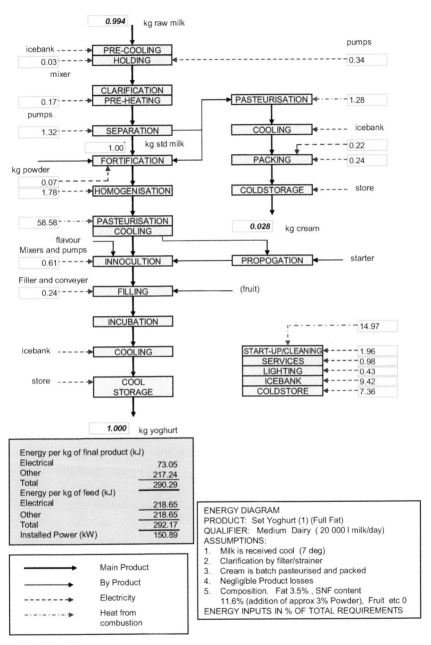

Figure 3.10 Energy flow diagram through a typical yoghurt processing facility.

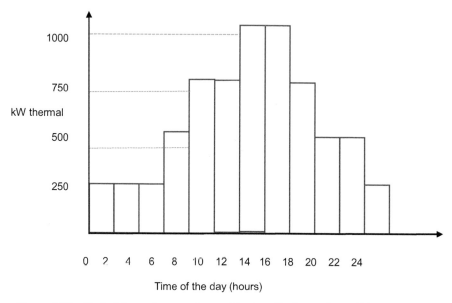

Figure 3.11   Typical thermal energy demand load profile for an air-conditioned building.

The highest demand of 333 kW$_{electrical}$ occurs during the period 14:00 to 18:00 and is known as the actual Maximum Demand (MDactual).

However, the electrical supply utility "see and experience" apparent power due to the fact that it must run a power station to deliver the energy in apparent power (kVA) to the customer. Figure 3.12 show the real power in kW$_{electrical}$ as well as the apparent power in kVA for a power factor of 0.8 schematically. For the majority of the industrial tariffs in South Africa the customer is billed on the apparent power consumption by taking the power factor into account.

Note that each specific tariff agreement for a company may state a minimum required power factor by the supplying utility and this needs to be checked by the energy auditor. If the customer's power factor is less than the specified minimum, there may be a penalty clause to be paid for this. This will be discussed in detail under the section on tariffs.

Since the actual use of the available generated energy is controlled by the plant operator/manager, the supply utility is required to keep enough generated energy available "on tap" throughout the day as per tariff agreement for the contractual period of the day. The cost of the energy generated by the utility, "waiting to be used", must be recovered from the consumer. The metric used is the highest measured energy demand, in South Africa over a 30-minute interval, considered for a period which normally spans a month. The utility thus measures the highest recorded kVA usage over an entire

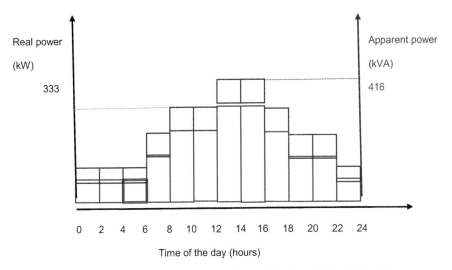

Figure 3.12 Typical electrical energy demand load profile for the building.

month, in half hour intervals sections in South Africa, and bill the customer at the end of each month for the highest Maximum Demand (MD).

The contractual agreement between the organisation and the electricity utility is the contractual Agreed Maximum Demand (AMD). This is also the deciding factor to for the supply utility to plan the size of their transmission and distribution lines as well as the size of the transformer to transport and deliver the energy to the customer's point of delivery. If the MD actual exceeds the agreed contractual value, there is usually a penalty to be paid for exceeding the agreement value. Depending on the specific tariff agreement this penalty could last for 12 months. It is highly advisable that energy auditors familiarise themselves with the relevant tariff agreements for each and every customer. This will be discussed in more detail under the tariff section

It is thus imperative that the energy auditor understand the tariff agreement and penalty clauses and ensure the correct measurement of the actual energy usage for each component on the energy chain is obtained, including the efficiency for each piece of equipment.

This energy could have been provided to other customers and for effective energy management to avoid exceeding the agreed maximum demand, the following steps are advisable:

i. Obtain the daily demand curves for the facility showing the time of use periods of maximum demand.

ii. Reduce the difference between real power (kW) and apparent power (kVA), which you pay for, through power factor correction to as near as practically and economically possible. Check that this includes the time of use period where maximum demand occurs.

iii. Use energy management principles to reduce the real power, followed by its subsequent reduction in apparent power, usage through consideration of the entire system and individual energy use equipment.

iv. Check the contract for the possible penalty clauses for overstepping the agreed maximum demand usage (see section on tariffs for details).

v.   Check the contract for the agreed minimum demand clauses (see section on tariffs for details).

Chapter 4

Fundamentals of Electrical Energy

Louis Lagrange

University of the Free State, South Africa

This module focusses on understanding the key aspects of electric energy and how to measure the usage of electric energy. It builds on the fundamental principles covered in Chapter 1. This relates to electric power and power quality, and the principles of measuring electric energy consumption.

4.1 Electrical Power and Electrical Power Quality

All materials are made up of one or more chemical elements such as copper or aluminium, while all elements are made up of specific types of atoms. The number of protons (positively charged) and electrons (negatively charged) identify and characterise the element. Protons as well as neutrons (no charge) are positioned in the centre of the atom while the electrons are arranged and travel in circular orbitals around the centre. The orbitals differ in distance from the centre and there are a certain number of electrons that can be accommodated in each orbital.

> *"A chlorine atom has seventeen electrons, seventeen protons and eighteen neutrons. A hydrogen atom has only one electron and one proton."*

When an atom has an equal number of protons and electrons, it is called neutral. The electrons in the outer orbital of an atom can be easily removed by an external force. When this happens, the atom has more protons than electrons, which gives it a positive charge and is then called an ion. Atoms can also have more electrons than protons, resulting in a negative charge.

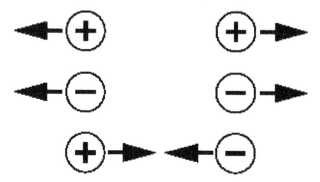

Figure 4.1   Forces of attraction and repulsion.

Particles with opposite electrical charges (for example, + and -) attract each other, while particles with like charges (for example, + and +) will repel each other. This is shown in Figure 4.1.

4.2 Electrical Voltage

Voltage is the pressure from an electrical circuit's power source that provide the "pushing force" to move charged electrons (current) through a conducting loop, enabling them to do work. In brief, voltage is an equivalent of pressure and is measured in volts (V).

"The term recognises Italian physicist Alessandro Volta (1745–1827), inventor of the voltaic pile—the forerunner of today's household battery. In electricity's early days, voltage was known as electromotive force."

The concepts of current and voltage can be explained by using an example of a water tank.

In this example, each of the elements of the water tank represent part of an electric circuit:

- The water represents the charge.

- The water pressure represents the voltage; and

- The water flow represents the current.

The water tank is a certain height above the ground. At the bottom of the tank is a hose, as shown in Figure 4.2.

The pressure ("pushing force") due to the height of the water above the reference point of the end of the hose represents the voltage while the water in the tank

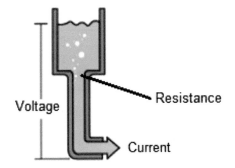

Figure 4.2 Water tank analogy to voltage and current.

represents the charge. Therefore, the higher the level of water is in the tank, the more pressure is available to move the water through the pipe and the resulting flow of water represents the movement of electrons, current.

4.3 Electrical Current

The term electricity refers to the flow of electrons through a material called a conductor. An energy force must firstly be established which result in the movement of electrons. This resulting movement of electrons create charge which is utilised to do work. Light bulbs, phones, radios and so on all make use of the movement of electrons to do work. Therefore, they all use one common basic power source, current, which is the movement of electrons.

The current can then be considered as the flow of energy in a conductor. There are different types of current, depending on the power source and the appliance used. When free electrons in a material (for example a metal) all move in the same direction, it is called a current. The amount of current that flows through a material is determined by the number of electrons Which pass through the conductor in one second. The symbol for current is **I**, and it is measured in ampere [A], which is commonly usually shortened to 'amps'.

One ampere means that 6.24×10^{18} electrons pass through a conductor in one second.

Current is the amount of charge flowing through a circuit during a certain period of time. Current is measured in amperes (A) and is usually represented by the letter 'I' in equations.

The tank in Figure 4.1 can be compared to a battery in a flashlight, where a certain amount of energy is stored and released on demand. Over time the flashlight gets dimmer as the batteries lose power because the voltage decreases. This is the same as the water from the tank being drained a bit,

Table 4.1   Summary of voltage and current.

	Current	**Voltage**
Definition	The rate at which charge flows in an electrical circuit.	The **potential difference** in charge between two points in a circuit.
Symbol	I	V
SI unit	Ampere	Volt
Measuring instrument	Ampere meter	Voltmeter
Relationship	Current is the result and voltage is the cause. Current cannot flow without voltage.	Voltage is the cause and current is the result. Voltage can function without current.

which causes the pressure to create flow at the end of the hose to decrease resulting in a decrease in the amount of water flow. Less pressure results in less water to flow, the same principle as in voltage and current. Table 4.1 summarises the characteristics of voltage and current.

4.4 Electrical Power

Power is the rate at which work is done. It is equal to the amount of energy (J) consumed per unit of time (s), thus Joule/second (J/s), measured in watt (W).

The formula to calculate electrical power from first principles is:

$$P \text{ [Watt]} = \text{Voltage [V]} * \text{current [I]}$$

The unit of power in watt is small and the unit of kilowatt is normally used

An example of how power is used in our everyday life is the rate at which a light bulb converts electrical energy into light and heat energy. The higher the wattage of the light bulb, the more power or electrical energy is used per unit of time.

Almost everything we use needs power to make it work. For example, power is used in the residential sector as well as in the commercial, transportation and industrial sectors. It is used for heating and cooling our homes, and it provides electricity for office buildings and the manufacturing of products that are needed in our day-to-day lives.

4.5 Demand

The concept of consumption and demand was addressed earlier. This section will focus on electrical demand. Consumption is the total amount of energy used in a specific building for specified period, measured in kWh and is measured by the electric meter.

The rate at which this energy is consumed is known as the demand and is measured in kilowatts (kW). Electrical energy demand is usually not measured for residential customers; it is mainly used for commercial customers where they are charged for both the energy consumed and how fast they use it. The highest electrical demand (maximum demand) is also the rate at which the electricity must be generated and kept "on tap" for the consumer. This amount of electricity to be generated to meet the amount of energy needed is called capacity. This concept is also used when designing a system or building and is done to make sure that electrical distribution equipment is properly sized. This promotes energy efficiency; the capacity of a power utility must be able to meet the demand so that customers do not sit without electricity.

When a toaster and a microwave are both switched on at the same time and it causes a fuse to fail, the circuit did not have enough capacity to meet the demand. However, if these appliances are used one after the other, the energy should be available for the appliances to work.

4.6 Types of Current Flow

There are two types of current due to two types of voltage, Direct current (DC) and Alternating current (AC). With a constant voltage the resulting flow of electric current is all in one direction, direct current (DC). This is found in low-voltage devices using batteries. When the voltage continuously alters and provides a "pushing force" first from one side of the conductor and then from the other side, the resulting flow of electrons follows this pattern and change direction of flow, called alternating current (AC).

4.7 Direct Current

In direct current the voltage continue to "push" in one direction and the current flows in one direction.

The current from a DC source will remain constant over time as long as the voltage does not change. For example, the graph of a 3 V AA battery shows it provides a constant voltage over time and therefore a constant current for as long as it remains charged (voltage is maintained).

DC sources can therefore be relied upon to provide constant voltages over time until a battery loses its charge when the voltage will drop away quickly and so will the current.

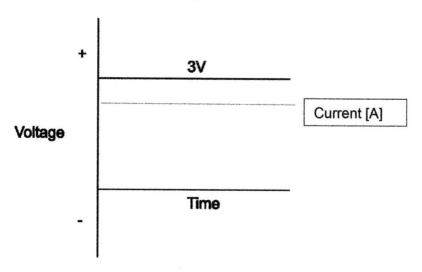

Appliances with a battery, or with an adapter to convert AC into DC like a charger that plugs into the wall or a universal serial bus (USB) cable all use DC as their power source.

Examples of appliances with a battery, an AC/DC adapter, or a charger that plugs into the wall are:

• Cell phones

• Flashlights

• Battery-operated devices

Most DC devices operate at low voltages (typically between 1.5 V and 24 V). Table 4.2 shows the different symbols used for DC.

Although the convention of current states electrons flow from the negative to the positive, actual current flows from the positive to the negative.

Figure 4.3 shows the normal flow and the electron flow in an electrical circuit.

4.8 Batteries

The batteries that we use in appliances such as flashlights, clock radios, clocks, cell phones, etc all work using chemical energy. This chemical energy separates the charges and thereby creates a positive and a negative terminal

Table 4.2 DC symbols.

Component	Symbol	Description
Cell		A cell supplies electrical energy. The larger terminal (left) is positive, and the shorter terminal is negative.
Battery		A battery consists of more than one cell joined together. The larger terminals are positive.
DC supply	+ −	Electrical energy that always flow in one direction.
Voltage meter	V	Voltmeter
Current meter	A	Amperemeter
Variable resistance		A diagonal arrow on any symbol means the values of that component can be varied.

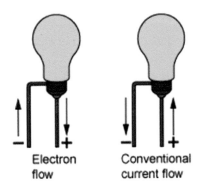

Electron flow   Conventional current flow

Figure 4.3 Flow of current.

with a certain potential difference (voltage) between them which provides the force to move the electrons.

A similar example would be the amount of work needed to lift an object onto a platform, which gives it some gravitational potential energy. Both work and potential energy are measured in joules, therefore the amount of work done is equal to the object's gravitational potential energy.

4.9 Alternating Current

When the voltage continuously alters and provides a pushing force, first from one side of the conductor and then from the other side, the resulting flow of electrons following the voltage also change the direction of flow, called alternating current (AC).

AC is generated using a device called an alternator which reverses its terminal polarities many times per second, causing the current to change direction as well. The form of the alternating current wave can vary, but the sine wave, as shown in Figure 4.4, is the most common form.

The sine wave has two axes:

- The direction as well as the magnitude of the voltage and/or current is shown on the vertical axis.

- The time duration is shown on the horizontal axis.

When the wave is above the horizontal axis denoting zero voltage (0 V), it is denoted as positive and current is flowing in one direction. When the wave is below the 0 V axis, current is negative and is flowing in the opposite direction. A sine wave moves through a 360°electrical degree cycle. One 360° cycle is also called one cycle. An alternating current has many of these cycles per second, called the frequency, measured in Hertz (Hz).

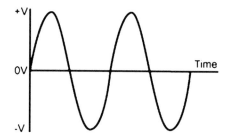

Figure 4.4   Sine wave.

AC is a very efficient method to power the electric motors found in appliances such as washing machines, refrigerators and dishwashers. Motors and generators are very similar devices; the main difference is that motors convert electrical energy into mechanical energy, whereas generators convert mechanical energy into electrical energy.

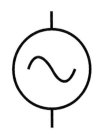

Figure 4.5 Symbol for an AC power supply.

Generators are used to produce electricity and the symbol shown in Figure 4.5 is mostly used to indicate AC power supplies.

Some of the advantages of AC include:

- Alternating current can travel through long distances and wires to reach buildings, homes, offices, etc. The efficient transport of electrical energy requires a high voltage and is known as Transmission voltages.

- If the generated electricity reaches homes, buildings, offices, the voltage is too high and the current too low for usage in everyday appliances. Substations lower the high voltage and transformers lower the voltage before it enters buildings. The electricity is thus transformed to a lower voltage and higher current and enters households and other buildings at 220 V.

- Transformers cannot change DC voltage, which makes it an advantage to use AC.

- Buildings, homes and offices are normally also supplied from the distribution network with AC electricity because the appliances require AC.

4.10 The Different Types of Loads

Electrical loads can be divided into different categories, as will be discussed in the sections that follow.

4.10.1 Electrical circuitry

An electric circuit is a path along which electrons flow from the current or voltage source. Electric current only flows in a closed path in the circuit. A closed path is a circuit where current can flow through a continuous path without any interruptions. In an open circuit, current does not flow and there are constant interruptions. Electric circuits use two types of power, AC and DC. The point where electrons enter an electric circuit is called the source of electrons, and the point where electrons leave the circuit is called the return, earth or ground. This point is called return because the electrons end up at the source when they have completed the path of the electric circuit.

4.10.2 Resistive loads

If the load in an electric circuit consists of a purely resistive element to convert current into different forms, for example, heat, it is known as a resistive load.

In such a case the direction and magnitude of the current follows the voltage closely and it is said to be in phase with the voltage. Figure 4.6 provides a schematic diagram of such an electric circuit, the voltage and current diagram, and the related formulas.

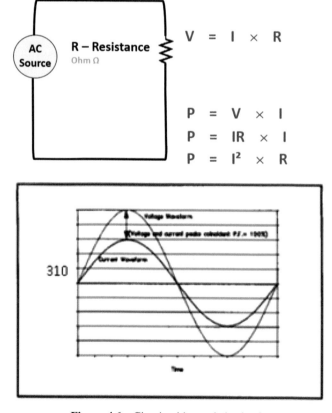

$$V = I \times R$$

$$P = V \times I$$
$$P = IR \times I$$
$$P = I^2 \times R$$

310

Figure 4.6 Circuit with a resistive load.

As the current rises to a steady state without any drastic changes, it can be said that resistive loads have very little current changes. To optimally use resistive loads, they could benefit from voltage optimisation. This is because resistive loads are used to convert current into energy at different voltages. Making use of voltage optimisation will help improve energy efficiency as well as conserve power and extend the duration which electronic appliances or equipment can last.

Figure 4.7 An electric heater using resistive elements.

Examples of resistive loads are:

*   Electrical heaters (see Figure 4.7)

*   Incandescent lighting

4.10.3 Inductive loads

If the load in an electric circuit consists of an inductor, electromagnetic waves are established in the surrounding air and the energy is temporarily "stored" in these waves. The electromagnetic waves are created due to the current flow through the inductor, and collapses when the direction of flow is reversed. In such a case the current does not follow the voltage closely, but when measured it will be reduced, said to lag behind the voltage. Figure 4.8 provides a schematic diagram of such an inductive electric circuit, the voltage and current diagram, and the related formulas

When the power for an inductive circuit is calculated, it becomes evident from Figure 4.8 that the value of the current to be multiplied with the voltage is reduced. The size of the reduction is provided by the factor cos θ

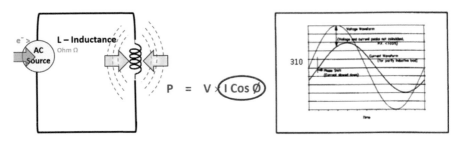

Figure 4.8 Circuit with an inductive load.

where θ is the number of degrees on the horizontal axis of the diagram. This is provided in the formula in Figure 4.8.

Inductive loads create electromagnetic fields and the inductance is measured in Henry.

Inductive loads work on two types of power, namely:

• Real power

• Apparent power

Real power is the actual useful work the equipment does when it is in operation, while apparent power is the energy that is obtained from the source and is used to produce magnetic fields. The total amount of power used by the device or equipment is measured by adding up the real and the apparent power.

4.10.4 Capacitive loads

These loads are the opposite of inductive loads and are used to resist the effect of inductive loads. They are therefore used to resist the changes in voltage and, in this case, the voltage lags behind the current. Capacitors consist of wires or metal plates separated by an insulator, and it stores the charge. The positioning of a capacitor in a circuit is indicated in Figure 4.9 and capacitance is measured in Farads.

Capacitors are very common and can be found in the following devices:

• Flashbulb.

• Heart defibrillator.

• Camera flash.

An example of a capacitance load is shown in Figure 4.10.

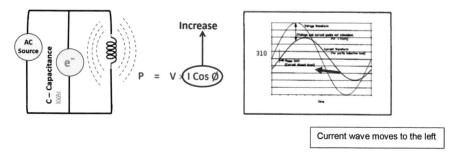

Figure 4.9   Circuit with a capacitive load.

Figure 4.10 A capacitance load found in a camera flashlight.

4.11 Electrical Power Factor

In AC circuits, the current and voltage are not always in phase with each other. The power factor (PF) provides a metric of how well they work together. The power factor ranges from 0 to 1 (from 0 % to 100 %). It can be explained by using a practical example such as a child being pushed on a swing by her dad. When the swing reaches the maximum height of the swing cycle, the dad gets a maximum result from the push, which is 100% PF. If the swing does not reach the maximum height, some of the PF is lost and therefore the result will be less than 100% PF.

The relationship between current, voltage, power and power factor are shown in the equations that follow.

$$Power(kW) = \frac{Voltage(V) \times Current(A) \times PF}{1000}$$

This can be written as:

$$kilowatt(kW) = \frac{Volts(V) \times Ampere(I) \times PF}{1000}$$

$$kilovoltampere(kVA) = \frac{V \times A}{1000}$$

The kilowatts and the kilovolt amps are related to each other by the power factor shown by the following formula:

$$PF = \frac{kW}{kVA}$$

It is important to bring the power factor is as close to 1 as possible to reduce energy losses and improve energy efficiency. Power factor is an indication of the <u>efficiency of use of the available power (apparent power which you pay for) to actual useful power in kW (which you obtain) for doing work.</u> The power you pay for but is not available for useful work is known as the reactive power.

A <u>power triangle</u> is a handy way to show the relationship between apparent power, real power and reactive power diagrammatically It can be expressed by representing the quantities as vectors. <u>Real/active power is shown by the horizontal vector</u> of the triangle and <u>reactive power is shown by the vertical vector</u>. The apparent power vector is the hypotenuse of the right angle that is formed when the real and reactive power vectors are connected.

Do you know what Pythagoras theorem states?

The longest side of a right- angled triangle is called the hypotenuse, which is always opposite the right-angle. If (a) and (b) are the lengths of the legs of a right triangle and (c) is the length of the hypotenuse, then the sum of the squares of the lengths of the legs is equal to the square of the length of the hypotenuse.

By using the theorem of Pythagoras, the relationship between these three vectors is determined using the following equation:

$$a^2 + b^2 = c^2$$
$$real\ power^2 + reactive\ power^2 = apparent\ power^2$$

An example of the power triangle is shown in Figure 4.11.

To understand the power factor the following terms are important:

- kW is the working power, which is also called actual power, active power or real power. This is the power that actually performs useful work and gives power to the equipment so that it performs its function.

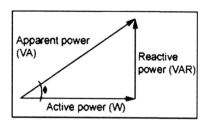

Figure 4.11 Power triangle.

- kVAr is the reactive power. This is the power that magnetic equipment such as transformers and motors need to produce the magnetising flux.

- kVA is apparent power. This is the 'vector sum' of kVAr and kW and is the power to be supplied by the utility and which you pay for.

Consider the following example to understand these terms better.
In the following figure, Matt is dragging a heavy load.

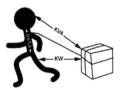

His working power or actual power (kW) is in the forward direction; this is where he wants his load to travel to. But Matt cannot drag the load in a perfect horizontal line, so his shoulder height adds some reactive power (kVAr) and the apparent power he is dragging the load with is kVA, which is the sum of kVAr and kW.

$$PF = \frac{kW}{kVA} = cos\,\theta$$

$$\frac{kVAr}{kVA} = sin\,\theta$$

Using the example of Matt's heavy load, note the following:

- kVAr would be very small (almost approaching zero).

- kW and kVA would be almost equal (Matt would not have to lose any power along his body height).

- The angle θ formed between kW and kVA would approach zero.

- Cos θ would then approach one.

- This means the power factor will approach zero.

Any equipment using electric motors to drive pumps, fans, conveyors, etc causes energy inefficiency by drawing additional currents. These are called inductive reactive currents. Although these currents produce no useful power, they increase the load on both the power utility and the customer's side (which you pay for). This inefficiency is expressed as the ratio of useful power to total power (kW/kVA) and is the power factor. Table 4.3 shows typical power factors found in a number industries in South Africa.

Table 4.3   Typical power factors of several industries in South Africa.

Industry	Power factor
Auto parts	75–80
Brewery	75–80
Cement	80–85
Chemical	65–75
Coal mine	65–80
Clothing	35–60
Hospital	75–80
Offices/buildings	80–90
Steel works	65–80
Paint manufacturing	65–70
Plastic	75–80
Metalworking	65–70
Electroplating	65–70
Foundry	75–80
Auto parts	75–80
Forging	70–80

A general average power factor in South Africa is 0.8. This means a 1 MVA transformer can only supply 800 kW or a customer can only make practical use of 80 A from a 100 A theoretical supply. If steps are not taken to improve the power factor, it could lead to energy inefficiency.

Most AC devices and equipment receive their supply from the apparent power, which is measured in kilovolt ampere (kVA). To have an efficient system, the power factor should be as close to 1.0 as possible. In many cases the electrical distribution has a power factor of much less than 1.0. This is a disadvantage to a power utility as it causes a loss of power.

Inductive loads cause a large kVAr. These inductive loads make up a large part of the power consumed in industries. Reactive power (kVAr) required by inductive loads increases the amount of apparent power (kVA) in the electricity distribution system.

The power factor of an electrical or electronic device or piece of equipment is the ratio of the power it draws from the main supply and the power it actually uses. An 'ideal' device has a power factor of 1.0 and it uses all the power it draws from the main supply. It would have a **linear load** and the PF would remain constant even if there is a change in voltage. Figure 4.12 shows the waveforms of a device with a PF of 1.0. From the graphs it can be

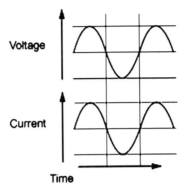

Figure 4.12 Input voltage and current waveforms for a device with a PF of 1.0.

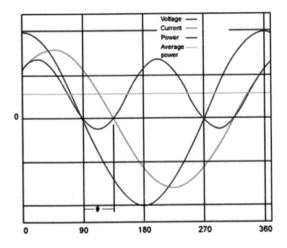

Figure 4.13 Graph of power factor of 0.7.

concluded that the voltage is perfectly in phase with the current and that both are sine graphs.

A device usually has a poor power factor when it either draws too much current out of phase with the supply voltage from the main supply or if it draws current in a non-sinusoidal waveform. When the device draws too much current, it is known as the displacement power factor. This type of problem is usually found in electrical motors driving industrial equipment such as fans, crushers, generators.

The non-sinusoidal waveform is known as the distortion power factor. This is usually found in devices such as computers, copiers and fax machines. Figure 4.13 shows an example of what the waveforms of a poor power factor looks like. From the graph it can be seen that the voltage and the current are not in phase (the current lags the voltage), and that the shape of the wave form is not sinusoid. This graph is for a power factor of 0.7.

A need for power factor improvement exists for the following reasons:

- Consumer: A consumer must pay for electricity charges for the maximum demand in kVA and the units consumed. If the power factor is improved, there is a reduction in the maximum kVA demand and the consumer will be saving on electricity bills, depending on the applicable tariff.

- Power utilities: A power utility has just as much concern about a poor power factor as the consumer. This is because the generators used in a power station are rated in kVA, but the useful output is dependent on the kW output. The output from the power station is calculated as shown in the following equation.

$$kW = kVA \times cos\ \theta$$

The number of units that a power utility can supply depends on the power factor: the higher the power factor of the generating utility system, the higher that kVA that can be delivered to the system. In conclusion, an improved power factor increases the capacity of the power utility.

From an economical view, if there is a reduction in the maximum kVA demand by improving the power factor, there can be substantial annual savings on the maximum demand charges. When the power factor needs to be corrected, there is an initial investment cost on the power factor correction equipment.

Reactive power (kVAR) required by inductive loads increases the amount of apparent power (kVA) in your distribution system as shown in the figure below. This increase in reactive and apparent power results in a larger angle θ (measured between kW and kVA).Therefore inductive loads (with large kVAR) result in low power factor.

Power factor correction should be considered when the power factor is low, as correction can yield the following benefits:

- Reduction in the cost of electricity with regard to demand charges

- Promotes energy efficiency

- Saves money in terms of energy costs and reductions

A low power factor results in power losses, which causes generators and motors to be energy inefficient. This leads to the overuse of energy, which in

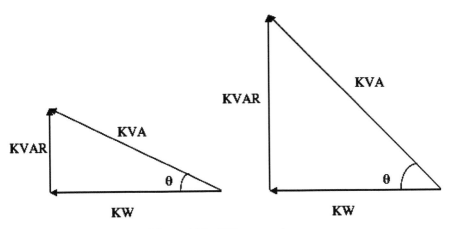

Figure 4.14 kVAr comparison.

turn leads to power losses. A low power factor is something that a company or consumer pays for as an extra or direct cost.

The reasons for power factor correction are discussed below.

4.11.1 Lower utility fees

Utility fees can be lowered by reducing peak kW billing demand. Inductive loads require reactive power, which is caused by a low power factor. This increase in reactive power (kVAr) causes an increase in apparent power (kVA). The building's low power factor therefore causes the power utility to experience an increase in its energy supply, resulting in an increase in transmission capacity to handle this extra demand, which of course must be borne by the consumer. Therefore, by raising the power factor less reactive power (kVAr) is used, which then requires less active power (kW) to be generated. This increases energy efficiency as well as saves money on electricity payments.

4.11.2 Power factor penalty is eliminated

Power utilities such as Eskom usually charge consumers an additional fee if the power factor is less than 0.95. This extra fee can be avoided by increasing the power factor.

4.11.3 Increase voltage levels in the electric system and distribution system

An uncorrected power factor causes energy losses in the distribution system. When power losses increase, it causes a drop in the voltage. High voltage drops causes overheating as well as failures in motors and other equipment. Therefore, by raising the power factor, voltage drops can be minimised, which, in turn, ensure that the motors and other equipment will run more efficiently.

An increase in system capacity can be achieved by adding more capacitors (kVAr generators) to the system. By doing this, the power factor is improved, resulting in less system losses.

Consider the following when thinking about energy demand.

A 100-watt light bulb burning for 10 hours use 1 000 watt-hours, or 1 kWh of energy. This means that when the light bulb is switched on, it requires or 'demands' 100 W from the power source. Therefore, the power source must always have 100 W available whenever the consumer turns the light on.

Similarly, ten 100-watt bulbs burning for 1 hour use 1000 watt-hours or 1 kWh in total. In both situations only 1 000 watt hours are used, but in the second situation the demand is much higher, and the power source should be able to provide for 10 light bulbs all operating at the same time. Therefore, the demand is 10 times more than in the first situation. The table that follows best explains this example.

Power ×	Time	= Energy Consumption
100 watt ×	10 hours	= 1 000 watt-hours or 1 kWh
(10 × 100 watt) ×	1 hour	= 1 000 watt-hours or 1 kWh

For example, if the power factor of a load was as low as 0.6, the apparent power would be 1.2 times more than the real power that is used by the load. The current in the circuit will also be 1.2 times more than the current required at a 1.0 power factor; therefore, the losses will be doubled.

Power utilities usually charge the consumer penalties if the power factor is less than 0.9–0.95.

A low power factor draws a lot of current from the power utility, more than necessary, and in a country like South Africa where energy is scarce, power utilities like Eskom must take other measures to prevent this from happening.

4.11.4 Power factor correction in linear loads

A high-power factor has a positive effect on the distribution system, which reduces distribution losses and improves the voltage regulation of the load.

The power factor should be adjusted to 1,0. Power factor correction is usually used in a power utility to improve the stability and efficiency of the distribution network.

In power utilities, an automatic power factor correction is used, which consists of several capacitors that are switched on by contactors as and when required. These contactors are controlled by a regulator, which measures the power factor in an electric network. Depending on the load and the power factor of that specific network, the power factor controller switches on the capacitors to make sure the power factor is maintained at a specific required value.

4.11.5 Power factor correction in non-linear loads

Rectifiers are examples of **non-linear loads** used in a power system. They are used in fluorescent lamps, welding machines and so on. How the power factor can be improved in these non-linear loads will be discussed below.

4.11.6 Passive power factor correction (PFC)

A simple way to control the current is to use a filter that passes current only at a line frequency, such as 50 Hz or 60 Hz. This filter consists of capacitors and inductors as shown in Figure 4.15.

The passive PFC has a disadvantage because large inductors and capacitors are needed in the circuit.

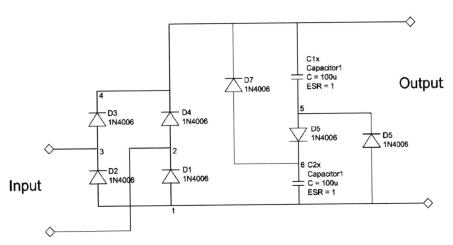

Figure 4.15 Valley fill circuit with passive PFC.

4.11.7 Active power factor correction

An active PFC is a type of power factor correction that uses power electronics, which changes the waveform of the current drawn by the device to improve or correct the power factor. Boost, buck, buck-boost, and the synchronous condenser are examples of an active PFC.

The active power factor correction can be one of two types, namely:

• The single-stage correction; or

• The multi-stage correction.

The advantage of power factor correction is that the power supplied using active PFC can adjust the operating voltage on AC power from 100 V (used in Japan) to 220–240 V (used in South Africa). This is, for example, very common in the power supplies used in laptops.

4.11.8 Dynamic power factor correction

Dynamic power correction is also known as real-time power correction. It is used to correct the power factor in cases of instantaneous load changes in large manufacturing sites. Dynamic power correction uses semiconductor switches called thyristors to quickly connect and disconnect the capacitors and inductors in the electric network to correct the power factor.

4.12 Demand Management

Apart from recovering production and transport costs, tariffs are compiled to shape the behaviour of consumers to follow a specific load profile. As a general statement this will be a straight line of constant demand but can differ depending on the mix of renewable energy generated at specific times of the day. Electricity producers can adopt different management strategies to influence the load profile of electricity use. This is referred to as Demand Side Management (DSM) or Integrated Demand Management (IDM) and three common strategies employed are:

   i. Load Shifting

   ii. Load Shedding

   iii. Energy Efficiency

Load shifting takes energy in the peak periods and shift the use to the valleys, i.e. different time. This does not imply any saving on the quantity of energy used but reduces the peak demand which is normally considered for many

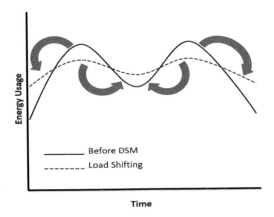

Figure 4.16 Load shifting as a demand side management strategy.

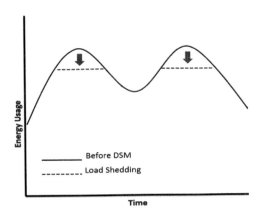

Figure 4.17 Load shedding as a demand side management strategy.

non-residential tariffs, resulting on a saving in demand cost. Figure 4.16 depicts such a strategy diagrammatically.

Load shedding aims at the protection of the electrical grid by shedding load in the peak periods through stopping the delivery of electricity to certain customers or geographical areas. This results in a reduction in demand, "energy saving" albeit at the cost of a reduced delivery to consumers with a resulting lowering of production. The loss of income is normally higher than the "saving" in energy cost. Figure 4.17 depicts such a strategy diagrammatically.

Energy efficiency aims to reduce both the demand as well as the energy used. It should lead directly to cost savings. It will also impact the environment through lowering fossil fuel consumption and lowering related emissions.

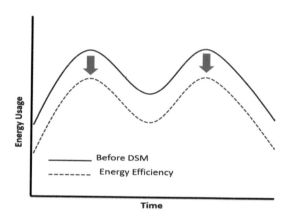

Figure 4.18   Energy Efficiency as a demand side management strategy.

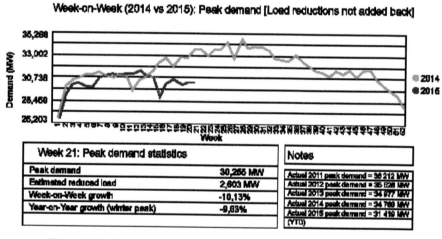

Figure 4.19   Weekly energy demand for South Africa in 2014 and 2015.

Figure 4.18 depicts such a strategy diagrammatically.

Figure 4.19 shows a comparison of the weekly energy demand for South Africa for the year 2014, as well as the amount of energy used for 2015 up to Week 21.

Energy demand management, also known as Demand-Side Management (DSM), is used to ensure that the electricity grid is stable and to balance supply and demand to ensure there is enough electricity to meet the demand of the consumers.

The objective of energy management is to educate the consumer about **energy surges** and to encourage the consumer to use less energy during peak hours. Peak demand management does not reduce the total energy consumption, but it does try to help keep the demand in balance with the supply. During the 1973 and 1979 energy crisis, the term 'DSM' developed.

4.13 Load Factor

A load factor is the measure of how much of the energy generated and "waiting, ready for consumption" was actually used by the consumer for a period of time.
The equation used to calculate load factor for a facility is:

$$Facility\ Load\ factor = \frac{Average\ load}{Maximum\ load\ in\ a\ given\ time\ period}$$

$$Load\ factor = \frac{kWh\ used}{Maximum\ load * hours}$$

Calculate the load factor of an industrial building using the following information:
Maximum load = 450 kW
Energy use = 154 400 kWh
Number of days in the total time period = 32 days

Solution

$$Load\ factor = \frac{kWh}{Maximum\ load * hours}$$

$$Load\ factor = \frac{154\,400\ kWh\ per\ 32\ day\ period}{450\ kW * 24\dfrac{h}{day} * 32\ days}$$

$$Load\ factor = 0{,}447$$

Therefore, to get the percentage of the load factor, you multiply your answer by 100:

$$0{,}447 \times 100 = 44{,}7\%$$

The load factor may be a daily, monthly or annual factor, but is usually less than one because the average load should be less than the maximum demand. The load factor is an important aspect to consider when determining the overall cost per unit of energy generated. The higher the load factor of a power utility, the less it will cost per unit of energy generated.

By analysing the load profile, the load factor can be improved by doing the following:

- Demand reduction: Demand is reduced by distributing the loads over different time periods.

- Increase production: Keeping the demand stable and increasing the energy production is a cost-effective way to increase production while maximising the use of the power generated.

4.14 Load Shifting

Through co-ordinated load management (activities made with respect to the total system) it is possible to avoid the unnecessary starting of production plants through the application of load shifting strategies. This strategy also manifests into environmental benefits.

If some form of co-ordinated load control is not co-ordinated between the producer, the distributor and the customer, action taken by the customer to reduce the cost of power demand may lead to a sub-optimisation of the total system. In this case, the revenue for the customer who has taken this action could be much higher than the reduced costs for the distributor and the producer. This happens if the customer's peak reduction takes place during hours when capacity is available at the production plant and in the distribution network.

The load curve analysis might provide an indication of :

- How peaks can be avoided, for example in the morning when switching on plants simultaneously or after lunch.

- How idle running machines can be switched off during the nights or weekends.

- How loads can be shifted to shave peaks and move loads to the valleys.

4.14.1 Demand response

Demand responses are the measures the consumer can take to reduce the amount of electricity used. This could be switching off all unnecessary appliances, consuming less electricity during peak hours and so on.

4.14.2 Dynamic demand

Dynamic demand is when there is a delay in the operating cycle of the appliance by a few seconds to increase the load. This is done by monitoring the power factor of the electricity grid.

Figure 4.20 Load shedding warning.

4.15 Load Shedding

When there is not enough electricity generated to meet the demand, it is necessary to interrupt and stop electricity supply in certain areas. This is called load shedding. It is done to avoid an excessive load in the power plant and to prevent the power plant and the distribution network from failing completely when the demand puts a strain on the capacity of the power generating plant.

4.16 Total Harmonic Distortion (THD)

As this is a complex concept it will be explained in two parts, namely:

- Harmonics, and

- Distortion.

Harmonics refers to a signal or wave where the frequency is a whole number (integer) multiple of the waveform fundamental frequency. For example, if a waveform has a frequency of 50 Hz, the 2nd, 3rd, 4th and 5th harmonic components would be 100 Hz, 150 Hz, 200 Hz and 250 Hz, respectively. Harmonics are important because they are what determine the amount of distortion the current will have when it reaches the user.

- Harmonics is a signal or a wave that is created in an object or instrument because of vibrations that occur in the object. Consider a power system with an AC source and an electrical load as shown in Figure 4.21.

This load on a system will take on one of the two basic types, linear or non-linear. The type of load chosen will determine the quality of power in the system, as the two loads draw current in two different ways as previously discussed. The linear type of load draws current that is sinusoidal

Figure 4.21   Power system with an AC source.

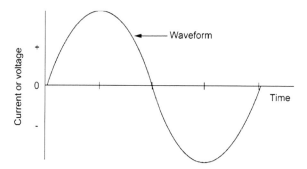

Figure 4.22   Linear load waveform.

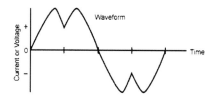

Figure 4.23   Non-linear load waveform.

and does not change the waveform, as shown in Figure 4.22. Most household appliances such as toasters, kettles, blow-dryers and so on fall into this category.

Non-linear loads can draw current that is non-sinusoidal, causing distortions in the wavelength. This is because the current wave deviates from the sine wave, causing voltage changes and therefore, changes in the waveform. This is shown in Figure 4.23.

As seen in Figure 4.24, when the waveform changes shape it can change the shape of the sinusoid. But no matter how complex the fundamental wave is, it consists of a merged number of waveforms known as harmonics.

Harmonics have frequencies (measured in Hz) that are integer multiples of the waveform fundamental frequency. How the waveform

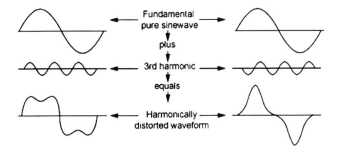

Figure 4.24 Harmonic distortion.

Figure 4.25 Examples of equipment where THD is present, in this case a microphone and an amplifier.

changes from the perfect sine wave to a wave with distortions is shown in Figure 4.24.

If the fundamental waveform frequency is 50 Hz, the first, second, third, fourth and fifth harmonic values will be 100 Hz, 150 Hz, 200 Hz and 250 Hz, respectively. Therefore, a **harmonic distortion** is the degree to which a waveform would deviate from the fundamental waveform (which is a perfect sinusoidal waveform).

The ideal sine wave has no distortions or alterations and, therefore, it has zero harmonic components.

Total harmonic distortion is the measurement of the harmonic distortion present in a system and is expressed as the ratio of the sum of the powers of the harmonic components to the power of the fundamental frequency. It is used to determine the linearity of audio systems and the power quality of electric power systems.

In an audio system, as in Figure 4.25, a lower distortion determines the accuracy and the quality of the sound produced from a loudspeaker, amplifier, microphone or any other audio equipment. In radio communications, a lower THD will produce an excellent signal without causing any disturbances to other electronic equipment. In power systems, a lower THD causes a reduction in current during peak times, leading to less heating, emissions and so on.

4.16.1 THD voltage

Total harmonic distortion is the sum of all the voltage components of the waveform compared to the fundamental voltage waveform. This is shown in the following equation:

$$HD = \frac{\sqrt{(V_{2^2} + V_{3^2} + V_{4^2} + V_{n^2})}}{V_1} \times 100\%$$

Where:

- V_n = *Individual harmonic voltage distortion values measured in volts*
- V_1 = *Fundamental voltage distortion value measured in volts*
- V_2 = *Second harmonic voltage distortion value measured in volts*

The formula above shows the calculation of THD on voltage signals where the final answer is expressed as a percentage. This percentage compares the harmonic components to the fundamental component. Note that the higher the percentage, the greater the disturbance in the signal.

4.16.2 Harmonic voltage distortions

Harmonic voltages can affect the operation of other devices or equipment which are connected to the same power supply. Various standards have been developed to judge the degree of harmonic distortion; one of these standards is based on IEEE 519 by the American Institute of Electrical and Electronic Engineers (IEEE). This standard identifies the sensitivity of electronic equipment in the building and determines how much voltage distortion is allowed.

Table 4.4 shows the facilities and how much THD is allowed in each facility, based on the percentages.

When voltage distortion occurs, it causes an interference with other devices or equipment. This happens because the strength of the magnetic field around the conductor is proportional to the pulse rate of the current in the conductor. These current pulses are fast-changing and transmit strong electric noise signals compared to the normal sinusoidal current, causing an audible 'hum' in the other devices present. It could also cause unreliable data

Table 4.4 THD allowed in different types of facilities.

Facility	THD (%)
Sensitive facilities	3
Airports/hospitals	
Telecommunication facilities	
General facilities	5
Schools/office buildings	
Dedicated facilities	10
Factories	

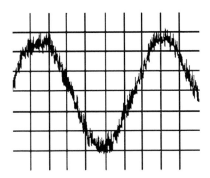

Figure 4.26 Voltage distortion.

transmission, poor displays on monitors and so on. Figure 4.26 shows a typical voltage distortion.

4.16.3 Harmonic current distortion

This is the measurement of the harmonic distortion present and is expressed as the ratio of the sum of the power of all harmonic current components to the power of the frequency current. The formula used to calculate this is shown below.

$$THD_C = Total\,Harmonic\,Current\,Distortion = \frac{\sqrt{I_2^2 + I_3^2 + I_3^2 + I_4^2 \ldots + I_n^2}}{I_1} \times 100\%$$

Where:

- I_n = *Individual harmonic current distortion values measured in ampere*

- I_1 = *Fundamental current distortion value measured in ampere*

- I_2 = *Second harmonic current distortion value measured in ampere*

Harmonics have been found in power systems from when generators were first produced. However, the current effect of harmonic components on systems were not significant due to the absence of non-linear loads in the 1960s. From then onwards non-linear loads became very popular and are now found in computers, computer components, fax machines, etc.

Harmonic distortion can have huge negative effects on electronic equipment. For example, high distortion can cause an increase in the power system, which causes higher temperatures in conductors and transformers. Harmonic distortion can also cause interferences in communication transmission lines due to the frequencies that clash. If this is not controlled and checked regularly, increased temperatures and interference can shorten the working period of the equipment and cause damage to power supplies.

4.17 Problems with Harmonics

Harmonic currents create harmonic voltages, and it is these harmonic voltages that cause problems with other equipment connected to the same secondary of the transformer where the harmonic originated. Harmonics are created by the increased use of non-linear devices such as UPS systems, solid state variable speed motor drives, rectifiers, welders, arc furnaces, fluorescent ballasts, and personal computers. The current drawn by these devices is not proportional to the supplied voltage; therefore, such loads are referred to as non-linear loads.

High voltage distortion, current distortion and high neutral-to-ground voltage caused by harmonics can result in equipment failure, which then leads to production downtime and costly repairs to the electrical distribution network. It is critical that the consumer is aware of the costly problems and hazards associated with high levels of harmonics, especially given the dramatic increase in the use of non-linear devices.

These harmonics can greatly impact the electrical distribution network along with all facilities and equipment connected to it.

The main problems associated with harmonics are:

a) Large load currents in the neutral wires of a three-phase system. This can cause overheating of the neutral wires which, in turn, can result in a potential fire hazard.

b) Interference in telecommunication systems and equipment.

c) Erratic operation of control and protection relays.

d) Tripping of circuit breakers and other protective devices.

e) Failure or malfunction of computers, motor drives, lighting circuits and other sensitive loads.

f) Overheating of standard electrical supply transformers, which results in costly down time, and repairs on or replacement of the transformer.

g) Poor power factor.

h) Resonance which produces over-current surges.

Resonance occurs when the system reactance (that is, the capacitive and the inductive reactance) are equal. There will be excessive currents if the resulting resonant frequency corresponds to the frequency on which electrical energy is present. This will cause serious problems as described above. Some indicators of resonance include overheating, frequent circuit breaker tripping, irregular fuse operation, capacitor failure, electronic equipment malfunction, flickering lights and telephone interference.

Traditional solutions to minimise harmonic distortion often involved one of the following methods:

a) Over-sizing or de-rating the installation.

b) Using specially connected transformers.

c) Using series reactors.

d) Using tuned passive filters.

However, the above solutions all had disadvantages in terms of higher utility costs because of the continued poor power factor. Today, the most common forms of harmonic mitigation involve either:

a) Passive harmonic filtering.

b) Active harmonic filtering.

c) Hybrid harmonic filtering.

4.18 Measuring Electrical Energy Consumption

Using measurements and converting the data through calculations provides an insight into the how and how efficient the available power is utilised as well as aid with both the identification and quantification of possible energy management opportunities. It provides an overview of the current efficiency of energy conversion as well as possible system problems and opportunities.

Figure 4.27   An example of a multi-meter.

This section prides examples of such measurements with solutions on how it is used in calculations.

4.18.1 Calculating power, energy and power factor in alternating current circuits

As an energy audit technician, you must be able to perform calculations to determine the energy efficiency of different electrical devices and machines. You must also be able to determine the effect power factor correction on the system(s).

In order to calculate the related metrics for an electrical system, fundamental input measurements are required, namely voltage and current. Figure 4.27 provides an example of a multi-meter which can be used to obtain these fundamental measurements.

The general formula to calculate power (rate of energy use) used in a system, is:

$$P = \frac{W}{t}$$

Where:
- P = *Power in watt (W)*
- W = *Energy in joule (J)*
- T = *Duration in seconds (s)*

How to calculate power
If a quantity of 60 J energy is used in 1 s, what is the power used?

Solution

$$P = \frac{W}{t}$$

$$P = \frac{60\,J}{1\,s}$$

$$P = 60\,W$$

Energy is the ability to do work and the general formula is expressed as follows:

$$W = Pt$$

Where:

- $W = Energy\ in\ joule\ (J)$
- $P = Power\ in\ watt\ (W)$
- $T = Duration\ in\ seconds\ (s)$

How to calculate energy

If the power which a system is using 40 W and it operates for a duration of 10 s, how much energy is released?

Solution

$$W = P \times t$$

$$W = 40\ W \times 10\ s$$

$$W = 400\ J$$

4.18.2 Calculate power, voltage, current and power factor in AC circuits

The concept of alternating current (AC) was introduced earlier. The change in direction of the voltage ("pushing force) causes the resulting flow of electric charge in the conducing material which then also change direction at the same interval.

The difference in the position of the current (lagging after voltage) due to the effect of an induction circuit, and the "correction movement" of the current to be more in phase with the voltage due to the addition of a capacitor was also shown. The related calculations to determine power factor and the size of a capacitor follows. The related figures are also replicated here for ease of reference.

Ohm's law

Power, current and voltage are all interlinked, and the same equation is used to calculate all three. This is based on Ohm's law.

> *Ohm's law is a law in electricity that states that the current in a circuit is equal to the potential difference divided by the **resistance** of the circuit.*

Ohm's law is the relationship between voltage, current and resistance, and how they are mathematically related.

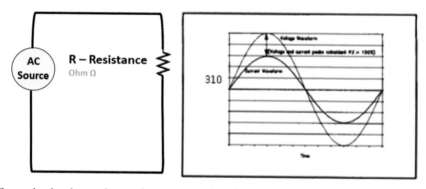

For a single phase alternating current circuit, Ohm's law states that the current flowing through a conductor is directly proportional to the voltage between the two points. This is equated as:

$$V = IR$$

Where:

$$V = Voltage\ (V)$$

$$I = Current\ (I)$$

$$R = Resistance\ (R)$$

The relationship between voltage, current and resistance, based on when one of the quantities remain constant, are as follows:

If the resistance (R) is constant and the voltage (V) applied to the circuit is increased, the current (I) will increase. However, if the voltage (V) is decreased, the current will also decrease. Therefore, when V increases, I increases.

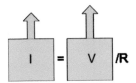

When V is decreased, I also decreases.

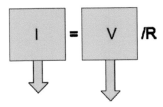

When the voltage is kept constant and the resistance applied to the circuit is increased, the current will decrease; if the resistance decreases, the current will increase.

When resistance (R) is increased, current (I) decreases.

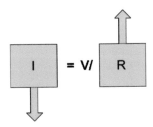

When the resistance is decreased, the current increases.

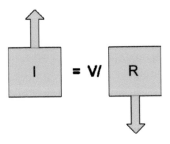

How to use Ohm's law to calculate current

Using Ohm's law and the two above mentioned statements where the current flowing through a 5 Ω resistor increases when the voltage is increased from 7 V to 15 V, this can be verified as follows:

Solution

When V = 7 V

$$V = IR$$
$$I = \frac{7V}{5\Omega}$$
$$= 1.4\ A$$

When V = 15 V

$$V = IR$$
$$I = \frac{15V}{5\Omega}$$
$$I = 3\ A$$

From this example it is evident if the voltage increases in a circuit, so does the current.

4.18.3 Voltage

"*Voltage is the electrical potential energy per unit charge.*

The unit of voltage is volts which is abbreviated to V.

Voltage is produced when the chemical energy that separates the charges, creates a positive and a negative terminal with a certain potential difference between them."

When a time-varying AC voltage is applied to a circuit, several laws are applicable. This includes Ohm's law as well as Kirchhoff's voltage law, which states that the sum of all the voltages in a circuit is equal to zero. It can also be defined as the voltage applied to a close circuit equals the sum of the voltage drops in that circuit. This law was defined by Gustav Kirchhoff and is used to determine the unknown voltages and current in a circuit. Kirchhoff's law is shown in Figure 4.28.

Now look at an example where Kirchhoff's law is applied.

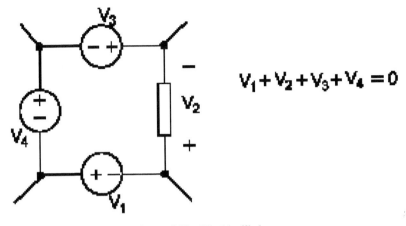

Figure 4.28 Kirchhoff's law.

$$V_1 + V_2 + V_3 + V_4 = 0$$

How to calculate voltage using Kirchhoff's law

In the first example, the source voltage must be determined. Source voltage is the sum of all the voltages in a circuit. Kirchhoff's law is applied by adding up all the voltages in the circuit to find the source voltage.

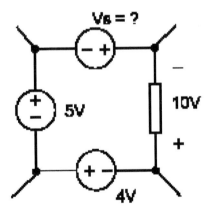

Solution

$$V_s = 10V + 5V + 4V = 19V$$

Therefore:

$$V_s = 19\ V$$

How to find missing voltage

The following figure shows how to find a missing voltage V_2.

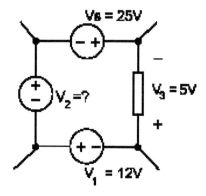

Solution

$$V_s = V1 + V2 + V3$$
$$25 = 12 + V2 + 5$$
$$V2 = 25 - 12 - 5$$
$$V2 = 8\ V$$

How to calculate unknown voltages in a complicated circuit

Look at how both Ohm's and Kirchhoff's laws are applied to solve unknown voltages in more complicated circuits.

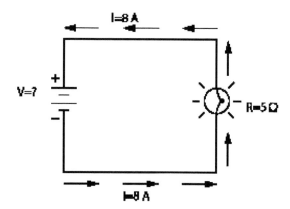

Solution

$$V = IR$$
$$V = 8\,A \times 5\,\Omega$$
$$V = 40\ V$$

4.18.4 Current

When finding unknown currents, the same laws apply. In that case it is Kirchhoff's current law, which states that the total current flowing into a circuit is equal to the total current that flows out of the circuit. This is shown in Figure 4.28; the current that flows in is a + b + c + d and the current that flows out is e + f. Both the sum of the input of the currents and the sum of the output currents are equal.

Now look at the following example.

How to calculate current with Ohm's law

The equation used to find current is the same equation used to find voltage; it is an application of Ohm's law.

$$V = IR$$
$$I = \frac{V}{R}$$

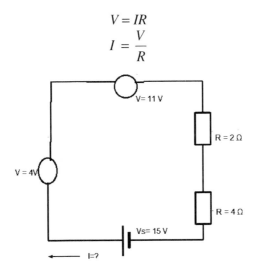

Solution

$$I = \frac{V}{R}$$

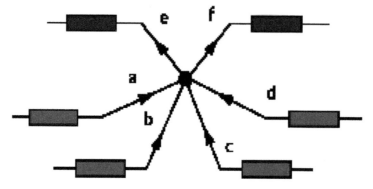

Figure 4.29   Total current in is equal to total current out – Kirchhoff's current law (KCL).

$$I = \frac{15}{(4 + 2)}$$

$$I = \frac{15}{6}$$

Therefore:

$$I = 2,5\ A$$

4.18.5 Power

Power is the ability to do work. In a circuit, the amount of electrical energy produced is equal to the power. This is measured in watts (W). Power in electrical systems can be calculated in several different ways and each different method will be discussed next.

Equation 1: When there is current flowing through a circuit while there is resistance, electrical energy is converted to heat. The amount of power produced in a circuit is dependent on the amount of resistance present, as well on the amount of current running through the circuit. This can be equated as follows:

$$P = VI = IRI = I^2 R$$

Where:
   P = Power in watt (W)
   I = Current in ampere (A)
   R = Resistance in ohm (Ω)

Equation 2: The second equation used to find power is derived in terms of voltage and current. It is expressed as follows:

$$P = VI$$

Where:
    P = Power in watts (W)
    I = Current in amperes (A)
    V = Voltage in volts (V)

Equation 3: The third equation is written as follows:

$$P = \frac{V^2}{R}$$

The three equations that are shown above together are known as Watt's law. This is how you apply this law:

Suppose the values of the current and resistance is known. In this case the first formula is used, which is:

$$P = \frac{V^2}{R}$$

If the current and voltage values are known, the second equation is used, which is:

$$P = I^2 R$$

If the voltage and resistance is known, then the third equation is used, which is $P = V^2/R$. The three circuits below will show you how to apply each equation depending on the available values.

How to calculate power
Find the power in the circuit shown in the following figure. In this circuit, only the current and the resistance values are known, therefore the first equation will be used to find the power.

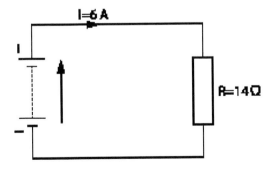

Solution

$$P = I^2 R$$
$$P = (6\,A)^2 \times (14\,\Omega)$$
$$P = 504\ W$$

How to calculate power

To calculate the power in the circuit in the following figure, the second equation will be used. This is because only the current and voltage values are known.

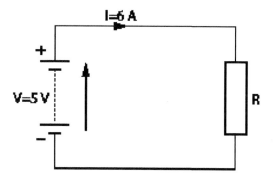

Solution

$$P = V \times I$$
$$P = 5\ V \times 6\ A$$

$$P = 30\ W$$

How to calculate power

Calculate the power in the circuit shown below. In this example, the third equation will be used. This is because only the voltage and resistance values are known.

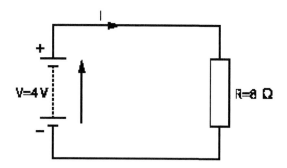

Solution

$$P = \frac{V^2}{R}$$

$$P = \frac{4^2}{8}$$

$$P = 2 \ W$$

4.19 Methods to Correct the Power Factor

The background to power factor and why it is advantageous to increase the power factor towards 1 have been discussed. It is important to improve the power factor as a consumer is billed on kVA. This does not apply to typical residential consumers where the kVA is already included in the tariff for kWh. Several different methods can be applied to improve the power factor of a facility.

The sources of reactive power, namely <u>inductive loads, result in a decrease of the power factor</u>. Some examples of these sources are:

• Transformers.

• Inductive loads (electric motors).

• Induction generators.

<u>Consumers of reactive power increase the power factor</u>. Some examples of these sources are:

• Capacitors.

• Synchronous generators.

• Synchronous motors.

<u>One method of improving the power factor is to install capacitors</u>. They decrease the magnitude of the reactive power (kVAr) and increase the power factor.

As shown in Figure 4.30, reactive power is caused by inductive loads acting at a 90° angle to the working power. As inductance and capacitance act at 180° to each other, capacitors store the reactive power and release the energy at a later stage back into the circuit, which in turn opposes the reactive energy released by the inductor. The presence of both an inductor and a capacitor create a balance in energy which, in turn, creates a continuous alternating transfer of energy between the two components. When the circuit is balanced, the inductor releases energy and the capacitor absorb the energy that was released.

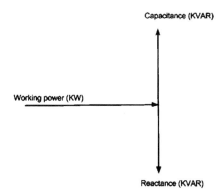

Figure 4.30   Capacitor cancelling out the effect of an inductor.

The power factor is increased by adding electrical capacitance to the electricity distribution grid or system. This can be positioned at or near the inductive load, or groups of loads, or it could be an addition cater for the entire facility.

Listed below are examples of how a capacitor cancels out the effect of the inductor.

- It minimises the operation of idling in motors; a low power factor is caused if induction motors are present.

- It prevents equipment from operating if it is above the rated or necessary voltage.

- It replaces standard motors with energy-efficient motors.

4.20 Calculating Energy Efficiency for Electrical Equipment

Energy efficiency, introduced in section 2, is the ratio between the useful energy output to the input energy procured. It is calculated as follows:

$$Energy\,efficiency\,in\,percentage = \frac{useful\,energy\,output}{procured\,energy\,input} \times 100$$

It is usually expressed as a percentage but can also be written as a decimal. It provides a metric of how efficiently or inefficiently the energy supplied (paid for) is converted into useful energy. Electrical equipment efficiency follows the same principle. The equation below shows how the efficiency of individual equipment, in this case an electric motor, can be calculated.

$$\eta_p = \frac{P_{out}}{P_{in}}$$

Where:

η_p = *electrical motor efficiency*

P_{out} = *mechanical shaft power output (Watt, W)*

P_{in} = *electric power input too the motor (Watt, W)*

How to calculate the efficiency of a motor

Calculate the efficiency of an electric motor that converts 25 kW of electrical energy into 20 kW of mechanical shaft power

Solution

$$Efficiency = \frac{Useful\ power\ out}{Total\ power\ in}$$

$$Efficiency = \frac{25}{20}$$

$$Efficiency = 0,8\ or\ 80\%$$

The conversion of energy into different streams of energy in a system can be visualised using a Sankey diagram of the conversion.

How to visualise the efficiency of equipment in a Sankey diagram

Use the squares on a piece of graph paper to work out the efficiency of the equipment shown by the Sankey diagram.

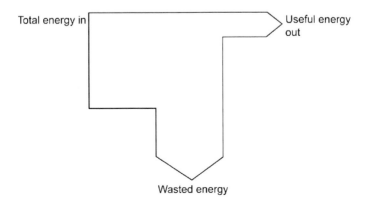

The efficiency of the equipment, according to the Sankey diagram, is illustrated in the following figure.

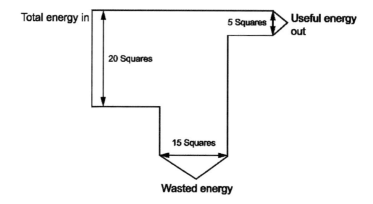

Solution
The efficiency of this device is calculated as follows:

$$Efficiency = \frac{Useful\ energy\ out}{Total\ energy\ in}$$

$$Efficiency = \frac{5}{20}$$

$$Efficiency = 0,25\ or\ 25\%$$

The calculation of the energy efficiency for a system as a whole, a sub-system and individual components was provided in section 2 and will not be repeated here.

4.21 Uninterruptible Power Supply

An Uninterruptible Power Supply (UPS), also called an uninterruptible power source, battery and/or flywheel backup, is an electrical apparatus that provides emergency power to a load when the input power source or mains power fails. A UPS differs from an auxiliary or emergency power system or standby generator because it will provide near-instantaneous protection from input power interruptions, by supplying energy stored in batteries, super capacitors, or flywheels.

The use of a UPS becomes important when there is an interruption in power supply or outage to continue to provide power (mostly to Information technology related equipment like computers) for a time. A UPS also provides protection when incoming power from the utility drops below or increase above safe voltage levels for the equipment. A UPS system convert AC power to DC power using a rectifier. The DC power is then used to feed an energy storage system like a battery pack or supercapacitor to store energy. In the event of an outage an inverter utilises the stored energy and convert it from DC power to AC power.

The different major types of UPS systems in the market are:

i. Passive standby/Offline – this is the simplest type and during normal operation the input power is fed directly to the output load with no filtering. A solid-state switch is used to transfer the load to the battery source when a power loss is detected.

ii. Line interactive - it acts similar to a standby UPS with the ability to adjust the output in response to possible over and under voltage scenarios. A solid-state switch is used to transfer the load to the battery source when a power loss is detected.

iii. On-line double-conversion - it uses double conversion power electronics where the battery system is always connected and does not require switching to the backup source.

The on-battery runtime of most UPS's is relatively short (only a few minutes) but sufficient to start a standby power source or properly shut down the protected equipment.

A UPS is typically used to protect hardware such as computers, data centres, telecommunication equipment or other electrical equipment,

Figure 4.31 A typical Uninterruptable power supply for an office.

because an unexpected power disruption to these could cause injuries, fatalities, serious business disruption or data loss. UPS units range in size from units designed to protect a single computer without a video monitor (around 200-volt-ampere rating) to large units powering entire data centres or buildings. The world's largest UPS, the 46-megawatt battery electric storage system (BESS), in Fairbanks, Alaska, powers the entire city and nearby rural communities during outages.

Chapter 5

Fundamentals of Thermal Energy

Albert Williams

Institute of Energy Professionals Africa, South Africa

Thermal energy involves the microscopic movement of atoms and molecules in everything around us. Thermal energy is often commonly referred to as heat. In fact, there are really two types of thermal energy. Thermal energy (commonly called heat) is energy in an object or system that involves the movement of atoms and molecules in the object. It is a type of kinetic energy because kinetic energy is energy due to motion. Thermal energy results in an object having an internal temperature that can be measured. A simple example of thermal energy is a heated plate on a stove. An element in the plate has thermal energy, and the higher you set the temperature, the more the internal energy of the element increases, meaning the temperature of the stove plate increases.

5.1 Types of Thermal Energy: Sensible and Latent

Sensible energy (or sensible heat) is energy that moves around or makes molecules and atoms in substances move. The substance becomes hotter when the movement increases. It is the type of energy that you can feel, either by touching the substance or by using a thermometer.

Latent energy (or latent heat) is the energy needed to change the phase or form of a substance. An example of this is when water (a liquid) changes to a different form (or phase), namely water vapor (a gas) or ice (a solid). The change of form happens when enough sensible heat is added. Latent energy is hidden (or latent) until the conditions are suitable for it to emerge. If enough heat is added to liquid water at 100°C, it will boil and become steam, which is a gas. If enough heat is removed from liquid water, it will become a solid we call ice. This happens at 0°C.

Two common forms of latent heat are:

• Latent heat of fusion

• Latent heat of vaporization

The latent heat of fusion or melting is the heat added to change a solid into a liquid. The temperature when this occurs is called the melting point. Energy must be supplied to a solid for it to melt. For a liquid to freeze the energy is released, because the liquid has a higher internal energy than the solid. The latent heat of fusion is 334 kJ/kg at 0°C and 101 325 kPa.

The latent heat of vaporization is the heat added to change the substance from the liquid phase to the gas phase. The temperature at which this occurs is the boiling point. The latent heat that is stored in a gas is much greater than that of the liquid. This means that steam holds a lot of energy, making it useful in thermal energy systems. The latent heat of vaporization is 2 257 kJ/kg at 100°C and 101.325 kPa absolute pressure.

Sensible heat cannot be added to a substance without limit. For any given substance there is a point that if we added enough heat, the form of the substance changes.

Put this way, at a certain temperature the movement of the molecules that make up the substance becomes so great that the form of the substance changes. This is what happens when ice is heated: eventually it melts and becomes liquid water. Again, at 100°C, water gets so agitated that it becomes water vapor.

Starting at the bottom left on Figure 5.1, as heat is added, the temperature of the ice increases according to its capacity to hold heat. At 0°C, the

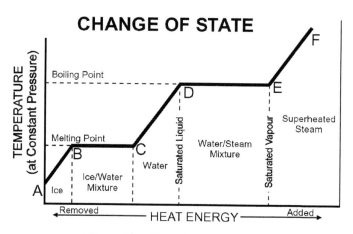

Figure 5.1   Phase changes for water.

temperature stops rising, but heat is still being added. Eventually, all the ice turns to water and the temperature starts to rise again. The heat added to melt the ice is called the latent heat of melting or fusion.

As more heat is added, the temperature of the water rises. The sensible heat in the water increases. But eventually the water cannot hold any more sensible heat, and the temperature once again reaches a plateau. Now water is being converted to water vapor. Heat is added and absorbed until all the water becomes a vapor.

The total amount of heat absorbed and hidden in the vapor on this plateau is called the latent heat of vaporization. Finally, when enough heat is added, and all the water is converted to vapor, the water vapor begins to absorb sensible heat and its temperature starts to rise again.

Looking at the increase in temperature, we can make some observations:

- The ability of the ice (solid), water (liquid) or vapor (gas) to absorb heat is called its heat capacity and this determines the rate of the temperature increase on the sloped sections of the chart. The higher the heat capacity of the substance, the less steep is the slope. The lower the heat capacity, the faster its temperature rises, and the greater the slope.

- The amount of heat that lies latent or hidden in the liquid or vapor is indicated by the length of the plateau sections. The longer the plateau, the greater the latent heat. The latent heat that is stored in water vapor is much greater than that of the liquid water. That is the reason that steam is so useful in thermal energy systems, it holds a lot of energy. The latent heat of vaporization is 2256.9 kJ/kg at 100°C and 101.325 kPa absolute pressure.

5.2 Concept of Useful Thermal Energy

Thermal energy is useful if it can do some work. In very simple terms, the ability to do useful work is related to increased temperature. Heat and thermal energy will only flow from a high temperature to a low temperature.

To determine useful thermal energy, the following should be considered:

- What object or system/substance is to be heated?

- What is the substance's temperature, and how much energy does it have?

- To what temperature does the substance have to be heated, and how much energy would this take?

- What is the temperature of the device or fluid used to heat the substance (this device or fluid must be hotter or have a higher temperature than the original substance)?

5.3 Temperature

The temperature (T) of a substance is how hot or cold it is compared to other objects. It can also be described as how much energy is involved in the movement of the molecules in a substance.

Temperature is measured in the following units:

- Degrees Celsius (°C)

- Degrees Fahrenheit (°F)

- Kelvin (K). It is the SI unit of temperature

On the Celsius scale, the freezing point of water is 0°C, and on the Kelvin scale it is 273.15 K. The boiling point of water is = 100°C or 373.15 K. To convert degrees Celsius, Fahrenheit or Kelvin to another temperature unit, the following equations are used:

- Celsius to Fahrenheit $= T_{(°F)} = T_{(°C)} \times \frac{9}{5} + 32$

- Fahrenheit to Celsius $= T_{(°C)} = (T_{(°F)} - 32) \times \frac{5}{9}$

- Celsius to Kelvin $= °C + 273,15$

Temperature may be measured in many different ways. A mercury or alcohol thermometer (in which a fluid expands as it warms) is the most common. Other devices such as a 'thermocouple' produce an electrical voltage that is proportional to the temperature or change their electric resistance with temperature.

In facilities we are increasingly using temperature loggers that record temperature over time in buildings. These provide a useful picture of the patterns and variation of temperatures experience in different spaces of a facility.

5.4 Pressure

Pressure is related to temperature. Pressure can be described as the push exerted by a substance upon its surroundings. The molecules in air move because of their energy. We can increase the amount of movement of the molecules by adding sensible energy or heat to a gas. When we heat a gas in a confined space, we create a pressure increase, or more push. For example, heating the air inside a balloon will cause the balloon to stretch as the pressure increases. It can be expressed mathematically as:

$$P = \frac{F}{A}$$

Where:
- $P = Pressure\ (Pa)$
- $F = Force\ (N)$
- $A = Area\ (m^2)$

When a gas is heated in a confined space, the pressure increases. For example, when the air inside a balloon is heated, the balloon will stretch as the pressure increases. The SI unit used to measure pressure is the pascal (Pa), which is equal to one newton (N) per square meter. One kilopascal (1 kPa) is equal to 1 000 Pa.

A system under pressure has the potential to perform work on its surroundings, which means that pressure can also be stored energy. Therefore, steam at high pressure contains more energy than at lower pressures.

Following are some of the concepts relevant to pressure:

- Atmospheric pressure: This is the pressure exerted by the weight of the atmosphere on the earth, as shown in Figure 5.2. Atmospheric pressure varies with altitude and weather. The average pressure at sea level is 101.325 kPa.

- Prevailing atmospheric pressure: The atmospheric pressure that exists at the point where measurements are taken.

- Gauge pressure: Defined relative to the prevailing atmospheric pressure (101,325 kPa at sea level), or as absolute pressure.

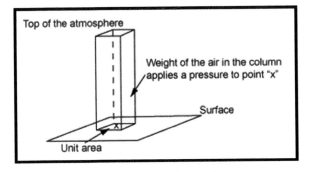

Figure 5.2 Demonstration of atmospheric pressure.

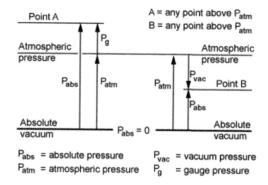

Figure 5.3 shows the relationship between these types of pressure.

Figure 5.3   The relationship between gauge, absolute and vacuum pressure.

Table 5.1   Air density correction factors.

Attitude (m)	Sea Level	250	500	750	1000	1250	1500	1750	2000	2500	3000
Barometer (kPa)	101.3	98.3	96.3	93.2	90.2	88.2	85.1	83.1	80.0	76.0	71.9
Air Temp (°C) 0	1.08	1.05	1.02	0.99	0.96	0.93	0.91	0.88	0.86	0.81	0.76
20	1.00	0.97	0.95	0.92	0.89	0.87	0.84	0.82	0.79	0.75	0.71
50	0.91	0.89	0.86	0.84	0.81	0.79	0.77	0.75	0.72	0.68	0.64
100	0.79	0.77	0.75	0.72	0.70	0.68	0.66	0.65	0.63	0.59	0.56
150	0.70	0.68	0.66	0.64	0.62	0.60	0.59	0.57	0.55	0.52	0.49
200	0.62	0.61	0.59	0.57	0.56	0.54	0.52	0.51	0.49	0.47	0.44
250	0.56	0.55	0.53	0.52	0.50	0.49	0.47	0.46	0.45	0.42	0.40
300	0.51	0.50	0.49	0.47	0.46	0.45	0.43	0.42	0.41	0.38	0.36
350	0.47	0.46	0.45	0.43	0.42	0.41	0.40	0.39	0.38	0.35	0.33
400	0.44	0.43	0.41	0.40	0.39	0.38	0.37	0.36	0.35	0.33	0.31
450	0.41	0.40	0.38	0.37	0.36	0.35	0.34	0.33	0.32	0.31	0.39
500	0.38	0.37	0.36	0.35	0.34	0.33	0.32	0.31	0.30	0.28	0.27

{Standard Air Density, Sea Level, 20°C = 1.2041 kg/m^3 at 101.325 kPa}

- Absolute pressure: This is the pressure measured at a certain point relative to a vacuum. A vacuum is absolute zero pressure. It is calculated as follows:

  Absolute pressure = Gauge pressure + Atmospheric pressure

Figure 5.3 shows the relationship between these types of pressure for different points A and B. The absolute pressure will be higher than the atmospheric pressure for point A, which is a point above the atmospheric pressure and absolute pressure is lower for any point below atmospheric pressure.

5.5 Phase Changes

There are various processes associated with changes of the state or phase of water:

Table 5.2 Processes of phases changes.

Process	Change of state/phase
Melting	Solid to liquid
Freezing	Liquid to solid
Evaporation	Liquid to gas
Condensation	Gas to liquid

5.5.1 Evaporation

Evaporation is the process through which a substance in its liquid form changes state to a vapor or gaseous form. This is achieved by adding heat as described previously.

5.5.2 Condensation

Condensation is the process through which a substance in its gaseous state changes state to the liquid form. This is achieved by cooling the substance. When the change of state occurs, the latent or hidden heat is released.

In the processes of melting and evaporation, energy or heat is added to the water. These changes in phase are endothermic. Freezing and condensation are processes where heat is released, meaning they are exothermic.

5.5.3 Steam

Steam refers to the gaseous phase of water (water vapor). It can carry large amounts of energy which makes it very useful in many applications, such as heat treatment, energy production, drying and many more. Superheated steam is steam at a temperature higher than the boiling point.

Properties of steam can be found in steam tables. Steam tables are collections of experimental data on temperature, pressure, volume and the energy contained in water and steam. The data is organized in columns. For example, the steam tables provide the temperature of steam if its pressure is known and the pressure of steam if the temperature is known.

5.5.4 Moist air and humidity

Humidity is the amount of moisture or water vapor in air. There are three measurements of humidity:

- Absolute humidity (AH): The mass of water vapor per unit mass of dry air.

- Relative humidity (RH): Given as a percentage, this is the actual water content of the air divided by the maximum moisture content of the air at the existing temperature. It is humidity at saturation.

- Specific humidity (SH): The mass of water vapor in a unit mass of moist air.

It is important to know how to calculate or read off the values of moist air and determine whether the properties of moist air are being addressed in a Heating, Ventilation, and Air Conditioning (HVAC) system. By doing this, you can detect where a fault is in your HVAC system if something fails. If you understand the properties of moist air, you will also be able to determine how to counter a failure based on the change in the properties of the moist air.

The properties of moist air are derived from the atmospheric air. The atmospheric air is the mixture of air and water vapors. The properties of moist air are:

- Atmospheric or barometric pressure;

- Partial pressure of dry air;

- Partial pressure of water vapor;

- Saturated air;

- Absolute humidity of air;

- Relative humidity of air;

- Specific volume; and

- Specific enthalpy.

Barometric: An instrument used in the study of atmosphere to measure the pressure that relates to the atmosphere of the earth.

Enthalpy: The amount of energy in heat that is released or used by the system at constant pressure.

Saturate: To absorb more liquid until it can no longer be absorbed

Each of the listed properties of air has a unique way of influencing the operation of the HVAC system. Air is used as the combination of both water vapor and dry air. It is important to note that the properties of air can also be denoted in terms of temperature. For example, the partial pressure of dry air can be denoted by dry bulb temperature.

The barometric pressure is the total measured pressure of the air and is measured using a barometer. This pressure is important because it will help you to know what the total pressure of the air is and during operation it can be used to determine the losses if the output is recorded.

If you cannot work out the total pressure with a barometer, you can calculate it by adding up partial pressures. To do this, you need to understand Dalton's law of partial pressures. Dalton's law of partial pressures can be used to calculate the individual pressures of gases within a gas mixture. Then these individual pressures can be added up to get the total pressure of the gas mixture. The next equation illustrates Dalton's law of partial pressures:

$$Pt = PP1 + PP2 + \dots PPn$$

In this equation, Pt is the total pressure and $PP1$ to PPn are the different partial pressures.

The partial pressure of dry air, represented by P_d, is a mixture of dry air and water vapor. The temperature of this dry air can be determined using a thermometer. This temperature is referred to as a dry bulb temperature because the bulb of the thermometer is dry during measurements. In contrast, the partial pressure of water vapor, denoted by P_w, is not combined with any of the gases in the air mixture. This is substantiated by Dalton's law of partial pressure because it says that gases may coexist without reacting chemically with each other. Therefore, Dalton's law states that, in this instance, the total pressure is described by the barometric pressure. In other words, the barometric pressure is the total pressure. This means that the total pressure, according to Dalton's law of partial pressures, can be calculated by adding the partial pressure of dry air and the partial pressure of water vapor:

$$P = P_d + P_w$$

This is great for the HVAC system because it means that the pressure and, therefore, temperature is trapped within the levels of the atmospheric pressure.

Remember that the air contains moisture regardless of the temperature and pressure. The air does not stop absorbing the moisture; however, if it is exposed to it under specific temperatures in a closed container, the excess moisture is converted to dew or fog and is no longer absorbed. This is the point where the air is referred to as the saturated air because all the moisture is absorbed. Since it can be established that the moisture content is dependent on the temperature, using Dalton's law of partial pressure, the partial pressure of water vapor is then represented as follows (the saturated air is denoted by P_{ws}):

$$P = P_d + P_{ws}$$

The absolute humidity or humidity ratio is the quotient of the total mass of the water vapor that is present in unit volume of air at any given temperature. The relative humidity of air is the quotient of the amount of water vapor in unit volume of unsaturated air and the amount of water vapor in unit volume of saturated air. It can further be represented in Dalton's law of partial pressure which describes it as a percentage form of the partial pressure of water vapor in unit volume of unsaturated air and the partial pressure of water vapor in unit volume of saturated air. The calculation for relative humidity (*RH*) is:

$$\%RH = \frac{P_w}{P_{ws}} \times 100\%$$

The specific volume represents the space that is occupied by the air. The warmer air, which is less dense than cool air, has a higher specific volume. The higher values of specific volume are associated with the partial pressure of dry air. The specific enthalpy which is also known as the content of the heat per unit mass, is the sum of the internal heat energy of the moist air with the inclusion of the water vapor and dry air mixture heat within.

5.6 Psychrometric Charts

A psychrometric chart is a tool used widely to determine the heat or cooling load calculations in addition to addressing problems encountered by air conditioners. The interpretation of a psychrometric chart involves understanding the properties of air because they are the focal point. The chart minimizes the time taken through calculations to analyse the behaviour of air through its properties. The chart is a shortcut to tedious and long calculations. The psychrometric chart requires only two properties of air to be able to determine the remaining ones because the properties are interrelated. An example of a psychrometric chart showing the lines and curves of air properties is shown in Figure 5.4.

The psychrometric chart, contains the following information:

- Dry-bulb temperature;

- Moisture content;

- Wet-bulb temperature;

- Dew-point temperature;

- Relative humidity;

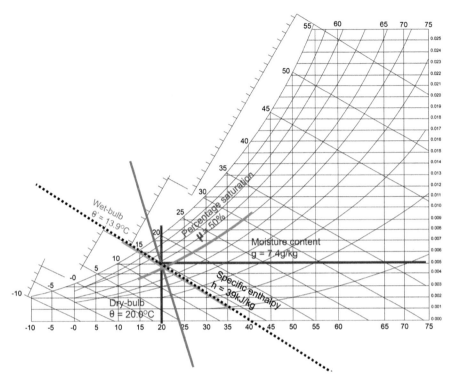

Figure 5.4 Psychrometric chart.

- Total enthalpy of the air; and

- Specific volume of the air.

The dry-bulb temperature (DBT) is represented on the horizontal axis with its lines drawn vertically up from the horizontal axis. The dry-bulb temperature moves from left to right when it increases. The vertical lines representing it show a constant dry-bulb temperature.

The moisture that is available in the air (dry air) is represented by a vertical line (dew point) at the far end of the horizontal axis. This horizontal line is drawn from the point the vertical line meets the curved line of wet-bulb temperature (WBT) towards the vertical axis representing the humidity ratio. Then all these horizontal lines between the wet-bulb temperature curve and vertical axis represents the moisture in the dry-air at a certain temperature.

The outward curve on the psychrometric chart represents the wet-bulb temperature. The wet-bulb temperature lines are the lines drawn from the curved scale diagonally downward towards the vertical axis. The lines parallel to this line also represent the wet-bulb temperature lines.

The dew-point temperature line is a constant dry-bulb temperature because it is related to the moisture in the dry-air. The constant dew-point temperature lines are the lines that are horizontal like the moisture lines.

The relative humidity (RH) lines are curved lines underneath the wet-bulb temperature lines and each of them represents the relative humidity in terms of percentage. The outermost curve of the relative humidity is the 100% and it is called the saturation curve. This is because the condition of air on this curve is fully saturated regardless of any value wet-bulb or dry-bulb temperature. This outermost line also represents the identical values of dry-bulb, wet-bulb and dew-point temperatures.

The measurement scale of the enthalpy of the air is represented on the outwards of the saturation curve. It consists of both the sensible and latent heat. The enthalpy of the air can be determined by first knowing what the value of the wet-bulb temperature is. The enthalpy of the air is thus found by locating the constant line passing through the given value of the wet-bulb temperature.

Specific volume of the air is used to determine the amount of air that must be handled by the cooling mechanism. It is represented by the constant lines from the saturation curve dropping down at an angle towards the vertical lines. These lines are not the same as those representing the wet-bulb temperature.

To determine all the properties of air, two properties of air must be known to start measurements of the remaining ones. The condition of the air will be determined by a point where all the lines meet or intersect.

For example:

- DBT = 20°C

- WBT = 10°C

- RH = 25%

5.6.1 Air temperature

Air temperature is defined as the temperature of air in the space around a person. The air temperature is also known as dry bulb temperature, which is measured by a bulb thermometer. In other words, it indicates the amount of heat in the air. A comfortable temperature range for thermal comfort is between 18°C and 26°C.

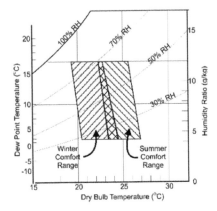

Figure 5.5   Psychrometric chart showing the comfort envelope.

5.6.2 Relative humidity

Humidity is the water vapor present in the air and relative humidity is the amount of water vapor in the air compared to the actual amount of water vapor that the air can hold at a specific temperature and pressure.

Figure 5.5 shows a psychrometric chart of the temperature and relative humidity ranges that are considered as good comfort zones for most people.

Since summer and winter weather conditions are markedly different, the summer comfort zone varies from the winter comfort zone. But the human body can adapt itself automatically to summer and winter conditions. Indoor air conditions that are quite comfortable in summer are decidedly uncomfortable in winter, and vice versa. As a tendency, there is a shift towards lower temperatures, with slightly higher relative humidity levels.

5.6.3 Mean radiant temperature

The radiant temperature is the temperature of the radiant heat in a room. The mean, which means the average, radiant temperature you experience varies based on how much of your body is in the sun's rays. Mean radiant temperature can also affect your thermal comfort because it affects how much heat you lose from your body. If the radiant temperature is too high, you will not lose any body heat and may feel too hot. If the radiant temperature is too low, you might lose heat in a room and become too cold.

5.6.4 Air flow movement

Air movement affects the amount of heat you lose from your body. When your body heat is too high, moving air can be used to cool and increase your comfort in a room. The variables that have been discussed can be used to maximize the thermal comfort while minimizing energy consumption. Some examples are provided next.

- Encourage people to wear light, loose-fitting clothing so that they will experience higher temperatures without discomfort. Similarly, encourage people to wear warmer clothes in winter so that they will experience cooler temperatures without discomfort. By using clothing to provide thermal comfort, you can save on energy costs that would be necessary to power a building's HVAC system.

- Direct air movement around people to provide a cooling effect for when a room becomes too hot. If the building envelope has large windows, these windows can be opened to allow for air movement and an increased thermal comfort. You will also save energy as an HVAC system will not be necessary.

- Insulation in a building can increase mean radiant temperatures, enabling lower air temperatures to be experienced without discomfort. This can help to save energy. Similarly, if a building is built with its windows facing the sun, the radiant temperature can warm a room when it is cold outside.

5.6.5 Infiltration loads in buildings

Infiltration is the entry of outside air into a building, which is similar to ventilation except that the entry of air with infiltration is unintentional or uncontrolled. The air outside the building leaks in through the building envelope through cracks and other openings, such as around window and door frames, underneath doors, through the wall air conditioning units, skylights and whenever a door or window is opened or left open.

Exfiltration is the uncontrolled or unintentional leakage of conditioned air to the outside through the same openings.

The main cause of infiltration and exfiltration is the pressure differences between the air inside and the air outside the building. During the cooling or the heating season, infiltration and exfiltration can be serious energy problems because when conditioned air leaks out, it mixes with outdoor air which must then be conditioned again as it re-enters the building.

5.7 Calculating Thermal Energy

The basic unit of thermal energy is the joule (J) defined as the work done (or mechanical energy needed) when a force of 1 newton is applied through a distance of 1 metre. The delivery of 1 J/s is equivalent to 1 watt. It can then be calculated as follows:

$$1 \, kWh = 3{,}6 \, MJ$$

Thermal energy is described as internal energy stored in a system that is responsible for its temperature. If the temperature of the object changes, the thermal energy input is determined as follows:

$$Qt = m \times Cp \times \Delta T$$

When there is a phase change in the system, ΔT is zero, but ΔQt is not zero, therefore the specific heat capacity ($\Delta Qt/m \cdot \Delta T$) will be undefined. However, the total amount of thermal energy needed to cause a phase change per kilogram of material is still important. This energy needed for the phase change is known as latent energy and is calculated as follows:

$$Latent\ energy = \frac{Thermal\ energy\ input}{Mass}$$

$$h = \frac{Qt}{m}$$

or

$$Qt = m \times \Delta h$$

When thermal energy is transferred from one object/surface to another (by conduction, convection and radiation) it is calculated using:

- Conduction: $q = -\frac{kdt}{dx}$
- Convection: $q = hc \times A \times dT$
- Radiation: $q = \sigma \times T^4 \times A$
- For objects other than ideal blackbodies the Stefan-Boltzmann Law can be expressed as: $q = \varepsilon \times \sigma \times T^4 \times A$

The value of thermal energy data in energy audits is to know all energy gain or loss of the systems.

5.7.1 Heat loss calculations

The process of calculating heat loss in buildings and rooms is described next. The following information is needed:

- The temperature inside the building or room;

- The ambient (outside temperature) and temperatures of surrounding spaces;

- The direct heat loss from the overall surface area of the structure; and

- Whether the heat loss is through natural or mechanical ventilation.

The difference in temperature between the indoor and outdoor air causes a transmission of heat energy through the solid components of the building envelope. The materials used in the building envelope can have a significant impact on the amount of energy required to maintain a suitable environment and temperature within the building. For example, glass or steel building walls are a major source of heat loss in the winter and heat gain in the summer and walls with masonry, insulation and cladding have more thickness and much higher insulating capabilities and, therefore, much lower heat loss and heat gain.

The thermal transmittance, which is denoted as the U-value, identifies the ability of a material to conduct heat from a high gradient to a low gradient. For example, aluminium has a higher U-value than wood and, therefore, a greater thermal conductivity. Thermal transmittance usually means that heat is being lost through a surface, because of the high U-value of the material. To reduce heat loss and thermal transmittance in a building envelope, materials with a low U-value must be during construction and material with insulation incorporated or added to the envelope. If you prevent heat from being lost, you will reduce the energy you need to continually heat your building.

The temperature increase required is determined from the difference between the ambient and internal temperatures as follows:

Temperature difference = internal temperature − ambient temperature

The heat loss for a structure is calculated by taking each surface in turn, calculating its overall area and multiplying by its thermal transmittance coefficient or U-value.

Heat loss through surface = width(m) × length(m) × Uvalue × temperature

where width(m) × length(m) = area of the surface (m²)

Note the area of windows and doors should be calculated and deducted from the area of the surface they are in and their heat loss should be calculated separately. Therefore, the total surface heat loss for the structure is the sum of all surface heat losses.

Total surface heat loss
= loss for walls + loss for roof + loss for floor + loss for windows + loss for doors

Heat loss through ventilation will vary depending on the extent to which the buildings or rooms are mechanically or naturally ventilated and the extent through which the air leaks through the building envelope due to, for instance, poorly fitting windows and doors. Ventilation heat loss calculations can be carried out using the air changes per hour and volumes of air in the building and the temperature difference between internal and external air and ventilation factors.

Ventilation heat loss = air changes × volume of air
∈ the building × temperature difference × ventilation factor

To heat one cubic meter of air by one degree Celsius, you need 0.33 watts of energy. This provides the value that will be used for the ventilation factor.

The example in Figure 5.6 shows how to calculate the total heat lost from a room in a building. Figure 5.6 represents the room, which is the bedroom, together with the dimensions, construction, air changes in the bedroom and temperatures in the adjacent spaces, including the external environment.

The heat loss from each structure/surface around the room is calculated as follows:

Heat loss through surface = Area × Uvalue × Temperature

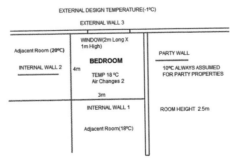

Figure 5.6 Room dimensions used to calculate heat loss.

Table 5.3 Solution to problem statement on heat loss.

Surface Element	Area (m²)	×	Temp/Diff	×	U Value (W/m²K)	=	Heat loss (W)	Total
External wall	5,5	×	19	×	0,92	=	96	
Window	2,0	×	19	×	5	=	190	
Party wall	10,0	×	8	×	2,1	=	168	
Internal wall 1	7,5	×	0	×	n/a	=	n/a	
Internal wall 2	10,0	×	−2	×	1,7	=	−34	
Floor	12,0	×	−5	×	1,36	=	−82	
Ceiling	12,0	×	19	×	0,34	=	78	416

Ventilation heat loss

Air Changes	× Room Volume (m³)	× Temp/Diff	× Vent Factor (W/m²K)	= Heat loss	Total
2	× 30	× 19	× 0,33	376	376
Total heat loss			792 W		

And ventilation heat loss is calculated from the following equation:

Ventilation heat loss = air changes × volume of air
        ∈ the building × temperature difference × ventilation factor

U-values of each surface can be obtained from tables provided by the manufacturers.

The solution Table 5.3 shows that the total heat losses from the room is 792 W, consisting of 416 W heat losses through the surface by conduction and 376 W from ventilation heat losses. The other ways in which heat loss can occur through a room include transmission and infiltration.

5.8 Energy Efficiency Measures in Thermal Processes

Before any assessment of possible savings can be made, the actual conditions of the equipment considered for heat recovery must be brought close to design conditions to avoid the false savings values. Performance or effectiveness of a heat recovery exchanger depends on its ability to recover:

• Sensible heat (dry bulb performance)

• Latent heat (humidity ration performance)

• Total heat

The energy efficiency considerations may include:

- Air stream arrangement - The counter flow configuration is the most efficient since it can theoretically achieve 100% recovery, given enough time, whereas parallel streams can only reach 50% at the best.

- Filtration and cleaning - For the outdoor air intake, the roughing filters should be provided to keep out large objects like birds, insects and paper from the heat exchanger.

- Face velocity and pressure drop -across the unit should be considered. An increase in static pressure will increase the horsepower requirements.

- Cross contamination - where even small amounts of cross contamination is not acceptable the use of the heat wheel will be out of the question.

- Controls - play an important role in efficient operation of the recovery system. The rotation of the heat wheel affects the performance of the unit as well as the tilt on heat pipe exchanger. Pressure differential switches check the condition of filters and the heat exchangers.

- Maintenance - How difficult is it to keep the equipment in top condition? How easy is the cleaning of the unit?

The performance of a waste heat recovery system should be based on the cost saving achieved through reduction in purchased energy. There is often a tendency to measure the system's performance on the quantity of energy recovered and transferred to user. For most plants, the two methods will provide the same result but not in all cases. E.g., in a chemical plant, an exothermic process may generate large quantities of medium pressure steam which is recovered and fed into the plant's steam piping distribution system. Steam is frequently vented however, because the plant's overall requirement for steam at that particular time is less than the amount recovered from exothermic process. The true savings provided by this recovery system is based on steam that is recovered and used, not just the recovered steam.

Chapter 6

Energy Management Systems and Industrial Energy Audits

Albert Williams[1] & Yolanda de Lange[1]

[1]Institute of Energy Professionals Africa, South Africa

6.1 Energy Management Systems (EnMS)

6.1.1 Overview

Energy Management Systems (EnMS) is a means for organisations to implement systems and procedures necessary to monitor, manage and control the effective and efficient use energy, and to establish long-term energy efficiency improvement processes and mechanisms. EnMS make use of a whole systems approach to provide the framework and means (not an end) towards assisting a company to build capacity and to focus on continuous improvement. As such it does not measure or guarantee energy savings or reductions on its own.

The International Standard of Energy Management System (ISO50001) was promulgated in 2011 and revised in 2018. Among the EnMS components, energy performance evaluation and the criteria to use plays a fundamental supporting role in measuring and evaluating the improvement of energy performance. Therefore, developing a mature and practical energy performance evaluation methodology becomes a key point to promote and implement EnMS.

The ISO50001 Energy Management Systems standard follows the ISO process approach of the PDCA (Plan, Do, Check, Act) cycle. There are several components per each of the main concepts, and a simplified categorization of this is given in the organogram in Figure 6.2.

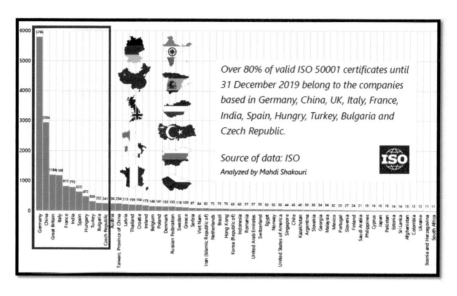

Figure 6.1   The number of valid ISO50001 company certificates per country as of 31 Dec 2019 (Source: Mahdi Shakouri).

Figure 6.2   ISO50001 Energy Management System at a glance (source: Mahdi Shakouri).

6.1.2 Energy performance indicators

One of the fundamental aspects is to determine the performance of the energy use systems and operations, using Energy Performance Indicators (EnPI's). The evaluation indicator, or metric, uses a specific common unit in order to compare levels of efficient operation.

A variety of energy performance criteria and subsequent different metrics are available for use in an EnMS and it provides management information from a high level overall view of the energy value chain down to specific processes and individual components. It is also used for continuous improvement of energy use.

Additional metrics that can be derived from energy performance data is the determination of related changes in greenhouse gas emissions, CO_2 reduction, and other related environmental metrics. Energy performance evaluation forms an important role in an energy management system for organizational level efficiency, and can also fulfil the following roles:

- Understand the current level of operation of the system or components depending on the chosen thermodynamic boundary.

- Identify the areas and/or intervention opportunities to carry out energy efficiency measures for the next step and improve energy efficiency continuously.

- Prioritise the areas and/or for interventions, including the possible ease, amount, cost and payback of each EMO.

- Evaluate whether the interventions function well and to what extent the goal has been achieved.

- Indicate when a system is moving away from accepted performance ranges and thus indicate possible problems or (eminent) equipment failures.

- Serve as basis of reward (or punishment) for energy efficiency policies, standards, interventions.

- Link energy performance with personnel management, and make responsibilities clear and arouse enthusiasm of energy efficiency improvement.

A typical process flow of how management systems promote continuous improvement through organisational practice and processes, development of teams to execute planning, evaluation, measurement and tracking is shown Figure 6.3.

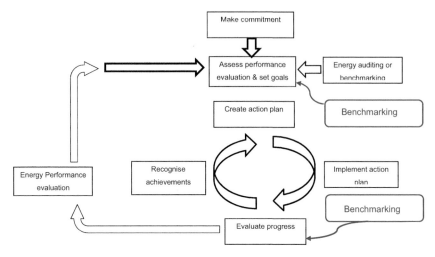

Figure 6.3   Energy performance in an Energy Management system (EnMS).

The evaluation of energy performance on a high level is normally associated with energy efficiency policies and standards, and is normally known as Energy Performance Benchmarking. It may even be mandated by government and may require buildings to display their benchmarking certificates. Benchmarking refers to relative performance, and because averages are used, care must be taken to interpret it with an understanding of possible inaccuracies and check for commonalities like occupancies, climates, sizes, operational parameters and so forth.

Benchmarking is one of the fundamental practices EnMS as it provides the confirmation that the interventions had an effect, and quantifies the efect on a holistic level. It is normally based on the comparison of management practices or on selected energy data. Two types of benchmarking can be used, namely:

- Practice benchmarking. Identify opportunities by comparing best energy management practices. It is a qualitative process comparing actions.

- Energy Benchmarking. Identify how well an entity performs, tracks the improvement over time, and positions the entity relative to other similar entities in terms of energy preformance. It is a quantitative process, is data driven and compares numbers.

Furthermore, benchmarking can be used for the following relative comparisons:

- Internal. Performance is compared against an internal baseline, e.g. other similar buildings within the organisation.

- External. Performance is compared against a metric outside of the organisation, e.g. best in class.

- Best available practices. Performance is compared to the best of available practices in the market outside of the organisation.

Generally, the steps involved in energy best practices benchmarking include:

- Identify areas for improvement that will benefit most from the benchmarking

- Research and identify key factors and variables used to measure the improvement

- Determine if the data is already available or how it will be obtained

- Analyse the data and identify the best practice/performance by selecting the best-in-class category (e.g., companies that perform each function at the lowest cost with the highest energy efficiency)

- Determine the conditions under which the best practices can be achieved and specify the action(s) that must be taken to achieve the desired results.

Implementing best practices: Set specific improvement targets and deadlines. Develop a continuous procedure to monitor, review and update the data and analyse it over time.

This will provide a basis for the monitoring, revision and recalibration of the measurements for further benchmarking studies.

The positioning of energy performance metrics to be used is provided within context of performing energy audits. Note that the determination of metrics is only finalized when the pre-assessment or preliminary audit has been completed and the audit mandate confirmed.

Energy performance evaluation means applying scientific criteria, methods and procedures, using correct metrics for the correct reason and in the correct way, as much as possible to ensure correct evaluations on energy performance achieved by organizations. The establishment of a practical energy performance evaluation methodology and continuous management is necessary to actually implement the plans and to realise savings.

6.1.3 Calculation of energy efficiency performance

Energy Performance Indicators (EnPI) can be used as a simple but relevant metric for benchmarking the energy performance of systems or processes against a known value for similar systems, either inside the company or outside of the company, or against best practices in the market. Energy Performance Benchmarking focusses on a comparative analysis of energy use per unit of physical production, a terminology also known as energy intensity.

Best benchmarking involves comparing the energy operation status of whole facilities, systems and/or processes with the best-in-class operations in the market. The EnPI's for benchmarking energy efficiency can be grouped as follows:

i High level Metrics

   a) Energy Use Index (EUI)

   b) Energy Cost Index

   c) Several models exist and some are available free of charge, e.g. Retscreen, PortfolioManager, EnergyStar, etc.

ii Productivity Metrics

   a) kJ/person, kWh/person

   b) kJ/kg product, kWh / kg product

   c) kJ/item manufactured, kWh/item manufactured.

   d) Energy Efficiency Ratio (EER) and Seasonal Energy Efficiency Ratio (SEER)

iii System Performance Metrics

   a) $kW_{electrical} / kW_{cooling}$

   b) $kW_{electrical}$ / litre of water pumped

   c) $kW_{electrical}$ / lumen produced (efficacy of lights)

   d) Window energy rating

The Energy Use Index (EUI) is calculated as the total energy consumed in a building over a year divided by total built up area in kWh/m²/year or MJ/m²/year. Take note the square meters refer specifically to conditioned space, and areas like parking garages and verandas needs to be left out. It is a simple and convenient high-level indicator for comparing a building to a norm as energy efficient or not. Although it provides an answer to the overall efficiency of energy use, it is at too high a measurement level to indicate specific energy management opportunity areas, processes or equipment.

Table 6.1   Typical EUI figures for buildings in the northern hemisphere.

Type of building	Typical annual energy use per m²
EUI Entertainment and public assembly	400 kWh m^{-2} a^{-1}
Theatrical and Indoor Sport	400 kWh m^{-2} a^{-1}
Places of Worship	110 kWh m^{-2} a^{-1}
Places of Instruction	400 kWh m^{-2} a^{-1}
Large shop (incl. shopping malls)	240 kWh m^{-2} a^{-1}
Offices	190 kWh m^{-2} a^{-1}
(average USA office = 293 kWh m^{-2} a^{-1})	
Warehouses	120 kWh m^{-2} a^{-1}
Hotel	600 kWh m^{-2} a^{-1}

6.1.4 High level benchmarking metrics

The ability to accurately measure current and forecast future energy consumption is an important strategy in achieving the objective of managing and reducing energy demand and cost, with the additional benefit of tracking and improving energy performance. This strategy requires several different methods and metrics of energy performance, widely referred to as indexes. Some of the more common indexes are presented here.

a) Energy use index

The Energy Use Index (EUI) is probably the most common type of Energy Performance Indicator (EnPI), and is considered the simplest and most relevant high-level indicator.

Process to determine the EUI:

- Formula: Energy Use Index (EUI) - MJ / annum / m² of conditioned space

- Convert the different fuels into MJ through the specific energy content of each

- Determine the area of conditioned space

- Calculate the EUI

- Compare the EUI with industry averages

b) Energy cost index

The Energy Cost Index (ECI) adds up the energy costs for all different types of energy used. It accounts for the fact that MJ$_{electric}$ is usually more expensive than MJ$_{natural}$ gas in the northern hemisphere (higher PoU cost). Beware ECI incorporates a variable that cannot be controlled, namely the variation in energy rates by location, season and/or time of use.

Process to determine the ECI:

- Formula: Cost of energy (USD) / annum / m² of conditioned space

- Use the same EUI data of the previous exercise

- Obtain typical costs for each energy source

- Calculate the ECI

c) Productivity metrics

In order to promote the efficient use of energy, governments worldwide have mandated minimum standards of energy preforming equipment. The metric compares the energy used to produce a unit number of deliverables (per unit of product) or unit number of people using the energy (per person). Indexes like kJ/person, kWh/person, kJ/kg product, kWh/kg product are common. Productivity Indexes provide a relative high level metric to compare the efficiency of a system/group of operations for comparison reasons, and from this metric more detailed audits of selected equipment can follow.

d) System performance metrics

System performance indexes uses a more detailed level of energy metrics, and the system boundaries can be carefully chosen to reflect the performance of systems, sub-systems and even individual equipment. It is still used as benchmark for comparison.

e) Typical system performance indexes

Typical system performance indexes in include $kW_{electrical}$ / $kW_{cooling}$, $kW_{electrical}$ / litre of water pumped, $kW_{electrical}$ / lumen produced (efficacy of lights), and window energy rating.

The ER ("Energy Rating") measures a window's overall performance, i.e., how well it: delivers solar heat gain in winter; prevents heat loss through the frame, the space between the panes of glass, and the glass itself; and. helps control heat loss due to air leakage.

6.2 Industrial Energy Audits

Energy audits are an approach used to determine how much energy a facility uses and to evaluate what measures can be taken to make it more energy efficient. It is important for the energy auditor to determine the following:

- What an energy audit is;
- What the main functions and benefits of an energy audit are;
- The various types of energy audits; and
- How to conduct an energy audit.

Energy audits form part of energy management and is one of the first steps towards identifying opportunities linked to energy efficiency improvement in a facility. An energy audit is defined as the systematic analysis of energy use and energy consumption within a defined energy audit scope, in order to identify, quantify and report on the opportunities for improved energy performance.

There are several aspects relating to an audit. When an energy audit is conducted on a building, it forms part of the building condition survey, used to evaluate the energy performance of the building, the same concept is applied to an industrial energy system. So, in short, an energy audit can be described as the action of developing an understanding of the energy-use patterns of a facility or system.

From a more quantitative point of view, energy audits can be described as systematic assessments of current energy-use practices from start to finish, considering the following four aspects:

- How and where energy enters the facility, system or equipment;
- The path of the energy and how it is used;
- The differences between inputs and uses if any; and
- How the energy efficiency can be improved.

This view of energy audits consists of a systems approach to energy auditing, where several independent systems are interrelated elements form a whole. In Figure 6.4, the system has a system boundary, inputs and outputs.

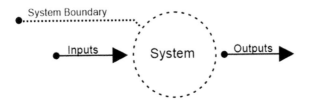

Figure 6.4   The components of a system.

A step-by-step method for preparing an energy flow diagram is outlined next:

Step 1 - Define the Facility's Energy System Boundary

Identify where energy enters (the incoming side of the system) and where it is considered unusable or lost (the outgoing side). In an industrial facility, the system boundary is often considered to be the shell of the building that encloses the equipment and processes. It may, however, extend beyond the building structure if parts of the process are outside the building.

Step 2 - Identify External Energy Sources

Identify and list all the external sources of energy that are used in the system (facility), or the particular part of the facility that is described by the energy flow diagram in Figure 6.4.

Step 3 - Identify Sub-Systems

Identify and list each of the facility's subsystems (processes, or energy-transforming equipment) such as boilers, washing, cooking and refrigeration equipment. Often a subsystem can be defined so that it encompasses a number of pieces of equipment. This will simplify the diagram. For example, a boiler subsystem would include the boiler, burner, condensate tank, flash tank, and fuel storage system.

Step 4 - Identify Subsystem Energy Inflows

Identify and list the inflows of energy to each subsystem. Also identify the source of each inflow. (The source will be either another subsystem or an external energy source.) For a boiler subsystem, the energy inputs are most likely to be fuel oil and electricity.

Step 5 - Identify Subsystem Outflows

Identify and list the balancing outflows for each subsystem. Include in this list an indication of whether the outflow is to another subsystem or to the external environment. Does the energy leave the system (plant) forever? In the case of a boiler subsystem, outflows would include the steam or hot water produced, and the hot flue gases -- the latter crossing the energy system boundary to the *external* world.

When viewing an energy audit as a system, you will learn the following:

•   Measurements and actions in one part of the system are an indication of what is happening in other parts of the system; and

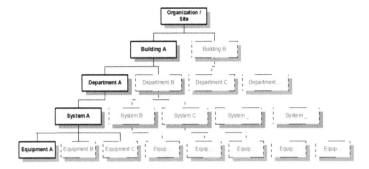

Figure 6.5 Energy consuming system, displaying one branch for the different levels in the system.

- If one part of the system is changed, it will affect other parts in the system. For example, if energy-efficient lighting is installed, the cooling loads for air conditioning may also be lowered.

Viewing an energy audit as a system may seem simple, but it is at times challenging to define a system with its boundaries. At the same time, it is sometimes difficult to quantify the energy input and output.

Looking at Figure 6.5 it is clear that an energy audit involving an entire energy consuming system may become really complex. For this reason, energy audits are often done in different layers or levels, starting with the top and working the way down.

Even though an energy audit may become quite complex as it increases in size, it still remains a method to evaluate the performance of an energy consuming element, whether it is a whole facility or just a single subsystem. It's main purpose also remains the same, namely, to look for ways to improve energy efficiency, be it technical or operational.

Although the purpose and definition of energy audits may stay the same, they can be used for different things such as:

- Condition surveys;

- Establishing the quality of equipment, as an energy label increases the value of equipment;

- Reducing energy costs for industrial facilities by applying energy-saving measures mentioned in the audits, saving money and improving efficiency; and

- Decreasing CO_2 emissions and contributing to sustainability initiatives.

When considering the different uses of energy audits, it becomes clear that conducting an energy audit has benefits in long term planning, saving money on energy costs and overall being able to enhance energy efficiency. Indirectly when the advised measures made in energy audits are applied, the environment will also be benefitted as CO_2 emissions will be lowered.

Now that you understand what the use, meaning and benefits of energy audits are, the focus will be on the different types of energy audits that can be conducted.

6.2.1 The types of energy audits

The American Society of Heating, Refrigeration & Air Conditioning Engineers (AHSRAE) defines the energy audits in different levels, i.e.: (i) Benchmarking – calculating energy / floor unit area, comparison to similar facilities, (ii) Level 1 – walkthrough audit (iii) Level 2 – energy survey and analysis, (iv) Level 3 – detailed analysis of capital-intensive modifications, and (v) Investment Grade audit – weighted risk and Energy Performance Contracts. Each of the respective audit stages need to be complete, before progressing to the next. Several different types of energy audits exist; however, it is the responsibility of the auditor to follow the energy audit process and merge the type(s) of audits into the process.

6.2.2 The energy audit process

The energy audit process is displayed Figure 6.6, which will help form an idea of the different steps in the process.

It is imperative to systematically work through the phases accordingly, before progressing to the next stage.

a) The purpose and elements of the energy audit planning

The intention of the energy audit planning section is for the energy auditor to lay out the different aspects of the project at hand including, but not limited

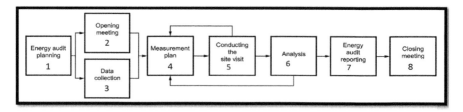

Figure 6.6   A schematic of the energy audit process.

to the elements of scope, objectives, timelines, boundaries, audit level and detail, evaluation criteria, process followed, regulatory commitments etc.

b) The purpose and elements of the opening meeting

During the initial meeting or opening meeting, the auditor collects important information about the organisation and building being audited. It is also important to build a relationship between the auditor and the client during this meeting and to reach an understanding of the aspects relating to the audit such as:

- The cost of the audit;

- Committing to the measures suggested in the audit;

- The schedule for the audit, including timeframes, deadlines and contact sessions; and

- Details between the auditor and organisation.

- Confirmation of the scope, boundaries and objectives.

c) The purpose and elements of the types of data to be collected

When the initial meeting is concluded, the next step is for the auditor to collect information before going on a site visit or walkthrough. The data that is gathered is usually obtained from the facilities manager or operator.

All the data must be reviewed by the auditor, serving as background information to the preliminary walkthrough. This data, when reviewed, will indicate to the auditor areas where specific attention should be given. For instance, if there are areas with periodic hikes in energy consumption, the auditor can inspect the areas to find a cause for the variance.

When reviewing the data, the following elements must be paid attention:

- The relation between seasonal variations in energy consumption and demand;

- Occupancy and production variations in relation to energy consumption and demand patterns;

- The relation between efficiency interventions and energy consumption and demand;

- The relation between operational changes, system changes and energy consumption and demand patterns; and

- The cost ratio between peak energy consumption costs and demand-related costs.

When considering the list of elements for which the data that is collected is used, the purpose of the data collection is clear. The purpose is for the auditor to precisely know the energy consumption and demand in relation to all aspects that may influence it and to recognize patterns in these relations.

d) Energy audit data sources

Data sources and the identification of data sources is an integral part of the audit plan design. In this section, the focus will be on the different kinds of data that may be used in the energy audit such as:

- Metered consumption data (including utility bills);

- Weather data (from websites or a weather station);

- Equipment data (including nameplate data);

- Ongoing demand and consumption (including sub-metering);

- Operation schedules and maintenance records (including interviews with key operator or facilities management personnel).

e) Historical energy consumption data

This data will typically come from utility bills, usually available from the financial department of the building or facility. The kWh and kVA figures are used from these bills to make the calculations. To ensure accuracy, there must also be differentiated between estimated and actual figures. Several utilities do not have smart metering devices installed; hence, the personnel members of the utility physically read the meters every one to three (or more) months; hence the months that are not read, are "estimated" based on the actual consumption readings of the facility.

The data that is collected here is of great significance because it can help the auditor get a full overview of energy consumption, and not just have single independent figures. With this data, average consumption can also be calculated, which can be compared to other averages from similar facilities, giving an indication of the energy performance of the facility or system.

f) Metered consumption data and utility bills

Metered consumption data can be obtained in facilities where smart meters are installed. These meters will generally provide the auditor with the necessary consumption (kWh) and demand (kVA) data, to do an analysis thereof.

The data obtained from the smart meters can also be compared with that of the utility accounts, to do bill verification. There are instances where a company is either over/under billed by the utility.

g) Weather data

As discussed in earlier modules, temperature and weather have an influence on the consumption of energy. Therefore, weather data is an important source of data when working towards the optimisation of energy efficiency within buildings. Data on average temperature, or 'degrees per day' data is available from the local weather office.

h) Equipment data

Equipment data, also called energy system nameplate data, is data containing the design energy characteristics of the equipment. This data is displayed on the nameplates of the equipment.

The nameplates containing the data are, however, sometimes located in areas difficult to access. For this reason, this data can also be collected by sub-metering e.g. a recording power meter. These meters can be applied on main incoming lines or on specific pieces of equipment.

i) Ongoing demand and consumption data

Ongoing demand and consumption data is data that can often be supplied by the electricity supply utility, such as local municipalities or the energy supplier. This data, when received from the utility provider, consists of historical data. As with the historical data previously discussed, this data must also be viewed in terms of actual and estimated figures. The data may also not always be from physical meter readings.

Facilities normally have meters on their main incomers (billing point), as well as several sub meters on site in order to measure their Significant Energy Uses (SEU), specific departments, cost centres, etc. This provides the energy auditor with a great platform to analyse historical data and identify relevant energy management opportunities.

j) Operation schedules and maintenance records

Data regarding the operation schedules and maintenance records can be obtained from building operational personnel, service contractors or the maintenance manager. This data will give the auditor an idea of how equipment in the facility is maintained and operated. This information becomes important later in the auditing process as it will give the auditor insight into how equipment may be managed more efficiently. When gathering this data, be wary of outdated information and ask different contractors, as one may not know everything.

k) The purpose and elements of the measurement plan

Throughout the audit process there are measurements and inspections done. Most of these occur during the detailed evaluation and analysis. The intention of the measurement plan is for both the auditor and the organisation to have a clear idea of what will be measured, when it will be measured, and how it will be measured. Some aspects that may be included in the measurement plan include:

- The areas of interest where measurement will take place (level of detail, specific points, etc.)

- The accuracy, reputability, and frequency of the measurement

- Variables that need to be considered

- Responsible person(s) to conduct the measurement

l) The purpose of conducting a site visit and the elements to be considered

The frequency of site visits and walkthroughs depend on the scope set out during the audit plan. The focus during the initial walkthrough includes assessment and inspection of the facility being audited with regards to:

- The general level of repair;

- Housekeeping (e.g. condition of equipment); and

- Operational practices relevant to energy efficiency.

The overall aim of the walkthrough is to identify energy management opportunities and aspects that should further be investigated regarding energy efficiency upon implementation of the audit. There are three broad purposes supporting the aim of the preliminary walkthrough. These are:

- To provide orientation regarding the entire facility regarding major energy uses;

- To identify areas within the facility that must be further examined regarding energy management opportunities, and also assisting in establishing the mandate and scope of the audit;

- To identify obvious areas where energy saving can be achieved with no further investigation, often linked to poor housekeeping.

When the preliminary audit process is completed and the audit mandate and audit scope are determined, a detailed walkthrough or site visit is done by the auditor. This site visit is much more detailed than the initial preliminary walkthrough. The auditor needs to develop a list of any additional energy management opportunities that could require further investigation and / or measurement.

m) The purpose and elements of analysis

The information that was gathered and collected during both the walkthroughs/ site visits, must be analysed for it to have value to the audit. Two types of analysis are conducted during the preliminary stage of the audit, namely:

- Analysis of energy consumption, cost and opportunities of improvement; and

- Comparative analysis (evaluating the identified opportunities).

n) Analysis of energy consumption, cost and opportunities of improvement

In this analysis, the focus is on energy bills and the tariffs linked to the bills. It exceeds the energy management opportunities that were identified in the preliminary walkthrough. During this analysis, auditors focus on energy sources, specifically the different energy per unit costs and the incremental cost, as well as the tariffs of energy.

The incremental costs lie within the tariffs or rate structures, which are very important as they influence savings that can be made when energy management options are considered.

There are three kinds of tariffs that must be kept in mind when analyzing costs and utilities apply various structures for their supply billing:

- Consumption tariffs: Consumption is charged at a fixed $/kWh rate, and may include a service fee for the meter;

- Demand tariff: Consumption is charged at a fixed rate together with the maximum demand that occurred in that month (this tariff also include service tariffs); and

- Time-Of-Use (TOU) tariff: Different rates are charged depending on the day/week/season of consumption.

The purpose of tariff analysis is to explore possible cost reductions that can be made. After this analyses, a client's tariff structure may change if lower costs are achieved.

The energy auditor will also be required to provide a ranked list of the energy management opportunities that were identified, starting off with no cost or low cost initiating and moving towards the expected energy savings where financial improvement and capital expenditure for each initiative is required.

o) Comparative analysis

In this stage of the analyses, energy use is compared from one period to another, one facility to another with a similar portfolio. Typical questions to be asked during these analyses are:

- How does the level of energy consumption compare to similar facilities and sites?

- What level of consumption is possible using best operating practices and performance benchmarks?

- How does the energy consumption compare on an annual base?

- How does site A compare to site B on an energy performance basis?

p) The purpose and elements of energy audit reporting

The audit report is what follows after all the collection and analysis of the data. The audit report is an important document as it reports and communicates information to the client regarding changes to be implemented. Without the audit report, an audit is fruitless because the audit reports the actions to be executed as determined through the audit process.

To ensure an audit report is not simply ignored, it should be written with the following goals in mind:

- To give a clear account of facts supporting the recommendations made; and

- To motivate readers to act on the recommendations made in the report.

There are guidelines and elements of focus guiding good report writing. Apart from these guidelines, the auditor must always review the report, pay attention to language use and spelling and assure that the writing style is appropriate. Throughout writing such a report, the focus must be to:

- Identify measures to reduce energy consumption;

- Reduce peak demand; and

- Reduce energy costs.

Table 6.2   Audit report framework.

Report section	Description
Executive summary	Give a summary of key findings.
	Name the recommended environmental management opportunities.
	Give a short account of the implementation, costs, savings and payback.
Technical section	State the audit mandate, scope and methodology.
	Give the facility description and observations made.
	Give calculations and explain assumptions made.
	Give audit recommendations.
Appendix	Data tables.
	Reference graphs used in calculation.
	Electricity and fuel tariffs.

Table 6.2 outlines a framework that may be used for an audit report.

When writing the scope of the audit, the auditor must give an exact account of what was covered in the audit, mentioning things that were included and excluded. In the audit methodology, the auditor simply explains how the audit was conducted; much detail is not necessary, but the thoroughness of the methodology must be ensured. In the methodology section, it is good to mention the standards, protocols and instrumentation that were used. This enhances the methodologies' credibility.

When giving the results, first give a full account of the results and only then the recommendations. Furthermore, when giving the results, it is useful to compare data, showing the difference between one area or building against another. In this way the result is contextualized. It is also useful to use colours and graphs in this section to keep the attention of the reader. The last part of the results should be written as a conclusion and summary that serves as an introduction to the recommendations.

In conclusion, it must be clear that the audit report is a very important tool of communication between the auditor and his client. If it is of a bad quality, all the effort that went into the rest of the process might just be disregarded by the client. As every client's requirements differ, it is the responsibility of the auditor to identify the needs of the client, and compile the report in a way that communicates the most effectively to the client.

q) The purpose and elements of the closing meeting

The closing meeting is similar in structure to the initial meeting, but instead of introducing the audit process and what will be done during the audit, the whole process is concluded. In the closing meeting there must be reflection on what happened during the audit process. The agenda for a closing meeting may include the following:

- After a brief introduction, key issues are summarized;

- Short-term findings are given, which may vary slightly from findings in the final report;

- A brief discussion of the above-mentioned findings;

- Time given for questions; and

- Contact details are exchanged, should any party have further questions.

It can therefore be deduced that the structure of the closing audit meeting consists of the following elements:

- Introduction;

- Feedback (including findings and limitations);

- Feedback discussion;

- Questions and answers (Q&A);

- Summary of Q&A; and

- The conclusion, thanking everyone.

The purpose of the closing meeting is therefore simply to conclude the audit and make sure that the findings are clear to all involved parties.

Chapter 7

Instrumentation and Control

Albert Williams

Institute of Energy Professionals Africa, South Africa

Control is an integral part of all systems that consume energy and is present in all energy systems. The control level and complexity of the energy consuming systems vary depending on the size and use thereof, as well as the function the system performs within the energy system.

These control systems may be as simple as a thermostat that controls the heating of water to a desired temperature or the control system may consist of a complex computerized system that simultaneously automate the control of multiple energy consuming systems and essential functions within a large plants or across multiple areas within a plant.

This chapter focusses on automatic control systems within energy systems with the focus on energy consumption and potential cost savings. Aspects that will be covered include the following:

- Control systems;

- Control loops;

- Components in control systems;

- Principles of efficiency through control; and

- Control applications.

7.1 The Need for Automated Control

Many processes and energy systems rely on operators to switch equipment on and off based on its setpoint demand or requirements. As the size of the energy systems increase, the manual switching of the energy consuming systems become more complex and it is often the case that equipment is left in operation when it is not required to operate outside of operational schedules. This

159

results in significant wastage of energy and present energy cost saving opportunities. This further results in increased maintenance costs due to unnecessary and increased operating hours of equipment. By design, energy systems operate under part-load conditions for most of the time throughout the year.

An automated control system becomes an essential tool under these conditions that may continuously vary, and which could be too complex to manage in a manual manner. The use of automation and control systems depend on the priorities of operation in conjunction with the financial feasibility of implementing and maintaining such a system. It entails a balancing act between maximum simplicity against maximum efficiency, both impacting on the cost of the automated control system.

The control offered by an automatic control system is essential to:

- Manage complex and repetitive functions within acceptable and regulated levels under changing conditions and varying demand or part-load conditions not suitable for manual control by operators

- Organise and sequence multiple processes and functions in a logical-, efficient-, diligent and repeatable manner whilst taking interactive effects into account; and

- Achieve consistent and repeatable operation of systems that is supplemented with enhanced control to Optimize energy use, energy cost and the subsequent environmental footprint of the plant and its operation.

It is evident that plant control systems and control automation can become very complex. The risk that this presents is that perceived complex systems could be bypassed or fall into disrepair if not operated and maintained by competent personnel. The plant control system could then present a false sense of optimized energy use whilst resulting in significant wastage with fluctuating parameter control outside of acceptable levels.

Essential components to an automated control system are its input- and output devices that enable the system to control various systems based on parameters that need to be controlled within the plant.

7.2 Control Components

Distinctions in input and output devices are made between the following:

- Switches;

- Sensors;

- Transducers;

- Controllers;

- Control devices; and

- Control loops.

The above-mentioned components work together to control the different energy systems within the plant. These components are explained in more detail next.

7.2.1 Switches

Switches are devices that have two states (on/off, open/closed) to control on-off electrical circuits as inputs or to actuate equipment in a binary manner.

7.2.2 Sensors

Sensors in a control system are used to sense and measure the controlled parameter or variable. They are the eyes and ears of a control system. The controlled variable is the parameter being measured and controlled (e.g. the temperature inside a process tank). The absence of sensors within a system makes it impossible to control the system.

Different types of sensors may be present in the control of a Heating, Ventilation and Air Conditioning (HVAC) system. Sensors are either binary (also referred to as two-position sensors) or analog. They can further be electrical or pneumatic.

Binary or two-position sensors return on/off, 0/1, true/false, full/empty, etc. signals. Typical binary sensors used in HVAC systems are:

- Flow switches which are activated by the flowrate of the fluid;

- Electric thermostats which are activated by the temperature around the space;

- Pressure switches which are activated by the difference in pressure around the space and the system; and

- Relays which are activated by a current or signal in one circuit to open or close another circuit.

Figure 7.1 illustrates a schematic of a two-position sensor mechanism. When a variable or disturbance is introduced, the switch opens.

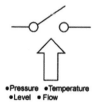

Figure 7.1   Two-position sensor mechanism.

Binary sensors can be used to:

•   Turn control devices on or off;

•   Open or close dampers; and

•   Enable and disable specific types of control devices.

Analog sensors convert a variable physical quantity into a signal the control system can understand. This could include temperature, pressure and humidity. It consequently returns a range of values. They usually operate in the 4-20 mA output standard due to noise immunity and other characteristics.

The analogue sensors are used to sense and measure:

•   Temperature;

•   Pressure;

•   Humidity;

•   Flow; and

•   Other specific variables.

They provide a variable output depending on the conditions monitored. The outputs such as voltage, current and resistance can be provided by analogue sensors as illustrated in Figure 7.2.

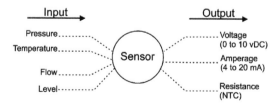

Figure 7.2   Analogue sensors inputs and outputs.

Sensors work in conjunction with transducers that convert a basic physical phenomenon into a form that is more useful to the instrument. Sensors are either passive or active input devices to the controller.

Passive sensors generate an output signal in response to some external stimulus. They do not need any additional energy sources and directly generate a signal in response to external stimuli. As an example, a thermocouple generates its own voltage output when exposed to heat. Passive sensors are consequently direct sensors which change their physical properties, such as resistance, capacitance or inductance, based on the external stimulus.

Active sensors require an external power supply (called an excitations signal) to function. This excitation signal is modified by the sensor to produce the output signal. Active sensors can also produce signal amplification. An example of an active sensor is an air pressure sensor that produces an electrical signal proportional to the pressure. These would typically be utilized in the form of a differential pressure sensor to measure on both sides of an air filter or throughout a ducting system. This is also a critical component in a variable-air volume system that utilise the sensor signals to open and close dampers to control the flow, and thus the temperature to specific areas within the building.

In the previously-mentioned cases, the sensor will send a signal to the controller. It is essential to ensure that sensors are well-maintained and regularly calibrated to ensure that the provide accurate measurements. It is further important that sensors are suited in terms of their complete measurement range they are supposed to operate in.

In Direct Digital Control (DDC) systems, the sensor provides information in digital form by means of an electronic communication system (using computers). The sensor will measure the input, and then send the electronic signal to the controller, which makes a change to the system according to the signal it received from the sensor. These sensors are used with any of the variables listed previously, but within an electronic DDC system.

7.2.3 Transducers

Transduces convert physical phenomena (such as energy, light, motion, position, temperature, etc.) to and from electrical signals. They are consequently utilized to convert a signal in one form of energy into a signal in another form and provide an interface for components within the automated control system to communicate with each other. Transducer is often utilized as a joint term for both sensors and actuators. The sensor, as the input device, would sense the different energy forms (such as temperature) by means of a thermocouple, a thermostat or a resistive temperature detector. The actuator, as the output device, then controls an external device such a heater, chiller plant, cooling coil or a fan (to control the temperature as an example).

7.2.4 Controllers

Controllers act as the "brain" of an automated control system by means of the data collected from sensors and then output signals to the various actuating and switching components within an energy system.

The function of the controller in the system is to compare the value of the controlled system (that is received from the sensor) with the setpoint, and generate a signal that responds to the difference of the two values. The setpoint is the desired steady-state of a controlled process and the goal of the control activity. Steady-state is defined as the state at which the state variables which define the behavior of the system are unchanging over time.

Control devices act on the output signal of the controller to effect a change in the system that influence the controller parameter measured by the relevant sensor. The controllers receive the output signal of a sensor as an input. This input signal is compared with a predetermined setpoint and evaluated for certain action. The output signal is generated to the control device to cause a corresponding control action.

Table 7.1   Examples of controllers.

Type of controller	Description
Electric/electronic controllers	For two-position control where the controller output may be simply an electrical contact or for proportional control where the output is a continuous signal that positions an electrical **actuator** or control device. With a DDC, the logic in a microprocessor translates the sensor input into an appropriate output signal on the basis of a design algorithm.
Pneumatic receiver/ controllers	For proportional control in sensors that generate a variable air pressure output.
Thermostats	For a combination of sensors and controllers with setpoints, differentials and ranges. They provide a signal directly to some controlled device, such as a water valve in a duct coil. They may be electric or pneumatic, have proportional or two-position output and various other characteristics.

7.2.5 Control loops

A control loop forms the core of automation. An activity is measured by sensors which provides an input signal to a controller. The controller decides what action is required and executes the required response through a set of actuators or control devices. The controller continues to receive input from the sensor to evaluate if the actuators or control devices had the desired effect. This process is repeated in a continuous loop of sensing, evaluating, actuating and repeating.

There are two types of control loops:

- Open-loop control; and

- Closed-loop control.

In the open-loop, the control variable is sensed and sent to the controller, which makes the control decision and sends the output signal to the control device. The action of the controlled device comes out as the output of the process. Therefore, open-loop control is simple and works on the input whilst the output has no effect on the control action.

Open-loop control assumes a fixed relationship between an external condition and the controlled variable. The disadvantage of the open-loop control strategy is that it does not consider variables that may affect the controller variable downstream of the controller device, such as variations in either airflow or water temperature, resulting in wasted energy or poor comfort control. Open-loop control system switches the building's lighting system on or off. Figure 7.3 illustrates the functioning of open-loop control.

In the closed-loop control system, the controller determines the actual change in the controlled variable, as measured by the sensor, and makes the controlled device actuate the variable back to the setpoint, or at least within the design range around the setpoint. Therefore, a closed loop is complex, it works on the output and modifies it to the desired condition in a continuous or repetitive manner. Closed-loop control senses the actual condition of the controlled variable. Closed-loop control is based directly on the condition of the controlled variable. A closed-loop provides better control than the open-loop strategy, resulting in more efficient use of energy and improved operational control.

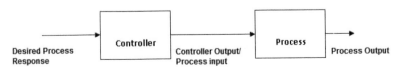

Figure 7.3 Open-loop control diagram.

In plant control systems, closed-loop control is the most common and preferred form of control used. An example of a closed-loop system is as follows: For example, if a temperature setpoint (the controlled value) is lower than the setpoint temperature, the difference in temperature will be sensed by the controller. This output signal is then sent to the control device. Depending on the system, the control device will then either reduce or suspend cooling or heating. The control device can consequently be a control valve on the cooling coils or an actuated damper or a variable speed drive controlling a fan. It could also be a switch that activates heating coils. Therefore, the control device manipulates the controlled medium, for example, water flow or airflow, and the controlled variable could be the temperature, pressure or humidity that is controlled by the control device. Figure 7.4 illustrates a simplified closed control loop.

An HVAC system can be used as an example to represent a building control system. Figure 7.5 illustrates a sensor that measures the air temperature in a room. The sensor then sends its output signal to the controller. The controller evaluates the output signal of the sensor against the programd setpoint to generate an output signal to a control device or actuator. Depending on the difference and position of the measured sensor output signal (temperature too high or too low), the controller will instruct the corresponding control device or actuator to perform actions that will result in a corresponding adjustment in the room temperature. This could consist of controlling the heating or the cooling system, or even the ventilation system that supplies air to the room.

Again, Figure 7.6 shows the block diagrams of an HVAC control system using the closed-loop approach. In this approach, the sensor measures the actual room temperature and feeds that information to the controller, which results in a hot water return (HWR) valve in a coil to increase the heat of the air being supplied to the room.

Figure 7.7 shows the block diagrams of an HVAC control system utilising the open-loop approach. In this example of the open-loop control, the

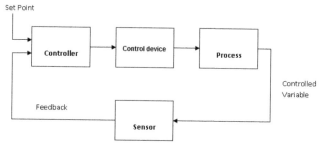

Figure 7.4   Schematic diagram of a closed-loop control.

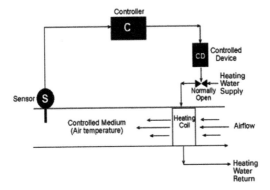

Figure 7.5 Basic loop for temperature control.

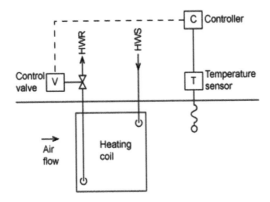

Figure 7.6 Closed-loop control.

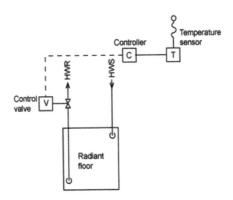

Figure 7.7 Open-loop control.

radiant floor heating system is switched on or off in response to the controller output signal. In this approach, the sensor measures the outside air temperature and feeds that information to the controller, which makes the control decision and sends the output signal to the control device to activate the radiant floor heating.

7.2.6 Control devices

Control devices may be electric, pneumatic or system powered. Examples of control devices or actuators are:

- Solenoid control devices;

- Electric motors;

- Pneumatic operators; and

- Electric-hydraulic actuators.

Solenoid control devices consist of a magnetic coil that operates a moving plunger. They are usually used for binary or two-position operation. An example of this type of control device is a solenoid control valve to control hot- or cold-water flow. In electric motors, the motor is used to operate a valve stem through a gear linkage to increase or decrease the flow of hot or cold water.

A pneumatic actuator is attached to a valve stem so that an increase in air pressure will move the valve stem and, in so doing, compress a spring that opposes the movement. When air pressure is reduced, the spring moves the valve stem in the opposite direction. In this way it converts energy into mechanical motion. Pneumatic operators are used to control the volume of dampers.

An electric-hydraulic actuator is similar in principle to the pneumatic operator, but it uses an incompressible hydraulic fluid rather than compressed air as the actuating medium. In HVAC systems, control devices are:

- Control valves that typically control hot- or cold-water flow; and

- Dampers that typically control airflow in an air-handling system.

7.3 Control Modes

The control mode of an automated building control system is important, regardless of the technology used. In most situations simple on-off control is adequate and appropriate. In other cases, the desired effect can only be achieved with modulating controls.

System capacitance refers to the rate of response of a system to a stimulus and inputs from a control system. Large capacitance systems tend to resist change and the effects of control are felt more slowly than systems with less capacitance. The control system's response time is consequently influenced by system capacitance.

Gain is an important control term associated with the sensitivity of the system. It is typically an adjustable value used to tune the controls within a control system. Consider a case where system capacitance is high. A quicker response is desired for a small input change to cater for large capacitance. Therefore, the gain is increased. Increased gain makes the input change more noticeable, and results in a stronger output reaction from the controller. The converse is also applicable.

A number of control modes are available for consideration as provided next. These control modes are influenced by system capacitance and gain strategies.

7.3.1 On/Off control

This control mode is often called "two position control" and is used with equipment that is either switched on or off. A nominal setpoint is established that is rarely achieved or maintained under steady-state conditions. A range of control values must consequently be allowed to avoid short-cycling the equipment. The smoothness of control depends strongly upon the system capacitance where systems with very low capacitance can commonly experience short-cycling problems under this control mode.

7.3.2 Floating control

Floating control is a hybrid combination of on/off control and modulating control. As with on-off control, there is a cut-in/cut-out control range. However, floating control systems have the ability to maintain a mid-position of the controlled device, instead of full-on or full-off. Between the cut-in and cut-out thresholds the controlled device merely holds its last position. The process variable is not actually under control within this range and is seen to float with the load until it crosses a threshold to get another incremental nudge in the correcting direction. Floating control is limited to system parameters that change slowly and gradually that do not require very strict control.

7.3.3 Proportional only control (P)

This is basic modulating control and entails a deviation sensing devise with a fixed gain. A control output is generated to control a process where the magnitude of the output signal and response is directly proportional to the size of the deviation from the setpoint. The gain of this control mode impacts on the proportional response of the system. If the gain is set too high, the response could be excessive which could result in hunting to occur where the controller output oscillates up-and-down without settling.

7.3.4 Proportional-plus-integral control (PI)

In this control mode an integral function is added to a proportional-only controller to eliminate the residual error. This control action adjusts the gain to a stronger and stronger value until the deviation has been eliminated.

The integral controller will not rest if any deviation exists. It is common to allow a small acceptable error band around the nominal setpoint to prevent low-level hunting.

7.3.5 Proportional-integral-derivative control (PID)

PID Control is used to address rapid changes in systems and Minimize overshoot and subsequent hunting. This is achieved by reacting to the rate of change of error (derivative) instead of the magnitude of the error (proportional) or the duration of the error (integral). In HVAC systems the derivative component is seldom used to avoid the potential for instability. HVAC processes are typically relatively slow acting and are tolerant of the temporary overshoot of PI control.

7.4 Sensor Types

Controlled facilities are equipped with numerous sensors, some of which are found in the energy equipment, and cannot be accessed outside the equipment. Sensing in facilities can improve the comfort, security and health and safety of the people within the premises and reduce energy consumption. The following are sensors for typical facilities:

- Thermostats;
- Electric meters;
- Water meters;

- Smoke sensors;

- Occupancy sensors;

- Light sensors;

- Carbon dioxide sensors; and

- Carbon monoxide sensors.

7.4.1 Thermostats

Thermostats are used for sensing the temperature in a system to allow the system to maintain the temperature at a desired setpoint. This can be achieved by using a programmable thermostat.

7.4.2 Electric meter

Electric power meters measure and display the electrical energy consumed in a facility. These meters are present for billing purposes by the utility company. Electric power meters on the main incoming supply, as well as the use of sub-metering of systems is a valuable tool to monitor a facility's electricity consumption, identify areas of focus for energy management, understand energy use and to apply measures to reduce electricity use at optimal levels.

7.4.3 Smoke sensors/detectors

Smoke detectors can sense smoke or fire and they will trigger a fire alarm. They are utilized as a safety measure.

7.4.4 Light sensors

Light sensors are examples of passive sensor devices that measure and convert radiant energy, whether visible or in the infra-red parts of the spectrum, into an electrical output signal that describes light intensity to a controller. Light sensors are also commonly known as "Photoelectric Devices" or "Photo Sensors".

Light sensors can often be combined with occupancy sensors. Light sensors are commonly encountered within outdoor lighting systems. It is also typically installed on peripheral lighting circuits to Optimize the use of natural light instead of making use of energy consuming lighting systems.

7.4.5 Occupancy sensors

Occupancy sensors detect when people are present in an area. This sensor will detect human activity and send a signal to a controller to automatically switch on the lights within the affected area. Occupancy sensors are designed to save energy by switching lights off when there is no activity within specific areas.

7.4.6 Carbon dioxide sensors

Measuring carbon dioxide is important in monitoring Indoor Air Quality (IAQ) in HVAC systems and can indirectly measure the number of people occupying the room. Carbon dioxide sensors help to maintain good air ventilation.

7.4.7 Carbon monoxide sensors

Carbon monoxide sensors detect the concentration of carbon monoxide in the air to prevent carbon monoxide poisoning. The sensors are designed to measure the carbon monoxide levels over time and sound an alarm before the levels reach a dangerous concentration.

7.5 The Principles of Efficiency with Control and Control Applications

Control systems are designed to maintain operating parameters within the systems they control. Control systems are further designed to help control or reduce energy costs. This is critical for plants that contain large and complex energy systems. Automated control performs complex functions where equipment operates on part-load conditions, or under conditions that continuously vary. The following will be discussed in this section:

• Principles of efficiency through control systems; and

• Principles of efficiency through control applications.

7.5.1 Efficiency through control

There are four basic ways to conserve energy through HVAC control systems:

• Operate the equipment only when needed;

• Sequence heating and cooling;

- Only provide the heating or cooling needed; and

- Supply the heating and cooling from an efficient source.

a) Operate equipment when needed

The equipment or energy systems should only be operated when needed. It is important to note that even the most efficient technology and systems waste energy if they are operated when they are not needed.

For example, the HVAC systems are operated only when there are occupants or when warming up or cooling of the area is required prior to occupancy to ensure that occupants arrive to a comfortable working environment. The same principle applies to fresh and recirculated air supplied to an area. A HVAC system should ensure that adequate IAQ is already in a steady-state prior to occupants arriving for work. Fresh air requirements and temperature setpoints can however be altered after "normal" working hours when the area is supposed to be unoccupied, taking cognisance of possible deviations in occupancy (after hours occupants and cleaning crews). This is typically referred to as setback control and can deliver significant energy and cost savings.

b) Sequence heating and cooling

Avoid the simultaneous operation of heating- and cooling systems to reduce energy waste. The design of control zones should eliminate simultaneous heating and cooling. This is however a very common situation found in HVAC control systems. Similarly, humidification and dehumidification should not be operating simultaneously. Humidification is when moisture (water vapor or humidity) is added to the airstream supplied to areas without changing its dry bulb temperature. The humidification process is used in conjunction with cooling or heating in the HVAC systems. Further note that heating and cooling control may impact on the humidification and dehumidification system within the same control system. These parameters and their interactive effects should be considered in conjunction with a psychometric chart when investigating for energy cost saving opportunities.

c) Provide the heating and cooling needed

An energy consuming system delivers a service to address a specific need within a facility. This need should be as closely addressed as possible, not more and not less. A fundamental principle of energy efficiency is meeting the needs of the requirement. In the case of an HVAC systems, this principle applies to the proper setting and calibration of temperature control systems, ventilation and fresh air demand.

d) Heating and cooling from efficient sources

The supply of heating and cooling can be Optimized to save energy and related costs. This does not necessarily have to entail the replacement or ret-rofitting of expensive equipment. It could include the supplemental use of hot or cold outside air, the use of natural light in areas to allow for the switching off of certain lighting zones, shading to decrease heat gain from the sun or waste heat recovery.

7.5.2 Efficiency through control applications

Control applications are applications used in automated control systems to improve operation, comfort, IAQ and safety, whilst optimising energy use. Control applications can also be used to reduce energy costs. The principles or options to conserve energy through control applications include:

- Programed start/stop;

- Optimized start/stop (optimal runtime);

- Timed occupant override;

- Load rolling;

- Duty cycling;

- Demand control;

- Temperature setback/setup;

- Alarms/monitoring;

- Energy monitoring;

- Optimisation of supply air temperature;

- Supply water optimisation; and

- Chiller/boiler optimisation.

Other control options include Building Automation Systems (BAS) which can also achieve energy reductions through the control of interior and exterior lighting and domestic hot water temperature which is matched to building demand.

a) Programed start/stop

Programed start/stop control applications are a control logic that schedule the start and stop of systems. The operating schedule Optimizes equipment use by allowing equipment to operate at appropriate times only. For example, you can program your equipment to avoid operation during times of peak electrical demand as part of a demand side management strategy. It is however essential to ensure that the critical and regulatory requirements are still met during these times (i.e. ventilation or lighting requirements, IAQ, water supply, etc.).

b) Optimized start/stop

This control logic determines the best time to start pre-cooling or preheating, based on current inside and outside conditions whilst taking the thermal mass of the area into account. The system also monitors temperatures to ensure that thermal comfort is Optimized.

c) Timed occupant override

This control application allows after-hours occupants to invoke the system override for comfort with a time limit that are applicable to the operation of the systems before it returns to the unoccupied control settings.

d) Load rolling

The fans, pumps and other components of an HVAC system are operated continuously during occupied periods to provide heating, cooling and ventilation for which they were designed. The capacity of this equipment is large enough to maintain occupant comfort during the peak load conditions on the coldest or hottest days of the year. It should be possible in some situations to switch off some of this equipment with no loss in occupant comfort.

e) Duty cycling

Energy activities can often and should be scheduled to avoid different sub-systems operating at the same time when their simultaneous operation is not essential to control and limit notified maximum demand (depending on the applicable tariff structure of the facility).

f) Demand control

Direct monitoring of system electrical demand and the shedding of specific loads that are non-essential is an important direct system monitoring strategy under demand-side management. The benefit of this strategy will also depend on the applicable utility tariff structure of the facility. It is also possible in some instances to prepare a system where storage capacity is available in advance to allow service levels to be maintained during peak periods whilst the system is fully or partially switched off during the peak periods.

g) Temperature setback/setup

Temperature setback involved the practice to change the temperature setpoint to a lower setting for a period when the area or space will not be occupied or require as much heating. In contrast, temperature setup is when you change the temperature to a higher setting when the space will not be occupied or require much cooling. Setback temperatures are applicable during the heating season (winter) whilst setup temperatures are applicable during the cooling season (summer) when the building is unoccupied. These practices can result in significant energy and cost savings.

h) Alarms/monitoring

Control software is available to initiate an alarm or specific action when a control limit has been exceeded. This can assist in maximum demand control and to maintain IAQ and comfort conditions.

i) Energy monitoring

Control systems usually record and gather data on fuel and electricity consumption, which is extremely useful during analyses with reference to key independent variables, such as degree-days, to assess cooling system performance under varying conditions.

j) Optimized ventilation

The blending of fresh air and return air can be controlled and varied by measuring indoor air contaminant levels (such as carbon dioxide) to reduce either the heating or cooling load.

k) Optimisation of supply air temperature

The supply air temperature can be controlled according to the heating and cooling needs of the area to result in energy and cost savings.

l) Supply water optimisation

In systems where the heating and cooling of the area or space is achieved by water coils in the supply air system, temperature control can be Optimized by controlling not only the flow of water in the coil, but the temperature of the water. An increase in the temperature of cooling water, for example, can reduce losses that arise because of the temperature difference between ambient water and water in the water distribution system.

m) Chiller/boiler optimisation

The chilled water temperature or hot water temperature at the chiller or boiler can be controlled to Optimize energy demand and consumption. Regular maintenance is essential to Optimize chiller/boiler efficiency.

Chapter 8

Energy Investigation Support Tools

Albert Williams

Institute of Energy Professionals Africa, South Africa

During an energy audit, historical data and the recording of energy inputs provide critical operational information and the baseline consumption data against which to gauge the success of energy efficiency efforts in the plant. The efficiency of each system, independent of any other has much to do with energy consumption. The manner in which different systems interrelate with one another is of at least equal importance. For example, even when operating and maintenance personnel do their utmost to make equipment and its operating characteristics as efficient as possible, energy still will be wasted if equipment is used improperly. Generally speaking, only a fraction of the potential savings will be realized unless the different inter-relationships are all taken into account.

To obtain the best information for a successful energy cost control program, the auditor must make some measurements during the audit visit. The equipment needed depends on the type of energy-consuming equipment used at the facility, and on the potential Energy Efficiency Measures (EEM's). For example, for a waste heat recovery EEM, the auditor must take substantial temperature measurement data from potential heat sources.

Some basic measuring instruments should be available to the auditor to improve the quality of the survey. Such instrumentation would include:

- portable digital thermometer or pyrometer to measure the temperatures of exposed surfaces of steam pipes, boilers and furnaces or refrigerating systems

- light meter to assess the level of illumination

- tachometer to check the RPM of rotating equipment

- psychrometer to establish the properties of air
- wattmeter to measure electrical power consumed
- voltmeter to measure system voltage
- ammeter to measure electrical current drawn
- combustion analyser to measure O_2, CO, CO_2, flue gas temperature
- leak detectors (e.g. ultrasonic) to detect steam or compressed air leaks

The other process variables that are important to know include *pressure, flow, air velocity, and fluid temperature*. These measurements can sometimes be obtained from process instruments, which must either be read manually or can be logged by Supervisory Control And Data Acquisition (SCADA).

8.1 Measurement of Power

Early in the audit planning it is essential to estimate the total energy use and cost to operate the system. This information will guide the process of planning the system audit. The commitment of time and money to conduct the system assessment must be reasonable given the potential cost savings.

$$\frac{kW \; nameplate \times load\,factor \times annual\,operating\,hours \times energy\;cost}{motor\,efficiency} = Annual\,energy$$

Nameplate kW power of an electric motor can be taken to determine the annual energy use cost of a motor, when taking the load factor, motor efficiency and energy cost into consideration.

It is important to estimate the annual operating hours for each motor as closely as possible. The result of this calculation is not intended to be used as baseline operating data, rather it is a rough estimate of energy use and cost to guide decisions made when planning a system audit. The commitment of time and money to conduct the system assessment must be reasonable given the potential cost savings.

Alternatively, the following calculation could be used to more accurately determine the annual energy cost of a three phase motor:

$$\frac{\sqrt{3} \times Voltage \times Motor\,Amperage \times Power\,factor \times hours \times cost}{1000} = Annual\,energy\;cost$$

Power in watts is line to line voltage multiplied by amperage. The factor of square root three must be applied for three phase circuits. In a three phase system the phases produce different amounts of power at any given moment in time. The phases are separated by 120 degrees and phases move through zero at different times. The correct power of a three phase system at any moment in time is calculated by applying the factor of the square root of three.

For induction motors, the voltage and current on each line of the 3 phases will be slightly out of phase and as a result the true power delivered is less than the apparent power (volts x amps), which is given as the power factor. Power factor is a ratio of true power to apparent power expressed as a fraction or percent. For example, if a 75 kW motor has voltage measured at 400 volts and 128 amps, the apparent power is 88.7 kVA. If the true power is measured at 78 kW, the motor's power factor is 0.88 (88%) [78 divided by 88.7].

Note that the power factor changes significantly with motor load. For example, at 50% of nameplate amperage, the motor's power factor may be 0.55 or 0.60 and therefore, true power is typically much lower that the Voltage x Amperage (apparent power) would suggest. That's why for actual baseline performance measurements made during a system audit, it is always best to make measurements with a true kW instrument rather than measuring volts and amps. Power factor variation as a function of percentage nameplate amperage is specific to a particular motor design. The motor manufacturer should be able to provide power factor versus percentage nameplate amperage curves for their motors.

Figure 8.1 Example of kW power measurement.

8.2 Measurement of Temperature

Temperature loggers are often used to record temperature. They give a useful picture of the patterns of, and changes in temperatures, in different parts of the building.

Temperature can be measured by various instruments, with examples in Figure 8.2

- Thermometers: The most common way to measure temperature is using a glass stem or bimetallic thermometer.

- The glass stem thermometer consists of fluid (mercury or alcohol) that fills a glass tube. The fluid expands as it warms.

- Bimetallic thermometers are made from two strips of metal bonded together in a coil, see Figure 8.3. The coil is attached to a hand or pointer on a scale, which rotates as the metals expand or contract with varying temperatures.

- Thermocouples: A thermocouple can also be used to measure temperature, see Figure 8.4. This device produces an electrical voltage related to the temperature.

Figure 8.2   Examples of different temperature loggers.

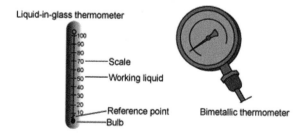

Figure 8.3   Types of thermometers.

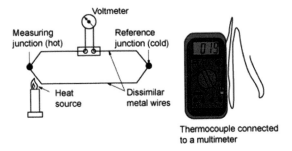

Figure 8.4 Thermocouple connected to a multimeter/voltmeter.

Figure 8.5 Infrared thermal camera.

- Resistance Temperature Detectors (RTD's): Sensors used to measure temperature by correlating the resistance of the RTD element with a specific temperature. In certain metals, the resistance increases as the temperature increases. The sensor is a small resistance wire that, when heated up, will change its internal resistance. This resistance change can then be measured to determine the temperature. A platinum 100 (PT 100) will have a 100 Ω at 0°C.

- Pyrometers: Non-contact thermometers. These instruments measure radiation without making contact with the object.

- Thermal-cameras are other options. The real temperature of an object can be found by measuring its emitted radiation. Infrared thermographs can also be used, see Figure 8.5.

8.3 Measurement of Pressure

Pressure gauges are most commonly used to measure pressure. Different gauges are used for different pressure measurements. The following instruments can be used to measure pressure:

Figure 8.6   Bourdon gauge.

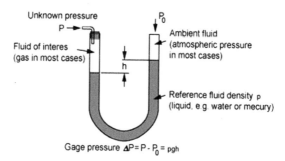

Figure 8.7   Manometer principle.

- Bourdon gauge. The Bourdon type pressure gauge, see Figure 8.6, works on the principle that a curved tube is trying to straighten itself out when pressurized. This motion is mechanically transferred to a hand that indicates the pressure.

- Manometer. It uses a column of liquid to measure pressure, see Figure 8.7

- Draft gauge

- Pressure transducer

It is important to do pressure measurements on fluids to verify the operating conditions of the apparatus or systems in the buildings. It is also necessary to investigate the pressure drop across the systems, because pressure drop amounts to energy loss. This will be relevant when assessing HVAC systems, fans and pumps.

8.4 Measurement of Humidity

A psychrometer is an instrument used to measure relative humidity by comparing the temperature sensed by a dry bulb to that sensed by a bulb completely enclosed by a saturated wick. At 100% RH, both bulbs should read the same temperature. Electrical conductivity meter, a hair hygrometer, or other hand-held units can also be used to measure humidity.

8.5 Measurement of Heat Capacity and Heat Storage

The heat capacity of most systems is not a constant. Instead, it depends on temperature as well as on the pressure and the volume of the system. Heat capacity can be measured at either constant pressure or at constant volume. The symbol for heat capacity is either C_p (measured at constant pressure) or C_v (at constant volume).

Following are the instruments that are used to measure heat capacity:

- Constant-volume calorimeter (also called a "bomb calorimeter", see Figure 8.8). This device measures heat capacity at constant volume (Cv) and consists of:

- A small cup to contain the sample

- Oxygen

- A stainless-steel sample bomb (by using stainless steel as a sample, the reaction will occur with no volume change)

- Water

Figure 8.8 Bomb calorimeter.

Figure 8.9   Constant-pressure calorimeter.

- A stirrer

- A thermometer

- The Dewar or insulating container (to prevent heat flow from the calo-rimeter to the surroundings)

- An ignition circuit connected to the bomb

- Constant-pressure calorimeter (also called an enthalpy meter), see Figure 8.9. This device is used to determine heat capacity at con-stant pressure (Cp). It measures the change in enthalpy of a reaction that happens in a solution where the atmospheric pressure remains constant.

The heat storage can be calculated using the following equation:

$$q = V \times \rho \times Cp \times dt = m \times Cp \times dt$$

Where:
- q = sensible heat stored in the material (kJ)
- V = volume of substance (m³)
- ρ = density of substance (kg/m³)
- m = mass of substance (kg)
- Cp = specific heat capacity of the substance (kJ/kg.°C)
- dt = temperature change (°C)

Figure 8.10 Example of combustion analyzer.

8.6 Combustion Measurement

The following instruments are recommended for assessing the combustion efficiency in most fuel fired equipment:

- Stack thermometer, to measure the flue gas temperatures,

- Digital thermometer, to measure the ambient and equipment surface temperatures,

- Smoke pump, to establish the flue gas conditions,

- Combustion testing kit, to measure oxygen ($\%O_2$) and/or carbon dioxide ($\%CO_2$) readings to calculate excess air and combustion efficiency, and

- Psychrometer, to measure the quality of the incoming combustion air.

The use of an electronic flue gas/combustion analyzer, see Figure 8.10, either hand-held or continuous type is an alternative which measures all the above parameters.

Simple combustion analyzer instruments, filled with liquid which absorbs CO_2 and O_2, can be used to give a quick assessment of the combustion efficiency. An example in Figure 8.10.

8.7 Measurements of Air Velocity

The following instruments could be used to measure the velocity of air, with an example in Figure 8.11.

- Anemometer - deflecting vane

Figure 8.11   Anemometer.

- Anemometer - rotating vane
- Pitot Tube
- Heated Thermocouple
- Hot Wire Anemometer

8.8 Measurements of Flow

There are a variety of flow meter types with examples in Figure 8.12.

- Differential pressure - orifice, venturi, nozzle, elbow
- Velocity - Magnetic, ultrasonic, turbine, vortex shedding, variable area (rotameter), pitot tube
- Open flow - Weir
- Positive displacement - gear, nutating disc
- Mass

In liquid flow measurement applications, most flow meters require a straight piece of pipe on their upstream side in order for a proper flow profile to be developed. Uneven flow profiles may skew the result of the measurement. If possible you should strive for 10 pipe diameters of straight pipe in front of the flow meter and preferably 5 diameters downstream as well.

In air flow measurement applications, the total pressure of an air stream flowing in a duct is the sum of the *static pressure* exerted on the sidewalls

Figure 8.12 Portable ultrasonic flow meter.

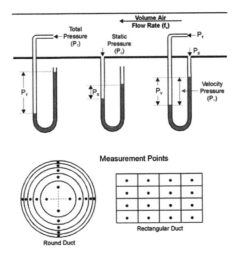

Figure 8.13 Pitot tube flow measurements.

of the duct and the *velocity pressure* of the moving air. In Figure 8.13, the illustrated pitot tube is a common device for measuring the velocity pressure. Measurements should be taken in accordance with traverse details shown. The velocity pressure should be calculated for each traverse position and the readings averaged. Using these measurements, the velocity of air in a duct can then be calculated.

8.9 Measurements of Compressed Air Systems

Without sufficient instrumentation on compressed air systems, it is impossible to determine whether they are operating efficiently. There have been many mentions of where energy is wasted; without a mechanism for detecting wastage, it is likely to continue and minimum energy costs will not be achieved.

The following list gives a guideline on areas to be measured when conducting a compressed air system assessment:

- kW power of each compressor at high frequency (one order of magnitude faster than e.g. the cycling event, i.e. if a compressor unloads 10 seconds after loading, power must be measured every 1 second)

- Pressure measurements on the discharge of each compressor

- Pressure on the primary receiver or wet receiver before treatment

- Pressure on the secondary receiver or dry receiver after treatment

- Pressure in the main header if different from the above

- Pressure at a significant user (in terms of size of production criticality)

- Pressure at the point furthest from the compressor house

- Pressure at the point where compressed air pressure problems are often experienced

- Pressure at high volume intermittent demand users

- Flow supply from each compressor

- Flow supply total from generation

- Flow demand to different plants

- Pressure dewpoint at the dryer to assess effectiveness of dryer

- Water temperature gauges in the compressor cooling jacket and the aftercooler, to detect any blockages that may be occurring

- Air temperature gauges at the outlet of the compressor and in the receiver, to help detect any fouling of the after-cooler heat exchanger

- Inter-cooler pressure and temperature gauges where applicable

- Blow off valve position on centrifugal compressors

- Inlet guide vane or inlet valve position

8.9.1 Compressed air flow measurements

In compressed air systems, airflow measurement is generally expressed as mass units per period of time, specifically in terms of volumetric flow rate. In Europe, the typical unit of measure is Nm^3/min (Normal cubic meters per minute). In the United States, the typical unit of measure is scfm (standard cubic feet per minute). Remember, if the unit of measure begins with "standard" or "normal", the unit is most likely referring to weight. If the unit of measure is just m^3/min, litres/sec, acfm or cfm, the unit is most likely a volume measure. For test equipment made in the United States, the calibration will set the air density at standard conditions*, which is 0.07423 lb/ft^3, and directly relates standard cubic feet per minute to a mass flow rate in lb/minute. For the DIN standard, the calibration would be set for 1.294 kg/m^3.

Flow transducers for compressed air generally fall into one or two broad categories: those that measure the gas velocity (e.g. meters per second) in the pipeline, and those that measure the mass velocity in the pipeline.

Thermal dispersion mass flow meters use temperature-sensing elements in the flow stream to measure mass velocity. One temperature sensor measures the temperature of the gas and the second is heated when current passes through the sensor. As gas flows over the heated element, the gas removes heat from the sensor. The rate of heat transfer varies with the fluid density, and also varies as the square root of the velocity at which the fluid flows past the wire. The power necessary to maintain temperature of the heated element is, therefore, related to the mass velocity of gas passing over the sensor.

The installation of an air flow meter on the main airline from the compressor house will give two very valuable pieces of information, see Figure 8.14:

- A true usage demand profile, and base leakage or minimum use information of the plant. This is preferable to estimating usage from the on/off-load running times of the compressors, as compressor output capacity must be assumed as design level, although it could be a long way from it.

- The overall generation efficiency coupled with electricity consumption readings i.e. input energy to output air for a given demand can be calculated and used for analysis. Care must be taken when trying to establish the efficiency of an individual compressor, because the meter will be reading plant demand, not compressor output.

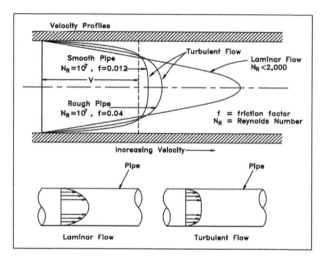

Figure 8.14   Pipeline's velocity profile over a range of flow rate (velocity) for both laminar and turbulent flow.

8.9.2 Leak detection in compressed air system

For ultrasonic leak detection, an ultrasound instrument that has frequency tuning capability is recommended, and the suggested frequency setting is 40kHz. For ultrasound instruments that are on a fixed frequency, or where frequency tuning is not a feature, 38kHz is usually the frequency setting that the instrument is fixed at.

There are different sources of high frequency sound that these ultrasound instruments detect. For compressed air and compressed gas leak detection, the source of the ultrasound is turbulence.

Turbulence is created when a compressed gas inside of a pipe or vessel exits to low pressure or atmosphere through a tiny crack or orifice. Turbulence is also created when there is air in-leakage, or vacuum leaks. With vacuum leaks, since most of the turbulence is on the inside of the leak, there is not as much ultrasound present; therefore, vacuum leaks are more difficult to find with ultrasound, but can still be possible if enough turbulent ultrasonic noise is present.

One thing to keep in mind while scanning for compressed air leaks out in the facility is the fact that high frequency sound is very low energy.

Because it is low energy, the sound will not travel through solid surfaces, but rather bounce and reflect off of solid surfaces. That is why it is important to scan in all directions with the ultrasound instrument, while adjusting the sensitivity. This will help to pinpoint the location of the compressed air leak.

Once the general area of the compressed air leak has been located, most ultrasound instruments will come with a focusing probe that can be slipped over the end of the airborne scanning module on the instrument to more finely narrow the field of view to more precisely identify the location of the leak. This method of compressed air leak detection using ultrasound is commonly referred to as the "Gross to Fine" method.

Chapter 9

Fuels, Furnaces, and Fired Equipment

Albert Williams

Institute of Energy Professionals Africa, South Africa

The standard of living in the majority of countries in the world largely depends on the use of fossil fuels. Any time the supply of the fossil fuels is endangered, a major economic crisis follows. It would seem logical that every country should try to reduce its dependence on fossil fuels by better utilization of the resource. So far the primary method of using fossil fuel is by burning, which is not the best way to utilize such a valuable source of energy. However, since combustion is the most popular way of fuel conversion, it is important for the technical personnel, who handle energy conversion equipment such as boilers, furnaces and kilns to understand the basic principles of a combustion process.

9.1 Fuel Fired Systems

Furnaces, dryers, boilers and kilns are used extensively in industry for diverse applications such as melting and heating metals, evaporating water or solvents and manufacturing lime for cement and in the pulp industries. Much of this equipment was installed when fuel was relatively cheap and little or no consideration was given to energy management. Even today, first cost and production capability are frequently the prime criteria for the selection of equipment, with energy management being relegated to a secondary role. The high cost of the fuels today demands a greater awareness for energy management techniques which can be applied to existing and new installations. Substantial savings in energy and cost can be realized by the application of these techniques. In many instances the return on invested capital makes the application of energy management one of the most attractive.

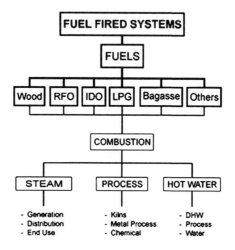

Figure 9.1   Fuel types and uses.

9.2 Fuels

The most important characteristics of the fuels is their calorific or heating value. Each fuel has a certain range of heating values depending on its origin. In the case of wood, bagasse and other biomass, the moisture content will determine the range of heating values. All fuels contain hydrogen which burns and produces water. This water normally leaves the plant as hot vapor at the temperature of exit gases.

This loss is significant because even small quantities of water absorb large quantities of heat when it evaporates. The net calorific value or Low Heating Value (LHV) is the gross calorific value or High Heating Value (HHV) less this loss. The difference between these two values is about 4% for coal, 5% for oils and 11% for natural gas. When comparing the efficiencies of different fuel burning equipment, it is important to establish the heating value of the fuels used during the tests.

9.2.1 Properties of solid fuels

Fuel fired equipment using solid fuels must be carefully designed for the fuel properties. Among these are calorific value, volatile content, ash content, moisture content, ash fusion temperature, grindability and agglomerating characteristics. For more information about these factors, consult reference manuals that deal specifically in various solid fuels.

Table 9.1 Stoichiometric combustion data for typical fuels.

Fuel Type	USA Coal	Botswana Coal	Zimbabwe Coal	No.2 Oil	No.6 Oil	Natural Gas	LPG	Bagasse	Pine Wood	Oak Wood
Ultimate Analysis										
Fuel (%b.w.)										
Carbon (C)	80.31%	59.71%	70.53%	87.20%	85.60%	69.26%	81.82%	23.40%	29.37%	37.34%
Hydrogen (H)	4.47%	3.30%	3.94%	12.50%	9.70%	22.68%	18.18%	2.80%	3.08%	2.97%
Nitrogen (N2)	1.38%	1.36%	1.54%	—	1.50%	8.06%	—	0.10%	0.06%	0.11%
Oxygen (O2)	2.85%	10.28%	2.96%	0.30%	0.50%	—	—	20.00%	20.85%	21.62%
Sulphur (S2)	1.54%	1.75%	2.03%	—	2.30%	—	—	—	0.06%	0.06%
Moisture (H2O)	2.90%	5.10%	6.00%	—	0.28%	—	—	52.00%	45.00%	45.00%
Ash	6.55%	18.50%	13.00%	—	0.12%	—	—	1.70%	1.60%	2.92%
Total Fuel	100.00%	100.00%	100.00%	100.00%	100.00%	100.00%	100.00%	100.00%	100.00%	100.00%
Combustion Air (%b.w.)										
Oxygen (O2)	23.31%	23.31%	23.31%	23.31%	23.31%	23.31%	23.31%	23.31%	23.31%	23.31%
Nitrogen (N2)	76.69%	76.69%	76.69%	76.69%	76.69%	76.9%	76.69%	76.69%	76.69%	76.69%
Moisutrue (H2O)	—	—	—	—	—	—	—	—	—	—
Total Combustion Air	100.00%	100.00%	100.00%	100.00%	100.00%	100.00%	100.00%	100.00%	100.00%	100.00%
Stoichiometric Flue Gas (b.w.)										
Carbon dioxice (CO2)	25.39%	26.03%	25.23%	20.93%	22.11%	15.20%	18.07%	22.80%	23.88%	23.91%
Nitrogen (N2)	70.63%	69.42%	70.33%	71.67%	71.40%	72.58%	72.07%	56.68%	59.97%	58.96%
Sulfur Dioxide (SO2)	0.27%	0.42%	0.40%	0.04%	0.32%	—	—	—	0.02%	0.03%
Moisutre (H2O)	3.72%	4.14%	4.04%	7.36%	6.17%	12.22%	9.86%	20.52%	16.13%	17.11%
Total Flue Gas	100.00%	100.00%	100.00%	100.00%	100.00%	100.00%	100.00%	100.00%	100.00%	100.00%
Mass Ratios										
Fuel (net)	0.9055	0.7640	0.8100	1.0000	0.9960	1.0000	1.000	0.4630	0.5341	0.5209
Fuel Moisture	0.0290	0.0510	0.6000	—	0.0028	—	—	0.5200	0.4500	0.4500
Fuel Ash	0.0655	0.1850	0.1300	—	0.0012	—	—	0.0170	0.0160	0.0292
Fuel (gross)	1.000	1.0000	1.0000	1.0000	1.0000	1.0000	1.0000	1.0000	1.0000	1.0000
Stoichiometric Air (dry)	10.6654	7.5974	9.3809	14.2786	13.1989	15.7071	15.5996	2.7799	3.5251	3.2215
Stoichiometric Air (moisture)										
Total Stoichiometric Air	10.6654	7.5974	9.3809	14.2786	13.1989	15.7071	15.5996	2.7799	3.5251	3.2215
Flue Gas (dry)	11.1686	8.0644	9.8363	14.1536	13.3219	14.6659	14.9634	2.9909	3.7819	3.4751
Flue Gas (moisture)	0.4313	0.3480	0.4146	1.1250	0.8758	2.0412	1.6362	0.7720	0.7272	0.7173
Total Flue Gas	11.5999	8.4124	10.2509	15.2786	14.1977	16.7071	16.5996	3.7629	4.5091	4.1924
Fuel HHV (kJ/kg)	32.800	24.000	30.000	45.200	12.570	50.770	50.390	9.300	11.550	10.700
Fuel Specific Gravity	n/a	n/a	n/a	0.87	0.98	0.13	n/a	n/a	0.73	0.85
Fuel Specific Gravity (kJ/kgC)	0.83	0.83	0.83	2.01	2.01	n/a	n/a	n/a	2.93	2.58
Flue Gas Specific Heat (kJ/kgC)	1.02	1.01	1.02	1.02	1.02	1.03	1.03	1.02	1.02	1.02

Specific Heat Constant: Dry Air = 1.02 kJ/kgC, Moisture (liquid) = 4.19 kJ/kgC, Moisture (Vapour) = 1.8 kJ/kgC, Latent Heat of Moisture = 2,500 kJ/kg

9.2.2 Properties of liquid fuels (Oil)

Fuel oil is classified by its viscosity, Sulphur content, heating value, pour point, flash point and specific gravity. The figure below gives characteristics of typically available fuels, together with data on combustion air requirements and storage temperature.

a) Viscosity

Viscosity, or resistance to flow, is expressed in the number of seconds it takes a liter of fuel to pass through a certain size hole at a certain temperature. The scales used are Redwood, Sybolt or Centistokes. Viscosity may be specified as maximum for Residual Fuel Oil (RFO) at 50°C as follows:

• 125 centistokes (1000 sec Redwood)

• 180 centistokes (1500 sec Redwood)

• 280 centistokes (2500 sec Redwood)

The most widely used grade is 125 centistokes.

b) Flash point

Flash point is a measure of fire hazard of bulk storage. Flash point is usually controlled to a minimum of 65.5°C for the following reasons:

• For handling this category of product, a minimum flash point is specified. The product is not expected to be volatile.

• If the flash point is lower than the specified value, then the viscosity may be too low, and this could make the product unsuitable.

• Addition of distillates such as kerosene with flash point of 38°C to heavier oils considerably increases the fire hazard.

c) Pour point

Pour point indicates the lowest temperature at which the fuel can be pumped. It is the temperature slightly above the solidification point.

d) Sulphur content

Upon combustion, the Sulphur in fuel is converted to Sulphur dioxide and ultimately to Sulphur trioxide. On cooling, Sulphur trioxide combines with water to form Sulphuric acid which is destructive to the chimneys. For this reason, the stack temperature should not fall below 150°C. Typically, maximum Sulphur content is 3.7% for 125 and 180 centistokes and 4.0% max for 280 centistokes.

9.2.1 Properties of gaseous fuels

Gaseous fuels may be analysed in terms of the chemical compounds they contain. Other properties by which the fuels are identified are:

a) Gas gravity
Gas gravity is a convenient measure of specific gravity of a gas relative to that of air (1.225 kg/m³).

b) Heating value
Although the heating value can be calculated from gas analysis, it is frequently measured by means of steady flow, constant pressure calorimeter in which the gas is burned in a water jacketed combustion chamber. The temperature rise in the water is a measure of the heat given off by the fuel.

c) Condensable hydrocarbon content
The term wet or dry as applied to natural gases indicates whether the quantity of contained condensable hydrocarbons (usually natural gasoline) is greater or less than 0.13 litres per cubic meter (0.1 gallon per 1000 cubic feet) of gas, respectively.

d) Sulphur content
The term sweet and sour refers to the Sulphur or hydrogen Sulphide content of the gas; sour gas being that which contains large proportion of Sulphur compounds.

The combustion process is the cornerstone to development in our civilization. From burning wood for warmth and cooking, to modern transportation which burns petroleum products, to generating electricity by burning solid fossil fuels, our modern world would collapse without conversion of fossil fuels to heat. Combustion is a complex subject and any substantive changes to the process should only be contemplated after consultation with the regulating bodies having jurisdiction, the manufacturer of the fuel burning equipment, the control system supplier and other trained specialists.

9.3 Combustion

Combustion or burning, by definition, is a process of conversion of chemical energy to thermal energy by very rapid oxidation of the component elements in fuels. The three main elements of fuels are: carbon, hydrogen and Sulphur.

Oxygen is obtained from combustion air which contains: 21% oxygen by volume (23% by weight) and 79% nitrogen by volume. During combustion, these elements are oxidized into carbon dioxide (CO_2), water vapor (H_2O) and Sulphur dioxide (SO_2) accompanied by the release of heat and light.

9.3.1 Combustion of carbon

Carbon can produce two compounds depending on the availability of the air supply:

* If enough air is supplied, carbon dioxide is produced. If the air is exactly right (stoichiometric conditions), the gaseous products equal the air quantity, i.e. 21% CO_2 and 79% nitrogen, plus release of heat.

* With a starved air supply, the carbon is partially burnt to carbon monoxide and the full calorific value of the fuel is not released. This is known as incomplete combustion; a dangerous condition in any fuel burning equipment. The figure below provides an estimate of combustion loss

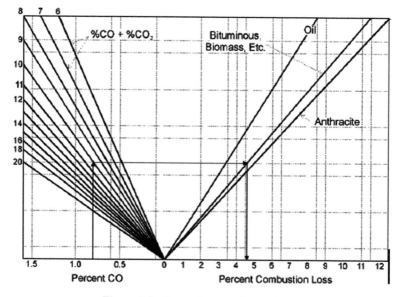

Figure 9.2   Incomplete combustion loss.

due to incomplete combustion which is indicated by the presence of CO in the flue gas. Note the loss indicated in this chart is in addition to normal combustion losses.

9.3.2 Combustion air requirement

Stoichiometric air is the theoretical amount of air required for complete combustion. In actual applications, however, it is impossible to get perfect mixing of the fuel and air. Thus, additional air, termed *excess air*, is required to burn the fuel safely and completely. The more refined the fuel, the less excess air is needed. Typical excess air values are:

Natural gas	5–10%
IDO (No.2 oil)	10–20%
RFO (No.6 oil)	10–25%
Coal	20–40%
Biomass (Bagasse)	30–50%

The effect of excess air on burning of oils is shown next. It can be seen that the CO_2 content is reduced from the stoichiometric 16% for perfect combustion to 12% at 30% excess air on dry basis (i.e. water vapor removed).

% Excess Air	% CO_2	% O_2
Nil	16%	0%
30%	12%	5%
50%	11%	7%
75%	9%	9.5%
120%	7%	12%

For more common fuels, the typical target values are:

Fuel	Max CO_2	Target CO_2	Target O_2
Coal	19%	14%	6%
Fuel Oils	16%	13%	4%
Natural Gas	12%	11%	2%

Although minimum quantities of excess air are required to ensure good combustion, too much excess air leads to lowered thermal efficiency as larger quantities of heated flue gases are produced and discharged to the atmosphere.

9.4 Optimizing Combustion Conditions

In order to burn fuels efficiently, it is necessary to introduce optimum quantities of air for combustion. To little air will cause smoking with consequent loss due to unburnt fuel. Because of visible smoke, this problem is usually corrected quickly.

The introduction of too much combustion air is more common in boilers, furnaces and vehicles, but less apparent, and therefore can continue undetected for long periods. The use of excessive quantities of air leads to substantial energy losses and can also cause operation problems, i.e. scaling in furnaces.

Control of the air/fuel ratio is very important particularly in high temperature exhausts i.e. furnaces and kilns, where stack losses can be up to 60% of the fuel input. A simple oxygen analyser and high temperature thermometer can detect high excess air quantities which can often be rectified by simple adjustment of the fuel control or the air fans.

9.5 Fuel Fired Equipment and Applications

9.5.1 Furnaces

The purpose of a process furnace is to supply heat to the contents in controlled manner. The furnace may be used for heating metals to a precisely controlled temperature for heat treatment or for melting. The furnaces are manufactured in many different types and sizes, some of which are described in this section.

Furnaces may be batch or continuous type. Furnaces, which generate heat by burning fuels, may be of the direct or indirect fired types. Furnaces are also heated by electric resistance or induction heaters.

a) Batch furnaces
The batch furnaces process the product in batches, which means that the furnace doors must be opened and closed at the beginning and end of each batch cycle. Since this is a significant source of energy loss, the loading and unloading times should be minimized. It is also important to load the furnace completely to minimize the energy loss per unit of product.

b) Continuous furnaces
Continuous furnaces process the product continually by moving it through the heating zones on chains or conveyors. Since the loading and unloading doors are open all or most of the operating time, there is a significant heat loss through these openings.

Continuous furnaces also may have a significant heat loss because of the conveying mechanism, which is heated to the operating temperature of the product. If the conveyor cools off outside the furnace before re-entering the loading area, the energy required to heat the conveyor is not used productively. Thus it is better if the conveyor stays within the heated furnace area.

c) Direct fired furnaces

The products of combustion are in direct contact with the product being heated in a direct fired furnace. The heat transfer process from the flame to the product is more effective than with the indirect heated furnace. The higher rate of heat transfer which can be achieved with direct fired furnaces can lead to a local surface overheating of the product, unless the furnace temperature is properly controlled.

d) Indirect heated furnaces

In indirect heated furnaces the heat is transferred through some form of heat exchanger. This type of furnace may be used to provide a controlled environment for oxidizing or reducing, by introducing an artificial atmosphere independent of the combustion process. Since the heat transfer from the flame to the product is not as effective as with the direct fired furnace, it can be expected that the flue gas temperature will be higher, resulting in higher heat losses unless heat recovery is used.

There are few special considerations for indirect fired furnaces which affect the heat balance calculations. If the controlled atmosphere is maintained inside the furnace, the heat input and output of the gas entering and leaving the furnace must be included in the heat balance. If heat is required for the preparation of the atmosphere, the energy required in the gas generator must be included as part of the total heat input to the furnace. Electrical energy used for refrigeration or other purposes in the gas generator must also be included.

9.5.2 Dryers

Dryers use heat to evaporate water or solvents from materials such as lumber, grain, ceramics, paints and carbon electrodes. The same principles of energy management described for furnaces also apply to dryers and much of the equipment is similar in concept. A major difference is in operating temperature, which is generally much lower than furnaces, as this avoids damage to the product. As a result, the direct fired heaters must operate with very high percentage of excess air. This means that excess air cannot be reduced to achieve the energy savings. Indirect fired dryers can operate at normal values of excess air within the combustion chamber. With direct and indirect fired heaters there is a large amount of heat in exhausted air in the form of evaporated water or solvent. Often the solvents must be incinerated before discharge to the atmosphere by burning additional fuel in the dryer discharge and raising the temperature to about 900°C. Recovery of the heat in the dryer exhaust can be achieved by a heat exchanger which is used to preheat the incoming air for drying with indirect fired dryers or the combustion air for firing in the direct dryers.

9.5.3 Kilns

There is no fundamental difference between furnaces and kilns from the energy management viewpoint. The ceramic and brick industries use station-ary kilns. The rotary kilns are used by the cement and pulp industries. Some rotary kilns burn pulverized coal or refuse-derived fuel. The large heat input to the rotary kilns provides opportunities for the insulation of heat exchang-ers to recover flue gas heat.

9.6 Flue Gas and Other Losses in Process Furnaces, Dryers and Kilns

Process requirements for some furnaces and dryers require high excess air values which cannot be reduced. Thus, flue gas heat loss is high, and cannot be reduced by lowering the excess air quantity. It is often possible in these applications to install a heat exchanger to preheat the incoming air with the flue gases leaving the furnace or dryer. The heat loss is then the heat in the flue gas after the heat recovery equipment. Flue gas analysis and temperature should be measured downstream of this equipment.

9.7 Burners

Burner design varies according to the type of fuel and the application objec-tives, but they must all do the following:

•   Direct fuel to the combustion chamber.

•   Direct air to the combustion chamber.

•   Effectively mix the fuel and air.

•   Once the burner has been ignited it must continue to ignite the incoming fuel.

9.7.1 Liquid fuel combustion

To burn oils, particularly the heavier grades efficiently, it is first necessary to break down the fuel into small droplets which can be quickly heated and mixed with air. A fuel droplet of lighter oils is vaporized by heat from the downstream flame and produces gases which readily react with oxygen. A fuel droplet of the residual oils partially vaporizes, and the gases burn readily, leaving a shell of liquid. The shell cracks with further heat leaving an empty ash shell which eventually breaks down. The whole process takes less than 2 seconds.

To atomize oil satisfactorily, it is necessary to control the viscosity of the oil. If the oil is too thick, large droplets will form and will not burn fully. If the oil is too thin, the droplets will be too small and evaporate too quickly, causing lift off from the burner, pulsations, etc.

9.7.2 Pressure jet burners

The pressure jet burner is essentially a nozzle through which the oil is pumped at high pressure (4 to 10 bars). The oil is introduced tangentially into a chamber through slots which cause the oil to spin through a small outlet orifice in a hollow cone. Different nozzles can be used to give varying outputs and flame shapes. Normally these burners are restricted to oil of less than 1000 secs viscosity, usually in an "On/Off" or "High/Low" mode. The main characteristics are:

- cheap to install,

- oilways are fine and must be cleaned,

- very sensitive to oil viscosity limited to 1000 secs,

- heat soak-back can cause coking up around the nozzle, and sensitive to draft variations.

9.7.3 Rotary cup burners

In this type, the oil is pumped into a tapered cup which is rotating at about 6000 rpm. The oil film flows to the tip where it is thrown off. Primary air is introduced at high velocity and atomises the film into droplets. The main characteristics are:

- high turn down ration (4:1) making the burner ideal for the fluctuating loads,

- moderate cost,

- not too sensitive to oil viscosity, and

- easy to clean.

These burners are widely used on boiler applications.

9.7.4 Air blast burners

Atomizing is achieved by introducing high velocity swirling air onto a stream of oil. With low air pressure burners, 20 to 30% of the combustion air is required for atomizing, with the remainder being introduced through different ports. The turn down ratio is usually about 4 to 2.1. Medium and high-pressure burners (7 bar air pressure) use less than 10% of the combustion air for atomizing, hence the turn down ration of 5:1 is easily achieved.

This type of burner is mainly used for furnace work where preheated combustion air can be used. Low pressure air 200°C, high pressure 400°C. The main characteristics are:

- good turn down ratio,

- easy to maintain, the high-pressure burners are almost self-cleaning,

- insensitive to draught, and

- flame shape controllable.

9.7.5 Common problems in burners

a) Solid fuel combustion

In a bed of burning solid fuel (wood, coal, peat, etc.) under-grate air combines with the carbon to produce CO_2 and CO. These hot gases rise through the bed

Table 9.2   Common problems in burners.

Condition	Cause	Action
Sparky Flame	Atomization	Check & Clean Nozzles
Flame Impingement	Incorrect Air Supply	Check Control Adjustments
Flame Pulsates	Too High Oil Temperature	Adjust Preheat
	Too High Air Velocity	
Smoke	Too Little Air	Adjust Air/Oil
		Seal Air Leaks
High Particulate	Atomization	Check Nozzle Preheat
	Fuel Input Too High	Reduce Fuel
		Check Design

and drive off the volatiles of the fuel (Hydrocarbons such as methane). Above the bed, secondary air is admitted which burns off the CO and the volatiles.

b) Optimizing combustion conditions

In order to burn fuels efficiently, it is necessary to introduce optimum quantities of air for combustion. To little air will cause smoking with consequent loss due to unburnt fuel. Because of visible smoke, this problem is usually corrected quickly.

The introduction of too much combustion air is more common in boilers, furnaces and vehicles, but less apparent, and therefore can continue undetected for long periods. The use of excessive quantities of air leads to substantial energy losses and can also cause operation problems, i.e. scaling in furnaces.

Control of the air/fuel ratio is very important particularly in high temperature exhausts i.e. furnaces and kilns, where stack losses can be up to 60% of the fuel input. A simple oxygen analyzer and high temperature thermometer can detect high excess air quantities which can often be rectified by simple adjustment of the fuel control or the air fans.

c) Control of thermal input - Overfiring

Losses can also occur due to the use of excessive amounts of fuel input into the furnaces or boilers, i.e. overfiring. This leads to high stack temperatures and avoidable energy losses. Overfiring is generally associated with incorrectly adjusted burners and/or with fouled heat transfer surfaces.

d) Control of thermal input - Underfiring

Low thermal inputs are easily detected because the boiler outputs will be low. However, overfiring and therefore excessive losses, are not apparent. A regular check of stack temperatures can ensure that the burner outputs are Optimized.

e) Fuel air ratio

Experience has shown that many burners are incorrectly adjusted, particularly under low load conditions. Wear on cams, linkages, fuel pump adjustments affect the performance of the energy conversion equipment. Regular combustion checks can identify any shortcomings in maintenance, cleanliness etc.

f) Flue gas temperature

High flue gas temperatures are associated with the following conditions:

- too high firing rate, usually due to incorrect setting of controls,

- fouled heating surfaces - in boilers it could be fouling of surfaces on fireside or scaling on surfaces on the water side or both.

Fouled heating surfaces impede the heat transfer resulting in more heat being rejected to the stack in form of higher flue gas temperature.

9.8 Thermal Efficiencies

Thermal efficiency is the ratio of useful heat output to the heat supplied to the plant. It is necessary to convert the units of output to the same units as the energy input.

- Thermal Efficiency = (Useful Energy Output / Heat Supplied to Plant) × 100

- Boiler Plant Efficiency = Heat Value of Steam / (Weight of Fuel Used × HHV) × 100

- Furnace / Kiln Efficiency = Heat Content of Product / (Weight of Fuel Used × HHV) × 100

- Diesel Generator Efficiency = kWh Converted to Heat Units / (Weight of Fuel Used × HHV) × 100

Thermal efficiency can also be defined as total energy input minus losses. In boiler plants and furnaces, these losses are mainly due to flue gas losses

Table 9.3   Seigert formula.

$$\%Loss = -\frac{K \times \Delta T}{\%CO_2} + C$$

Where:

% Loss	=	*total flue gas loss as % of the fuel's gross energy (HHV),*
K,C	=	*constants for fuel type (see table below),*
%CO_2	=	*CO_2 as percent (by volume) of dry gas in flue gas,*
ΔT	=	*temperature difference (°C) between flue gas and combustion air (refer to Figure 13.4)*

SEIGERT CONSTANTS

Fuel Type	K	C
Fuel Oil	0.56	6.5
Coal	0.63	5.0
Natural Gas	0.38	11.0

and radiation from the plant. Since boilers and furnaces are normally kept at constant temperatures, the radiation losses should be fairly constant. If a value of radiation is assumed, the Seigert formula can be used to quickly obtain the thermal efficiency to take into account air fuel ratio and exhaust temperature.

Thermal Efficiency = Total Input - Total Losses:

- Flue gas losses - use nomograph or Seigert formula

- Radiation losses - use standard values

    o 2 - 5% for boilers

    o 10% for furnaces and kilns

- Blowdown losses (refer to 11.1.8 Blowdown losses)

9.9 Air Pollution Control - Process and Equipment

The combustion processes for heat generation, transportation and chemical processes emit pollutants that are harmful to the environment. The three most common effects of the air pollution are:

- Greenhouse effect

- Acid rain

- Ground level ozone

9.9.1 Greenhouse gas effect

Sun's short-wave radiation penetrates the atmosphere and heats up the earth. The warmed earth radiates back the excess heat in form of long wave lengths radiation because of much lower surface temperatures. Water vapor and greenhouse gases such as carbon dioxide, nitrous oxides and methane absorb the infrared radiation, thus heating the atmosphere and the earth's surface. The heating of the atmosphere by blocking the escape of infrared radiation is known as greenhouse gas effect which is responsible for global warming.

9.9.2 Acid rain

Acid rain results from combining of nitrogen and Sulphur oxides with atmospheric water vapor. These pollutants originate from coal burning, metal smelting, vehicles and all other fuel burning activities. Nitric oxide and Sulphuric oxides, when combined with water vapor, form nitric and Sulphuric acids that return to the earth as acid rain, snow or fog that leads to acidification of lakes and other surface waters.

9.9.3 Ground level ozone

Ground level ozone is produced by the chemical reaction between nitrogen oxides and Volatile Organic Compounds (VOC) and is the key NOx and VOC related air quality problem. NOx is formed by burning fossil fuels. VOCs are formed mainly from the evaporation of liquid fuels, solvents and organic chemicals. Ozone damage to crops and vegetation can be significant. Ozone sensitive crops include beans, tomatoes, potatoes, soybeans and wheat.

9.9.4 Reduction of pollutant emissions from combustion process

The emission of pollutants from combustion processes can be reduced by four different methods:

- Energy efficiency improvements
- Refinements and modifications to the combustion process
- Flue gas treatment
- Switching to cleaner fuels or alternative energy source.

9.9.5 Energy efficiency improvements

Changes to the combustion system that reduce fuel usage have the additional benefit of reducing pollutant emissions. Measures to reduce fuel consumption are desirable because cost savings accrue as fuel usage is reduced.

9.9.6 Refinement to the combustion process

Modifications can be made to the combustion process for the purpose of reducing the pollutant emissions. However, the changes may have a little or no effect on combustion efficiency. Some of the methods used include flue gas recirculation, staged air combustion and staged fuel combustion. All three methods are designed to delay the availability of oxygen to the fuel. Flue gas recirculation has added benefit of cooling the flame below the temperature where most NOx formation takes place.

9.9.7 Flue gas treatment

Flue gas treatment equipment is available that can remove NOx and SOx from the flue gas stream, but it is quite expensive. SOx can be removed from the flue gas through use of a chemical scrubber that works by spraying a solution through flue gas stream. The spray chemically neutralises the SO_2 in the gas and removes it from the stream before releasing it to the atmosphere.

9.9.8 Fuel switching

Different fuels have significantly different emission characteristics. Where circumstances warrant, emissions can be reduced by switching to lower Sulphur fuels or by changing fuels altogether.

9.10 Energy Efficiency Measures

Energy Efficiency Measures (EEM's) is a term used to represent identified opportunities that can be recommended to management, operating and maintenance personnel, in order save energy and/or money.

9.10.1 Maintain proper burner adjustment

It is good practice to have an experienced burner manufacturer's representative set up burner adjustments. Furnace operators can then identify the appearance of a proper burner flame for future reference. The flame should be checked frequently and always after a significant change in operating conditions affecting the fuel, combustion air flow or furnace pressure.

9.10.2 Check excess air and combustibles in the flue gas

A continuous O_2 and combustibles analyzer is the best arrangement, but cost is high. Sampling tests with a combustion analyzer or by other chemical means can be a reliable guide for proper combustion conditions. Re-adjustment of the fuel/air ratio control should be done promptly if required.

9.10.3 Keep heat exchange surfaces clean

This is required more frequently with oil fired furnaces and for these applications, the use of permanently installed steam or air sootblower may be justified.

9.10.4 Replace/Repair missing and damaged insulation

Heat radiation from a furnace with inadequate insulation can be easily detected during the plant survey.

9.10.5 Check furnace pressure regularly

Air leakage into or gas leaking out of a furnace can be controlled by maintaining a slight positive furnace pressure. The control dampers in the furnace flue gas ducting or related controls should be readjusted if the furnace pressure is not at a correct value.

9.10.6 Schedule production to operate furnaces at or near maximum output

It may be possible to operate the furnace at maximum load every other day, instead of at 50% load continuously. Alternatively, the work may be switched to a smaller furnace which can operate near full load continuously.

9.10.7 Replace damaged furnace doors or covers

Furnace doors or covers which are warped or damaged can be a source of considerable leakage of air into or gas out of the furnace. These should be replaced by doors or covers with tight fitting seals.

9.10.8 Install adequate monitoring instrumentation

The minimum requirement is to have the ability to determine the energy used per unit of output, so that significant deviations from this can be identified and corrective action taken. The fuel or watt meter may be a portable instrument which can then be used on several furnaces. Additional instrumentation will be required to identify individual losses. Measurements of flue gas temperature and oxygen content can be used to indicate the flue gas loss. If a heat exchanger is used to recover the heat from the flue gas, the temperature of the gas and air in and out of the heat exchanger can be used to check the performance.

9.10.9 Recover heat from equipment cooling water

It is often possible to use the warm water discharge from equipment coolers for the purposes such as process washing. In some systems the water discharge may be too cool to be useful. In these instances, the installation of a water flow control valve and temperature controller may be helpful. The water flow is controlled automatically from the water temperature at the cooler outlet so that the water temperature is high enough to be useful, while maintaining proper cooling. The control system will also reduce water use.

9.10.10 Install a heat exchanger in the flue gas outlet

The cost of a heat exchanger is significantly affected by the temperature of the gas entering the unit. Careful consideration should be given to introducing cold air into the gas stream, if required, to lower the gas temperature enough to use economic materials. Stainless steels or alloys cannot be used for temperatures above 950°C.

If the recovered heat is to be used to preheat combustion air, the burner manufacturer should be consulted to determine the maximum allowable temperature. Frequently it will be as low as 250°C. It is unlikely that it will be higher than 400°C since that would require alloy steels instead of carbon steel. If it is not practical to preheat the combustion air if it may be possible to heat the process water or to install a waste heat boiler to utilize the heat energy in the flue gas.

Chapter 10

Heat Exchange Systems

Albert Williams

Institute of Energy Professionals Africa, South Africa

The transfer of thermal energy or heat is driven by a temperature difference. The rate at which heat moves from a high temperature body to a body at a lower temperature is determined by the difference in temperatures and the materials through which the heat transfer takes place.

10.1 Concepts of Conduction, Convection and Radiation

There are three fundamental processes by which heat transfer takes place. These are:

- conduction,

- convection and

- radiation.

All heat transfer occurs by at least one of these processes, but typically, heat transfer occurs through a *combination* of these processes. All heat transfer processes are driven by temperature differences and are dependent on the materials or substances involved. Figure 10.1 and Figure 10.2 demonstrates the process graphically.

10.1.1 Conduction

Conduction is the heat transfer between two objects that are in contact with each other. The hotter object will heat the cooler object. The molecules of the object with a higher temperature have more energy, and they bump into the molecules of the cooler object. In this way they transfer some of their energy,

215

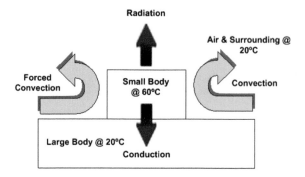

Figure 10.1   Heat transfer processes.

Figure 10.2   Heat transfer processes examples.

causing the temperature to increase. Conduction can also be described as heat flow through materials. In buildings, conduction happens through walls, ceilings/roofs and floors. The heat flow through materials can be described using the terms discussed next and Figure 10.3.

Conductivity (k): This is the amount of heat transmitted in time through the material. It is defined using the following equation (Fourier's Law):

$$q = -\frac{k \times dT}{dX}$$

Where:
q = heat flux – the amount of energy through unit area per unit time (W/m²)
dT/dX = the temperature gradient
k = conductivity coefficient (W/m.°C)

Conductance (U): This is the number of watts that flow through 1 m² of a given thickness of homogenous material when the temperature drop is 1°C. The units for conductance are W/m² °C.

Resistivity (R): This is how effective a solid is as an insulator. R is the reciprocal for conductance (U) (R = 1/U) and is measured in hours. It is the time needed for 1 W to flow through 1 m² of a material of a given thickness. The

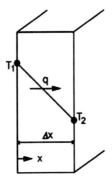

Figure 10.3   Heat conduction through a certain material.

units are m^2 K/W or m^2 °C/W. Resistance is useful when comparing insulating materials, since the greater the R-value, the better the insulator.

The amount of heat transferred by conduction depends on:

• The temperature difference of the objects.

• The properties of the materials involved.

• The thickness of the material.

• The contact surface area.

• The duration of the transfer.

Metals are good conductors of heat/thermal energy because they are dense, which means that their molecules are close together. Gases are bad conductors because their molecules are far apart.

10.1.2 Convection

Convection is the heat transfer caused by the motion of fluid media from a warmer surface to a cooler surface. In buildings this happens around windows and doors. The heat transfer through convection was first described by Isaac Newton and the relationship is called Newton's law of cooling. The equation for convection can be expressed as:

$$Q = hc \times A \times dT$$

Where:

q = Heat transferred per unit time (W)

A = Heat transfer area of the surface (m2)

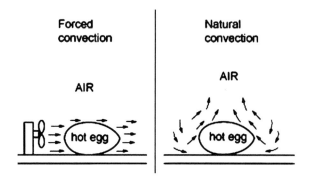

Figure 10.4   Natural convection and forced convection.

hc = Convective heat transfer coefficient of the process (W/m2K or W/m2°C)

dT = Temperature difference between the surface and the bulk fluid (K or °C)

The convective heat transfer coefficient (hc) depends on the type of media, gas or liquid, the flow properties such as velocity, viscosity and other properties related to flow and temperature. There are two types of convection heat transfer, see Figure 10.4:

- Natural or free convection: The fluid is heated by conduction. It expands as it is heated and becomes less dense and rises. The cold fluid moves down, causing a circulatory movement of the fluid past the heated body.

- Forced convection: The movement of the fluid is forced by an external source such as a fan, a pump or stirrer.

10.1.3 Thermal radiation

Thermal radiation is a heat transfer process where energy or heat is emitted in all directions from a heated surface in the form of electromagnetic waves. Sunlight is an example of thermal radiation. Figure 10.5 demonstrates the concept.

Thermal radiation interacts with a substance in the following processes:

- Absorption: Radiation enters the body, gets absorbed and becomes heat.

- Transmission: Radiation passes through the body.

- Reflection: Radiation bounces off the body.

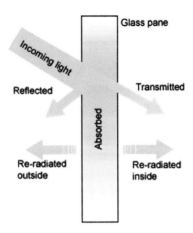

Figure 10.5   Incoming radiated light on a wall, which is transmitted, reflected and reradiated.

Objects receive thermal radiation when they are struck by electro-magnetic waves, thereby agitating the molecules and atoms. More agitation means more energy and a higher temperature. Energy is transferred to one body from another without contact or a transporting medium such as air or water. In fact, thermal radiation heat transfer is the only form of heat transfer possible in a vacuum.

Typical units of measure for rate of radiant heat transfer: Watts per square meter (W/m^2). The radiation of heat can be described by the reference to the so-called 'black' body.

The emissivity of a surface is its ability to emit energy. Emissivity is the ratio of the thermal radiation from a surface to the radiation from a black body at the same temperature. A black-body is a body that absorbs all incident radiation falling on its surface, while black-body radiation is radiation emitted by a black body at thermal equilibrium, which is at a constant temperature.

The emissivity constant depends on the type of material and the temperature of the surface. A list thereof is shown in Table 10.1. It lies in the range $0 < \varepsilon < 1$. The emissivity of some common materials is:

Oxidised iron at 200°C– $\varepsilon = 0.64$
Polished copper at 25°C – $\varepsilon = 0.03$

The equation for radiation can be expressed as:

$$q = \sigma T^4 A$$

Where:

    q = heat transfer (W)
    σ = 5.6703 × 10⁻⁸ (W/m².K⁴) – The Stefan–Boltzmann constant
    T^4 = absolute temperature Kelvin (K)
    A = area of the emitting body (m²)

For objects other than ideal blackbodies, the Stefan-Boltzmann law can be expressed as:

$$q = \varepsilon \times \sigma \times xT^4 \times A$$

Where:

    ε = emissivity of the object
    q = heat transfer (W)
    σ = 5.6703 10⁻⁸ (W/m².K⁴) – The Stefan-Boltzmann constant
    T = absolute temperature Kelvin (K)
    A = area of the emitting body (m²)

Table 10.1   Emissivity coefficients for materials.

Surface Material	Emissivity Coefficient
Aluminium Oxidised	0.11
Aluminium Polished	0.05
Aluminium Anodised	0.77
Aluminium Rough	0.07
Asbestos Board	0.94
Black Body Matt	1.00
Brass Dull	0.22
Brass Polished	0.03
Brick Dark	0.9
Concrete	0.85
Copper Oxidised	0.87
Copper Polished	0.04
Glass	0.92
Plaster	0.98
Tile	0.97
Water	0.95
Wood Oak	0.9
Paint	0.96
Paper	0.93
Plastics	0.91 Av
Rubber Nat Hard	0.91
Rubber Nat Soft	0.86
Steel Oxidised	0.79
Steel Polished	0.07
Stainless Steel Weathered	0.85
Stainless Steel Polished	0.15
Steel Galvanised Old	0.88
Steel Galvanised New	0.23

10.2 Specific Heat Capacity

Heat capacity of a certain system or substance is the amount of heat needed to raise 1 gram of substance by 1 degree. It is expressed in units of kJ/kg.°C. For example, the specific heat capacity of water is 4.19 kJ/kg.°C, which means 4.19 kilojoules of heat or energy is needed to increase the temperature of 1 kg of water by 1°C.

Usually, the heat capacity of a substance is known from tables. The question is how much heat will be required to raise its temperature by a certain amount. The following equation is used:

$$Q = M \times Cp \times (T_2 - T_1)$$

Where:

Q = Heat/energy (kJ)
M = Mass (kg)
C_p = Specific heat capacity (kJ/kg°C)
T_2 = Final temperature
T_1 = Initial temperature

The specific heat capacities of different materials/substances are known and shown in Table 10.2.

Water has a very high heat capacity while metals generally have low heat capacities. The heat capacity and the heat conductance of the materials are plotted in Figure 10.6.

The high heat capacity of water is because of the hydrogen bonding among the molecules. Hydrogen bonds are broken when the heat is absorbed, and this causes the molecules to move freely. The high heat capacity means that it takes a longer time for a material to heat and to cool, which in turn, means it is harder to make the temperature change. See Table 10.3 with material properties of the different substances.

Table 10.2   Specific heat capacities for selected materials.

Specific heat capacities of selected materials	
Material	**C (J/kg. °C)**
Aluminium	897
Concrete	850
Diamond	509
Glass	840
Helium	5193
Steel (below 700°C)	500
Water	4181

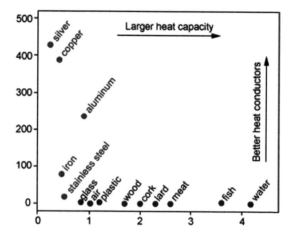

Figure 10.6   Heat capacities and the heat conductance of different materials.

Table 10.3   Material properties of different substances, including C_p values.

Material	Temperature Range (°C)	Density -ρ- (kg/m³)	Specific Heat -Cp- (J/kg°C)	Energy Density (kJ/m³°C)
Aluminium	max. 660 (melting point)	2700	920	2484
Cast Iron	max. 1150 (melting point)	7200	540	2389
Fireclay		2100 – 2600	1000	2100 – 2600
50% Ethylene Glycol - 50% Water	0 – 100	1075	3480	3741
Dowtherm A	12 – 260	867	2200	1907
Draw salt - 50% NaNO₃ - 50% KNO₃) (by weight)	220 – 540	1733	1550	2686
Granite		2400	790	1896
Liquid Sodium	100 – 760	750	1260	945
Molten Salt - 50%KNO₃ - 40% NaNO₂ – 7% NaNO₃ (by weight)	142 –540	1680	1560	2620
Taconite		3200	800	2560
Therminol 66	–9 – 343	750	2100	1575
Water	0 – 100	1000	4190	4190

10.3 Insulation

Insulation is used in industry and in manufacturing processes to prevent heat loss or heat gain. Although its primary purpose is an economic one, it also provides more accurate control of process temperatures and protection of personnel. It prevents condensation on cold surfaces and the resulting corrosion.

The most significant analysis of insulation involves determination of economical thickness. As in most engineering decisions, it is a trade-off between the insulation cost and the value of energy saved. The first step should be to eliminate all bare surfaces hot or cold by providing the optimum amount of insulation.

Exposure to moisture is perhaps the factor most often missed in the selection and maintenance of an insulating system. To understand the importance of moisture in the insulation, it is helpful to keep in mind that:

• insulation saturated with water transfers heat approximately 15 to 20 times faster than dry insulation.

• insulation which is saturated with ice transfers heat approximately 50 times faster than dry insulation.

These relative factors make it clear that critical attention must be paid to vapor barrier selection, installation and maintenance. Insulation is the energy stabilizer - it keeps the wanted energy in and the unwanted energy out. It protects, controls and saves. Insulation is widely used:

• to reduce heat loss, safety, process control, and reduce condensation

• used for safety (e.g. boilers) and also energy saving

Insulation does not stop heat loss - it just slows it down:

• saving is difference in loss between bare and insulated losses

• "rule of thumb" about 90% reduction in heat loss with insulated over bare

If the exposed surface is too hot to touch - it is wasting energy!

Benefit of Insulation

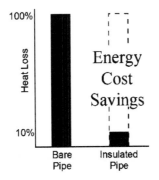

Figure 10.7 Benefit of Insulation.

The purpose of any insulating material is to retard heat flow. To calculate the flow of heat through conducting or insulating material the following equation can be used:

$$Q = \frac{\Delta T \times A}{(R + R_s)}$$

where:

Q = *heat flow (Wh/h or W)*
ΔT = *temperature difference across the medium (°C)*
A = *surface area (m²)*
R_s = *surface resistance (m².°C/W)*
R = $1/U$ = *thermal resistance (m².°C/W)* = $\dfrac{t}{k}$
where t = material thickness (m)

As discussed earlier, thermal resistance "R" is defined as the opposition to the passage of heat through the medium or in this case, through the insulating material. Thermal conductivity "k", on the other hand, is used to express the quantity of heat which will flow across a unit area with the temperature difference of 1°C. (Units are W/m°C). Surface Resistance "Rs" is the opposition to heat flow through the boundary layer between the insulation and the ambient air. The level of resistance provided by this surface film depends on the amount of heat flow through the layer. The Rs value can be estimated from Figure 10.8.

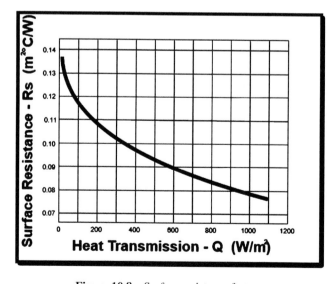

Figure 10.8   Surface resistance factor.

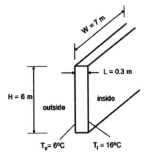

Figure 10.9 An example of heat loss through a wall.

Note that the heat flow (Q) depends upon the surface resistance (Rs) value. From the figure above, Rs depends upon the Q. Thus, a trial-and-error solution must be used to converge upon final Rs and Q values.

Heat loss through convection is common in heated or cooled air streams that provide ventilation and exhaust in industrial buildings. This estimation method considers the sensible heat in the air as well as the moisture in the air. Heat loss can also happen when warm air flows into a cooler environment and the cooling system must account for the intake, as in Figure 10.11 and Figure 10.15

10.3.1 Heat loss through a wall

The wall of a house, 7 m wide and 6 m high is made from 0,3 m thick brick with $k = 0,6 W/mK$. The surface temperature on the inside of the wall is 16°C and that on the outside is 6°C. Find the total heat loss through the wall.

Solution
For one-dimensional steady state conduction:

$$Q = UA \times (T_2 - T_1) watts$$

$$Q = \frac{k}{thickness} \cdot Area \cdot (T_i - T_o)$$

$$Q = \frac{0.6}{0.3} \cdot (6 \times 7) \cdot (16 - 6) = 20W \ / \ m^2$$

$$Q = 840W$$

10.3.2 Heat loss from a pipe

A 20 mm diameter copper pipe is used to carry heated water, the external surface of the pipe is subjected to a convective heat transfer coefficient

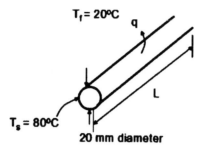

Figure 10.10   An example of heat loss through a pipe.

of $h = \frac{6W}{m^2} \cdot C$ find the heat loss by convection per metre length of the pipe when the external surface temperature is 80°C and the surroundings are at 20°C. Assuming black-body radiation what is the heat loss by radiation?

Solution

$$q_{conv} = h \times (T_s - T_f) = 6 \times (80 - 20) = 360 \ W/m^2$$

For 1 m length of pipe:

$$Q_{conv} = q_{conv} \times A = q_{conv} \times 2\pi r = 360 \times 2 \times \pi \times 0.01 = 22.6 \ W/m$$

For radiation, assuming black-body behavior:

$$q_{rad} = \sigma \times (T_s^4 - T_f^4)$$

$$q_{rad} = 5{,}67 \times 10^{-8}) \times (353^4 - 293^4)$$

$$q_{rad} = 462 \ W/m^2$$

For 1 m length of pipe:

$$Q_{rad} = q_{rad} \times A = 462 \times 2 \times \pi \times 0.01 = 29.1 \ W/m^2$$

A value of $h = 6 \ W/m^2K$ is representative of free convection from a tube of this diameter. The heat loss by (black-body) radiation is seen to be comparable to that by convection.

10.3.3 Heat loss from an industrial freezer

An industrial freezer is designed to operate with an internal air temperature of −20°C when the external air temperature is 25°C and the internal and external heat coefficients are 12 W/m^2C and 8 W/m^2C, respectively. The walls of the freezer are composite construction, comprising of an inner layer of

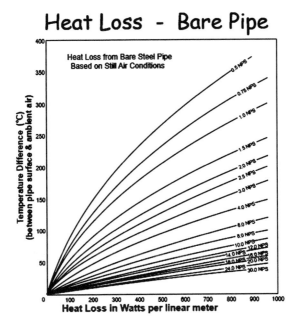

Heat Loss - Bare Pipe

Figure 10.11   Heat loss from a bare steel pipe.

plastic ($k = 1$ *W/m · C* and thickness of 3 mm), and an outer layer of stain-less-steel ($k = 16$ *W/m · C* and thickness of 1 mm). Sandwiched between these two layers is a layer of insulation material with $k = 0.07$ *W/m · C*.

Find the width of the insulation that is required to reduce the convective heat loss to 15 *W/m²*.

Solution

$$q = U\Delta T$$

Where U is the overall heat transfer coefficient given by:

$$U = \frac{q}{\Delta T} = \frac{15}{25 - (-20)} = 0,333 W/m^2 K$$

$$U = \left[\frac{1}{h_i} + \frac{thickness_p}{k_p} + \frac{thickness_i}{k_i} + \frac{thickness_s}{k_s} + \frac{1}{h_0} \right]^{-1} = 0,333$$

$$U = \left[\frac{1}{h_i} + \frac{thickness_p}{k_p} + \frac{thickness_i}{k_i} + \frac{thickness_s}{k_s} + \frac{1}{h_0} \right] = \frac{1}{0,333}$$

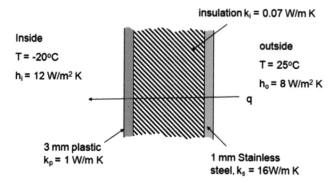

Figure 10.12   An example of heat loss from an industrial freezer.

$$thickness_i = k_i \times \left\{ \frac{1}{0,333} \times \left[\frac{1}{h_i} + \frac{thickness_p}{k_p} + \frac{thickness_s}{k_s} + \frac{1}{h_0} \right] \right\}$$

$$= 0,07 \times \left\{ \frac{1}{0,333} \times \left[\frac{1}{12} + \frac{0,003}{1} + \frac{0,001}{16} + \frac{1}{8} \right] \right\}$$

$$thickness_i = 0,195m \ (195mm)$$

10.3.4 Insulating materials

In buildings, insulation prevents both heat loss and heat gain. Insulation materials form the thermal envelope of a building or a cover on equipment and piping. Insulation comes in different types and forms. The type indicates the internal structure and composition, while the form is the overall shape or application.

The following types are normally found:

- Fibrous insulation, see Figure 10.13. Composed of small diameter fibers which divide the air space. Glass fiber and mineral wool are the most widely used insulations of this type.

- Cellular insulation, see Figure 10.14. Composed of small individual cells separated from each other. The cellular material may be glass or foamed plastic such as polystyrene, polyurethane and elastomeric. Cellular insulation has the advantage of staying in shape and position longer than fibrous materials. It is also nicer to work with. Rockwool however, can stand higher temperatures.

- Granular insulation, see Figure 10.16. Made up of small nodules which contain voids or hollow spaces. Gas can be transferred between the

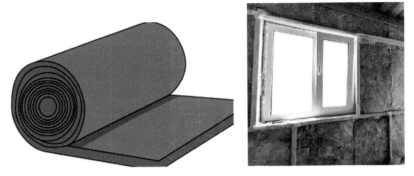

Figure 10.13 Fibrous type insulation.

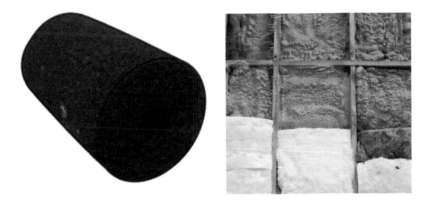

Figure 10.14 Cellular type insulation.

individual spaces. This type of insulation can be produced as a loose, flowable material or combined with a binder and fibers to make a rigid insulation.

Insulation material is supplied in the following formats:

- Rigid board comes in blocks, sheets and preformed shapes. Cellular and granular insulations are produced in these forms.

- Flexible sheet of which there are cellular and fibrous insulations.

- Flexible blankets are fibrous insulations are produced in the form of flexible blankets.

- Cement (insulating and finishing) is produced from fibrous and granular insulations and cement. They may be either hydraulic air setting or air-drying types.

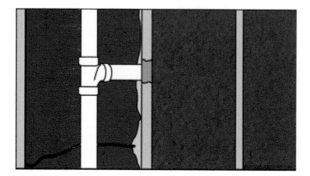

Figure 10.15   Fibrous insulation versus cellular insulation.

Figure 10.16   Granular type insulation in an attic.

- Foams which are poured, or froth foam used to fill irregular areas and voids. Spray is used for flat surfaces.

The following is a general inventory of the characteristics and properties of major insulating materials used in industrial, commercial and institutional installations:

- Calcium Silicate is a granular insulating material made of lime and silica, reinforced with organic and inorganic fibers and molded into rigid forms. The temperature range covered is from 38 to 982°C. Flexural strength is good. Calcium Silicate is water absorbent. However, it can be dried out without deterioration. The material is non-combustible and used primarily on hot piping and surfaces. Jacketing is generally field applied.

- Cellular Elastomeric insulation is composed principally of natural and synthetic elastomers, or both, processed to form a flexible, semi-rigid or

rigid foam with predominantly closed cell structure. Upper temperature
limit is 104°C.

- Cellular glass is fabricated into boards, pipe covering and other shapes.
  The service temperatures range from −40 to 482°C. This material has a
  low thermal conductivity at low temperatures, low abrasion resistance,
  good resistance to substrate corrosion, and good sound absorption
  characteristics.

- Fibrous glass is manufactured in variety of forms including flexible
  blankets, rigid and semi-rigid boards and pipe covering. Service temperatures range from −73 to 538°C depending on binder and structure.

- Foam plastic insulations are predominantly closed cellular rigid materials. Thermal conductivity may deteriorate with time due to aging
  because of the air diffusing into the cells. Foamed plastics are generally
  used in lower and intermediate temperature ranges.

- Mineral fiber and mineral wool are produced by bonding rock and slag
  fibers with heat resistant binder. The upper service temperature limit
  can reach 982°C. The material is non-combustible and is used in high
  and intermediate temperature ranges less than 200°C.

- Refractory fiber insulations are mineral and ceramic fibers, including
  alumina and silica, bound with extremely high temperature binders.
  They are manufactured in blanket or rigid brick form. Thermal shock
  resistance and temperature limits are high (up to 1000°C).

Table 10.4 shows a summary of common insulating materials and their
properties.

10.3.5 Protective coverings and finishes

Protective coverings are needed in insulation to protect the material from
moisture entry and mechanical or chemical damage, which is important for
the efficiency and service of the insulation. The choices of protective covering, also regarded as jacketing, and finish materials are based on the mechanical, chemical, thermal and moisture conditions of the insulation, and the cost
and appearance.

Protective coverings are divided into six functional types:

- Weather barriers. The weather barrier prevents water from entering
  the insulation. If water is deposited within the insulation, its insulating

Table 10.4   Common insulating materials.

Type	Form	Temp. range	k-Factor (W/m.K)	Notes
Armaflex	Pipe covering (HVAC, cold)	Up to 70°C	0,04	For cold applications
Calcium silicate	Pipe covering (block segments)	Up to 649°C	0,087 @ 260°C	High compressive strength, good cutting characteristics, water absorbent, non-combustible
Cellular glass	Pipe covering (block segments)	Up to 427°C	0,077 @ 150°C	Good strength, water and vapor resistant, non-combustible
Glass fibre	Pipe covering (board, blanket)	Up to 455°C Up to 538°C	0,037 @ 24°C 0,033 @ 24°C	Good handling and workability. May be water-absorbent. Some are non-combustible
Mineral fibre	Pipe covering (board)	Up to 649°C	0,037 @ 24°C	Non-combustible, good workability, water absorbent
Rigid PU foam panels	Cold storage	Up to 70°	0,04	For cold storage, or roofs
Styrofoam	Insulation on buildings	Up to 70°	0,04	Comparatively cheap material for buildings

properties will be significantly reduced. Applications consist of either a jacket of metal or plastic or a coating of weather barrier mastic.

- Vapor retarders. Vapor retarders do not allow moisture vapor from the atmosphere to enter or penetrate the surface of the insulation. Joints and overlaps must be sealed with a vapor-tight adhesive or sealer. Vapor retarders are available in three forms. The first is rigid jacketing, which is reinforced plastic, aluminium or stainless steel fabricated to exact dimensions and sealed vapor tight. The second is membrane jacketing which is metal foils, laminated foils or treated paper which is generally factory applied to the insulating material. The third is a mastic application of either the emulsion or solvent type, which provide a seamless coating but require time to dry.

- Mechanical abuse covering. Metal jacketing provides the strongest protection against mechanical damage from personnel, equipment and machinery. The compression strength of the insulation material should also be considered when assessing mechanical protection.

- Low flame spread and corrosion resistant coverings. When selecting material for potential fire hazard areas, the insulation material and the jacketing must be considered as a composite unit. Most of the available types of jacketing and mastic have a low flame spread rating. This information can usually be obtained from manufacturer's data. Stainless steel is the most successful in resisting the corrosive atmosphere, spills and leaks. Mastics are also generally resistant to corrosive atmospheres.

- Appearance coverings and finishes. Various coatings, finishing cements, fitting covers and jackets are chosen primarily for their appearance value in exposed areas. Typically for piping, jacketed insulation is covered with a reinforcing canvas and coated with a mastic to give it a smooth, even finish.

- Hygiene coverings. The coatings and jackets must present a smooth surface which resists fungal and bacterial growth, especially in food processing areas and hospitals. High-temperature steam or high-pressure water wash-down conditions require jackets with high mechanical strength and temperature ratings.

10.3.6 Accessories

The term accessories are applied to the following devices or materials:

- Securing the insulation or jacketing. Insulation jacketing refers to an outer cover that is wrapped around insulation to protect it from moisture and damage. The jacketing also supports and secures the insulation.

- Insulation reinforcement for cement and mastic. The basic and fault protection that is provided by substantial insulation between live parts and accessible parts.

- Water flashing prevents any water from entering the insulation.

- Stiffening that applies metal lath and wire netting to high temperature surfaces before insulation is applied.

- Sealing and caulking to seal joints or seams.

- Expansion and contraction compensation for manufactured overlapping or slip joints, bedding compounds and flexible sealers.

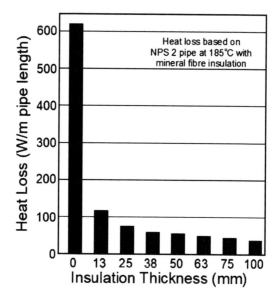

Figure 10.17   Economic insulation thickness.

10.3.7 Insulation energy efficiency measures

- Repair damaged insulation,

- Repair damaged coverings and finishes,

- Maintain safety requirements.

- Insulate non-insulated pipes.

- Insulate non-insulated vessels.

- Add insulation to reach the recommended level.

- Upgrade existing insulation levels.

- Review economic thickness requirement.

- Limited budget upgrade.

10.3.8 Vapor loss from open processing tanks

Open tanks with exposed liquid surfaces can cause substantial energy loss through evaporation, even when the liquid temperatures are much lower than boiling point. Figure 10.18 provides a means for estimating energy loss from surface evaporation.

One possibility to reduce the evaporation loss from any heated, open top vessel is to cover the surface of the liquid with a floating inert material.

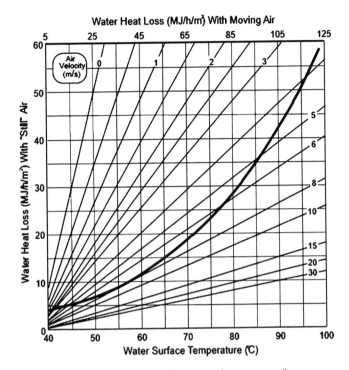

Figure 10.18 Heat loss from open hot water surface.

Make sure the covering material does not contaminate or degrade the process or end product. Many types of foam material in form of chips, spheres or hollow beads are commercially available.

As a rule of thumb, a covering will reduce the energy loss to about 10% of the open surface loss.

Example

A small chrome plating plant realized a significant reduction in energy loss through evaporation by covering the exposed liquid surfaces of its plating tanks with 5 × 5 cm polystyrene chips.

The plant operates four open-top, rectangular tanks with an area of 1.7 m² each. Three of the tanks contain either copper, nickel or chromium solutions necessary for chrome plating and the fourth tank contains water for rinsing. The four tanks are heated for 8 hours a day, 4 days per week to temperatures in the range of 60°C.

From Figure 10.18, the "still air" energy loss from the open surface is approximately 11.5 MJ/h/m². The heat loss after the expanded polystyrene chips were placed on the liquid surfaces amounted to about 1.0 MJ/h/m².

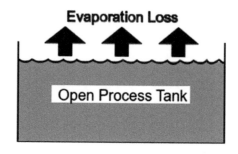

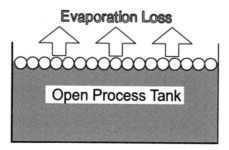

Figure 10.19   Reducing heat loss from an open processing tank.

The annual energy saving is:

$$= 6.8 \ m^2 \times (11.5 - 1.0) \ MJ/hr/m^2 \times 32 \ hr/wk \times 50 \ wk/yr$$
$$= 114\ 240 \ MJ/yr \ (114.2 \ GJ/yr)$$

Additional savings may be achieved during the heat-up period.

How to read Figure 10.18: Select water surface temperature from scale at bottom of graph and extend up to heavy curved line. To find heat loss at "still" air condition (1.16 m/s), extend horizontally to read the heat loss scale at the left edge of the graph. To find heat loss at specific air velocity, extend horizontally (left or right) from heavy curved line to intersect specific air velocity line, then extend up to read heat loss scale at top of graph.

10.4 Heat Recovery with Heat Exchangers

Waste energy, usually in form of waste heat, is present in almost all industries and plant operations. In many situations, opportunities exist to recover this waste in a form that may be used to reduce plant's overall requirement for purchased energy. The key to waste heat recovery is to be able to identify both the potential sources and suitable uses for waste energy, and then to find a practical, cost effective means of coupling each source and use.

The economic recovery of waste heat depends on the following factors:

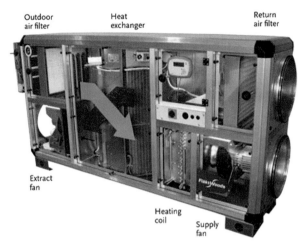

Figure 10.20 Cross flow heat exchanger in a HVAC system.

- A suitable end-user for the waste heat.

- An adequate quantity of waste heat.

- An adequate quality of heat to suit the end-use.

- The cost of transferring the waste heat to the end-user.

Heat exchangers are used to transfer heat from one medium to another through a dividing wall. The most common types of heat exchangers are shell and tube heat exchangers and plate and frame heat exchangers. These are constructed in various materials to account for corrosion potentially caused by the media they have to work with.

10.4.1 Shell and tube

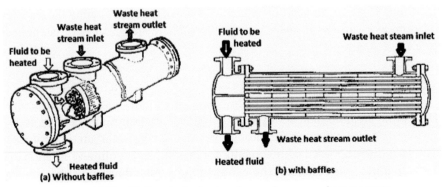

Figure 10.21   Shell and tube heat exchanger for process heat recovery

10.4.2 Plate and frame

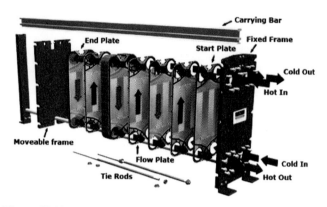

Figure 10.22   Plate type heat exchanger to recover heat from water.

10.4.3 Heat wheel

The heat wheel has been used for over 70 years for preheating combustion air in large boilers. For structural strength, the wheel is usually divided into sectors which are filled with metal wool. That is, small aluminium or stainless-steel wires are formed, knitted or mesh-packed. The wire material does not affect the heat transfer capacity.

Heat transfer is a function of surface area. The more wire packed in, the better the heat transfer. Unfortunately, the resistance to the flow also increases. Only the diameter of the wheel increases with increased volume flow rate (m³/s). The thickness of the wheel does not change; it stays at about 0.3 to 0.45 m. The pressure drop for every size wheel of a particular manufacturer is relatively the same.

The heat wheel will mainly transfer sensible heat and only very little moisture (latent heat). In many industrial applications the humidity level of incoming fresh air may not be critical. Yet, in space conditioning the transfer of humidity warrants serious consideration. There are 2,256 kJ of latent heat in a kg of steam.

10.4.4 Heat pipes

Heat pipes are used industrially for cooling dies, bearings, tool clamps, transformers or for transferring the automotive exhaust heat to carburetor air intake. The heat pipes are used commercially for heating and cooling ventilation air.

In a heat pipe system, the exhaust and intake ducts must be side by side (refer figure below). Both ducts are transverse by a heat pipe, which

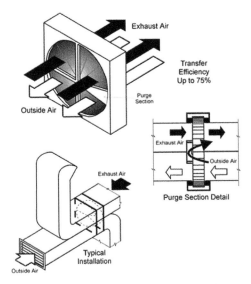

Figure 10.23 Rotary wheel air-to-heat exchanger.

picks up heat on one side, transferring it to the other. The conventional heat pipe is constructed from aluminium or copper piping about 1.6 cm in diameter. This pipe or tube is filled with a measured amount of refrigerant and a wick. The heat at one end will evaporate the liquid refrigerant into a warm vapor. This vapor travels to the other end of the tube where it condenses and returns via the wick. In condensing it gives up the heat of vaporization. The refrigerant evaporates on the warm side and condenses on the cool side. The wick capillary action moves the liquid back to the warm side. To assist this flow, the tubes are slanted toward the warm side. The entire unit is supported on a pivot. The different degrees of tilt make it possible to regulate the heat transfer. Maximum tilt is around 6 degrees.

The heat is not carried along the pipe by conduction. The heat pipe is a completely reversible isothermal device; isothermal meaning equal temperature. Thus, the pipe is actually at equal temperature at either end. The heat pipe does not transfer humidity.

10.4.5 Run around system

This system comprises two liquid-to-air exchangers, somewhat similar to the radiators in the car, interconnected by two pipes. The circuit usually contains glycol as a transfer medium. A pump keeps the fluid flowing round and round which is why this exchanger is referred to as "run-around" system.

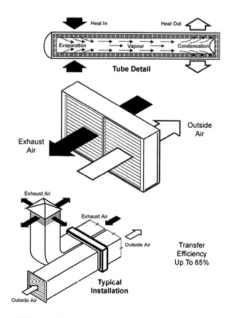

Figure 10.24 Heat pipe heat exchanger.

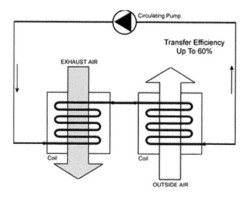

Figure 10.25 Closed circuit "Run Around" System.

This unit requires piping and a constantly running pump. The heat exchanger requires more maintenance than is required for wheels, baffles or heat pipes. Only sensible heat is transferred and the unit is up to 50% efficient. Temperatures range from 0°C to 90°C.

10.4.6 Plate or Baffle type heat exchanger

The baffle type heat exchanger requires the intake and exhaust ducts to be side by side. Cross contamination is zero, as long as there is no physical

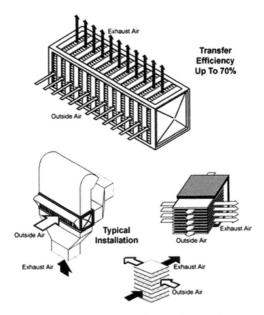

Figure 10.26 Plate or Baffle type heat exchanger.

defect in the unit. The unit consists of closely spaced corrugated metal plates in a box, through which the supply and exhaust air flows in alternate rows. Heat is transferred through the plates by conduction. Where plates are bedded in the resin, the operating temperatures are limited to about 80°C. For a welded or crimped stainless-steel exchanger, the temperature limit may go to 800°C.

10.4.7 Heat pumps

The heat recovery equipment discussed so far can be considered straight heat exchangers. This means that the incoming fresh air or liquids will not reach the temperature of the waste heat source. The heat pump overcomes this problem to some degree. It reclaims the heat units and stacks them. As a result, the reclaimed heat is of higher temperature than the waste medium. To achieve this, 30% to 50% in electrical energy must be added. The liquid in the evaporator absorbs heat from the waste heat source and vaporizes. The vapor is then compressed, raising the temperature. Thereafter it goes to the condenser where the absorbed heat is given up to the fluid to be heated.

The unit works basically as a reverse refrigeration cycle. With normal waste heat source temperatures, the COP (Coefficient of Performance) for heat pumps runs between 3 to 4. This simply means that for every 1 kWh

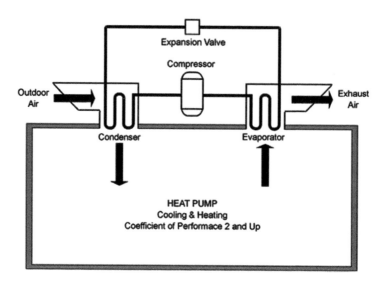

Figure 10.27   Heat pump system.

input the unit delivers heat equivalent of 3 to 4 kWh, generally at lower temperatures (50 to 150°C).

10.4.8 Waste heat boilers

Hot exhaust gases either from industrial processes or from commercial boilers are ducted into waste heat boilers to heat water for sanitary or space heating applications. In high temperature inputs the waste heat boilers can generate steam for process use. Traditionally, the heat recovery was limited to reclaiming the sensible heat only because of problems with cold-end corrosion. Nowadays the waste heat boiler manufacturers offer a full range of equipment to recover all latent heat with exhaust gas temperature near the ambient levels, called a condensing heat exchanger.

The potable hot water generated by waste heat boilers is suitable for food processing, meat packing, chemical industries, dairies and hospitals. Potential savings range from 15 to 22% of fired fuels.

10.4.9 Recuperators

There are many types of recuperators used in industry, the largest ones probably in the glass industry. On a smaller scale they are often called economisers and their main application is in preheating the feed water for boilers or preheating the combustion air.

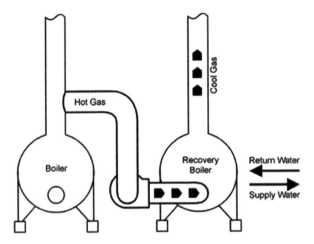

Figure 10.28 Waste heat boiler.

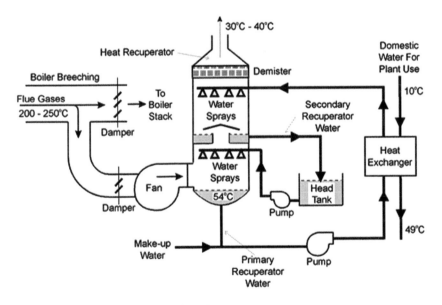

Figure 10.29 Direct contact recuperator.

10.4.10 Heat recovery ventilation systems

The ventilation system of an HVAC system affects the indoor air quality. Indoor air quality is about the air introduced into a certain environment, so that the quality can meet the required standards in excess of the air that is already present in the environment. The provision of high-quality indoor air is centered on the following:

- Proper control of air temperature;

- Restoration of oxygen;

- Removal of moisture; and

- Removal of odours, smoke, heat, dust, airborne bacteria and other unwanted gases like carbon dioxide.

All these provisions of indoor quality air prevent the stagnation of the interior air and makes sure that the air circulation is up to standard. Ventilation is regarded as one of the best methodologies used to improve the indoor air quality. The two types of ventilation which are used widely in buildings are mechanical or forced ventilation and natural ventilation.

Mechanical ventilation is mostly used indoors to regulate surplus humidity, odours and contaminants through the outside air. The regulation of humidity and other contaminants in humid climates requires a lot of energy for the success of the process. The same applies to the removal of excess moisture from the ventilation air. This led to other means of technology being introduced to make sure that the regulation of the mentioned parameters is upheld but not at the expense of energy.

In mechanical ventilation, the principle of ventilation is that it increases the energy required for either cooling or heating and, as such, a mechanism needs to be devised to Minimize the energy consumption. The heat recovery ventilation system has been introduced for this reason and it involves the exchange of heat between the incoming and the outgoing air. This has led to even more breakthroughs like the energy recovery ventilation system where the humidity is exchanged between the incoming and outgoing air. An example of the exchange ventilation system is shown in Figure 10.30.

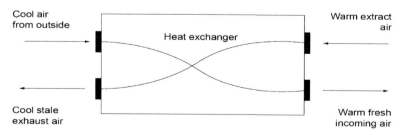

Figure 10.30   Heat recovery ventilation system.

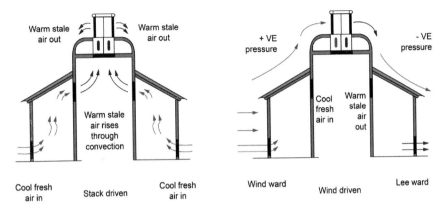

Figure 10.31   Natural ventilation system.

10.4.11 Mechanical and natural ventilation

Mechanical ventilation is also used in environments where there is smoke and odours. This ventilation is normally controlled using fans which basically need to be designed in relation to flow rate, noise level and exhaust vent size. The fans are used to aid ventilation and remove the smoke and odours from the indoor air.

In contrast, natural ventilation uses natural openings like windows and doors. It is mostly used for ventilating smaller spaces. The natural ventilation in complex systems or industrial areas is performed by allowing the warm air to exit the enclosure or building through the upper openings to the atmosphere. This process is called the stack effect. The cooler air used to ventilate the area is then collected from the outside through openings like windows in the lower areas. The natural ventilation can take place as either stack or wind driven. Natural ventilation systems are shown in Figure 10.31.

Chapter 11

Steam Systems

Albert Williams

Institute of Energy Professionals Africa, South Africa

Steam is used for heating and process work as it is an ideal carrier of heat. Its three main advantages as a heat transfer medium are as follows:

- It transfers heat at constant temperature. This is extremely useful when dealing with heat sensitive materials. The temperature of steam is dependent upon the steam pressure. This results in a simple method of temperature control.

- Steam carries a very high heat content. Relatively small pipes can carry a great amount of heat. Steam at low temperature contains about twenty-five times as much heat as the same weight of air or flue gases at the same temperature. It is compact in terms of heat content per unit volume. This means heat can he conveyed in simple piping systems.

- It is convenient. Steam is generated from water which is cheap and plentiful. The heat in steam can be used again and again. Steam can generate power first and can then be used for heating.

Steam is often used carelessly resulting in systems becoming poorly maintained and thus inefficient. Even in the best regulated establishments there is bound to be some unavoidable wastage of heat, but having allowed for this comparatively small loss, it is necessary to see that the rest of the heat is put to good work.

Often it is not noticed that a 'wisp' of steam is leaking from a joint, that insulation is missing, that steam traps are blowing steam and that boiler operators blow down the boiler on the basis of previous practice. Possibly, or even probably, the equipment using the steam is not giving optimum performance because it contains air or is waterlogged due to faulty steam trapping.

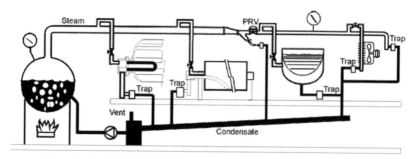

Figure 11.1   Generic steam system.

The production rate then falls. In giving up its heat the steam condenses, but still retains some of the energy originally put into it by burning fuel in the boiler. This energy can be recovered and put to good use. Steam utilisation efficiency is not as easily measured as the thermal efficiency of a boiler and as a result, it is frequently neglected.

A neglected steam system can cause concern about its cost effectiveness both in terms of energy cost and productivity. The methods required to achieve optimisation are neither difficult nor costly. Few firms know what their steam costs are, yet this must be an important part in the costing of any product. Too often these are regarded as unavoidable overheads, although the return on capital expenditure to improve the steam system can be high.

Fuel conversion systems, such as boilers, extract energy from primary sources (fuels) and convert it into secondary form of energy such as steam, hot water or hot air. The main task involved in assessing these systems is to determine their fuel conversion efficiency. The combustion of fuels comprises the major part of the steam generating process.

11.1 Generation

11.1.1 Steam

The term steam often refers to a mixture of water and vapor. Strictly speaking, steam is water vapor. At the beginning of the vaporization plateau there is 0% vapor and 100% water. At the end of the plateau, there is 100% vapor and 0% water. In the middle, there is 50% vapor and 50% water. The water in the middle may be in the forms of very small droplets, just like fog. Steam quality, indicated as a percentage between 0% and 100% is simply a reference to the proportion of vapor in the steam.

Steam has many properties which have been extensively studied and tabulated. Steam tables provide values for the energy content of steam at various conditions. Typical units related to steam measurement are:

- Conditions: Temperature (°C) and Pressure (kPa)

- Mass: kilograms (kg)

- Mass Flow: kilograms per hour (kg/hr)

- Energy Content: kilojoules per kilogram (kJ/kg)

11.1.2 Sensible heat and latent heat

Before getting into the energy saving opportunities, it will be useful to understand how steam is raised and the two types of heat associated with it, sensible and latent heat. When heat is added to a kilogram of water, its temperature rises by 4.19°C for each kJ of heat added (1°C for each kilocalorie).

This rise in temperature can be detected by the senses and is called sensible heat (419 kJ/kg of heat is required to convert water from 0°C to 100°C). At normal atmospheric pressure, any further addition of heat to water at 100°C will not increase the temperature but will cause some of the water to boil into steam. To change all the water into steam, 2 257 kJ/kg (537 calorie/kg) of heat would have to be added. The additional heat cannot be felt by the senses as a rise in temperature and is called the latent heat of vaporization. Thus, a total of 2 676 kJ/kg of heat is required to turn water at 0°C into steam.

If water is subjected to pressure greater than one atmosphere it will not boil at 100°C (212°F) but at a higher temperature. This temperature is related to the steam pressure and, as can be seen from Figure 11.2, the lower the steam pressure the higher the proportion of latent heat per unit weight of steam.

This physical fact has an important bearing on fuel economy. The higher the steam pressure, the higher the steam temperature. This relationship can be used to achieve a temperature required by a process, critical in some cases, by matching it with the correct steam pressure. For greater accuracy, these relationships are normally given in the form of steam tables (at the end of this module).

So, if pressure is reduced to give greater economy it must be ensured that productivity is not upset by the lower temperature. Steam which does not increase in temperature when heat is added is known as saturated steam. It is a mixture of water and steam. Steam that does increase in temperature when heat is added is known as superheated steam. It is pure steam with no

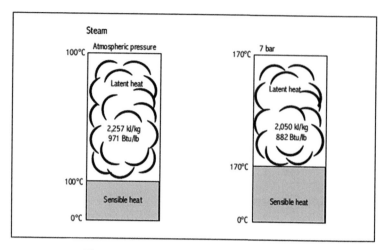

Figure 11.2 Temperature related to pressure.

water. Wet steam contains water droplets. Dry steam does not contain water droplets. Superheated steam is used in power stations where high steam temperatures give a better thermal efficiency (more kilowatt-hours of electricity per unit of fuel consumed).

Process steam is nearly always saturated steam. Many processes employing steam as the heating medium only make use of latent heat. Therefore, it is necessary to Optimize the availability of latent heat and the driving force, by good steam pressure control. Additionally, the heat in the condensate rises with steam pressure, and so the higher the steam pressure used for a process the greater the need to recover heat from the condensate in order to maintain high levels of efficiency.

As heat energy is added to water, the temperature of the water increases until the boiling point is reached (refer to Figure 11.3). This heat, which increases the water temperature, is called sensible heat. When the boiling point is reached, the addition of further heat causes some of the water to change to steam, but the steam and water mixture remains at the boiling point temperature. At atmospheric pressure, the boiling point of water occurs at 100°C. The heat which converts the water to steam at a constant boiling temperature is called latent heat. When the steam has been fully vaporized at the boiling temperature, it is called dry saturated steam. This means that there are no droplets of moisture within the steam vapor.

When water is heated at a pressure above atmospheric, the boiling point will be higher than 100°C and the sensible heat will be greater. For every pressure there is a corresponding boiling temperature, and at this temperature

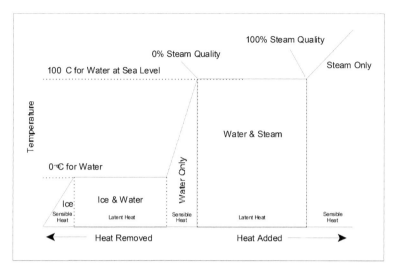

Figure 11.3 Phase changes of water.

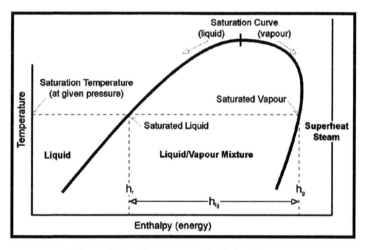

Figure 11.4 Temperature - Enthalpy diagram.

the water contains a fixed, known amount of heat. Enthalpy is the expression used to identify the energy content of the water, steam and water mixture or steam on a unit mass basis.

Under the enthalpy heading above, there are three columns; enthalpy of the liquid (h_f), enthalpy of evaporation (h_{fg}) and enthalpy of steam (h_g).

• Enthalpy of liquid (h_f) is a measure of the amount of heat energy contained in one kg of water at a specific temperature.

- Enthalpy of evaporation (h_{fg}) (correctly called the latent heat of vapor-ization) is the quantity of heat energy required to convert one kg of water to one kg of steam at a given pressure.

- Enthalpy of steam (h_g) is the total heat contained in dry saturated steam at a given pressure. This quantity of energy is the sum of the enthalpy of liquid (h_f) and the amount of energy required to evaporate one kg of water at the saturation temperature (h_{fg}).

$$h_g = h_f + h_{fg}$$

Where
- h_g = Enthalpy of dry saturated steam (kJ/kg)
- h_f = Enthalpy of liquid (kJ/kg)
- h_{fg} = Enthalpy of evaporation (kJ/kg)

Most boilers are designed to produce dry saturated steam.

11.1.3 Steam quality

The enthalpy cannot be directly obtained from steam tables when there is moisture in the steam. The steam quality can be expressed in equation form:

Steam Quality = Mass of Steam Vapor / Mass of Steam Vapor and Water Mixture

A steam quality of 0.98 means that there is 2% moisture in the steam. The heat content of 1,000 kPa and 0.98 quality steam can be calculated using steam tables.

11.1.4 Superheated steam

As long as water is present, the temperature of saturated steam will corre-spond to the figure indicated for that pressure in the steam tables. However, if heat transfer continues after all the water has been evaporated, the steam temperature will again rise. The steam is then called "superheated" and this superheated steam can be at any temperature above that of saturated steam at corresponding pressure.

Saturated steam will condense readily an any surface which is at lower temperature, so that it gives up the enthalpy of evaporation which, as we have seen, is the greatest proportion of its energy content. On the other hand, when superheated steam gives up some of its enthalpy, it does so by virtue of a fall in temperature. No condensation will occur until the saturation temperature has been reached.

The rate at which we can get energy to flow from superheated steam is often less than we can achieve with saturated steam, even though the super-heated steam is at a higher temperature. Because of its non-condensing prop-erty, is the natural first choice for power steam requirements, while saturated steam is ideal for process and heating applications.

11.1.5 Example of the effects of increasing surface area

From the point of view of steam economy, the lower the steam pressure, the lower the steam consumption for a given amount of heat. It is also true, how-ever, that the lower the steam pressure, the lower the temperature and there-fore the lower the rate of heat flow from a given surface area. This difficulty can sometimes be overcome by increasing the amount of heating surface.

A heating system working at a pressure of 5.5 bar can be made to give the same heat output at a pressure of 2.4 bar simply by increasing the heating surface by 25%. If for instance a room contains four lengths of heating pipe, then the total heating surface will be increased by 25% if an extra length of pipe is added. By doing this, a saving of 4% is made. Further reduction in pressure to 0.34 bar and an increase in the heating surface of 75% would result in a saving of 7%.

This principle should be borne in mind when designing heating sys-tems, such as fitting heating coils in hot water tanks and installing heat pipes for air heating.

There are two points to be considered:

• As the boiler operating pressure is reduced the specific volume of steam increases rapidly as the operating pressure falls below 7 bar. The rapid rise in the specific volume of steam promotes carry-over of liquid water, which is not a good heat conductor.

• It is not possible to increase the heating surface in all kinds of steam plant and equipment.

11.1.6 Boiler types

Steam is generated in boilers, i.e. pressure vessels where water is turned into steam on a continuous basis by application of heat. The classifications of boilers are:

• Low pressure boilers operate in the range up to 3 bars pressure.

- Medium pressure boilers operate in the range up to 10 to 15 bars pressure, mainly in industrial processes.

- High pressure boilers operate above 15 bars, mainly in power generating applications.

The principal boiler types are the firetube, watertube, coiltube and electric.

a) Firetube boilers

These are essentially shell-and-tube heat exchangers where combustion gas passes through tubes which are immersed in water. Firetube boilers usually burn natural gas or oil, although some, with a firebox type of combustion chamber, can be installed on top of a coal or wood stoker. They can generate dry saturated steam or hot water up to a maximum of 1,700 kPa (17 bar) gauge. The output ranges from 350 to 28,000 MJ/h. Boilers are shop assembled and delivered with integral burner, forced draft fan and controls.

Since firetube boilers operate at low pressures, the boiler water temperature is correspondingly low, ranging from 110 to 200°C. By ensuring that the combustion gas contacts as much of the heat transfer surface as possible, the flue gas temperature can be reduced to within 50°C of the boiler temperature. This minimizes the flue gas heat loss and can result in boiler efficiencies in excess of 80%.

b) Watertube boilers

The watertube boiler is capable of firing any type of combustible material in a wide range of capacities. Watertube boilers operate at pressures up to 30,000 kPa (300 bars) and can produce steam at up to 565°C. Watertube boilers pass the combustion gases around tubes carrying water. This type is generally used in sizes from 2 ton/h to about 500 ton/h as manufactured units and in larger sizes with field-erected assemblies.

Normally the steam drum of the watertube boiler contains a sophisticated system of steam/water separators to produce high quality steam at the outlet. Steam with less than 1% entrained water droplets are common for such boilers.

c) Coiltube boilers

Coiltube boilers are essentially forced circulation water tube boilers which generate steam from water circulated through a single tube or multiple coiled tubes surrounding the combustion chamber. This type is used in sizes up to about 10ton/h. Coiltube boilers require a continuous forced circulation of water through the tubes and usually have an inertial type steam/water separator at the steam outlet. The quality of steam leaving the boiler depends on the efficiency of the separator and the steam may contain up to 10% water droplets by weight.

d) Electric boilers
Hot water or steam can be generated in boilers where water is heated electrically with immersion coils. Electric boilers are more efficient than fuel fired boilers because there are no flue gas losses to the stack. Electrical energy is often not competitive with other fuels, but this should be checked particularly with respect to off-peak tariffs.

New three-pass firetube boilers, with ratings of 1,600 to 16,000 MJ/h are available with electric heaters as well as gas or oil burners. These boilers are considerably more expensive but provide the flexibility of fuel switching with the use of gas during the day and electricity at night.

11.1.7 Combustion losses
Combustion losses due to combustion inefficiencies can be calculated by means of the Seigert formula.

11.1.8 Blowdown losses
Blowdown is a necessary operation for a boiler plant to maintain correct water conditions. The water fed into the boiler contains dissolved materials

Table 11.1 Seigert formula.

$$\%Loss = -\frac{K \times \Delta T}{\%CO_2} + C$$

Where:
% Loss	=	*total flue gas loss as % of the fuel's gross energy (HHV),*
K,C	=	*constants for fuel type (see table below),*
%CO$_2$	=	*CO$_2$ as percent (by volume) of dry gas in flue gas,*
ΔT	=	*temperature difference (°C) between flue gas and combustion air (refer to Figure 13.4)*

SEIGERT CONSTANTS

Fuel Type	K	C
Fuel Oil	0.56	6.5
Coal	0.63	5.0
Natural Gas	0.38	11.0

and as the water is evaporated into steam these are left to concentrate in the boiler either in a dissolved or suspended state.

It is, therefore, necessary to control the level of concentration of the solids and this is done by the process of 'blowing down', where a certain volume of water is drawn off and is automatically replaced by feedwater, thus maintaining the optimum level of Total Dissolved Solids (TDS) in the water. If not carried out, boiler failure may occur and there will be carry-over and foaming, the latter resulting in a large quantity of water being carried forward in the piping system to the process.

This problem calls for the careful monitoring and supervision of the water conditions in all boilers, particularly the modern shell type packaged units which are even more vulnerable than earlier types because of their small water capacity and limited steam space in relation to their output. It is important to recognize that blowdown can, if incorrectly carried out, be a significant source of heat loss second only to the heat carried out of the boiler in the flue gases.

There are two aspects to consider:

- The first and most important is that the quantity of blowdown should not exceed the minimum amount necessary. Anything in excess is a waste of energy. Proper control is most important.

- When this has been achieved the recovery of heat from the blowdown should be examined to see whether it is economical to do so. On average about 50% of the heat may be recoverable.

a) Methods of blowdown
There are two methods of blowdown, see Figure 11.5 to Figure 11.6.

- Intermittent - taken from the bottom of the boiler to remove any sludge that has settled. This is generally a manual operation carried out once

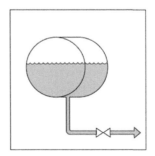

Figure 11.5   Blowdown drain valve.

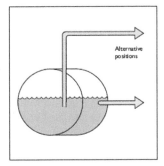

Figure 11.6   Boiler blowdown points.

per shift in a series of short, sharp blasts, with the amount of blowdown being estimated from the reduction of level in the gauge glass. This was the traditional method utilized with shell boilers.

- Continuous - as a bleed from a source near the nominal water level. In more recent years this has become 'step-continuous', the valve being opened or closed cyclically from a time signal, or from a signal derived from some property of the boiler water such as electrical conductivity.

In modern practice, both intermittent and continuous blowdown methods are used: the former mainly to remove suspended solids which have settled out; the latter to control TDS. It is important to carry out the intermittent blowdown sequence at periods of light load. It is also important that this should not be neglected, otherwise, with unfavorable water, sludge may build up beneath the boiler furnace tubes to such an extent that heat transfer is impeded, and the furnace tubes fail.

b) How much do you blowdown?

The following provides a simple checklist for estimating the quantity of blowdown from a boiler, if not already known:

- If the TDS level of the boiler feedwater (mixture of condensate return and make-up) can be obtained, the required percentage of blowdown may be calculated.

- For existing plants, the present blowdown method may consist of blowing down, say, 25mm from the gauge glass at regular intervals. This may be converted to a volume by estimating the water surface area of the boiler (width x length), and multiplying this by the frequency of blowdown, to give an equivalent continuous blowdown flowrate.

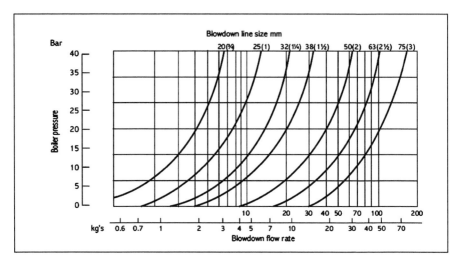

Figure 11.7   Blowdown flow rates.

Remember that this will be related to the present average steam generation rate.

• Alternatively, the existing blowdown method may consist of opening the bottom blowdown valve for a given time at certain intervals. For the standard fullbore valve the flowrate is controlled by the length and bore of the blowdown line, and the boiler pressure. Figure 11.7 may be used for estimating the flowrate when the valve is open - and from the figure obtained, an equivalent continuous blowdown flow rate may be calculated. Again, this will be related to the average generation rate.

NOTE: The blowdown flowrate given in Figure 11.7 is in kg/second, not kg/hour as is commonly used for boiler generating rates.

c) What does it cost?

To buy water, treat it, pump it into a boiler, heat it to boiling point and then throw it away may be necessary to satisfy the requirements of steam quality. Unless it is properly controlled, however, it can be very wasteful of energy and money. It should also be remembered that constant quality of water should not be taken for granted and intermittent blowdown practices may fail to cope with such a difficulty. The costs of blowdown are seldom obvious because they are hidden in the overall boilerhouse costs, in water and its treatment costs and in fuel costs.

11.1.9 Feedwater treatment

The quantity and quality of the condensate returned to the boiler plant will directly affect the extent and cost of the feedwater treatment. The feedwater conditioning and handling system must continuously satisfy certain conditions to discourage operating problems.

The feedwater treatment and equipment may include the following:

- Filters to remove suspended matter from condensate.

- De-aerating heater to preheat the boiler feedwater and remove the dissolved oxygen, carbon dioxide and other non-condensable gases.

- Water softener and/or demineralizers to remove scale forming dissolved solids from raw feedwater required to make up lost condensate. In demineralization, ion exchange removes ionized mineral salts. Demineralization can yield pure water required by high pressure boilers.

- Blowdown tanks to allow blowdown of sediment from the boiler caused by chemical treatment of make-up water.

- De-alkalizers remove the alkalinity in the form of bicarbonates from raw water make up. Bicarbonates break down into carbonates and CO_2. CO_2 leaves the boiler with the steam and forms acidic condensate, which causes corrosion of condensate piping system.

- Chemical treatment to:

  o keep suspended and dissolved solids and sludge in a form that can be removed through blow down.

  o reduce corrosion by preventing the build-up of oxygen and carbon dioxide in the water.

  o control pH.

  o prevent foaming conditions within the drum which allows water carryover with the steam.

11.1.10 Condensate tanks

Condensate tanks or receivers are designed to hold the returned condensate and treated make-up water. They can be pressurized or vented to the atmosphere. Vented tanks lose from 2 to 10% of the heat in the condensate as flash steam. The cost of the treated boiler water that must be replaced and the pumping cost must also be considered. A pressurized tank avoids these losses, but a low-pressure steam system must be available to absorb the vented steam. An alternative is to cool the condensate with cold make-up water to reduce or eliminate flashing of the condensate.

11.1.11 Flash tanks

Flash tanks are used to separate condensate and flash steam that is produced when condensate is reduced in pressure. This may be done so that plant discharges can be reduced to atmospheric pressure before being disposed as effluent or to produce quantities of low-pressure steam for heating or deaerating purposes. If a plant discharge produces a consistent flow of significant quantities, some attempt should be made to recover heat by using the flash steam to heat domestic or service water.

11.1.12 Flash steam heat recovery

Flash steam is as good, as useful and often drier than steam which comes direct from a boiler. In many situations it can be recovered and put to good economic use with the aid of simple equipment. When steam condenses in a pipe or vessel, it forms condensate which is at the same temperature as the steam.

Flash steam is released from hot condensate when its pressure is lowered, rather than by further addition of heat. Even water at ordinary room temperature of 20°C would boil if the pressure was lowered below 0.02 bar(a) - and water at 170°C will boil at any pressure below 6.9 bar(g). The steam released by the flashing process is just the same as the steam released when heat is added to saturated water while a constant pressure is maintained.

For example, if a load is applied to a boiler, and the boiler pressure drops a little, then some of the water content of the boiler flashes off to supplement the steam which is being produced by the supply of heat from the boiler fuel. Because it is all produced in the boiler, the steam is all referred to as "live steam". Only when the flashing takes place at relatively low pressure, as at the discharge side of steam trap, is the name flash steam used. Unfortunately, this usage has led to the erroneous conclusion that flash steam is in some way different from and less valuable than, so called live steam.

In any system where it is sought to maximize efficiency - which should mean in all systems - flash steam will be separated from the condensate. It can then be utilized at low pressure, to help supply any low-pressure load. Every kilogram of flash steam used in this way is a kilogram which does not have to be supplied directly by the boiler. It is also a kg which will not be vented to the atmosphere.

The reasons for the recovery of flash steam are just as compelling, both morally and economically, as those for recovering condensate.

In general, the standard methods of condensate recovery make no real use of the heat in the flash steam which is available at the steam traps. The correct way to use the flash steam, and at the same time to get over many of the difficulties of condensate which is too hot to handle, is to fit a flash vessel either in the common condensate return system or after the traps on big high pressure steam using units. The flash given off from this can be taken to a low-pressure system or unit.

The important basis of flash steam formation is the temperature and heat content of the condensate as it leaves the trap. If thermostatic traps or any other types are used which hold back the flow of condensate until it has given up some of its sensible heat, allowance must be made in calculating the amount of flash steam available. It must also be realized that recovery of flash steam at a low pressure imposes a similar back pressure on the general condensate return system. This could be of importance where the high-pressure plant is thermostatically controlled.

The flash steam formed at the traps travels with the condensate along the return lines. If the pipes are uninsulated much of the steam will condense and the heat will be lost to the air. If the pipes are insulated, quite a lot of steam will reach the feed tank. If the condensate return is above the water level, the flash will escape to the air; if the return is below the vessel should be fitted with a pressure relief valve to prevent excess pressure build up should the demand for low pressure steam drop below the rate of flash formation. Ideally, the flash vessel should be fitted in a situation where there is a continuous demand for all the flash available.

Maximum heat recovery is best obtained by keeping the system pipework to a minimum, thus avoiding unnecessary heat losses. For this reason, a number of small, self-contained recovery units around the plant are generally better than one major unit. The flash vessel and all interconnecting pipework should be insulated.

11.2 Distribution

Before contemplating changes to steam and water distribution systems, due consideration should be given to the end-use of the steam and hot water. As noted previously a good match to the requirement must be achieved. Then it

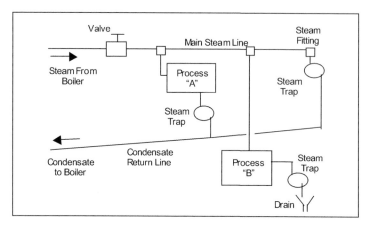

Figure 11.8   Steam distribution system.

is appropriate to consider the efficiency of the systems providing steam and hot water starting with the distribution.

The purpose of the steam and hot water distribution systems is to efficiently deliver steam and hot water from a boiler plant to process and building heating equipment and, in the case of steam, to return condensate to the boiler for re-use. A simple schematic of a steam distribution and condensate system is shown in Figure 11.8.

Energy efficiency measures in steam and hot water systems result from reducing the frequent loss of steam and condensate from these systems:

•   Steam leaks

•   Excessive pressure drop in steam lines in undersized lines

•   Excessive standby losses due to oversized lines

•   Steam lost due to failure of steam traps

•   Condensate sent to drain rather than returned

•   Heat loss from un-insulated pipes valves and fittings

Begin by questioning each aspect of the systems design and operation. The flow chart provided in Figure 11.9 provides a logical approach to assessing the efficiency of the distribution systems and application of the appropriate energy saving action.

Reduction of steam leakage must be a first priority. The high energy content of steam makes leaks costly and the effort to reduce and ideally eliminate such leaks extremely cost effective.

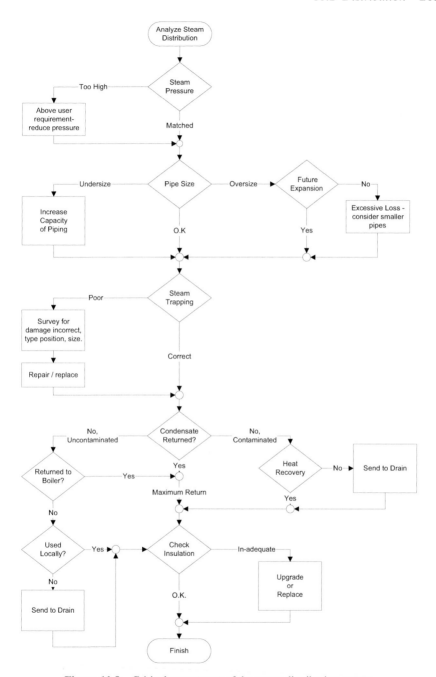

Figure 11.9 Critical assessment of the steam distribution system.

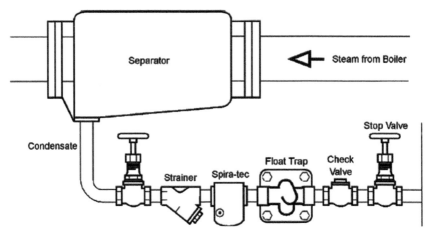

Figure 11.10   Steam separator at take-off from boiler.

Saturated steam should be distributed with a minimum loss of heat, a minimum pressure drop and at a velocity not exceeding 25 m/s, to minimize the damage to the system due to the water-hammer effect. The distribution system should ideally include, steam separators, traps with strainers and air vents. It should have an adequate slope in the direction of the flow to ensure removal of the condensate and air. It is usually economical to distribute steam at boiler working pressure with pressure reduction, if required, immediately ahead of the user equipment.

11.2.1 Condensate return

a) The importance of condensate recovery

Steam condenses after giving up its latent heat to the process being heated. This condensate carries with it a sizeable proportion of the original heat content put in by the fuel - around 20%. It is wasteful to throw this away so either an alternative use for it must be found in another process or it must be retained within the steam system. Condensate that has not been in direct contact with the process is chemically pure and therefore needs little water treatment apart from pH adjustment.

Experience from many industrial and commercial sites has shown that much less importance is given to the condensate recovery system than to the steam system. All too often condensate is not returned to the boiler house and is discharged to drain. Investment in condensate recovery systems including pipes, valves, transfer pumping equipment and insulation has, on many occasions, been shown to produce quick returns.

The enthalpy of the steam is the total heat contained in the water and the vapor. It is assumed in this method the steam is saturated. This means that it has not been heated beyond the point of turning all the water to a vapor, i.e. it is not superheated.

b) Equation for rate of heat transfer:

$$Q = M \times h \quad \text{in units of kilojoules (kJ)}$$

Where

- *Q = Heat Flow*
- *M = Steam Flow*
- *h = enthalpy (kJ/kg)*

c) Condensate Return Exceptions

There are some exceptions usually associated with large-scale sites where the capital cost of installing and operating condensate collection is prohibitive. One such exception usually occurs where there is a relatively small load a long way from the boiler house. Another exception is where the length of pipe run, even when well insulated, is so long that there would be no useful heat content left in the condensate at the boiler house. In some cases, however, it may still be economic to return cold condensate over long distances because of the high cost of raw water and feedwater treatment.

Even when it is uneconomic to return the condensate to the boiler house, its energy content should not be discarded unless there is no alternative. The heat content of the condensate can, for example, be used either directly or indirectly for process hot water generation.

Unfortunately, the condensate can sometimes become contaminated by contact with some other substance being processed. Contaminated condensate, if returned to the boiler, often results in fouling of the heat transfer surfaces, thereby reducing efficiency. In the worst cases catastrophic failure of the boiler can result from overheating of the metal as a result of this fouling. In most cases the amount of contaminated condensate is small and does not justify the expense of buying and maintaining heat recovery equipment. In those exceptions where the quantities are significant and where there is a use for process hot water, a simple heat exchanger can be used to avoid wasting the energy involved. It must be remembered, however, that the heat exchanger will also suffer from fouling by the contaminated condensate, but regular cleaning should be simpler to arrange in this situation.

The one rule that must apply, and which overrides all considerations of energy conservation, is that wherever there is any doubt as to the purity of the condensate it must not be returned directly to the boiler feedwater.

d) Condensate return savings

The steam distribution system in a large heating plant only returned about 70% of the total steam condensate to the boiler plant. The average steam consumption was 45,000 kg of steam per hour. Thus, the make-up water requirement was on the order of 13,500 liters per hour. This represented a significant heat and water loss in hot condensate and increased water treatment costs. A survey of the equipment revealed that almost 1/3 of the condensate being sent to drain was not contaminated and could be re-used in the boiler, which equates to 4,000 liters per hour of condensate that could be returned to the boiler.

Thermal energy savings could be calculated from the energy in the water sent to drain:

Given:

Condensate	4,000 liters/hr
Operation	6,000 hours/year
Condensate Temperature:	95°C
Mains Water Temperature	10°C
Boiler Efficiency:	82.0%
Fuel Energy Cost:	$415/GJ

Annual Savings:

Energy $= M \times (T_{Condensate} - T_{Mains}) \times C_p$

Where M $= 4,000$ liters/hr x 1 kg/liter x 6000 hrs/year
$= 24,000,000$ kg/year

Energy $= 24,000,000$ kg/year x $(95 - 10)$ C x 4.19 kJ/kg °C
$= 8,547,600,000$ kJ /year or 8,547.6 GJ/year

Annual Cost Savings $=$ Fuel Energy Cost x (Energy ÷ Boiler Efficiency)
$= \$415/GJ \times (8,547.6 \text{ GJ} \div 0.82)$
$= \$4,325,920$/year

As can be noted, the cost of lost condensate is not insignificant. In addition to the energy savings, there could be water and sewerage charges depending upon the source of mains water and chemical savings due to reduced water treatment.

11.2.2 Steam leaks

Another common loss of steam energy is leaks or venting to atmosphere. The discharge of steam may have a purpose if the steam is contaminated, but it still represents an energy flow and a potential opportunity for heat recovery. The energy lost in a leak or venting of steam can be estimated from the diameter of the leak.

In general, if the steam flow, is known then the equations given below may be used directly. Common methods of determining steam flow would be from a metering station – at a boiler plant or elsewhere in the distribution system. Steam metering is expensive and not extremely reliable. If the flow from a leak or vent is unknown the method provided below allows an estimate of the flow based upon easily measured data.

Table 11.2 shows the approximate annual losses of steam through holes of various diameters. Because it is difficult to relate a leaking flange gasket to a hole size, another commonly referenced measure is the visible plume length of a steam leak.

a) Steam leaks checklist

- Monitor safety valves and boiler crown valves for passing steam. Monitoring the vent pipes for excess temperature serves as a quick check.

- Give high priority to repairing steam leaks.

Table 11.2   Steam loss through orifice discharging to atmosphere.

Orifice Diam (mm)	Steam Loss (kg/h) when steam guage pressure (kpa) is:											
	15	30	60	100	150	300	500	700	900	1400	1700	1900
0.8	0.18	0.21	0.25	0.32	0.40	0.63	0.95	1.27	1.58	2.37	2.85	3.16
1	0.28	0.32	0.40	0.49	0.62	0.99	1.48	1.98	2.47	3.71	4.45	4.94
2	1.14	1.28	1.58	1.98	2.47	3.95	5.93	7.91	9.88	14.8	17.8	19.8
3	2.56	2.89	3.56	4.45	5.56	8.90	13.3	17.8	22.2	33.4	40.0	44.5
4	4.55	5.14	6.33	7.91	9.88	15.8	23.7	31.6	39.5	59.3	71.2	79.1
5	7.10	8.03	9.88	12.4	15.4	24.7	37.1	49.4	61.8	92.7	11.1	124
6	10.2	11.6	14.2	17.8	22.2	35.6	53.4	71.2	89.0	133	160	179
7	13.9	15.7	19.4	24.2	30.3	48.4	72.6	96.9	121	182	218	242
8	18.2	20.6	25.3	31.6	39.5	63.3	94.9	127	158	237	285	316
9	23.0	26.0	32.0	40.0	50.0	80.1	120	160	200	300	360	400
10	28.4	32.1	39.5	49.4	61.8	98.8	148	198	247	371	445	494
11	34.4	38.9	47.8	59.8	74.7	120	179	239	299	448	538	598
12	40.9	56.3	56.9	71.2	89.0	142	213	285	356	534	640	712
12.7	45.8	51.8	63.8	79.7	99.6	159	239	319	399	598	717	797

- Costs can soon mount up with only a few leaking valve glands.

- Operate a documented system for reporting and rectifying steam leaks.

Visible steam leaks give employees the impression that site management does not care about energy efficiency. In the same way as leaving lights switched on steam leaks do not motivate staff to save energy. The main difficulty associated with rectifying steam leaks is operational, as access to cold lines rarely occurs at convenient times.

Techniques involving the pressure injection of fast setting resins into leaking flanges are available. Valve selection also plays a part: a bellow design can justifiably be used for critical valves in certain process areas. This type of valve, which incorporates a double seal, allows on-line removal of the main gland, if necessary, without affecting operations.

b) General cautions

The methods detailed in this section are simple estimation methods and should only be used as a first approximation for energy use in a given situation. They can help identify potential energy saving opportunities, but proper engineering calculations should be used to verify and refine the initial estimates before actually changing the systems involved.

The methods discussed assume static or non-changing conditions over the time period specified. For estimations that may involve monthly or yearly time periods over which conditions change periodically (i.e.: daily, nightly, weekly, or seasonally), it will be necessary to repeat the estimation for a number of shorter time periods over which conditions are assumed to be constant.

11.2.3 Insulation

Insulating unlagged sections of pipework and fittings is one of the simplest and most cost-effective ways of increasing the energy efficiency of a heat distribution system. The payback period is typically less than a year. Checklist for insulation:

- Check insulation thickness regularly and as fuel prices increase, calculate whether extra thickness is justifiable.

- Check for waterlogging as this reduces insulation values.

- Check for loose fitting sections of insulation as these allow air to circulate between the insulation and the pipes.

- Cover hot liquid surfaces with either a lid or a blanket of plastic balls. Measure the surface temperature of all warm surfaces regularly. As a rough guide, all insulated pipes, insulated surfaces, bare surfaces of tanks, etc. inside buildings should be well below 60°C.

- As another rough rule of thumb, if you cannot touch a surface without getting burned, the payback for insulating will be less than 1 year.

- Insulate steam supply pipes to unit heaters, etc. left uninsulated on the grounds that the heat loss contributes to space heating. Without insulation, overheating can occur in mild weather. Heat losses at high level can also accentuate temperature gradients within a building.

a) Choice of insulation material

Depending on the specific conditions and pipework locations, different types of insulation are available to enable a durable and effective installation to be made. With most pipework pre-formed mineral wool with aluminium cladding performs well. Flanges should be either boxed in or given flexible covers.

Uninsulated pipes in an occupied area should never be justified on the grounds that they may contribute to space heating. Space heating should always be controlled: a circulation pipe is not controlled particularly if it is running continuously to serve process needs from the same circuit. Space heaters are designed to direct heat to an area through radiation or directed convection currents. A hot pipe at high level and next to a wall loses much more heat through the roof than can possibly be directed down to floor level.

b) Economics of insulating pipework

The economic thickness of insulation for pipework in heat distribution systems depends on:

- cost of fuel/heat

- annual operating hours

- pipework temperature and diameters

- ambient temperature

- cost of insulation material, and

- required payback period.

For a given return on investment, the lowest combined cost of insulation and heat loss is required. The heat loss graph given below shows the heat losses

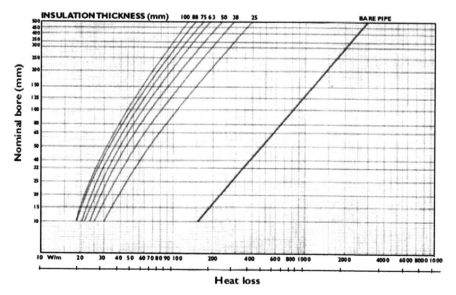

Figure 11.11   Heat loss for pipes with a surface temperature of 150°C with varying insulation thicknesses.

for pipes with a surface temperature of 150°C with different thicknesses of insulation.

The cost of the heat loss over the selected evaluation period, can then be compared with the installation cost of different thicknesses of insulation. Installation costs should be obtained from an insulation supplier or contractor. Such calculations demonstrate the substantial cost of leaving pipes completely uninsulated and the significant savings achieved by only 25-50 mm of insulation.

c) Insulating valves and flanges

All the flanges and valves should be included when calculating heat loss from total lengths of uninsulated pipework. In terms of heat loss, a flange is equivalent to 0.5 m of pipe, while a valve may be equivalent to 1 m of pipe. Insulating a pipe reduces the heat loss by approximately a factor of ten.

Thus, an uninsulated flange is equivalent to a five-meter length of insulated pipe and an uninsulated valve is equivalent to ten meters of insulated pipe. Although the pipework distribution system may have excellent insulation on the pipes themselves, all the flanges and valves may have been left bare. Completing the insulation with flange and valve covers could halve distribution heat losses.

Insulation is one of the best ways of preventing leaks because it reduces temperature differentials and the stresses associated with them. Any leaks will still become apparent very quickly.

A modified approach is required for both flange and valve insulation. While it is generally a simple task to remove standard mineral fiber insulation with its aluminium pop-riveted cladding. It is often time consuming to refit it properly. The additional expense of flexible and tailored valve covers with quick-release fasteners for insulating pipe fittings is worthwhile as they are much more likely to be replaced. When employing contractors, their written terms of reference should include a requirement to replace insulation after working.

d) Condensate lines insulation

Table 11.3 shows the loss from bare pipes. The boiler feed tank into which the condensate is finally delivered should be adequately insulated and fitted with either:

- a lid containing a vent to atmosphere;

- a floating blanket of hollow plastic balls on the surface of the water.

11.2.4 Steam pressure

Steam should be generated at the pressure necessary to meet the maximum required by the equipment in the system. In practice the pressure chosen offers a balance between capital costs and the overall energy efficiency of the system. The benefits of distributing at high pressure are:

- High pressure distribution minimizes the size of pipe required. As the pressure increases, the specific volume of steam decreases. At

Table 11.3 Heat emission from pipes.

Temperature difference	Theoretical heat emission from a single horizontal bare steel pipe free exposed in ambient air at temperatures between 10°C and 20°C.W/m								
					Pipe size				
°C	15mm	20mm	25mm	32mm	40mm	50mm	65mm	80mm	100mm
55	59	70	88	110	118	150	180	210	260
60	66	78	98	120	130	170	200	230	290
70	80	95	120	160	160	200	240	280	350
80	96	110	140	170	190	240	290	330	410
90	110	130	160	200	230	270	330	380	480
100	130	150	190	230	260	320	390	450	550

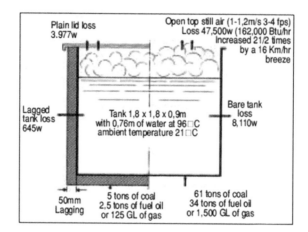

Figure 11.12   Effect of insulation of condensate tank (Source: TLV Co Ltd).

atmospheric pressure 1 kg of steam occupies 1.67m² but at 7 bar It only occupies 0.24m² so a much smaller pipe can be used to carry the same quantity of steam. A smaller diameter pipe means that capital costs are reduced.

- High pressure distribution minimizes the amount of insulation material required. Although this is related to smaller pipe diameter, this benefit is not always achieved as, with increasing steam temperature, the minimum recommended insulation thickness increases.

Set against these advantages are a number of other factors:

- The possibility exists of having to use thicker walled, more expensive pipework at the higher pressure. This will also apply to all fittings such as flanges etc.

- Steam leakage losses are higher. As a general statement, leakage losses increase in Proportion to the pressure; they are twice as much at 10.0 bar as at 5.0 bar.

- The potential for producing flash steam increases and this goes to waste unless a low-pressure sink can be operated in parallel with the high-pressure equipment.

- Heat losses are higher. They increase approximately in proportion to the steam saturation temperature, e.g. heat loss per m at 10.0 bar is some 15% more than at 5.0 bar. This must be set against the benefit of the smaller diameter pipework.

Steam reduced in pressure via a Pressure Reduction Valve (PRV) may have to be de-superheated before being used in a process. When the pressure of a volume of saturated steam is reduced, the heat content is not lost. The excess heat above that which the saturated steam at the new pressure can hold turns into sensible heat in the steam, raising its temperature. In cases where maximum temperature is a critical process parameter this excess heat must be removed at a point where, often, no other user is available. This heat is therefore lost to the system, thereby reducing its overall efficiency.

Determining the pressure for small distribution systems is relatively simple: it should just meet the user requirement unless future expansion of the system or new equipment requiring higher pressures is envisaged. For systems where only a small quantity of high-pressure steam is required but where large quantities of low-pressure steam are used, the possibility of separating the two should be considered. A high-pressure steam generator dedicated to the high-pressure steam using equipment could be a more energy efficient option.

In summary:
High Pressure - Leakage and Flash Steam Losses.
Low Pressure - Large Surface Heat Losses.

11.2.5 Steam pipes

a) Pipe sizes
Once the necessary system pressure has been determined, the pipes must be correctly sized. If the pipe is too small, insufficient steam at a high enough pressure will get through to the process. Too large a pipe simply means that surface heat losses are increased or more insulation is required. Either way the overall system efficiency drops. Proper sizing of the steam lines means selecting a pipe diameter which gives the minimum acceptable pressure drop between the boiler and the user.

For many years, designers and engineers used simple 'rule of thumb' methods to determine the pipe sizes for a particular application. These criteria were evaluated from actual situations and generally still hold good. To begin the process of determining required pipe size, it is usual to assume a velocity of flow.

For saturated steam from a boiler, 20 – 30 m/s is accepted general practice for short pipe runs. For major lengths of distribution pipework, pressure drop becomes the major consideration and velocities may be slightly less. With dry steam, velocities of 40 m/s can be contemplated - but remember

Table 11.4   Mass flow (kg/hour) of steam in pipes for a pressure drop of 0.25 bar/100 m.

Steam Press. (barg)	Pipe diameter (mm)											
	20	25	40	50	65	80	100	125	150	200	250	300
0.3	14.4	31.8	95	201	354	63	1162	2041	3211	6722	11703	19514
1.0	18.2	38.4	116	245	427	680	1410	2485	3892	8165	44234	23814
2.1	21.8	45.5	140	294	520	825	1706	2994	4708	9852	17200	28713
3.1	25.0	35.6	159	337	591	944	1905	3429	5389	11240	19650	32741
4.1	27.2	59.1	177	376	659	1053	2196	3810	6015	12519	21854	36469
5.5	30.8	65.9	95	422	740	178	428	4273	6722	14016	24494	40824
6.9	34.0	72.7	218	460	806	1287	2621	4681	7375	15377	26753	44700
8.3	37.3	79.5	241	506	890	1415	2939	5117	8083	16874	29475	48988
10.3	40.3	86.3	259	544	961	1524	3157	5552	8763	18289	31897	53071
13.8	45.5	99.9	295	623	1097	1747	3620	6341	9988	20875	36279	60691
17.2	50.9	109.0	327	689	1214	1932	4001	7022	11077	23052	40143	67223
20.7	54.4	117.8	354	740	1295	2068	4273	7484	11784	24630	43001	71578

that many steam meters suffer wear and tear under such conditions. There is also a risk of noise from pipes. Table 11.4 lists the mass flow of steam in pipes for common saturated steam pressures and a pressure drop of 0.25 bar/100 m.

b) Pipe sizing system design

It is just as important to ensure that the correct size of pipework is installed for the condensate as it is for steam, and for basically the same reasons. If the pipe is too small, more energy is needed to overcome the back pressure generated within the system, i.e. condensate pumps will need to generate higher heads.

If the pipe is oversized the installation cost will be higher and the surface heat losses greater. Accurate sizing of condensate pipework is much more difficult than the equivalent for steam. Under normal operating conditions some of the condensate will 'flash' to steam in the pipework.

The proportion involved is normally small in weight but occupies a relatively large volume, and an understanding of this form of two-phase flow is required when determining the correct pipe size. Fortunately, years of practical experience have produced a rule of thumb that all condensate pipework should be sized for water flow under start-up conditions. Under these conditions steam condenses rapidly, and the consumption will be at least twice that of normal operation. Experience has shown that pipes sized in this way will be adequate to carry the mixed flash steam and condensate under operating conditions.

Table 11.5 Condensate/Flash steam capacity in relation to pipe size.

Pipe sizemm	CapacityKg/h
15	160
20	370
25	700
32	1 500
40	2 300
50	4 500
65	9 000
80	14 000

Table 11.5 gives the maximum capacity of pipes in common practice. This is based on a pressure drop of 0.8 mbar per meter run of pipe. However, the table and the rule of thumb given above only apply for steam system pressures up to 14 bar. At higher pressures, the quantity of extra flash steam occurring in the pipework is much greater and requires the condensate pipework to be even more generously sized.

The best way of dealing with the additional flash steam occurring in high pressure systems is to recover it at a lower pressure and to use it elsewhere within the process. The alternative is to install a closed pressurized condensate return system. Such systems are, however, expensive to install because every piece of equipment must be able to withstand the high pressures involved. Furthermore, many components within such a system, form pressure vessels and so are subject to insurance inspection.

c) Pipe layout

In a well-designed system, the condensate return will not impose an unreasonable back pressure on the steam traps. This is essential, especially during start-up when the traps have to vent first large quantities of air from the system and then large volumes of water.

It is rarely possible to gravity feed condensate back to the boiler feed tank. It is conventional to install condensate receivers at low level, thereby minimizing the back pressure on the steam traps, and then to pump the condensate back to the boiler house. Either electric pumps, or an automatic pumping trap, can be used. Whichever is selected, it must be able to cope with condensate that is near its boiling point. All condensate collecting vessels should be properly vented because they are not manufactured as pressure vessels and cannot withstand full steam pressure when a steam trap fails.

d) Lifting condensate

All good reference books state that condensate should never be lifted from a low-level outlet to a high-level collecting vessel or pipe. In practice, however, often the only convenient place to install condensate pipework is at high level.

The steam pressure at the trap has itself to be used to lift the condensate. The condensate exerts a back pressure of 1 bar for each 10 m of lift. This in turn reduces the pressure differential across the trap which means that it can pass less condensate. If a trap has to lift condensate 10 m from a vessel with steam at 3 bar, it can only pass approximately 65% of the amount it would pass if the condensate were to be discharged to atmosphere. To overcome this problem larger steam traps must be used.

If the differential pressure across the trap is allowed to fall too low it will not operate, especially under start-up conditions, and this will result in waterlogging. Another instance where this quite often occurs is where thermostatic control of a process vessel such as a jacketed-pan is required. If this is achieved by throttling the steam supply the steam pressure falls too low to operate the trap.

e) Feed pump problems

Improving the amount of condensate returned to the boiler house may lead to other problems. The feed tank temperature will now be high, and this may result in problems of cavitation and vapor locking at the boiler feed pump. To overcome these problems, the pump must have sufficient net positive suction head: this, in simple terms, can be expressed as the height of the feed tank above the feedwater inlet to the boiler.

f) Other pressure losses

When the steam route changes in direction or the steam flow is disturbed, steam suffers a drop in pressure. Thus, the number of bends and valves affects the pressure drop along a given length of pipe. It is most convenient to express this pressure drop through various fittings in terms of 'equivalent straight length of pipe'.

Table 11.6 shows that the equivalent figures depending on the pipe bore. When making initial estimates on pipe size, there is therefore a need, if the diameter changes, to repeat the calculations for pressure drop with revised equivalent lengths.

Valves, elbows, bends and tees should be totaled, and equivalent lengths added to the actual pipeline length for each distinct section of pipework. At this point, rationalization of existing layouts to remove all unnecessary tees

Table 11.6 Resistance of standard pipe fittings measured as equivalent pipe length (meters).

Pipe size (mm)	Standard elbow (90°)	Standard Bend (90°)	Tee (flow through branch	Gate valve (open)	Globe valve (open)
50	1.5	0.6	3.0	0.7	17
65	2.0	0.8	4.0	0.85	22
80	2.4	1.0	4.8	1.0	27
100	3.0	1.2	6.0	1.3	34
125	3.75	1.5	7.5	1.6	43
150	4.5	1.8	9.0	2.0	51
200	6.0	2.4	12.0	2.6	68

and elbows should be considered. Long swept bends are preferable to elbows; valves can be selected for minimum pressure drop.

g) Pipe drainage

The fact that steam is produced from water which is relatively cheap and plentiful is a definite advantage. The fact that, as steam cools it reverts to water, is not. Condensate in a steam line is at least a nuisance but can be potentially disastrous. At the very least condensate lying in the bottom of a pipe effectively reduces that pipe's cross-sectional area so requiring increased velocities and causing a higher pressure drop. In the worst case, the condensate layer becomes deep enough to be picked up by the steam and forced as a bullet or plug down the pipe.

These high velocity slugs have difficulty passing round bends and through fittings. In extreme cases this water hammer can lead to sudden failure of the pipe or of fittings such as valves. If the condensate is carried forward into the process machines there is again the possibility of damage. Wet steam builds up a thick film on heat transfer surfaces reducing the effectiveness of the process machines. It also leads to excessive erosion and wear on the pipework and fittings of the machine, increasing maintenance costs. The excess condensate must be removed by the existing steam traps, possibly overloading them and leading to early failure.

Good steam pipework layout ensures that there is provision for removing condensate from the distribution system before it can cause a problem. For this provision to be effective the pipes must be installed so that the condensate flows towards these drain points.

General guidelines for the effective draining of condensate and layout of steam lines:

• The steam mains should be laid with a falling slope in the direction of steam flow of not less than 125 mm for every 30 m of pipe length. This ensures that the condensate always flows to where the next drain point is sited.

- Drain points should be provided at intervals of 30–45 m along the steam main. The actual distances will vary, depending on how often a branch pipe occurs and how often there is a change in the level or direction of the steam main. In a straight run of pipe carrying dry steam, drain points and steam traps should be 45 m apart. Installing them at more frequent intervals may seem to be making the system safer but the penalty is the increased possibility of failure and steam venting. If the steam produced by a boiler plant is very wet the drain points and trap sets must be at more frequent intervals.

- Condensate will always collect where there is a low point in the system, so a drain point is required at each of these. At any bend there is an increased likelihood of entrained condensate droplets being deposited on the walls of the pipe, this is especially true where a steam main rises. A drain point is therefore required.

- A sump should be provided at a drain point in the main steam lines. The simplest method is to use an equal 'T' connection, the bottom limb forming the sump.

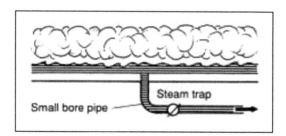

Figure 11.13   Incorrect drainage of steam main.

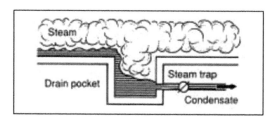

Figure 11.14   Correct drainage of steam main.

- The choice of steam trap is important for the main steam lines. Inverted bucket traps or thermodynamic (TD) traps should be used wherever possible.

- Branch lines taken from the main should always be connected at the top of the pipe. This largely prevents any carryover of condensate into the branch.

- Pipework and insulation are heavy. If the pipe is not adequately supported at regular intervals sagging will occur. This creates low points for the build-up of condensate. The type and frequency of support required will depend on the diameter and wall thickness of the pipes.

- Steam pipework does not remain at working pressure and temperature all the time. At start-up and shut-down the metal of the pipework expands and contracts. If no allowance is made for this movement a considerable amount of stress is set-up which can lead to cracking and ultimately to failure. To overcome this problem, expansion loops with smooth swept bends are installed at intervals in the steam main. Smaller steam mains and branches may also require expansion allowance: in these cases, bellows-type expansion joints are commonly used.

- All steam using equipment operates best with dry steam but for some equipment dry steam is essential. As their name implies remove, the entrained droplets of water from the steam. These should be installed before essential equipment and, again, should be properly drained and trapped.

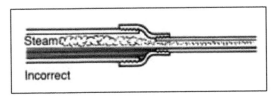

Figure 11.15   Incorrect fitting of reducers on steam main.

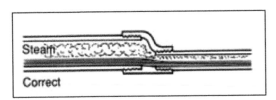

Figure 11.16   Correct fitting of reducers on steam main.

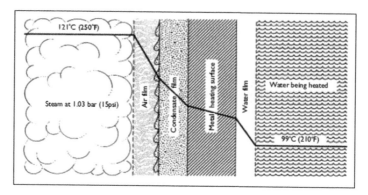

Figure 11.17   Effect of high resistance to heat flow.

- The practice of fitting a concentric reducer on a steam main and when changing system pipe diameters is a common cause of waterhammer and should be avoided.

11.2.6 Heat transfer from steam

The heat transfer rate from condensing steam to a surface is very high but can be seriously impeded by films of air or water. Appropriate air and steam condensate removal techniques will improve the overall efficiency of heat transfer.

The metal wall is the heating surface of any process steam plant in which the steam does not come into direct contact with the material being heated. Firstly, on each side of this wall will be a scale film which creates considerable resistance to the flow of heat to the product. Often it is possible (and it always pays) to clean the surface regularly.

Two further films, air and water, must be removed as rapidly and completely as possible otherwise heat transfer and process output efficiencies are reduced. The effect of air and water films on process output is not an isolated occurrence. It occurs in all steam-heated processes and will continue to occur, unless some action is taken to reduce the thickness of the air and water films on condensing surfaces.

11.2.7 Steam traps

a) The purpose of steam traps

A steam trap is a device that fulfils three important functions:

- To remove condensate (water),

- to remove air, and

- to retain steam.

It removes the condensate formed either within the steam pipework or within the process equipment. It must be able to do this at least as quickly as the condensate is formed or the system will become waterlogged. In the case of the steam pipework this would lead to water hammer and the risk of damage to pipework and fittings. In process equipment, waterlogging means that the steam cannot get in to heat up whatever requires heating, therefore the process stops or at least slows down significantly.

As its name suggests one of the functions of a steam trap is to prevent large amounts of steam escaping. However, some traps require small amounts of steam to escape to operate correctly.

A steam trap should enable any gases in the system to escape. If the gases remain, they will take up part of the space that the steam should occupy: this reduces the carrying capacity of pipework and prevents the steam from reaching the heat transfer surfaces of process equipment. In the worst cases a pipe or piece of equipment can become air-locked so that even the condensate cannot be released.

The gases that must be removed comprise first the air that fills the system when it is cold and drained down. In addition, during normal operation some non-condensable gases can get into the system either by being dissolved in the feedwater or as a result of the breakdown of chemicals in the feedwater.

b) Classification of steam traps

There are many types of steam traps in use today, not all of which can perform well the functions previously outlined. Before the principal types of traps available are examined in detail, it will aid in understanding of their operation if they are classified by their main categories.

There are three main categories:

   i. Mechanical.

   ii. Thermostatic.

   iii. Thermodynamic.

Mechanical traps work on the principle of differentiating between the density of steam and condensate. For example, some mechanical traps use a float that will rise as the condensate level rises, opening a valve, but will not become buoyant in the presence of steam only, keeping the valve closed. Some mechanical traps will not, however, vent air and non-condensable gases, unless some form of thermal element is incorporated within the trap. Such elements are miniature versions of those used in thermostatic traps.

Thermostatic traps operate by sensing the temperature of condensate. As steam condenses, the condensate so formed is at steam temperature, but as it flows to the steam trap it loses temperature. When the temperature has dropped to a specified value below the steam temperature, the thermostatic trap will open to release the condensate.

Finally, the third category is the thermodynamic type, which operates on the difference between the flow of steam over a surface, compared to the flow of condensate over the same surface. Steam, or for that matter a gas, flowing over a surface creates a low-pressure area, this phenomenon being used to move a valve towards the seat and eventual closure.

In the three categories outlined, different modes of operation are employed, though each mode is working on the same basic principle within its category.

c) Steam trap characteristics

In determining which steam trap to use for a specific application, it is useful to try to match the characteristics of the trap to the heat requirement for the equipment in question. Therefore, a summary of trap characteristics will assist the specifier to make such a selection.

d) Dirt

On large sizes of traps, additional protection against dirt in the steam system is essential. "Y"type strainers should be installed, but always with the strainer

Table 11.7 Different trap types and their characteristics.

Different Trap Types and Their Classification		
Mechanical	Float-Thermostatic	Free Float
	Inverted Bucket	Float with Lever
		Free Ball-bucket
		Cylindrical Bucket
Thermostatic	Expansion	Liquid
	Balanced Pressure	Wax Capsule
	Bimetallic	Bellows Type
		Diaphragm
		Bimetallic
Thermodynamic	Disc	Exposed Chamber
	Impulse	Air Insulated
		Steam-jacketed
		Orifice and Piston

Table 11.8 Summary of trap characteristics.

Type	Advantages	Disatvantages	Applications
Balanced Pressure	Small, Lightweight, No Adjustment required for changes in pressure. Good at air venting Unaffected by back pressure.	Can be damaged by water hammer. Cannot be used for superheated steam. Will be damaged by freezing if not installed to self-drain. Will hold back condensate until it cools to several degrees below Saturated steam temperature.	As an air vent for all steam equipment using saturated steam. Steam heated radiators. Small sizes of process plants where a slight amount of condensate within the steam space will not affect the output. Steam tracing.
Bimetalli	Small. Good for air venting at high pressure. Will with withstand water hammer. Can be used for high pressure steam.	Requires adjustment over a wide pressure range. Will hold back condensate until it subcools. Reacts slowly to load changes. Can be affected by back pressure.	Low temperature tracing. Instrument enclosures. As a high pressure air vent. As a standard air vent.
Free Float Thermostatic	Simple construction. No link mechanism to wear and cause sticking. Rapid and automatic adjustment to variations in condensate flow rate and pressure. Vents air on start-up. Can incorporate steam-lock release valve. With 3-point seating can be used for draining superheated steam mains.	Can be damaged by very excessive water hammer. Can freeze in exposed conditions.	All heat exchangers and process plants requiring maximum efficiency. Batch processes requiring fast warm up.

Continued

Table 11.8   *Continued*

Type	Advantages	Disatvantages	Applications
Inverted Bucket	Reasonably rugged construction. Withstand a fair degree of water hammer.	Vents air slowly. Can be damaged by freezing. Will lose the water seal and blow steam if there is a rapid drop in pressure. Wastes steam on light loads. Is not recommended for use on superheat.	For draining steam mains. Small items of process plant operating under fairly steady conditions.
Thermodynamic	Simple Compact rugged construction. Withstands water hammer, freezing and superheat. Some have special bimetal vent to vent air on start-up. High capacities per size of trap. Operates over wide pressure range without a change of orifice. Unaffected by vibration.	Cannot be used on very low inlet pressures. Cannot operate on back pressures greater than 80% of inlet pressure. Unless air vent is fitted, it will air bind. Without air-jacket the trap will cycle rapidly in adverse ambient conditions e.g. rain or snow.	Draining all classes of steam mains especially where high pressure or superheat exists. Small items of process plant where vibration or movement exists. Steam tracing.

screen at either the 3 o'clock or 9 o'clock position. Otherwise, in large strainers, condensate, which can be picked up by a surge in steam flow, will collect and cause water hammer within the steam trap.

When constructing drain points for steam mains, these should normally be the size of an equal-tee up to 100 mm (4") pipe size and a dirt pocket left in the bottom of the pipe. Never take the connection to the trap from the bottom of the pocket, but always partly up the side. Drain points for mains larger than 100mm (4") should normally be not less than 2 to 3 pipe sizes smaller, with the minimum being 100mm (4").

e) Group trapping
Naturally, no one wants to spend more money than necessary when installing steam equipment, but care must also be taken that what is perceived to be an economic measure, does not turn out to be a major disadvantage for the efficiency of the process. Just such a case occurs when attempts are made to group several items of steam plant to one steam trap.

f) Checking the performance of steam traps
Correct operation of steam traps is essential because they provide a vital link between the steam and condensate services. A single continuously leaking 12.5 mm (0.5 inch) steam trap can waste thousands of rand a year.

g) Steam trap checklist
- Maintain steam traps adequately.

- Instigate a regular inspection and servicing routine.

- Replace internal parts, if possible, from time to time.

- Confirm that the most suitable types are being used for particular applications, paying attention to ease of repair and/or replacement.

Steam trap failure in the closed position is usually indicated by poor plant performance, although it can go unnoticed on steam mains. Failure in the open position is also not always obvious. Traps usually discharge into a common condensate return system. While live steam at the collecting tank indicates that there is a problem, it will not distinguish the particular defective trap.

h) Visual inspection of traps discharging open-ended
Thermodynamic traps, conventional balanced pressure traps, and inverted bucket traps handling moderate loads all discharge open-ended. An untrained eye can usually decide whether the trap is working correctly by looking at

the trap discharge. Traps with a blast or intermittent discharge are particularly easy to check. When the trap is closed, only a wisp of steam should be visible. This is caused by the evaporation of any drops of hot condensate left in the outlet connection.

When the trap is discharging, a quantity of flash steam will normally leave the outlet with the condensate. This should not be mistaken for live steam. Float traps, bi-metallic traps and some balanced pressure traps with stainless steel elements generally, but not always, give a continuous discharge. With these types of trap, it is more difficult to tell if they are working correctly.

If there is a short transparent zone in the discharge with a bluish hazy appearance, this suggests that the trap is blowing steam. If a trap discharging to atmosphere is stuck wide open, then the noise and unvarying discharge provide a strong indication that something is wrong.

i) Testcocks
Fitting a test cock on the downstream side of a trap allows the discharge to be diverted to atmosphere. The trap will then discharge open-ended and performance can be assessed as described above.

The drawback with this solution is that the trap is relieved of back pressure. This will alter the effective setting of bi-metallic traps, and if high enough, will render impulse or thermodynamic traps inoperative. The test is therefore not entirely conclusive, and the results must be considered accordingly.

j) Sight glasses
An alternative is to observe the discharge through a sight glass - a window fitted on the downstream side of a trap. This method is generally effective in the case of traps having a blast discharge since the on/off characteristic is clear.

k) Temperature measurement
Although temperature-sensitive crayons and the latest pyrometers have been used, these methods are of limited use. However, they will detect a trap causing serious waterlogging.

The temperature of the condensate and flash steam on the downstream side of a correctly working trap is normally around 100°C. However, since the temperature is controlled by the line pressure, the condensate and live steam on the downstream side of a defective trap will have the same temperature. In this situation, temperature measurement gives no guide to trap performance.

l) Noise

While thermodynamic traps have a distinctive and regular 'click', which can be detected by an untrained ear, many traps have no distinctive signal. Condensate and flash steam immediately downstream of the trap orifice can sound the same as condensate and live steam at the orifice. Both sounds are affected by mass flow and pressure.

A defective trap under light load conditions gives a lower signal than a correctly functioning trap under full load conditions. However, a 'scan' across the base of a trap can produce an astonishing spread of different signals. Other problems arise due to interference from the sound of adjacent traps transmitted through the pipework. Ultrasonic leak detectors can be effective with some traps, although they may need careful tuning to match, or suit, trap conditions.

m) Electrical conductivity

A recent device, which utilizes the electrical conductivity of condensate, involves fitting a sensor chamber containing an inverted weir on the upstream side of the steam trap. When the steam trap is working normally, condensate flows under the inverted weir which has a small hole at the top to equalize the pressure on each side.

The presence of condensate is detected by a sensor on the upstream side. The completeness of the electrical circuit is checked by plugging a lead from the sensor into a portable indicator; a visual signal (green or red) indicates whether the trap is working correctly or not. If the trap fails in the open position, then a relatively large volume of steam will flow towards the trap. This depresses the water level on the upstream side of the weir and exposes the sensor. The electrical circuit is broken and the portable indicator signals that the trap has failed.

This method has the advantage that a positive signal is provided, which can be interpreted without the need for experience or personal judgement. Use of suitable wiring allows the test point to be installed remotely from the sensor chamber. This can be useful in the case of the traps located at high level or in ducts which would otherwise be inaccessible. Various versions of this equipment are also able to identify traps that have gone cold due to a faulty trap, a blocked strainer or a closed valve upstream.

n) Indirect method

Steam metering provides a 'standard' figure when everything is operating correctly. A significant rise in steam consumption therefore indicates that the traps are beginning to pass steam. However, steam metering usually applies to a relatively large machine or area, making it difficult to determine which traps are giving trouble. Nevertheless, it is a useful prompt that individual traps should be checked.

11.2.8 Routine maintenance of traps

Steam traps should be examined and, if necessary, serviced on a regular basis. Although this approach is applied routinely to larger pieces of plant, it is rarely extended to steam traps. The work depends on the type of trap. For example, a balanced pressure thermostatic steam trap has an element which is designed for easy replacement. While changing these elements, say every two years, may seem wasteful in terms of time and materials, it removes the need for trap checking and should ensure a trouble-free system with no losses through defective traps.

To be cost-effective, routine maintenance should include the renewal of any suspect parts. This avoids spending time and materials cleaning and reinstating partially fatigued parts, such as bellows, only to produce a trap that will require checking and be prone to fatigue.

Generally, it is only the internal moving parts which will wear, as the body of the trap usually lasts as long as the plant to which it is fitted. It is therefore advantageous to be able to renew the internals of a steam trap from time to time. The value of this measure depends greatly on the ease with which new parts can be fitted and the reliability of the refurbished trap. The elements of most thermostatic traps can generally be changed by removing a screwed-in seat. Replacement is simple and the remade trap reliable. However, if the joint between the trap body and the seat (the weakest point) has been allowed to blow steam, remaking will be impossible.

Another factor is site conditions. Small float and inverted bucket traps are designed so that the cover, with the internals attached, can be taken to the workshop for attention without the need to disturb the pipework. This is preferable to renewing the seats of inaccessible traps welded into the pipework.

On some sites, high labor costs will rule out the repair of all but the largest traps. In these cases, it is therefore essential that the traps themselves can be changed easily. While flanged connections provide one solution, flanged traps are more expensive than the equivalent screwed ones and the mating flanges are an additional expense. Alternatively, traps with swivel connections can be fitted; in this case, the joint between the trap and the pipeline is maintained by only two bolts.

11.3 End-Use

Normally, saturated steam is used in industrial and space heating applications. Two basic types of heating occur in steam heating equipment. These are *direct* and *indirect* heating.

With direct heating, the product or material to be heated is in direct contact with the steam and in most cases, no condensate is recovered. An example of direct heating is the heating of the liquid by directly injecting it with steam. The steam and condensate mix with the product. If steam injection is used to heat an aqueous solution an allowance must be made for the diluting effect of the condensate.

Indirect heating separates the steam and product. In most cases the condensate from the steam is recovered and reused for boiler feed water or other hot water requirements. Examples of indirect heating include:

- Steam-to-liquid heat exchangers
- Product heating in storage tanks
- Air heaters

It must be noted that situations may occur where condensate is not recovered from indirect heated equipment. In instances such as heating vegetable oils, glucose or preheating fuel oils in heat exchangers, a failure in the heat exchanger could allow the heated material to mix with the condensate. If this condensate was then returned as boiler feedwater, this condensate would foul the internal heat transfer surfaces of the boiler.

The three basic types of indirect steam heated equipment are the steam coil, jacketed vessels and heat exchangers. Normally for jacketed vessels or steam coils the liquid to be heated is not flowing. For heat exchangers the steam and liquid are flowing.

Unit heaters are heat exchangers that use steam or hot water forced through metal tubes, to heat air blown over the tubes (refer to the figure

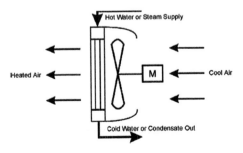

Figure 11.18 Typical unit heater.

below). Normally the tubes are finned or passed through thin metal plates to increase the surface area and heat transfer rate. A low room temperature signal from a thermostat starts the fan and blows air over the heated surfaces, increasing the heat transfer rate to the air. As soon as the thermostat senses the desired temperature, the fan shuts off.

11.4 Energy Efficiency Measures

11.4.1 Boiler house – Operation opportunities

- Regularly check water treatment procedures.

- Maintain the Total Dissolved Solids (TDS) of the boiler within recommended limits, for the pressure range of the boiler.

- Operate at the lowest steam pressure or hot water temperature that is acceptable to the boiler design and distribution system requirements.

- Condition fuel for optimum combustion.

- Minimize load swings and schedule demand where possible to maximize the achievable boiler efficiencies.

- Regularly check the efficiency of the boilers.

- After the boiler tune-up start recording and analyzing the flue gas temperature for signs of heat transfer surfaces fouling.

- Regularly monitor the boiler excess air.

- Install performance monitoring equipment.

- Relocate combustion air intake to the top of the boiler house to use the heated air and save energy.

- Recover blowdown heat.

- Reduce boiler excess air where possible.

11.4.2 Boiler house – Maintenance opportunities

- Keep burners in proper adjustment.

- Check for and repair leaking flanges, valve stems and pump glands.

- Maintain tightness of all air ducting and flue gas breeching.

- Check for hot spots on the boiler casing that may indicate deteriorating boiler insulation that should be repaired during the annual shutdown period.

- Keep fireside surfaces of the boiler tubes clean.

- Replace and repair missing or damaged insulation.

- Replace boiler observation or access doors and repair any leaking door seals.

11.4.3 Boiler house – Retrofit opportunities

- Install preheater

- Upgrade burner

- Install turbulators in fire tube boiler

11.4.4 Steam distribution system opportunities

- Establish steam trap maintenance and procedures.

- Check and correct steam and condensate leaks.

- Train operating personnel.

- Check control setting.

- Shut down steam and condensate branch system when not required.

- Recover condensate where economically feasible.

- Overhaul the pressure reducing stations.

- Reduce the direct use of steam where possible by using the heat exchanger.

- Remove unused steam and condensate pipes.

- Reduce system pressure where possible.

- Relocate the equipment to shorten the length of piping.

- Institute steam trap replacement program

- Optimize pipe sizes

- Recover flash steam

- Eliminate steam use where possible
- Stage the depressurization of condensate
- Recover heat from condensate
- Meter all steam and condensate flows

11.4.5 End-use equipment opportunities

- Seal leaks at valves, fittings and gaskets.
- Repair damaged insulation
- Maintain equipment strainers and traps.
- Clean heat transfer surfaces.
- Ensure that steam quality is adequate for the application.
- Ensure that the steam pressure and temperature ranges are within the tolerances specified for the equipment.
- Ensure that the traps are correctly sized to remove all the condensate.
- Ensure that the heating coils are sloping from the steam inlet to the steam trap to prevent the coil flooding with condensate.
- Shut down equipment when not required.
- Provide lockable type covers for control equipment such as thermostats to prevent unauthorized tampering.
- Operate equipment at or near capacity whenever possible. Avoid running multiple units at reduced capacity.
- Convert from direct to indirect steam heated equipment and recover condensate.
- Modify process, if possible, to stabilize steam or water demand.
- Evaluate wastewater streams leaving a facility for heat recovery opportunity.

Table 11.9   Saturated steam tables.

Gauge Pressure bar	Absolute Pressure bar	Temperature °C	Specific Enthalpy			Specific VoluC (V_g) m³/kg
			Water (h_f) kJ/kg	Evaporation (h_{fg}) kJ/kg	Steam (h_g) kJ/kg	
	0.05	32.88	137.82	2423.7	2561.5	28.192
	0.10	45.81	191.83	2392.8	2584.7	14.674
	0.15	53.97	225.94	2373.1	2599.1	10.022
	0.20	60.06	251.40	2358.3	2609.7	7.649
	0.25	64.97	271.93	2346.3	2618.2	6.204
	0.30	69.10	289.23	2336.1	2625.3	5.229
	0.35	72.70	304.30	2327.2	2631.5	4.530
	0.40	75.87	317.58	2319.2	2636.8	3.993
	0.45	78.70	329.67	2312.0	2641.7	3.580
	0.50	81.33	340.49	2305.4	2645.9	3.240
	0.55	83.72	350.54	2299.3	2649.8	2.964
	0.60	85.94	359.86	2293.6	2653.5	2.732
	0.65	88.01	368.54	2288.3	2656.9	2.535
	0.70	89.95	376.70	2283.3	2660.0	2.365
	0.75	91.78	384.39	2278.6	2663.0	2.217
	0.80	93.50	391.66	2274.1	2665.8	2.087
	0.85	95.14	398.57	2269.8	2668.4	1.972
	0.90	96.71	405.15	2265.7	2670.9	1.869
	0.95	98.20	411.43	2261.8	2673.2	1.777
	1.00	99.63	417.46	2258.0	2675.5	1.694
0	1.013	100.00	419.04	2257.0	2676.0	1.673
0.05	1.063	101.40	424.9	2253.3	2678.2	1.601
0.10	1.113	102.66	430.2	2250.2	2680.4	1.533
0.15	1.163	103.87	435.6	2246.7	2682.3	1.471
0.20	1.213	105.10	440.8	2243.4	2684.2	1.414
0.25	1.263	106.26	445.7	2240.3	2686.0	1.361
0.30	1.313	107.39	450.4	2237.2	2687.6	1.312
0.35	1.363	108.50	455.2	2234.1	2689.3	1.268
0.40	1.413	109.55	459.7	2231.3	2691.0	1.225
0.45	1.463	110.58	464.1	2228.4	2692.5	1.186
0.50	1.513	111.61	468.3	2225.6	2693.9	1.149
0.55	1.563	112.60	472.4	2223.1	2695.5	1.115
0.60	1.613	113.56	476.4	2220.4	2696.8	1.083
0.65	1.663	114.51	480.2	2217.9	2698.1	1.051
0.70	1.713	115.40	484.1	2215.4	2699.5	1.024

Continued

Table 11.9 *Continued*

Gauge Pressure bar	Absolute Pressure bar	Temperature °C	Specific Enthalpy			Specific VoluC (V_g) m³/kg
			Water (h_f) kJ/kg	Evaporation (h_{fg}) kJ/kg	Steam (h_g) kJ/kg	
0.75	1.763	116.28	487.9	2213.0	2700.9	0.997
0.80	1.813	117.14	491.6	2210.5	2702.1	0.971
0.85	1.863	117.96	495.1	2208.3	2703.4	0.946
0.90	1.913	118.80	498.9	2205.6	2704.5	0.923
0.95	1.963	119.63	502.2	2203.5	2705.7	0.901
1.00	2.013	120.42	505.6	2201.1	2706.7	0.881
1.05	2.063	121.21	508.9	2199.1	2708.0	0.860
1.10	2.113	121.96	512.2	2197.0	2709.2	0.841
1.15	2.163	122.73	515.4	2195.0	2710.4	0.823
1.20	2.213	123.46	518.7	2192.8	2711.5	0.806
1.25	2.263	124.18	521.6	2190.7	2712.3	0.788
1.30	2.313	124.90	524.6	2188.7	2713.3	0.773
1.35	2.363	125.59	527.6	2186.7	2714.3	0.757
1.40	2.413	126.28	530.5	2184.8	2715.3	0.743
1.45	2.463	126.96	533.3	2182.9	2716.2	0.728
1.50	2.513	127.62	536.1	2181.0	2717.1	0.714
1.55	2.563	128.26	538.9	2179.1	2718.0	0.701
1.60	2.613	128.89	541.6	2177.3	2718.9	0.689
1.65	2.663	129.51	544.4	2175.5	2719.9	0.677
1.70	2.713	130.13	547.1	2173.7	2720.8	0.665
1.75	2.763	130.75	549.7	2171.9	2721.6	0.654
1.80	2.813	131.37	552.3	2170.1	2722.4	0.643
1.85	2.863	131.96	554.8	2168.3	2723.1	0.632
1.90	2.913	132.54	557.3	2166.7	2724.0	0.622
1.95	2.963	133.13	559.8	2165.0	2724.8	0.612
2.00	3.013	133.69	562.2	2163.3	2725.5	0.603
2.05	3.063	134.25	564.6	2161.7	2726.3	0.594
2.10	3.113	134.82	567.0	2160.1	2727.1	0.585
2.15	3.163	135.36	569.4	2158.5	2727.9	0.576
2.20	3.213	135.88	571.7	2156.9	2728.6	0.568
2.25	3.263	136.43	574.0	2155.3	2729.3	0.560
2.30	3.313	136.98	576.3	2153.7	2730.0	0.552
2.35	3.363	137.50	578.5	2152.2	2730.7	1.544
2.40	3.413	138.01	580.7	2150.7	2731.4	0.536
2.45	3.463	138.53	582.8	2149.2	2732.0	0.529

Continued

Table 11.9   *Continued*

Gauge Pressure bar	Absolute Pressure bar	Temperature °C	Specific Enthalpy			Specific VoluC (V_g) m³/kg
			Water (h_f) kJ/kg	Evaporation (h_{fg}) kJ/kg	Steam (h_g) kJ/kg	
2.50	3.513	139.02	585.0	2147.6	2732.6	0.522
2.55	3.563	139.52	586.9	2146.3	2733.2	0.515
2.60	3.613	140.00	589.2	2144.7	2733.9	0.509
2.65	3.663	140.48	591.3	2143.3	2734.6	0.502
2.70	3.713	140.96	593.3	2141.9	2735.2	0.496
2.75	3.763	141.44	595.3	2140.5	2735.8	0.489
2.80	3.813	141.92	597.4	2139.0	2736.4	0.483
2.85	3.863	142.40	599.4	2137.6	2737.0	0.477
2.90	3.913	142.86	601.4	2136.1	2737.5	0.471
2.95	3.963	143.28	603.3	2134.8	2738.1	0.466
3.00	4.013	143.75	605.3	2133.4	2738.7	0.461
3.10	4.113	144.67	609.1	2130.7	2739.8	0.451
3.20	4.213	145.46	612.9	2128.1	2741.0	0.440
3.30	4.313	146.36	616.4	2125.5	2741.9	0.431
3.40	4.413	147.20	620.0	2122.9	2742.9	0.422
3.50	4.513	148.02	623.6	2120.3	2743.9	0.413
3.60	4.613	148.84	627.1	2117.8	2744.9	0.405
3.70	4.713	149.64	630.6	2115.3	2745.9	0.396
3.80	4.813	150.44	634.0	2112.9	2746.9	0.389
3.90	4.913	151.23	637.3	2110.5	2747.8	0.381
4.00	5.013	151.96	640.7	2108.1	2748.8	0.374
4.10	5.113	152.68	643.9	2105.7	2749.6	0.367
4.20	5.213	153.40	647.1	2103.5	2750.6	0.361
4.30	5.313	154.12	650.2	2101.2	2751.4	0.355
4.40	5.413	154.84	653.3	2098.9	2752.2	0.348
4.50	5.513	155.55	656.3	2096.7	2753.0	0.342
4.60	5.613	156.24	659.3	2094.5	2753.8	0.336
4.70	5.713	156.94	662.3	2092.3	2754.6	0.330
4.80	5.813	157.62	665.2	2090.2	2755.4	0.325
4.90	5.913	158.28	668.1	2088.1	2756.2	0.320
5.00	6.013	158.92	670.9	2086.0	2756.9	0.315
5.10	6.113	159.56	673.7	2083.9	2757.6	0.310
5.20	6.213	160.20	676.5	2081.8	2758.3	0.305
5.30	6.313	160.82	679.2	2079.8	2759.0	0.301
5.40	6.413	161.45	681.9	2077.8	2759.7	0.296

Continued

Table 11.9   *Continued*

Gauge Pressure bar	Absolute Pressure bar	Temperature °C	Specific Enthalpy			Specific VoluC (V$_g$) m³/kg
			Water (h$_f$) kJ/kg	Evaporation (h$_{fg}$) kJ/kg	Steam (h$_g$) kJ/kg	
5.50	6.513	162.08	684.6	2075.7	2760.3	0.292
5.60	6.613	162.68	687.2	2073.8	2761.0	0.288
5.70	6.713	163.27	689.8	2071.8	2761.6	0.284
5.80	6.813	163.86	692.4	2069.9	2762.3	0.280
5.90	6.913	164.46	695.0	2067.9	2762.9	0.276
6.00	7.013	165.04	697.5	2066.0	2763.5	0.272
6.10	7.113	165.60	700.0	2064.1	2764.1	0.269
6.20	7.213	166.16	702.5	2062.3	2764.8	0.265
6.30	7.313	166.73	705.0	2060.4	2765.4	0.261
6.40	7.413	167.29	707.4	2058.6	2766.0	0.258
6.50	7.513	167.83	709.7	2056.8	2766.5	0.255
6.60	7.613	168.38	712.1	2055.0	2767.1	0.252
6.70	7.713	168.89	714.5	2053.1	2767.6	0.249
6.80	7.813	169.43	716.8	2051.3	2768.1	0.246
6.90	7.913	169.95	719.1	2049.5	2768.6	0.243
7.00	8.013	170.50	721.4	2047.7	2769.1	0.240
7.10	8.113	171.02	723.6	2046.1	2769.7	0.237
7.20	8.213	171.53	725.9	2044.3	2770.2	0.235
7.30	8.313	172.03	728.1	2042.6	2770.7	0.232
7.40	8.413	172.53	730.4	2040.8	2771.2	0.229
7.50	8.513	173.02	732.5	2039.2	2771.1	0.227
7.60	8.613	173.50	734.7	2037.5	2772.2	0.224
7.70	8.713	174.00	736.8	2035.9	2772.7	0.222
7.80	8.813	174.46	738.9	2034.2	2773.1	0.219
7.90	8.913	174.93	741.0	2032.6	2773.6	0.217
8.00	9.013	175.43	743.1	2030.9	2774.0	0.215
8.10	9.113	175.88	745.2	2029.3	2774.5	0.212
8.20	9.213	176.37	747.2	2027.6	2774.8	0.210
8.30	9.313	176.83	749.3	2026.1	2775.4	0.208
8.40	9.413	177.27	754.3	2024.5	2775.8	0.206
8.50	9.513	177.75	753.3	2022.9	2776.2	0.204
8.60	9.613	178.20	755.3	2021.3	2776.6	0.202
8.70	9.713	178.64	757.2	2019.7	2776.9	0.200
8.80	9.813	179.08	759.2	2018.2	2777.4	0.198
8.90	9.913	179.53	761.1	2016.6	2777.7	0.196

Continued

Table 11.9 *Continued*

Gauge Pressure bar	Absolute Pressure bar	Temperature °C	Water (h_f) kJ/kg	Evaporation (h_{fg}) kJ/kg	Steam (h_g) kJ/kg	Specific VoluC (V_g) m³/kg
				Specific Enthalpy		
9.00	10.013	179.97	763.0	2015.1	2778.1	0.194
9.10	10.113	180.41	765.0	2013.5	2778.5	0.192
9.20	10.213	180.83	766.9	2012.0	2778.9	0.191
9.30	10.313	181.26	768.7	2010.5	2779.2	0.189
9.40	10.413	181.68	770.6	2009.0	2779.6	0.187
9.50	10.513	182.10	772.5	2007.5	2780.0	0.185
9.60	10.613	182.51	774.4	2006.0	2780.4	0.184
9.70	10.713	182.91	776.2	2004.5	2780.7	0.182
9.80	10.813	183.31	778.0	2003.1	2781.1	0.181
9.90	10.913	183.72	779.8	2001.6	2781.4	0.179
10.00	11.013	184.13	781.6	2000.1	2781.7	0.177
10.20	11.213	184.92	785.1	1997.3	2782.4	0.174
10.40	11.413	185.68	788.6	1994.4	2783.0	0.172
10.60	11.613	186.49	792.1	1991.6	2783.7	0.169
10.80	11.813	187.25	795.5	1988.8	2784.3	0.166
11.00	12.013	188.02	798.8	1986.0	2784.8	0.163
11.20	12.213	188.78	802.3	1983.2	2785.5	0.161
11.40	12.413	189.52	805.5	1980.5	2786.0	0.158
11.60	12.613	190.24	808.8	1977.8	2786.6	0.156
11.80	12.813	190.97	812.0	1975.1	2787.1	0.153
12.00	13.013	191.68	815.1	1972.5	2787.6	0.151
12.20	13.213	192.38	818.3	1969.9	2788.2	0.149
12.40	13.413	193.08	821.4	1967.2	2788.6	0.147
12.60	13.613	193.77	824.5	1964.6	2789.1	0.145
12.80	13.813	194.43	827.5	1962.1	2789.6	0.143
13.00	14.013	195.10	830.4	1959.6	2790.0	0.141
13.20	14.213	195.77	833.4	1957.1	2790.5	0.139
13.40	14.413	196.43	836.4	1954.5	2790.9	0.137
13.60	14.613	197.08	839.3	1952.0	2791.3	0.135
13.80	14.813	197.72	842.2	1949.6	2791.8	0.133
14.00	15.013	198.35	845.1	1947.1	2792.2	0.132
14.20	15.213	198.98	848.0	1944.6	2792.6	0.130
14.40	15.413	199.61	850.7	1942.3	2793.0	0.128
14.60	15.613	200.23	853.5	1939.8	2793.3	0.127
14.80	15.813	200.84	856.3	1937.4	2793.7	0.125

Continued

Table 11.9   *Continued*

Gauge Pressure bar	Absolute Pressure bar	Temperature °C	Specific Enthalpy			Specific VoluC (V$_g$) m³/kg
			Water (h$_f$) kJ/kg	Evaporation (h$_{fg}$) kJ/kg	Steam (h$_g$) kJ/kg	
15.00	16.013	201.45	859.0	1935.0	2794.0	0.124
15.20	16.213	202.04	861.7	1932.7	2794.4	0.122
15.40	16.413	202.64	864.4	1930.4	2794.8	0.121
15.60	16.613	203.21	867.1	1928.0	2795.1	0.119
15.80	16.813	203.79	869.7	1925.7	2795.4	0.118
16.00	17.013	204.38	872.3	1923.4	2795.7	0.117
16.20	17.213	204.94	874.9	1921.2	2796.1	0.115
16.40	17.413	205.49	877.5	1918.9	2796.4	0.114
16.60	17.613	206.05	880.0	1916.7	2796.7	0.113
16.80	17.813	206.61	882.5	1914.4	2796.9	0.111
17.00	18.013	207.17	885.0	1912.1	2797.1	0.110
17.20	18.213	207.75	887.5	1909.9	2797.4	0.109
17.40	18.413	208.30	889.9	1907.7	2797.6	0.108
17.60	18.613	208.84	892.4	1905.5	2797.9	0.107
17.80	18.813	209.37	894.8	1903.4	2798.2	0.106
18.00	19.013	209.90	897.2	1901.3	2798.5	0.105
18.20	19.213	210.43	899.6	1899.1	2798.7	0.104
18.40	19.413	210.96	902.0	1896.9	2798.9	0.103
18.60	19.613	211.47	904.3	1894.8	2799.1	0.102
18.80	19.813	211.98	906.7	1892.6	2799.3	0.101
19.00	20.013	212.47	909.0	1890.5	2799.5	0.100
19.20	20.213	212.98	911.3	1888.4	2799.7	0.0986
19.40	20.413	213.49	913.6	1886.6	2799.9	0.0976
19.60	20.613	213.99	915.8	1884.3	2800.1	0.0967
19.80	20.813	214.48	918.1	1882.2	2800.3	0.0958
20.00	21.013	214.96	920.3	1880.2	2800.5	0.0949
20.50	21.513	216.15	925.8	1875.1	2800.9	0.0927
21.00	22.013	217.35	931.3	1870.1	2801.4	0.0906
21.50	22.513	218.53	936.6	1865.1	2801.7	0.0887
22.00	23.013	219.65	941.9	1860.1	2802.0	0.0868
22.50	23.513	220.76	947.1	1855.3	2802.4	0.0849
23.00	24.013	221.85	952.2	1850.4	2802.6	0.0832
23.50	24.513	222.94	957.3	1845.6	2802.9	0.0815
24.00	25.013	224.02	962.2	1840.9	2803.1	0.0797
24.50	25.513	225.08	967.2	1836.1	2803.3	0.0783

Continued

Table 11.9   *Continued*

Gauge Pressure bar	Absolute Pressure bar	Temperature °C	Specific Enthalpy Water (h_f) kJ/kg	Specific Enthalpy Evaporation (h_{fg}) kJ/kg	Specific Enthalpy Steam (h_g) kJ/kg	Specific VoluC (V_g) m³/kg
25.00	26.013	226.12	972.1	1831.4	2803.5	0.0768
26.00	27.013	228.15	981.6	1822.2	2803.8	0.0740
27.00	28.013	230.14	990.7	1813.3	2804.0	0.0714
28.00	29.013	232.05	999.7	1804.4	2804.1	0.0689
29.00	30.013	233.93	1008.6	1795.6	2804.2	0.0666
30.00	31.013	235.78	1017.0	1787.0	2804.1	0.0645
31.00	32.013	237.55	1025.6	1778.5	2804.1	0.0625
32.00	33.013	239.28	1033.9	1770.0	2803.9	0.0605
33.00	34.013	240.97	1041.9	1761.8	2803.7	0.0587
34.00	35.013	242.63	1049.7	1753.8	2803.5	0.0571
35.00	36.013	244.26	1057.7	1745.5	2803.2	0.0554
36.00	37.013	245.86	1065.7	1737.2	2802.9	0.0539
37.00	38.013	247.42	1072.9	1729.5	2802.4	0.0524
38.00	39.013	248.95	1080.3	1721.6	2801.9	0.0510
39.00	40.013	250.42	1087.4	1714.1	2801.5	0.0498
40.00	41.013	251.94	1094.6	1706.3	2800.9	0.0485
42.00	43.013	254.74	1108.6	1691.2	2799.8	0.0461
44.00	45.013	257.50	1122.1	1676.2	2798.2	0.0441
46.00	47.013	260.13	1135.3	1661.6	2796.9	0.0421
48.00	49.013	262.73	1148.1	1647.1	2795.2	0.0403
50.00	51.013	265.26	1160.8	1632.8	2793.6	0.0386

Chapter 12

Motors and Drives

Albert Williams[1] & Eustace Njeru[2]

[1]Institute of Energy Professionals Africa, South Africa
[2]Energy and Petroleum Regulatory Authority, Kenya

The electric motor is perhaps the most ubiquitous of electrical equipment. They account for an estimated 67% of all the electrical energy consumed in industrial plants. Motors are extremely rugged and durable, highly reliable and tolerate much abuse and neglect. Because they provide such sterling service and generally operate in the background there is a tendency to take them for granted, and there is little incentive to understand their operating characteristics.

In this Chapter we will cover the basics of electric motor theory and operating characteristics as well as discuss techniques for energy conservation. This will enable you to assess the performance of the electric motors in your plant, and take steps to minimizing their energy consumption and operating costs. A saving of 5% of the cost of the energy consumed by electric motors at your plant is not unrealistic.

12.1 Electric Motor Types

All industrial electric motors can be broadly classified as either Direct Current Motors, Synchronous Motors or Induction Motors. All motor types have the same four operating components: Stator (stationary windings), Rotor (rotating windings), Bearings, and Frame (enclosure). All motors convert electrical energy into mechanical energy by the interaction between the magnetic fields set up in the stator and rotor windings.

12.1.1 Direct-Current motors (DC)

DC motors, as the name implies, use direct, *i.e.* unidirectional, current. Used in special applications, they only represent about 10% of motors used in industry, *e.g.* where high torque starting or where smooth acceleration over a broad speed range is required. They are used in textile plants where correct tensioning of the fabric being processed between a series of drives is essential. They are expensive machines and in many applications are being replaced by AC induction motors controlled by variable-speed drives (VSD)

12.1.2 Synchronous motors

AC power is fed to the stator of the synchronous motor. The rotor is fed by DC from a separate source. The rotor field locks onto the stator rotating field and rotates at the same speed. The speed of the rotor is a function of the supply frequency and the number of magnetic poles in the stator. They are expensive motors with limited application, generally where low-speed and high power drives are required, *e.g.* compressors.

12.1.3 Induction motors

In induction motors a magnetic field is *induced* in the rotor windings by the magnetic fields set up in the stator by AC power supplies. Unlike synchronous machines, they are supplied from only one power source. The rotor conductors are all connected to end-rings on the rotor. At standstill the induction motor is analogous to a transformer with a short circuit secondary winding. The induction motor always runs at a slightly slower speed than the supply system synchronous speed.

They are the cheapest and simplest type of electric AC motor, and the 3-phase squirrel cage motor, so called because the rotor windings look like a squirrels' cage, is the workhorse of industry. It is rugged and reliable, and is by far the most common motor type used in industry. They drive pumps, blowers and fans, compressors, conveyers and production lines. This is the motor type which is the focus of this chapter.

The 3-phase induction motor has three windings each connected to a separate phase of the power supply.

12.2 Motor Nameplate Data

Motor nameplates provide a lot of useful design and performance data.

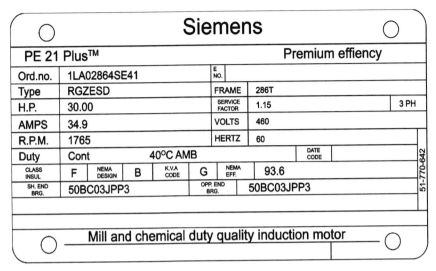

Figure 12.1   Motor nameplate.

12.2.1 kW or HP

Rated kW or horsepower is the power the motor is designed to deliver at its shaft with rated frequency and voltage applied at its terminals with a *service factor* of 1.0.

12.2.2 Service factor

Normally 1.0 or 1.15. Fractional motors may have a SF as high as 1.4. A SF of 1.0 means that the motor insulation may be seriously injured if motor is required to deliver greater than rated power. For a SF greater than 1.0 the motor may be run at rated power times the SF without serious injury to the insulation. However, if the motor is run continuously above its rating, shortening of insulation life will result. SF must not be confused with momentary overload capacity.

12.2.3 Efficiency

The efficiency at rated output. Energy efficient motors will be identified on the nameplate.

12.2.4 Amps

The current drawn by the motor at rated voltage and frequency with full rated power delivered to its shaft.

12.2.5 Volts

The motor rated voltage. The voltage that should be present at the motor terminals when delivering rated power.

12.2.6 Slip

The difference between the motor speed and synchronous speed.

12.2.7 RPM motor speed

The speed of the output shaft when delivering rated power; synchronous speed less slip. 'Synchronous speed' is the theoretical value of the speed that is calculated using the AC frequency and amount of motor poles. The difference between the two speeds is called the slip.

The equation used to calculate the synchronous speed of the motor is as follows:

$$Synchronous\, speed = \frac{60\, seconds \times Frequency\, of\, the\, electrical\, supply}{Number\, of\, pole\, pairs}$$

For example, if the frequency of the electrical supply is 50 Hertz with 4 poles (2 pole pairs), the synchronous speed of the motor is:

$$Synchronous\, speed = \frac{60\, seconds \times Frequency\, of\, the\, electrical\, supply}{Number\, of\, pole\, pairs}$$

$$Synchronous\, speed = \frac{60\, s \times 50\, Hz}{2}$$

$$Synchronous\, speed = 1\,500\, rpm$$

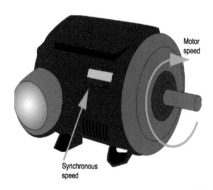

Figure 12.2   Motor and synchronous speed.

12.2.8 Motor pole

The number of electromagnetic windings that a motor has.

12.2.9 Hertz

The frequency of the supply system for which the motor is designed.

12.2.10 Duty

Duty is either Intermittent or Continuous. Intermittent will include a time after which the motor must be shut down and allowed to cool to prevent injury to the insulation. Continuous means that the motor may be run continuously for years.

12.2.11 Bearings

Indication of antifriction bearings installed.

12.2.12 Temperature

The maximum ambient temperature based on its insulation class.

12.3 Torque

The torque is related to the speed of the motor and is the primary parameter that is taken into consideration when the electrical motors are designed. The relationship between the torque and speed is based on the synchronous speed and load torque. The torque of the motor is divided into four categories:

- Starting torque;

- Accelerating torque;

- Breakdown torque; and

- Full-load torque.

In the USA, the National Electrical Manufacturers Association (NEMA) define different classes of electrical motors which all start in different ways. Figure 12.3 depicts class A and B motors.

Starting torque, which is marked point A on Figure 12.3, is plotted when the rotor is at rest. This condition occurs during starting the motor when the

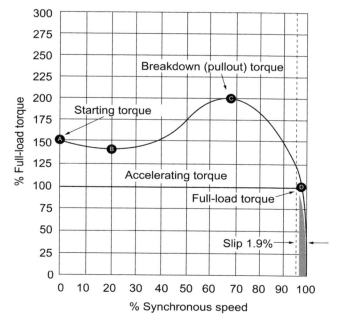

Figure 12.3   Torque and speed characteristics.

rated voltage and frequency are applied. It is also known as the locked rotor torque. For the rotor to be at rest when the voltage and frequency are applied, the motor must have been off. The voltage and frequency are applied to the stationary part of the motor, i.e. the stator, before reaching the rotor. This means that there is a delay between the moment when the voltage and frequency is applied, to the moment when the rotor starts turning. The delay causes the motor to create 150% of the full-load torque. Note that the starting torque of a motor differs based on the type and the design of the motor.

The rotation on the rotor is caused by the attraction of the magnetic field. For class A and B motors, this causes the rotor to start accelerating. When the motor starts to pick up speed, the torque starts to decrease from the starting torque to point B on Figure 12.3. This is called the accelerating torque. The torque increases further to a maximum torque which is approximately 200% of the full-load torque. At this point, the torque can no longer increase any further and, as such, the speed needs to decrease. This is the breakdown or pullout torque. Any further loadings beyond the 200% of the full-load torque can stall the motor or cause it to suddenly slow down.

If the speed continues to increase after the breakdown torque has been reached, torque starts to decrease until point D on the figure is reached. This is the full-load torque and the speed that matches it is not 100% of the

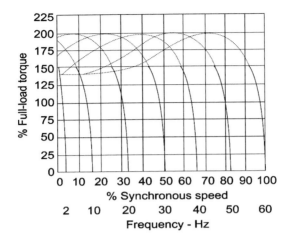

Figure 12.4 Starting torque at various rated conditions.

synchronous speed. This is the actual speed of the motor because the full-load torque is reached. This is where the motor is operating at its rated voltage, frequency and load. The speed that the motor is running at is called the slip speed or the actual motor speed and it is through the slip that the torque is developed.

The difference in the starting torques signifies that different applications of electrical motors require unique behavior from the motor. If the rated conditions of the motor are varied, the starting torque of the motor can be in excess of 600% of the full-load torque. This is illustrated in Figure 12.4. This can be achieved by adding a variable speed drive to the motor in which the voltage and frequency of the input can be increased.

12.4 Power

There are different ways to rate electrical motors and 'power' indicates the size of the motor. The power rating (in W, kW or MW) represents the input power or the rated power of the motor. A motor can be operated beyond its rated speed, but not beyond its rated voltage. To do this, the frequency can be increased beyond its rated value; this will increase the synchronous speed which is directly dependent on the frequency. This is illustrated in Figure 12.5

The change in both the frequency and voltage leads to a constant torque which is achieved until the rated conditions are reached. The voltage remains constant after the frequency has exceeded its rated value. This results in constant power and a decrease in torque due to a decrease in voltage-to-frequency ratio. The voltage-to-frequency ratio can be determined by using the next example.

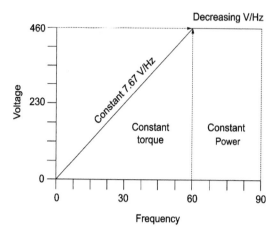

Figure 12.5 Constant power.

How to calculate frequency ratio

For a motor that is rated 414 V and 54 Hz, what is the voltage to frequency ratio?

Solution

$$voltage - to - frequency\,ratio = \frac{Voltage}{Frequency}$$

$$voltage - to - frequency\,ratio = \frac{414}{54}$$

$$voltage - to - frequency\;ratio = 7{,}67\frac{V}{Hz}$$

12.5 Motor Losses

Motor losses consume electrical energy but do not provide useful mechanical power. They occur in four areas. The percentage losses indicated are for 3000 rpm motors, and 1500 rpm motors in brackets.

12.5.1 Core loss

Approx. 18% (22%) of total loss at full load. Core losses represent the energy required to magnetize the core material (hysteresis) and are expended by small electric currents that flow in the core (eddy currents). Core loss of a motor is constant and is independent of the motor load current, and thus accounts for a much higher percentage of the losses at low motor loads.

12.5.2 Stator and rotor resistance (I2R) Loss

Approx. 42% (56%) of total loss at full load. Resistance or heat loss is the I2R loss in the stator windings due to the current I flow through the motor conductors of resistance R. Heat loss of a motor is proportional to the square of the stator and rotor current and is reduced by load reduction.

12.5.3 Friction and windage loss

Approx. 30% (11%) of total loss at full load. This loss results from friction within the shaft bearings and from the resistance to air being circulated through the motor by cooling fans.

12.5.4 Stray load loss

Approx. 10% (11%) of total loss at full load. Stray load loss results from leakage of magnetic flux, and depends on the rotor slot design. Like I2R losses they are dependent on the square of the load current and tend to increase with motor load.

12.6 Motor Efficiency

The efficiency of a motor is the ratio of its mechanical power output to its electrical power input. This ratio represents how effectively the motor converts electrical energy to mechanical energy, and is a measure of the motor losses. As with all electric equipment operating under optimum conditions motor efficiencies are high; generally, above 80%.

Typical AC polyphase motor efficiencies peak at about 75% loading and drops significantly when loading is below about 30%.

12.6.1 Energy efficient motors

The motor losses described above can be reduced by motor manufacturers through improved motor design and the use of more and better materials. Inevitably the cost of an energy efficient motor is more expensive than a standard motor having the same rating. However, this extra cost may be justified by a reduction in the motor operating costs.

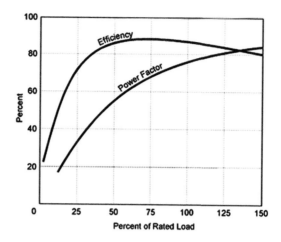

Figure 12.6 Efficiency/power factor vs load for a typical 3 phase induction motor.

a) Stator and rotor loss reduction

Such loss can be reduced by using larger diameter conductors for the stator and rotor windings and by using copper instead of aluminium to reduce the winding resistance.

b) Core loss reduction

Hysteresis loss is reduced by using low-loss silicon "electric" steels in the core. Eddy current loss is decreased by making core laminations thinner. Core loss reduction results in less magnetizing current and a corresponding improvement in the motor power factor.

c) Friction and windage losses

Friction is reduced by using high quality bearings. Windage is reduced by using smaller fans. Energy efficient motors generally run hotter than standard motors even though reduced stator/rotor losses results in less heat generation.

The benefits from higher efficient motors are more significant for smaller motors.

12.7 Motor Loads

The motor loads are used to check whether the motor will be able to meet the torque requirements of the load. This is achieved by comparing the speed and torque curve of the motor against the speed and torque curve of the load. The curves are shown in Figure 12.7.

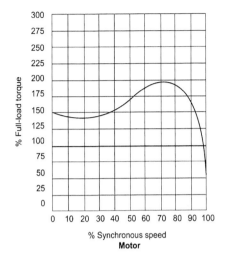 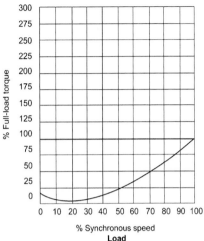

Figure 12.7 Speed-torque curves,

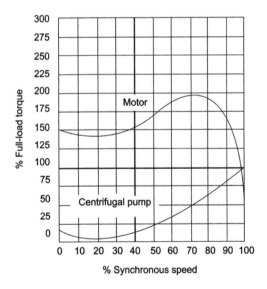

Figure 12.8 Load torque requirements.

The load of the motor is selected so that it can be started and operated by the motor. An electrical motor that is capable of a starting torque of 150% of full-load torque, cannot be used to run loads requiring starting torques of 200% of full-load torques. A fully functional motor that can deliver the desired torque requirements of the load is shown in Figure 12.8.

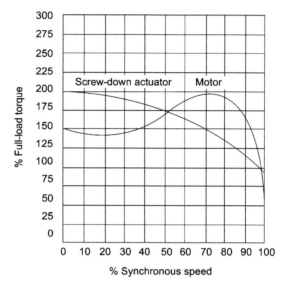

Figure 12.9   Load torque requirements.

An instance where the torque requirements of the load cannot be met by the motor are shown in Figure 12.9.

12.8 Motor Rewinding

In industry it is common practice to rewind motors that have suffered winding failure. Rewinding a motor, if done correctly, can result in many more trouble free hours of operation. In fact, the motor can be rewound with larger conductors to a higher efficiency than before, by reducing the I^2R losses. On the other hand, if improper burnout procedures are used to remove the old windings, *i.e.* using a hand-held torch, and subjecting the motor core to abnormally high temperatures may result in core operating losses increasing by up to three times the original value. The increased losses and subsequent increase in full load current and winding temperatures could result in premature motor failure.

Once a decision has been made to rewind a motor it should be recognized that the motor represents an energy investment and the rewind should be done without causing a deterioration of its efficiency.

12.9 Motor Protection

Many motor failures can be averted and their useful life extended if they are provided with adequate controls and protection.

12.9.1 Overcurrent protection

Overcurrent protection is provided by fuses or a circuit breaker set to interrupt the power supply to the motor when the current drawn by the motor is excessive, due to a short circuit fault or a very heavy overload. This protection is usually located at the line end of the motor feeder.

12.9.2 Overload protection

Overload protection is in addition to overcurrent protection and safeguards the motor from mechanical overloads. This protection located at the motor and will comprise overload relays, thermal overloads, electronic overload relays or fuses. Overload relays open the motor controller when the load current becomes too high. Thermal overloads have heaters that closely approximates the actual motor heat build-up or heat detectors in the motor windings that disconnects the motor when the temperature gets too high. Electronic overloads and time delay fuses operate in a similar way. The thermal and electronic overload devices have the advantage of a "memory" that cannot be reset until the motor has cooled down.

12.9.3 Other protection

Line voltage monitoring relays detect conditions of a) voltage unbalance, b) phase failure, c) phase reversal, and d) under-voltage, all conditions injurious to motors.

12.10 Electric Motor Standards Compared to Actual Measurement

This section discusses electrical motor standards to ensure the understanding of motor to meet a specific standard. The motors are constructed and built to adhere to the International Electrotechnical Commission (IEC), Comité Européen de Normalisation Électrotechnique (CENELEC), Verband der Elektrotechnik (VDE) regulations and Deutsches Institut für Normung (DIN) standards, among others. The application for the motor often coincides with the standards set out for the motor. For example, the motor can be tested for hours on end when the standards are set out. However, this does not take into consideration the factors that might be relevant at the application of the motor.

The standards governing the motors include the following:

• Cooling;

- Degrees of protection;

- Standard voltage ranges;

- Tolerances;

- Mounting arrangements; and

- Dimensions and power standards.

The standards governing cooling clearly state and list possible ways to cool the motor without using external mechanisms like fans. However, in reality, motors may experience an increase in temperature even though the standard states that they can cope with the particular application. This can happen because the motor will react differently based on its operating environment. In other words, electric motor standards need to be checked against actual

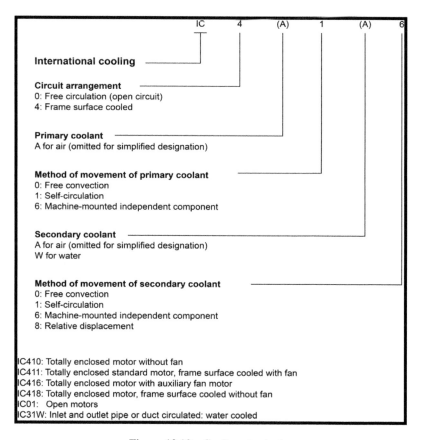

Figure 12.10 Cooling standards.

job-site conditions and results. Therefore, cooling standards need to be applied with the environment.

Differentiating between motor standards and actual operating needs to be taken into consideration as it will affect the efficiency of the motor and the associated maintenance costs. A motor that overheats may need additional protocols to reduce its temperature, in order to reduce long-term costs associated with cooling, maintenance and repair.

12.11 Energy Efficiency Measures

12.11.1 Motor load scheduling

a) Switch off unproductive motors (reduce energy)
In many facilities electric motor drives are run continually and independently of the production load. Simply by switching off motor drives when they are not required can result in significant energy cost savings. The potential savings can readily be calculated from the motor drive power demand as measured during idle running, an estimate of the shut down time, and the kWh cost.

b) Schedule motor operations to lower overall demand
An analysis of the electricity consumption and plant demand profile may indicate that it is possible to stagger the operation of two motor drives or reschedule the motor drive to operate during non-peak periods, thus lowering the demand peak which would otherwise occur.

12.11.2 Motor drive maintenance and alignment

Operation of a motor is affected by maintenance. As already stated, induction motors are rugged devices, but simple regular maintenance and inspection will not only provide longer motor life but can also save on operating costs.

a) Temperature
The most important factor affecting the life of a motor is the temperature of the insulation. Increasing the insulation temperature by 10% will reduce the motor life by half. Ensure motors are well ventilated.

b) Dirt
If screens, filters or air vents become clogged motors may overheat and eventually fail.

c) Moisture

Intermittent use or standby motors are prone to problems with moisture in the windings. Motors in a damp environment should be run for a couple of hours a week to drive off moisture. The winding insulation resistance measurement is a good indicator of the presence of moisture. Remedial action should be considered if the insulation resistance is less than 1 Mega-Ohm per kV.

d) Greasing

Over-greasing of antifriction bearings increases friction causing bearings to overheat and motor losses to increase, and is the most common cause of bearing failure. Bearings should be filled no more than 30%.

e) Vibration

A noticeable increase in motor drive vibration is an indication of trouble. Checks should be made of mounting bolts, shaft alignment, bearings. Vibration can be difficult problem to resolve and the assistance of the motor manufacturers may be necessary. Motor drive vibration increases motor losses.

f) Starting

Excessive starting is a prime cause of motor failure through overheating from high staring currents. For motors below 150 kW, the maximum starting time with a high inertia load is 20 seconds. The motor should not exceed more than 150 start-seconds a day.

g) Belt drives

Typical belts, synchronous and V-belts, used in industry today incur energy losses due to windage, flexing and slippage. The use of cogged or notched V-belts increases drive efficiency with savings ranging from 2% to 4%.

12.11.3 Motor power factor correction

An induction motor uses magnetizing current to convert the electrical energy into mechanical energy. This magnetizing current or reactive current component of the total current lags behind the applied voltage by 90° and results in a phase displacement, i.e. the motor power factor, between the supply voltage and the motor current. As illustrated in Figure 12.11, this reactive current can be taken from the supply utility in which case it will be included in demand charges, or it can be generated by capacitors installed on the demand side of the tariff metering. Ideally, the capacitor should be located as close as possible to the motor; either at the motor terminals, or at the starter. The capacitor

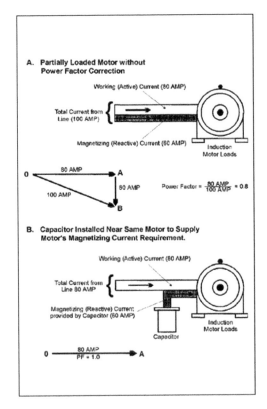

Figure 12.11   Power factor correction.

would be switched by the motor controller. Economics dictate that individual capacitor installations are normally only feasible for motors larger than about 30 kW.

To avoid overvoltage from self-excitation when the motor and capacitor are switched off, the power factor correction should be limited to 0.98. The size of the capacitor cable should be the same as the motor supply cable as both are protected by the same overcurrent protection. It is noted that the capacitor size calculated is the sum of the capacitors required on each of the three phases.

12.11.4 Balance motor phase voltages

Temperatures and losses increase in proportion to the square of the voltage unbalance:

% loss increase = % temperature rise = 2 x (% voltage unbalance)^2.

Thus a 2% voltage unbalance will result in an 8% increase in losses. Motor losses under balanced load conditions can be calculated from motor nameplate (manufacturer's) efficiency.

12.11.5 Energy efficient motors

There are many benefits from operating energy efficient induction motors:

- Lower operating costs

- Lower demand charges

- Lower branch circuit losses

- Improved bearing life

- Lower heat generation, lower operating temperatures

- Longer lifetime

- Improved power factor

- More susceptible to voltage imbalances

- Lower operating temperature

However, energy efficient motors have a higher initial cost than standard motors; in the order of 20% to 25% more. Generally, installing energy efficient motors can only be justified for new installations or where the existing motor must be replaced and where the annual operating hours of the motor will be high. The extra cost usually cannot be justified for replacing a damaged standard motor versus rewinding. However, each case should be examined separately.

12.11.6 Cost implications of motor replacement versus maintenance

There are cost implications that are associated with both the replacement and maintenance of a motor. Whether to replace or maintain a motor depends on which option yields benefits with respect to production disturbance and quality output and efficiency. The electrical motor incurs unnecessary costs if it is replaced before reaching its end-of-life time. The main cost of electrical motors arises because production had to be stopped to maintain the motor. Furthermore, maintenance costs become more necessary when the equipment starts to age because the equipment efficiencies start to deteriorate.

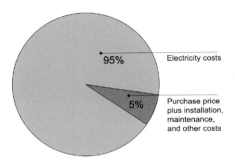

95%   Electricity costs

5%   Purchase price
plus installation,
maintenance,
and other costs

Figure 12.12   End-of-life costs of a motor.

The costs associated with maintaining the electrical motor or equipment are also increased as a result of the electricity the motor uses after it reaches its end-of-life time. Figure 12.12 depicts the costs associated with maintaining a motor that is operating beyond its end-of-life period.

The maintenance of the motor requires a detailed program that makes sure that all the problems experienced by the motor are addressed accordingly. The preventive maintenance program is one of the best ways to make sure the motor is guarded against sudden failure. This program is not costly because it is carried out by the personnel in the maintenance team or operators. This program includes:

• Routine inspection; and

• Lubrication.

Factors such as repair costs, replacement costs and production downtime are considered when deciding whether to replace or repair a motor. Before deciding, do the following:

• Check the cost of repairing an old motor against replacing it with a new one;

• Check whether the costs are viable for the remainder of the end-of-life;

• Identify which parts need to be replaced based on the size of the motor; and

• Verify whether the motor is a standard motor or not.

The costs associated with replacing a motor may be less than compared to operating an existing operating motor, if life cycle costs are taken into consideration.

Chapter 13

Fan Systems

Albert Williams

Institute of Energy Professionals Africa, South Africa

Fans are subject to more misuse, abuse and faulty applications than virtually any other type of equipment. The result of ineffective utilization is high energy cost which can be reduced to yield sizeable savings. The fans provide the motive power to circulate the heating or cooling medium in most of the systems in use today. In selected applications specially designed fans are used for materials handling. The control of the energy consumed by fans is very important to the overall efficiency of the system.

13.1 Fan Types

A fan is a device that causes flow of a gaseous fluid by creating a pressure difference on the medium to be transported. The gaseous fluid transported by the fan is most often air and/or toxic fumes (whereas blowers may transport a mixture of particulates and air).

A blower is similar to a fan, except that it can produce a much higher static pressure. Sometimes higher pressure is achieved by a multistage impeller arrangement. Engineering practice distinguishes fans and blowers for low pressure and centrifugal compressors for high pressure. The demarcation between blowers and compressors is set at a 7% increase in the density of air from blower inlet to blower outlet. The fan and blower definitions and formulae, which assume incompressibility, apply below this demarcation with insignificant error.

There are two basic types of fans. *Centrifugal fans* move air by the centrifugal force that is produced by moving the air between the rotating impeller blades, and by the inertia generated by the velocity of the air leaving the impeller. *Axial fans* move air by the change in velocity of the air passing over the impeller blades. There is no energy added to the air by centrifugal forces.

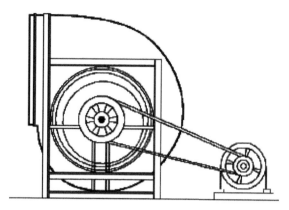

Figure 13.1   Centrifugal fan.

13.1.1 Centrifugal fans

Centrifugal fans are widely used in industry and changes the direction of the airflow perpendicular to the drive shaft. Centrifugal fans are used for higher pressure and low flow applications.

The fan impellers are generally forward curved, straight, or backward curved. The detail design of the impeller is determined by the application of the fan and can have an impact on the fan efficiency and allowable dust loading.

a) Forward curved

Forward curved fans are used in most low pressure systems and run at slower speeds than backwardly inclined wheel types. This type of fan, at constant speed, will show considerable horsepower increase as the system's static pressure decreases, resulting in the possibility of motor overload.

b) Backward Inclined

The backwardly inclined wheel is used in high pressure duct system applications and is non-overloading under normal conditions. This fan will have less blades in the wheel and they may be flat or slightly curved in comparison to the closely spaced blades of the forward curved fan which are never flat. Backward inclined fans will have a higher efficiency in their design range and will usually operate at considerably higher speeds.

c) Airfoil

Airfoil fans have a special backward curved air foil type blade. These fans have the highest efficiencies and operate at very high RPM, from 1750 to

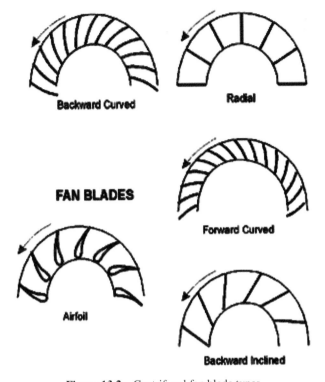

Figure 13.2   Centrifugal fan blade types.

3000. They are found on all system types - low, medium and high pressure; but are also the most expensive and should be installed in clean air streams.

d) Radial blade

Radial blade fans are used for material handling and have self-cleaning blades. These are the least efficient of the centrifugal fans.

13.1.2 Axial fans

Axial fans are differentiated from centrifugal fans, by moving the air parallel to the drive shaft. Axial fans are generally used for low pressure and high flow applications.

a) Propeller fans

The propeller type fan, either direct or belt driven with flat or slightly curved blades, is usually used in places where they operate against very low pressures

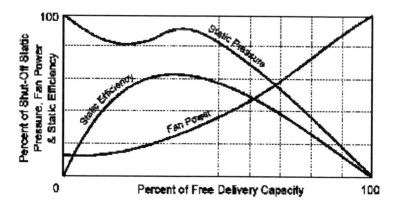

Figure 13.3   Forward curved blade fan performance.

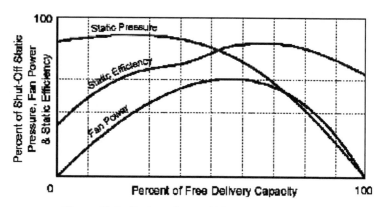

Figure 13.4   Backward curved blade fan performance.

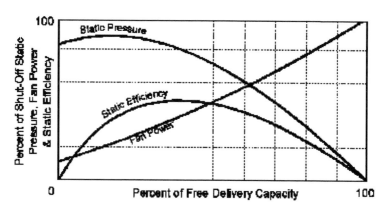

Figure 13.5   Radial blade fan performance.

Table 13.1   Centrifugal fan performance characteristics.

Fan Type	Maximum Flow (1000 L/s)	Maximum Pressure (Pa)	Maximum Power (kW)	Efficiency Range (%)	Users
Forward Curved	100	750	11	72–76	Washroom exhausters Building ventilators Building exhausters Boiler forced draft
Airfoil	425	3500	2240	84–91	Ventilating Air supply
Flat Radial Blade	70	5000	450	70–72	Fluge gas recirculation Hot primary air
Modified Radial Blade	70	4000	450	78–83	Boiler induced draft Handling gas streams with moderate dust loading Sawdust and chips Grain dust
Open Radial Blade	70	4000	450	65–70	Long shavings Rags and wool Papers shreds and stringy material
Backward Inclined Backward Curved	175	2200	450	77–80	Commercial and industrial ventilation Ventilation, air conditioning and heating Boiler forced draft

and are very seldom connected to a duct system. They are mostly used to move large volumes of ventilation air through large openings in the walls or roofs where the outlet has a small pressure loss.

b) Tubeaxial fans

The tubeaxial fans are more efficient than propeller fans and are capable of higher differential pressures. Tubeaxial fans have four to eight airfoil or curved blades. The housings are cylindrical tubes formed so that the running clearance between the blade tips and the tube are minimal. The construction results in tubeaxial fans having higher efficiencies than propeller fans. Ease of installation, reasonable cost and low maintenance are the main advantages of tubeaxial fans. They are used in certain industrial applications such as drying ovens, paint spray booths and fume exhaust systems.

c) Vaneaxial fans

Other axial fans have blades of an air foil design and can be operated against pressure. They are usually direct driven and operate at higher speeds than the propeller fans. On this type of fan, the horsepower curve will rise sharply

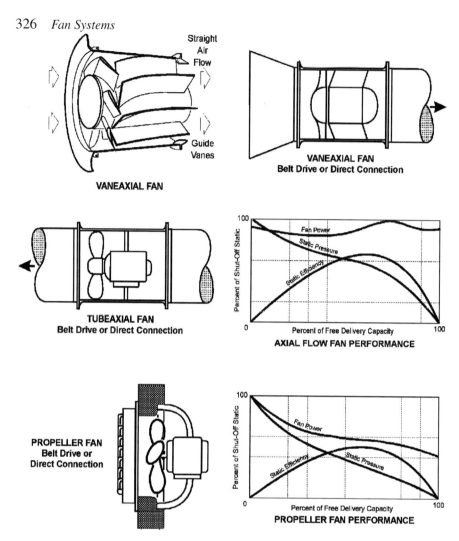

Figure 13.6   Axial fans and their performance curves.

with an increase in speed and/or system resistance, therefore the motor can be easily overloaded.

13.2 Fan Performance

13.2.1 Airflow measurement

The total pressure of an air stream flowing in a duct is the sum of the static pressure exerted on the sidewalls of the duct and the velocity pressure of the moving air. In Figure 13.7, the illustrated pitot tube is a common device for

Table 13.2 Axial fan performance characteristics.

Fan Type	Maximum Flow (1000 L/s)	Maximum Differential Pressure (Pa)	Maximum Power (kW)	Uses
Propeller	57	300	15	Ventilation in factories, power plants, and agricultural buildings Personnel cooling fans or as a low cost ventilator
Tubeaxial	47	500	60	Transferring large volumes of air at low differential pressure. Exhausting spray booths.
Vaneaxial	118	5500	112	Mine ventilation Tunnel ventilation Fume exhaust

measuring the velocity pressure. Measurements should be taken in accordance with traverse details shown. The velocity pressure should be calculated for each traverse position and the readings averaged.

Several factors can affect the accuracy of the field measurements.

- Air flow not at right angles to the measurement plane.

- Non-uniform velocity distribution.

- Irregular cross sectional shape of the duct or passageway.

- Air leaks between the measurement plane and the fan.

Field Performance Measurements, Publication 203 by the Air Movement and Control Association (AMCA) provides information about equipment and procedures for more precise fan performance measurements.

13.2.2 Pressure measurements

The total differential pressure across the fan can be calculated from the measured data:

$$DP_{total} = Ps_{outlet} + Pv_{outlet} - Ps_{inlet} - Pv_{inlet}$$

where:

- *DP = total differential pressure [Pa]*
- *Ps_{outlet} = static pressure at outlet [Pa]*
- *Pv_{outlet} = velocity pressure at outlet (Pa)*
- *Ps_{inlet} = static pressure at inlet [Pa]*
- *Pv_{inlet} = velocity pressure at inlet [Pa]*

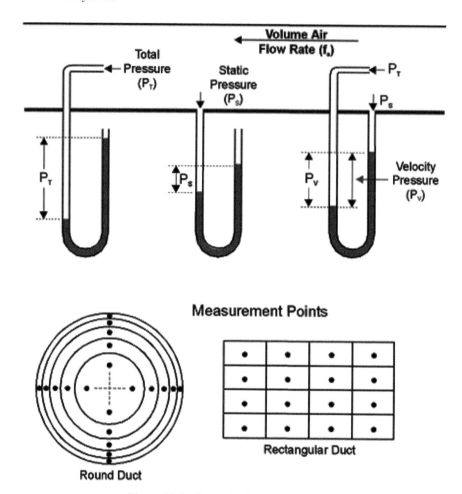

Figure 13.7   Pitot tube flow measurements.

The total fan static differential pressure can also be calculated

$$DP_{static} = Ps_{outlet} - Ps_{inlet} - Pv_{inlet}$$

The effect of inlet and outlet conditions have not been included in these equations however, they provide a reasonable basis for the further calculation of fan power and static efficiency.

13.2.3 Fan power requirement

The work done by a fan can be measured by the quantity of air it delivers, and the pressure against which this air is delivered. The theoretical power (W_t)

required to move a given volume of air (Q) against a total pressure (P$_t$) can be calculated as follows:

$$W_{total} = \frac{Q \times P_{total}}{1000 \times \eta}$$

Where:
- W_{total} = theoretical power required to move air [kW]
- Q = air flow [L/s]
- P_{total} = total pressure against which air is moved [kPa]
- η = fan efficiency

The overall fan efficiency relates the theoretical output against the electrical power supplied to the fan system and includes fan losses, belt drive losses, and motor losses. Note that the efficiency stated by most fan manufacturers is for the fan unit alone; (i.e. the theoretical output as a ratio of the power input to the fan shaft).

13.2.4 Fan performance curves

Fan performance information is available from the manufacturers on all production fans in the form of "fan performance curves". Figure 13.8 shows a typical curve.

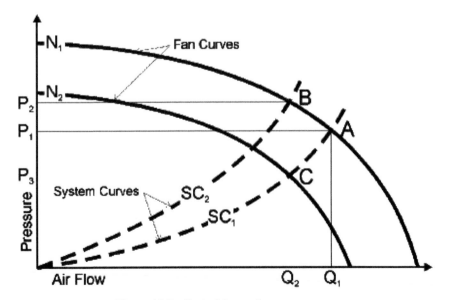

Figure 13.8 Typical fan performance curve.

A fan operates along a performance given by the manufacturer for a particular fan speed. At fan speed N_1, the fan will operate along the N_1 performance curve as shown in the schematic in Figure 13.8. The fan's actual operating point on this curve will depend on the system's performance characteristics.

In any fan system, the resistance to air flow (pressure) increases when the flow of air is increased. The pressure required by a system over a range of flows can be determined and a "system performance curve" can be developed (shown as SC_1). This system curve can then be plotted on the fan curve to show the fan's actual operating point at "A" where the two curves (N_1 and SC_1) intersect. This operating point is at air flow Q1 delivered against pressure P1.

Two methods can be used to reduce air flow. One is to restrict the air flow by partially closing a damper in the system. This action causes a new system performance curve (SC_2) where the required pressure is greater for any given air flow. The fan will now operate at "B" to provide the reduced air flow Q2 against pressure P2.

The air flow could also be decreased by leaving the damper fully open and reducing the fan speed to N_2. The fan would operate at "C" to provide the same Q_2 air flow but at a lower pressure P_3. Reducing the fan speed is a much more efficient method to decrease air flow since less power is required and less energy is consumed.

13.2.5 Density consideration

Fan performance data, unless otherwise specified, is based on dry air at the standard atmospheric pressure of 101.325 kPa (29.921 in. Hg) and a temperature of 20°C. The density at standard test conditions is 1.2 kg/m³.

In most applications, fans process moist air at temperatures and pressures other than standard conditions; therefor the air density must be corrected to obtain the actual fan performance. For fans processing moist air, the moisture content of the airstream is determined by measuring the wet bulb temperature or the dew point temperature or relative humidity. Wet bulb and dry bulb temperatures are most often determined at fan inlet conditions, using a sling thermometer. When the airstream exceeds 82°C the dew-point temperature is more reliable to determine the moisture content. Density, when the dry bulb temperature falls between 5°C and 38°C, may be determined by using the psychrometric chart.

13.2.6 Fan laws

The fans operate under a predictable set of laws concerning speed, power and pressure. A change in RPM speed of any fan will predictably change the pressure rise and power necessary to operate it at the new RPM.

If only the RPM is changed the following will take place:

First law:

i. $\dfrac{Flow_1}{Flow_2} = \dfrac{Speed_1}{Speed_2}$

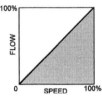

Air volume in cubic meters per second will vary directly as the revolutions per minute (RPM).

Varying the RPM by 10% decreases or increases air delivery by 10%.

Second law:

ii. $\dfrac{Flow_1}{Flow_2} = \dfrac{Speed_1}{Speed_2}$

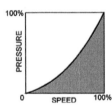

Static pressure will vary as the square of the RPM.

Varying the RPM by 10% decreases or increases the static pressure by 19%.

Third law:

iii. $\dfrac{Flow_1}{Flow_2} = \dfrac{Speed_1}{Speed_2}$

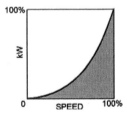

Fan power (kW) will vary as the cube of the RPM.

Varying the RPM by 10% decreases or increases the power requirement by 27%.

13.3 Flow Control

Air handling systems are usually engineered for 100% design flow, but many times could operate with less flow. Let's say that 50% flow is required for some time. What are the options? Operate with constant volume, control the flow with dampers or air inlet vanes, or install one of the adjustable speed drives? Figure 13.7 shows the approximate energy use by different control systems at 50% flow conditions.

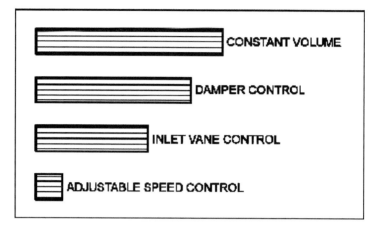

Figure 13.9   Energy used at 50% flow.

Some observations about these methods:

• Constant volume waste energy.

• Dampers may be noisy and have limited turn down.

• Inlet vane control restricts flow even when wide open.

• Variable speed drives can re-adjust the fan to exact needs through speed control. This reduces fan noise and more importantly, saves the most energy. However, will the extra cost be justified?

When the cost of speed control must be justified through energy savings alone, there are several pieces of information required. The most obvious are:

• Fan kW (not the motor kW);

• Cost of electricity (including demand and power factor penalties);

• Installed cost of equipment.

Some less obvious information requirements are:

• Hours / year from 0 - 60% flow

• Hours / year from 60 - 80% flow

• Hours / year from 80 -100% flow

Figure 13.10 shows typical Power vs Flow curves that are based on the % power required by the fan to produce design flow, i.e. 100% design flow

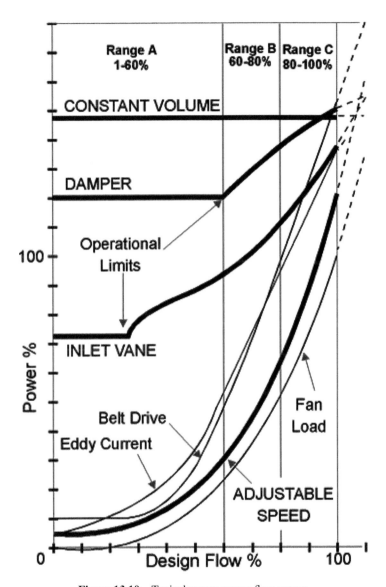

Figure 13.10   Typical power versus flow curves.

requires 100% power at the fan input shaft. These curves are based on a fan which is 10% oversized. The fans are usually oversized because:

• filters clog and leaks develop,

• design engineers are conservative,

• the next smaller sized fan could not meet design flow requirements.

All curves are based on the use of an AC motor with 90% efficiency at full speed, full load, and typical reduction in efficiency for reduced loads. If the preliminary investigation indicates a good potential savings with the use of the variable speed drive, a speed control specialist should be consulted to work out the details.

13.3.1 System effect factors

The fan is normally tested with open inlets and straight duct attached to the outlet; this results in uniform airflow into the fan and efficient static pressure recovery at the fan outlet. If these conditions are not matched in the actual installation, the performance of the fan degrades; this must be allowed for when selecting a fan.

The fans are sensitive to their application in the distribution system. This characteristic is called "system effect" and involves air movement at the inlet and outlet connections of the fan. The changes in direction of flow at the outlet or inlet of the fan will adversely affect the fan performance. Dampers very close to the inlet or outlet, and branch ducts very close to the discharge, will also have an adverse effect on fan performance. Typical conditions are shown in the next figures.

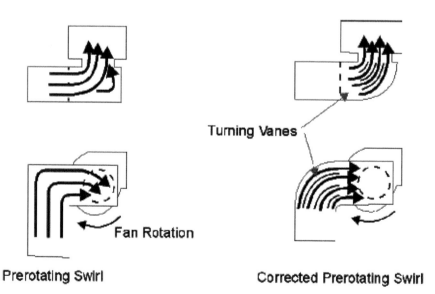

Figure 13.11   Pre-rotating swirl.

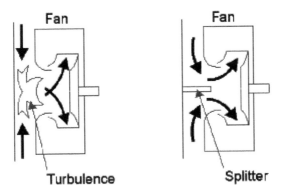

Figure 13.12 Air-splitter.

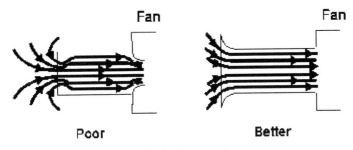

Figure 13.13 Inlet conditions.

13.4 Energy Efficiency Opportunities

Balancing of an air handling system normally requires services of an experienced specialist and is generally performed after the system is installed. For the purpose of this section, it is assumed that, the existing air handling system was initially balanced and has been operating efficiently. Over the years however, the components of the system wear down. The fan wheels get out of balance due to dirt accumulation and start to vibrate and become noisy. Bad bearings on the fan shaft can cause vibration as well as damaged fan wheels. Dirty filters can reduce air flow considerably reducing the motor load and creating false savings. It is evident that the first step in assessing the air handling systems is to bring them up to design operating conditions through proper maintenance.

13.4.1 Maintenance opportunities

• Check fan for correct rotation

• Check and adjust belt drives on fans regularly. Improper alignment of the fan drive sheaves can cause excessive power requirement and

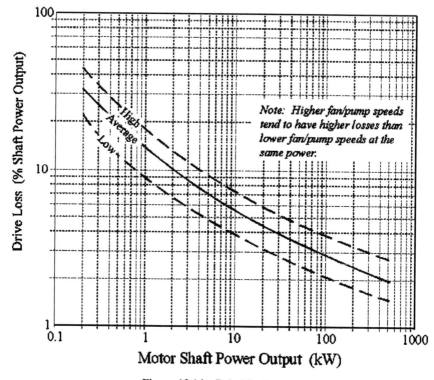

Note: *Higher fan/pump speeds tend to have higher losses than lower fan/pump speeds at the same power.*

Figure 13.14   Belt drive losses.

damage to belts. Properly aligned and tensioned belt drive systems will have mechanical losses as indicated in Figure 13.14. Misaligned and loose belts will have losses of power outside the indicated limits. High speed fans will have losses close to the upper limits of the curve and low speed fans will have losses close to the lower limit of the curve.

- Lubricate fan components according to manufacturer's instructions. Lubrication of fan components, such as couplings, shaft bearings, adjustment linkage and adjustable supports, must be maintained with proper lubricants and at intervals recommended by the manufacturer.

- Clean fan components regularly. Fans, particularly those handling dirty air, should be cleaned regularly to maintain their efficiency. Contamination on blades and housing interior causes higher static pressure loss in the fan, thereby reducing their efficiency.

- Correct excess noise and vibration to ensure smooth and efficient operation. The noise and vibration of the fan can be caused by one or more factors:

  o Fan wheel out of balance

  o Bad bearings

  o Insufficient isolation

  o Misaligned shaft seal

  o Corrosion between shaft and bearing

- Correct leaks. Energy is lost when air leaks from loose connections, improperly sized damper shaft openings and unsealed expansion connections. These and similar conditions at fan suctions and discharges should be corrected.

- Replace loaded air filters. Loaded air filters is a common cause of poor performance in fan systems. Filter manufacturers provide recommendations for the pressure drop at which their filters are considered fully loaded for various air velocities at the inlet to the filters. Filters should be replaced before their pressure drop reaches the loaded values for the particular air velocity. Balancing a system with loaded filters will result in excessive air flow and higher fan energy consumption when the filters are replaced.

- Implement a maintenance programme. A maintenance programme for fans should be tailored to the specific needs of the facility. This type of programme could include the following actions:

  o Daily; observe fan sounds, vibration, bearing temperature, and reading of installed gauges and meters.

  o Monthly; check drive belt alignment, belt tension, and lubricate the fan bearings.

  o Semi-annually; inspect fan shaft seals, check inlet and outlet dampers, check inlet vanes, drain and refill oil lubricated bearings.

  o Annually; check lubrication lines to assure proper movement of grease or oil, check fan auxiliaries, recalibrate all associated instrumentation and carry out performance tests.

  o Replace worn components.

13.4.2 Low cost opportunities

Implemented low cost opportunities are energy efficiency actions that are done once and for which the cost is not considered great. The following are typical energy efficiency measures in this category:

- Reduce fan speed to suit optimum system air flow with balancing dampers in their maximum open position for balanced air distribution.

- Improve fan inlet and outlet duct connections to reduce entrance and discharge losses.

- Shut down fans when not required.

13.4.3 Retrofit opportunities

The retrofit opportunities are the ones for which the implementation cost is significant. Many of the projects in this category, with the exception of replacement of oversized motors, require detailed analysis by specialists. The following are typical energy efficiency measures in the retrofit category:

- Add variable speed motor to allow fan output to follow system requirements.

- Replace outdated equipment with new units sized at optimum efficiency.

- Replace oversized motors.

- Install a microprocessor-based energy management control system.

Chapter 14

Pump Systems

Albert Williams

Institute of Energy Professionals Africa, South Africa

In order to make liquid move through pipes and channels, energy has to be imparted to the liquid. The energy, usually mechanical, provided by prime mover is transferred to the liquid by devices called pumps.

The pumps react within the system almost in the same manner as fans. The pump laws are similar to fan laws. In the case of the fan, the fluid being moved through the system is air or other gases; the pump fluid is water or other liquids. The pumps are usually direct driven by being coupled directly to the shaft of the motor and their speed is not easily changed.

14.1 Pump Types

Pump types can be grouped under two main categories; centrifugal (dynamic) and positive displacement. Figure 14.1 provides a classification of the various types of pumps found in industrial, commercial and institutional facilities.

14.1.1 Centrifugal pumps

Centrifugal pumps are dynamic devices that impart kinetic energy, or energy of motion, to a liquid by the spinning motion of an impeller. The simplified radial flow centrifugal pump shown in Figure 14.2 has rotation vanes that move the liquid outward from the centre of the impeller into the scrolled casing. Some of the kinetic energy is converted to pressure, forcing the liquid out of the discharge.

Centrifugal pumps are used throughout industry in a wide range of applications. *Radial flow* pumps are the most common type of centrifugal.

An *axial flow* centrifugal pump imparts energy to the liquid by a lifting action of propeller shaped vanes, resulting in an axial discharge.

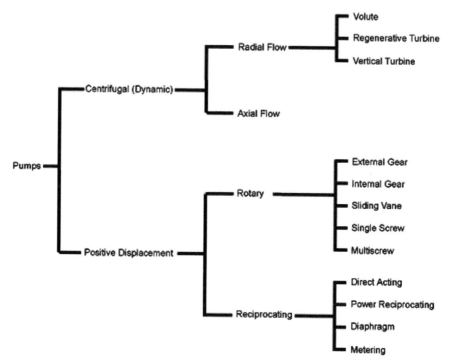

Figure 14.1   Classification of pump types.

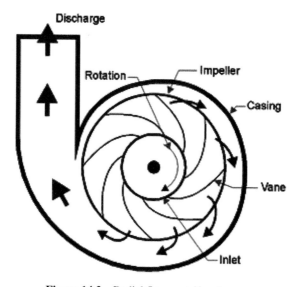

Figure 14.2   Radial flow centrifugal pump.

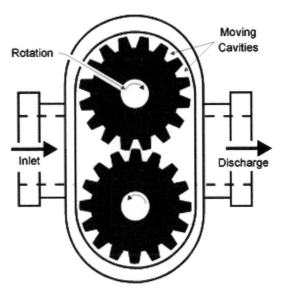

Figure 14.3 Positive displacement pump.

Mixed flow centrifugal pumps provide a combination of radial and axial action. The energy of the liquid is increased by a combination of radial forces and lifting action.

Volute and diffuser pumps are common examples of radial flow centrifugal pumps.

14.1.2 Positive displacement pumps

Positive displacement pumps operate by trapping the liquid in various forms of pump cavities and displacing it to pump discharge. They provide an essentially constant volumetric rate of flow for a particular pump speed independent of pressure difference and liquid characteristics. A typical gear type positive displacement pump is shown in Figure 14.3.

This operation is accomplished either by rotary or reciprocating action. Gear (shown in Figure 14.3) and screw types are common examples of rotary pumps while reciprocating, diaphragm and plunger pumps are common reciprocating types.

14.2 Pump System Fluid Relationships

Pump operating characteristics discussed in this section apply for water at standard conditions of 20°C at sea level. Although the density, and thus the specific gravity of water decreases with an increase in temperature, calculations using standard conditions are considered sufficiently accurate for estimating purposes.

The performance of a pump is defined by the flow and the head. The head differential required across a pump to move a flow of liquid within a system is called the *total dynamic head*. This head will be expressed as "metres of water". Head refers to the equivalent height of fluid column that can be supported by a given pressure. For example, water in a 1m × 1m × 1m vessel would have a volume of 1m³ and a mass of 1,000 kg. The pressure exerted on the vessel bottom (1m² area) would be 1,000 kg/m². This pressure could be converted to kPa (pressure) or it could be expressed as the pressure equivalent to 1 metre water column which is the height of water exerting the pressure. If the same vessel contained another fluid with a different specific gravity, the head would still be 1 metre but the equivalent pressure would change because of the different fluid mass.

The relationship between head and equivalent kPa pressure is:

$$H = \frac{P}{9.81 \times SG}$$

Where:
- H   = head of fluid [m]
- P   = equivalent pressure [kPa]
- SG   = specific gravity of fluid [g/cm³]
- 9.81 = gravitational constant [m/s²]

For water, with a specific gravity of 1.00, 1 metre head equals 9.81 kPa pressure.

The total dynamic head required for a pump depends on friction head, velocity head, and static head:

$$Head_{total} = Head_{friction} + Head_{velocity} + Head_{static}$$

14.2.1 Friction head

Friction head is the friction and inertia pressure losses caused by the resistance to the flow of fluid through a piping system. It depends upon the type, size and length of pipe as well as the type and number of pipe fittings. Generally, friction head is proportional to the square of the flow rate. With no flow, friction losses are zero. Friction head is not related to elevation head or surface pressure.

14.2.2 Velocity head

Velocity head is related to kinetic energy. It is the equivalent head associated with the velocity of a fluid. The relationship between fluid velocity and velocity head is:

$$H_v = \frac{v^2}{2g}$$

Where:
- H_v = velocity head [m]
- v = fluid velocity ([m/s]
- g = 9.81 standard gravitational constant [m/s^2]

Friction losses are caused by a change in velocity head. The velocity head is small for typical systems (normally less than 0.5m) and can be ignored in preliminary calculations for most medium to high pressure system applications. It should always be considered however, in gravity or low-pressure applications.

14.2.3 Static head

Static head is the head across a pump when there is no flow. It is the sum of *elevation head* and *system pressure* differences. Elevation head is the difference in elevation between the liquid surfaces at the source and the destination locations. System pressure is the absolute pressure to which the surface fluids are subjected at the source and destination locations. Static head is the difference between two components, namely: the *static suction head* which is the static pressure at the pump inlet and the *static discharge head* which is the static pressure at the pump outlet.

The various types of head pressures are illustrated in Figure 14.4. In each of the three examples, the friction head depends on the flow as well as the pipe size, length and fittings. In the first system (left), the source and destination liquids are both open to atmosphere so there is no system pressure differential across the pump due to relative surface pressures. The destination level however is much higher than the source so the pump must provide an elevation head differential equal to the height difference between the two levels. The total head differential required across the pump is the combined elevation head and friction loss. Since the source is lower than the pump, the suction head (at pump inlet) is less than atmospheric pressure (negative gauge pressure).

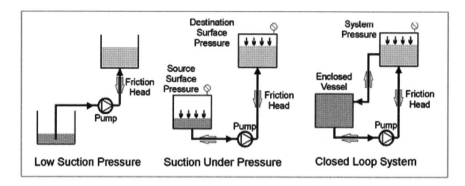

Figure 14.4   Typical head pressures.

In the second system (centre), the pump must offset the system pressure differential between the source and destination liquids and the elevation head differential between the two as well as the friction pressure loss.

In the closed loop system (right), the source and destination liquids are interconnected and there is no system pressure differential across the pump. The source level appears to be lower than the destination but because of the interconnection, the elevation head of the higher level is transferred to the lower and there is no elevation head differential across the pump. The total head differential across the pump on this system is the loss due to friction.

14.3 Pump Performance Characteristics

14.3.1 Pump and system performance curves

The performance of a centrifugal pump can be defined by the following variables: impeller diameter, pump speed, flow rate, head, power, and fluid characteristics. Manufacturers' data on these performance is usually available in graph form with a separate graph being provided for each pump type, pump size, and pump speed, based on water as the pumped fluid. As shown below, the graph is usually presented with flow rate along the horizontal axis and total head along the vertical axis.

The pump's performance with a specific impeller size is shown as a continuous curve between no-flow condition (highest head) and full-flow (zero head). This is the pump's performance curve for a specific impeller size. Other lines are shown for other impeller diameters. Normally the manufacturer recommends that only the middle region of these lines be used since the outside areas at each end of the curve may provide unstable operating conditions. In addition, the graph will indicate efficiency lines and the area of

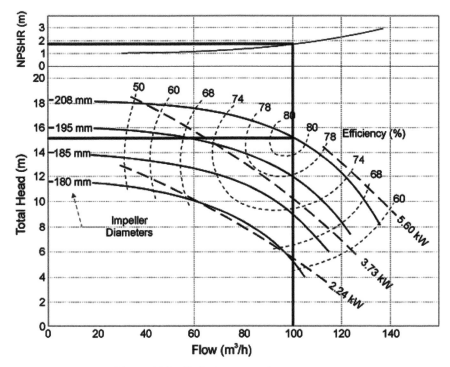

Figure 14.5 Typical pump performance curves.

maximum efficiency as well as power requirement curves. Most graphs also provide a means of determining the Net Positive Suction Head Requirement (NPSHR). As indicated in Figure 14.5, the most efficient operation (80%) is with a 208 mm impeller diameter at 100 m³/h flow rate with 15 m total head. The power requirement is approximately 5.4 kW. The NPSHR at this operating point is 1.7 m head.

The performance variables for a centrifugal pump are related by the Affinity Laws which manufacturers use to develop the fan performance graph. Similar to the basic fan laws, the pump affinity laws presented in Table 14.1, relate the performance variables for any dynamically similar series of pumps. The variables are: impeller size (D), rotational speed (N), fluid density (δ), volume flow rate (Q), static head (Ps) or total head (Pt) and power (W). These laws may be applied to condition changes in a system where the system performance curve is not altered. They may not be used where piping changes produces a new system performance curve. Also, these laws should not be used for analysing systems with a significant static head component unless the change is small, say less than 10%.

Table 14.1   Centrifugal pump affinity laws

Variable N (D and δ constant)

$$Q_1 = Q_2 \times \left(\frac{N_1}{N_2} \right)$$

$$P_1 = P_2 \times \left(\frac{N_1}{N_2} \right)^2$$

$$W_1 = W_2 \times \left(\frac{N_1}{N_2} \right)^3$$

Variable D (N and δ constant)

$$Q_1 = Q_2 \times \left(\frac{D_1}{D_2} \right)$$

$$P_1 = P_2 \times \left(\frac{D_1}{D_2} \right)^2$$

$$W_1 = W_2 \times \left(\frac{D_1}{D_2} \right)^3$$

Variable δ (N and D constant)

$$W_1 = W_2 \times \left(\frac{\delta_1}{\delta_2} \right)$$

where:
- D = impeller diameter
- N = pump speed
- δ = fluid density
- Q = flow rate
- P = total head
- W = power.

Note the laws relating to variable impeller diameter apply only to changing the diameter of a given impeller within a given pump. They do not apply for geometrically similar impellers.

Positive displacement pumps provide a constant volumetric flow, independent of pressure and fluid characteristics. A pressure relief device is normally installed at the discharge to limit the total head to the maximum rating of the pump. Manufacturer's performance data for these pumps is usually in tabular form listing flow rate, total head and power. Positive displacement pumps are often used for liquids other than water and the assistance of a qualified expert may be required for pump selection in these applications.

The power requirement for these pumps is affected by flow rate, pressure, and fluid characteristics. The affinity laws do **not** apply to positive displacement pumps. Table 14.2 indicates the performance relationships with changes in total head, pump speed or fluid density.

Table 14.2 Positive displacement pump laws

$$Q_1 = Q_2 \times \left(\frac{N_1}{N_2}\right)$$

$$W_1 = W_2 \times \left(\frac{P_1}{P_2}\right)$$

$$W_1 = W_2 \times \left(\frac{Q_1}{Q_2}\right)$$

$$W_1 = W_2 \times \left(\frac{\delta_1}{\delta_2}\right)$$

14.3.2 Pump power requirements

Assuming the pump is 100% efficient, the *theoretical, absorbed* or *ideal* power (W_t) required to move a given flow of liquid (Q) against a given total pressure or *head* (H_t) can be determined by the following relationship:

$$W_{theoretical} = \frac{Q \times H_t}{102}$$

Where:
- W_t = *theoretical or absorbed power required to move water at 100% efficiency [kW]*
- Q = *given liquid flow rate [liters / second]*
- P_t = *given total pump pressure or head [m]*
- *102* = *conversion of units*

The above relationship can be expanded to take into account the pump efficiency (η_p), belt drive efficiency (η_d) and motor efficiency (η_m) as follows (efficiencies expressed in decimal form):

$$W_{theoretical} = \frac{Q \times H_t}{102 \times \eta_p \times \eta_d \times \eta_m}$$

The overall efficiency (η) for the pump unit is expressed as the ratio of output to input as follows:

$$\eta_{overall} = \frac{Power\,output}{Power\,input} = \frac{Theoretical\,power}{Actual\,power}$$

The efficiency stated by most pump manufacturers pertains to the pump unit alone and is based on the theoretical power output from the pump as a ratio to the power delivered to the pump shaft. Other losses must be considered in determining the overall efficiency of the pump which would relate the theoretical power output to the actual power input from the electrical supply. Electric motor efficiency, which relates the electrical input supplied to the motor with the power delivered to the motor shaft, is discussed in section 12: MOTORS AND DRIVES. Figure 14.6 provides an estimate of belt drive efficiency which relates shaft power between the motor and the pump.

In energy system optimization work, the most frequent requirement is to estimate the change in power (and energy usage) that will result from changes in head or flow. Ideally, performance curves are available for the pump and the performance curve can be determined for the system and superimposed on the pump curve graph. The existing and proposed operating points can then be located from the graph where the pump and system performance curves intersect. Changes in total head, flow rate and power can then be read directly from the graph.

Performance curves are often not available for the pump and the calculations required to derive the system performance curve can be very time consuming. In these situations, the change in power and energy usage can be estimated for centrifugal pumps by using the affinity laws presented in Table 14.1. It must be remembered however, that the new operating point derived from the affinity laws may not coincide with the system performance curve. Thus, the actual operating point (on the system curve) may be slightly different than the derived operating point. The error, however, is usually not significant for minor changes in pump settings.

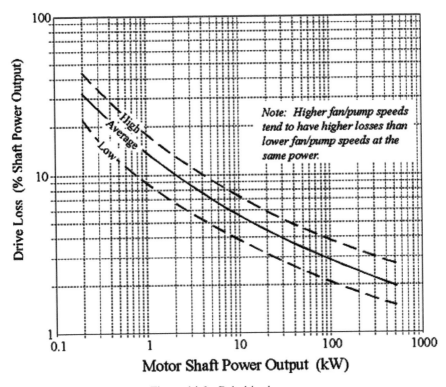

Figure 14.6 Belt drive losses.

14.3.3 Multiple pump systems

Two or more pumps may be installed either in "series" or "parallel". To establish the combined pump curve for pumps in series, the combined total head is the sum of individual pump heads at equal flows. The flow rate through each pump is the same. To establish the combined pump curve for pumps in parallel, the combined flow is the sum of individual pump flows at points of equal head. The head increase across each pump is identical. Refer to Figure 14.7.

14.3.4 Cavitation and NPSH

Cavitation in centrifugal pump occurs when pressure in the suction line falls below vapour pressure, vapour forms and moves along with the liquid. These vapour bubbles (cavities) collapse when they reach higher pressure areas causing noise and vibration. The larger the pump, the greater the noise and vibration. If a pump is operated under cavitation conditions for a sufficient length of time, impeller vane pitting will occur. The violent collapse of

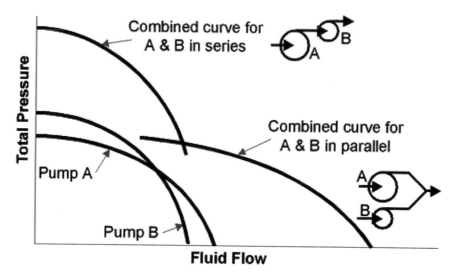

Figure 14.7   Combined curves for multiple pumps.

vapour bubbles forces liquid into vapour filled pores of the vane metal at high velocity. This produces high-intensity surge pressures on small areas which can exceed the tensile strength of the metal and actually blast out particles giving the metal a spongy appearance. The noise and vibration can also cause bearing failure, shaft breakage and other fatigue failure in the pump.

The other major effect of cavitation is a reduction in the efficiency of the pump. The reduction in efficiency may occur before vapour pressure is reached, particularly in petroleum-based liquids when ethers and entrained air are liberated. In general, cavitation indicates insufficient available Net Positive Suction Head available (NPSH$_a$). Excessive suction pipe friction combined with low static suction head and high temperature contribute to this condition. If the system cannot be changed it may be necessary to change to a different pump with low NPSH requirements. Larger pumps may require a booster pump to add pressure to the available NPSH.

NPSH$_a$ is calculated using the following equation:

$$NPSH_a = H_a \pm H_z - H_f + H_v + H_{vap}$$

Where:
- H_a = Atmospheric pressure (Includes tank pressure if tanks are sealed)
- H_z = Vertical elevation in meters
- H_f = friction loss through the suction pipe and fittings (Always negative)

- H_v = Velocity head at pump suction (Generally negligible and can be ignored)
- H_{vap} = Vapor pressure of water (Pressure required to keep water in its liquid state)

In order to avoid cavitation, $NPSH_a$ should be approximately 3% more than the rated $NPSH_r$ (Net Positive Suction Head required).

14.4 Pump Maintenance

The type of shaft seals used on centrifugal pumps and quality of maintenance performed can have a significant effect on the overall efficiency of the pump. Friction at the shaft seal uses a portion of the shaft input power and the leakage past the seal represents a loss of pumped liquid. The most common types are *packing gland* and *mechanical seal.*

14.4.1 Packing glands

Packing glands seals consist of multiple rings of flexible, low friction packing material compressed to achieve intimate contact with the shaft and pump casing. Forced lubrication is usually provided between the shaft and the packing rings. Lubrication methods include controlled leakage of pumped liquid, forced flushing by a separate liquid and controlled force feeding of oil and grease. In all cases the power used, the liquid lost, and the maintenance life of the seal depends on skilled adjustment of the retaining ring pressure on the packing rings. This packing has a low first cost but a high operating and

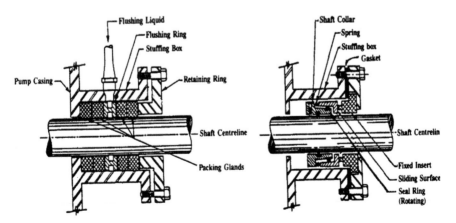

Figure 14.8   Typical pump seals.

maintenance cost. *As a rule of thumb, the power usage by packing glands is about six times greater than for mechanical seals.*

14.4.2 Mechanical seals

Mechanical seals consist of spring-loaded rings of rigid, low friction material sliding against finely finished mating surfaces. The seal rings may be made of a self-lubricating material or the seal surfaces may be lubricated by slight leakage of the pumped liquid. The type of seal has a relatively high cost but their power consumption is much lower than packing gland seals (see Figure 14.9), resulting in significant operating cost savings. Special types of mechanical seals are available for retrofitting existing pumps that have packing glands. Mechanical seals can be economically justified for most pumps but they have been used most frequently for pumps handling valuable or hazardous liquids.

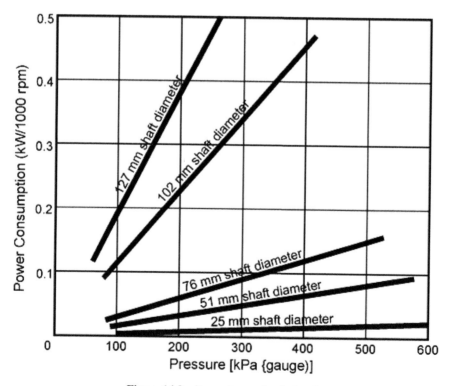

Figure 14.9   Power for mechanical seals

14.5 Energy Efficiency Measures

14.5.1 Housekeeping - Maintenance

Implemented housekeeping opportunities are energy management actions that are done on a regular basis, but never less than once a year.

Check packing glands

Pump packing glands should be checked periodically for correct adjustment and tightness. Depending upon the packing material, liquid temperature, shaft speed and allowable liquid leakage, an optimum tightening of the packing may be established by monitoring the rate of dripping from the packing. Pump and packing material manufacturers can provide guidance on packing tightness for specific applications. With few exceptions, packing must leak slightly for lubrication or excessive energy will be used and mechanical damage to the shaft will occur.

Check critical tolerances

The efficiency of a pump is affected by the amount of leakage past the impeller from the discharge to the suction. Some pumps have replaceable wear rings with small clearances between moving surfaces to minimize leakage and maintain serviceability. Mechanical seals are used with critical tolerances to stop leakage and to stop air from being drawn into the liquid flow. These tolerances can be affected by erosion of the impeller and wear rings when pumping liquids that contain the abrasive particles. The clearances and surfaces must be checked and maintained periodically to keep the pump efficiency high.

Check and adjust drives

Open drives, such as belts and flexible couplings, provide long service when properly designed and maintained. The following actions should be carried out regularly:

- Maintain alignment of pulleys and couplings.

- Check tension of belts.

- Lubricate bearing.

- Replace or repair damaged belts, pulleys, clutches, drive keys and couplings.

Proper tensioning for various types of belts is usually described in handbooks and catalogues available from component manufacturers.

Clean pump impeller

Pumps, particularly those moving dirty liquids, should be regularly cleaned to maintain the efficiency of the pump. Refuse collected on impeller and the housing of the pump causes higher static pressure losses in the pump itself, reducing its efficiency.

Shut down pump when not required

Savings in both energy and maintenance cost can be achieved by shutting down pumps when liquid flow is not required in the system. Heating water circulating pumps can normally be shut down during the summer months and process cooling water pumps can often be shut down when the process is not operating.

Establish maintenance program

A maintenance program for pumps should follow manufacturer's recommendations and be tailored to the specific needs of the facility. The program could include the following actions:

- Daily; monitor pump sound, bearing temperature, stuffing box or mechanical seal leakage, and gauge and meter readings.

- Semi-annually; check free movement of the stuffing box glands, inspect the packing, check the pump and driver alignment, drain and refill oil

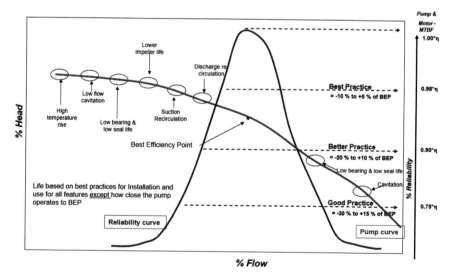

Figure 14.10   Effects on pump life from variability from its Best Efficiency Point (BEP).

lubricated bearings, check quantity and consistency of the grease in grease lubricated bearings and lubricate the gland bolts.

- Annually; clean, inspect and lubricate bearings and their seals; examine the packing and the shaft sleeve; recalibrate all associated instrumentation, and check pump performance against the design ratings.

- Replace worn components when tests indicate loss of performance.

- Adjust impeller clearance on pumps when tests indicate loss of performance power requirement and repair records on each pump.

Maintenance personnel must have the capability and experience to service, repair and troubleshoot the pumps and distribution systems. Training should be provided covering new equipment, changes to the facility and new procedures.

14.5.2 Retrofit opportunities

Many of the opportunities in this category may require detailed analysis which should be carried out by specialists. The following are typical examples in the retrofit category:

- Install variable speed controller on pumps to better match liquid flow demand (A predominantly friction head system is better suited than a predominantly static head system for the installation of a VSD.).

- Replace outdated equipment with new units sized at optimum efficiency.

- Replace oversized motors.

- Install microprocessor energy management control system.

Chapter 15

Compressed Air Systems

Albert Williams

Institute of Energy Professionals Africa, South Africa

While an important energy consumer in industrial facilities, compressed air systems are also found in buildings, for example to supply air to pneumatic control systems.

Compressed air has the most expensive energy conversion in industry, and it is rare that enough attention is paid to the maintenance that these systems require. As typical compressed air system efficiencies range from 5 to 15 % the cost of energy in the form of compressed is at 5 – 8 times that of electricity. Small changes to the systems can provide large savings opportunities with quick payback periods. With the high cost of the delivered energy form, actions to reduce the end-use are most important.

Compressed air systems are widely used in industry, accounting for some 10% of all industrial electrical power consumption, and approximately 18% of industrial electric motor consumption. Electricity is the largest cost in producing compressed air. Initial capital costs are usually exceeded by electricity costs after a short period, about one-year (depending on the type of compressor, manufacturer and the electricity charges). For a lifecycle of 10 years, the cumulative costs of compressed air comprise of 10% maintenance, 10% capital and 80% energy.

Life cycle costing should be used because the lifetime electricity costs are much greater than the initial costs of the compressors. Overall system efficiency should be considered and not only the motor or compressor efficiency. To achieve this least cost solution for compressed air systems, users should select systems based on appropriate economics to determine compression, treatment, distribution, control and monitoring.

There are many reasons why compressed air as a source of power is preferred over other forms of energy. It is clean to use, can be stored, and

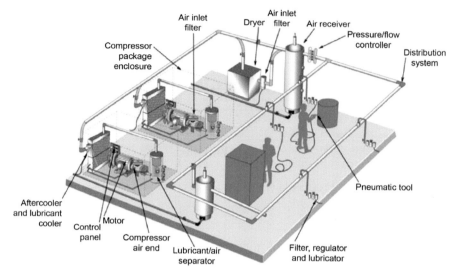

Figure 15.1   Typical generic industrial compressed air system.

does not pose a health or fire hazard. There is a tendency to treat it as a free commodity. It is not a cheap power source and its mismanagement can result in significant energy waste.

The factors most commonly found responsible for demand side energy loss are air leaks, inappropriate use of compressed air, and artificial demand – when system pressure is higher than required for productive end use. A properly designed and maintained compressed air system can contribute significantly to improving the energy efficiency of an operation.

Compressed air systems comprise three main areas:

- Compressed air supply (or generation) (i.e. compressor, separator, aftercooler, primary storage tanks, pressure-flow control valve),

- Distribution and treatment (piping, distribution network, drying, filtration, secondary storage tanks)

- Compressed air demand (end-users, equipment service lines).

15.1 Supply Side

Air Compressors are mechanical devices which draw in air and discharge it at a higher pressure, usually into a piping system or storage tank. Compressors can be described as either displacement (using pistons or rotors) or dynamic (using impellers or blades). In the former group,

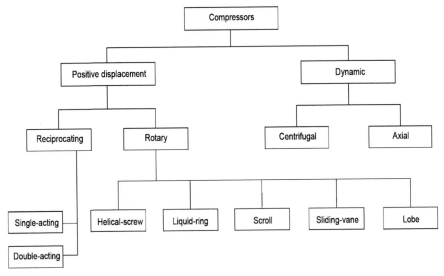

Figure 15.2   Categories and types of compressors.

reciprocating and rotary screw compressors are the most common types utilized. Although compressors are driven by a variety of prime movers, including internal combustion and steam engines, in this text only electric motor drives are considered.

The displacement compressors are further divided into rotary and reciprocating compressors. The reciprocating compressors are either single-acting or double-acting compressors, while rotary compressors can be helical-screw, liquid-ring, scroll, sliding-vane or lobe compressors.

In a positive-displacement compressor, the volume of the compressor chamber is mechanically reduced to increase the pressure of the air or gas. The dynamic compressors supply velocity energy to the gas through its high-speed rotating impellers. The impellers convert the velocity energy into pressure energy.

Compressed air is costly because of the power and energy required to operate the compressor. The required power is for the most part determined by the system pressure, the air initial temperature and pressure, and the integrity of the system. All these factors can be controlled within given constraints to Minimize energy costs.

The higher the pressure of the compressed air required, the more expensive it is to deliver. For a system at 7 barg, *an additional six percent in operating energy costs is required for every additional 1.0 bar in operating pressure.*

15.1.1 Specific power for various compressor types

While the basic compressor design is a significant factor in determining compressor efficiency, other design factors also affect the full load specific power of an air compressor. Factors include:

*   Drive motor efficiency

*   Mechanical drive losses; e.g. belt drive, gear drive

*   Compressor speed and frictional loss

*   Internal leakage (slippage) and resultant volumetric efficiency.

*   Internal compressor valves, port size, airflow passages, and pipe size.

As a result, with-in and compressor type there is a range of specific power depending on the individual manufacturer's compressor design and operating characteristics. When considering compressor performance, it is necessary to contact the compressor manufacturer for rated performance and factory test performance data.

Specific power measurements above as an indication of air compressor efficiency applies only to the full load operating condition. That is to say the compressor is delivering full rated capacity at the rated discharge pressure.

In multiple compressed air systems, most compressors operate at less than full load rated capacity for the majority of time. Air compressors are equipped with capacity control regulation. Most capacity controls respond to air pressure at the compressor discharge. When the air pressure reaches a predetermined set point the compressor stops producing air. System pressure will usually then fall until it reaches a lower pressure set point and the air compressor again begins compressing air. Other capacity control systems operate in a progressive fashion. As discharge pressure increases the

Table 15.1   Specific power for various compressor types.

Specific Power for Various Compressor Types (typical range)			
Volumetric flow rate (free air delivery)	kW / m³ / min	kW / 100 l/sec	kW / 100 cfm
Receip. Single Acting (sgl stage)	7.8 – 8.5	47 – 51	22 – 24
Receip. Single Acting (2 stage)	6.4 – 8.1	38 – 49	18 – 23
Receip. Double Acting (sgl stage)	8.5 – 10.2	51 – 61	24 – 29
Receip. Double Acting (2 stage)	5.3 – 5.7	32 – 34	15 – 16
Lubricated Screw (sgl stage)	6.0 – 7.8	36 – 47	17 – 22
Lubricated Screw (2 stage)	5.7 – 6.7	34 – 40	16 – 19
Lubricated Free Screw (2 stage)	6.4 – 7.8	38 – 47	18 – 22
Centrifugal (3 stage)	5.7 – 7.1	34 – 42	16 – 20

compressor progressively reduces it output. If pressure. If discharge air pressure decreases the compressor will progressively increase its delivered air-flow until it reaches full load capacity.

15.1.2 Positive displacement compressors

a) Rotary screw positive displacement compressors

The most common type of rotary compressor is the helical twin screw-type (also known as rotary screw or helical lobe). Male and female screw rotors mesh trapping air and reducing the volume of the air along the rotors to the air discharge point.

Rotary screw compressors have comparatively low initial cost, compact size, low weight, and require less maintenance. Rotary screw compressors are available up to 1000 kW and may be air or water cooled. Less common rotary compressors include the single screw, the rotary vane, the liquid ring and the scroll-type.

b) Reciprocating compressors

Reciprocating compressors have pistons and work like bicycle pumps. A piston, driven through a crankshaft and connecting rod by an electric motor, reduces the volume in the cylinder occupied by the air or gas, compressing it

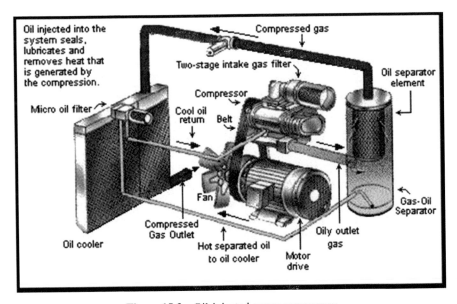

Figure 15.3 Oil-injected screw compressor.

to a higher pressure. Single-acting compressors have a compression stroke in only one direction, while double-acting units provide a compression stroke as the piston moves in each direction.

Smaller compressors are usually mounted on air receivers. It is possible to get non-lubricated piston compressors for duties such as food, air conditioning and pharmaceutical production. However, in these cases it is more common to use an oil-injected compressor with filtration to remove the oil carried over from the compressor.

15.1.3 Dynamic compressors

These compressors raise the pressure of air or gas by imparting velocity energy and converting it to pressure energy. Dynamic compressors include centrifugal and axial types.

Each impeller, rotating at high speed, imparts primarily radial flow to the air or gas, which then passes through a volute or diffuser to convert the residual velocity energy to pressure energy. Some large manufacturing plants use centrifugal compressors for general plant air, and, in some cases, plants use other compressor types to accommodate demand load swings while the centrifugal compressors handle the base load.

Mixed flow compressors have impellers and rotors, which combine the characteristics of both axial and centrifugal compressors. Axial compressors consist of a rotor with multiple rows of blades and a matching stator with rows of stationary vanes. The rotating blades impart velocity energy, primarily in an axial plane. The stationary vanes then act as a diffuser to convert the residual velocity energy into pressure energy. This type of compressor is restricted to very high flow capacities and generally has relatively high compression efficiency.

For efficient operation, it is important to state the site ambient temperatures and pressures, and the design flow and pressure when specifying dynamic compressors. The energy requirements and control ranges of these compressors are seriously affected by operation outside design conditions.

Generally, for energy efficiency at full and part load, the more stages of compression the better. Centrifugal machines are more energy efficient than screw compressor for applications over approximately 60 m³/min. Centrifugal compressors are very reliable and efficient if properly applied and maintained.

15.1.4 Compressor lubrication

Displacement compressors can either be lubricant free or lubricant injected. The purpose of lubrication or oil in a compressor is to provide lubrication, to seal the gap between rotors and casing, to cool down, and to clean and absorb some of the particles entrained in the intake air. It is actually not uncommon to have the compressed air from a lubricant injected compressor be of a lower particle level than lubricant free compressors.

Irrespective of which compressor is used, it is still vital that appropriate filtration is in place to deliver the required quality level at the end user. Lubricant-free rotary screw and reciprocating compressors usually have higher capital costs, lower efficiency due to higher rotor/piston speeds and more friction, and higher maintenance costs than lubricant injected compressors.

15.1.5 Inlet air temperature

Reducing the temperature of the compressor intake air will reduce the compressor power required to achieve the same air discharge pressure and capacity. This can often be accomplished by simply installing an air intake duct from outside the building instead of drawing air from the warmer plant environment.

The location of the air compressors on site can have a bearing on the amount of energy used by the compressor. Cool, clean, dry intake air will lead to more efficient compression. Where possible, air should be taken from outside the building because its temperature will be lower. Lower temperature air is denser and the mass of air that can be compressed by the machine is increased. The air inlet should be protected against the entry of rain and wind-blown dust, which would clog filters and waste energy.

Ducting between air intake and compressor should be short, straight and have a generous diameter. The condition of the air entering the compressor is extremely important, since fouling of inlet filters and high ambient air temperatures can result in significant energy wastage. For every 4°C drop in intake temperature, there is a 1% increase in efficiency. For every 25-mbar pressure lost at the inlet, the compressor efficiency is reduced by 2%.

15.1.6 Inlet air pressure

If the pressure of the inlet air can be raised (i.e. reduced pressure drop at inlet), there will be a decrease in the required compression power for the same air flow capacity and discharge pressure. This can be accomplished in various ways, such as replacing intake filters, or revising ductwork. For every 25-mbar pressure lost at the inlet, the compressor efficiency is reduced by 2%.

15.1.7 Compressor control

Compressed air system controls match the compressed air supply with system demand (although not always in real-time) and are one of the most important determinants of overall system energy efficiency. Proper control is essential to efficient system operation and high performance. The objective of any control strategy is also to shut off unneeded compressors or delay bringing on additional compressors until needed.

All units that are on should be run at full load, except for one unit for trimming. (This is because the energy costs per unit of compressed air rise markedly when the compressors are running at less than full load.) Compressor systems are typically comprised of multiple compressors delivering air to a common plant air header.

The combined capacity of these machines is sized, at a minimum, to meet the maximum plant air demand. This is not necessarily the sum of all the maximum machinery demand, as equipment loading may be at different intervals. System controls are almost always needed to reduce the output of the individual compressor(s) during times of lower demand.

Compressed air systems are usually designed to operate within a fixed pressure range and to deliver a volume of air, which varies with system demand. System pressure is monitored and the control system decreases compressor output when the pressure reaches a predetermined level. Compressor output is then increased again when the pressure drops to a lower predetermined level. The difference between these two pressure levels is called the control range.

In the past, individual compressor controls and non-supervised multiple machine systems were slow and imprecise. This resulted in wide control ranges and large pressure swings. As a result of these large swings, individual compressor pressure control set points were established to maintain pressures higher than needed. This ensured that swings would not go below the minimum requirements for the system. Today, faster and more accurate microprocessor-based system controls with tighter control ranges allow for a drop in the system pressure set points. This advantage is that a precise control system is able to maintain a much lower average pressure without going below the minimum system requirements. Narrower variations in pressure not only use less energy, but also improve production quality control.

Caution needs to be taken when lowering average system header pressure because large, sudden changes in demand can cause the pressure to drop below minimum requirements, leading to improper functioning of equipment. With careful matching of system controls and storage capacity, these problems can be avoided.

The type of compressor being used largely determines the type of control specified for a given system and the facilities' demand profile. If a system has a single compressor with a very steady demand, a simple control system may be appropriate. On the other hand, a complex system with multiple compressors, varying demand, and many types of end-uses will require a more sophisticated strategy. In any case, careful consideration should be given to both compressor and system control selection because they can be the most important factors affecting system performance and efficiency. For energy efficiency, it is important to consider the control of individual machines and the way in which multiple installations meet the demand in terms of flow and pressure requirements. For a relatively low capital outlay, a modern compressor control system can save on average 18%, and up to 57% of the total generation costs. And, in some cases improved pressure control will also result in productivity gains.

15.1.8 Individual compressor control

a) Rotary screw compressor control

Rotary screw compressor manufacturers have developed a number of different types of part-load control strategies in order to deliver a reduced amount of air during periods of reduced demand:

- Load/unload, which open and closes the inlet valve in response to increases or reductions in air demand

- Inlet valve modulation, which throttles the inlet valve

- Variable displacement control, which reduces the effective length and area of the rotor in which compression takes place

- Variable Speed Drive (VSD), which changes the motor frequency or similar technologies

Start/stop is the simplest control available and can be applied to either reciprocating or rotary screw compressors. The motor driving the compressor is turned on or off in response to the discharge pressure of the machine. Typically, a simple pressure switch provides the motor start/stop signal. This type of control should not be used in an application that has frequent cycling because starts will cause the motor to overheat and other compressor components to require more frequent maintenance.

Automatic dual control stops the compressor after a period of no-load running (e.g. end of production day or weekend), usually 15 - 45 minutes, and then automatically restarts the machine on a demand for air. The offload running time is essential, unless a soft starter is fitted, to protect the drive motor from too many starts. Soft start controls are available which provide a variable start time with Minimized starting currents, and which eliminate current surges thereby preventing motor damage.

Load/unload control allows the motor to run continuously but unloads the compressor when the discharge pressure is adequate. An unloaded rotary screw compressor will consume 15 - 35% of full load power when it is unloaded while delivering no useful work. As a result, some load/unload control schemes can be inefficient.

Inlet valve modulation (throttling) control allows the output of a compressor to be varied to meet flow requirements. Throttling is usually accomplished by closing down the inlet valve, thereby restricting inlet air to the compressor. This control method, when applied to displacement compressors, is an inefficient means of varying compressor output. Rotary screw machines are often fitted with both two-step unloading and modulating control with a manual or automatic change over switch.

Variable displacement control on rotary screw compressors can vary their compression volumes (ratio) using sliding or turn valves. These are to provide more accurate pressure control with improved part-load efficiency.

Using Variable Speed Drive (VSD) motors to drive piston and screw compressors offers many control and efficiency advantages. In the past costs have been prohibitive; however, new advances in electronics and control gear are making these systems more popular. Care should be taken not to reduce the compressor speed to the extent that it is inadequately lubricated. It is not recommended to install a VSD on an already existing fixed speed machine, due to the inherited complexities. Rather consider purchasing a compressor which has a built-in VSD as manufactured by the OEM.

b) Piston compressor control

Piston machines with two or three-step inlet suction valve unloaders, on- or off-line inlet valves, or five-step clearance pocket unloading, give the best efficiencies at part loads. Piston, vane and screw machines with variable inlet throttle valves that modulate over a close pressure range are not efficient on low loads, because they are positive displacement machines and throttling causes an increase in compression ratio.

Some compressors are designed to operate in two or more partially loaded conditions. With such a control scheme, output pressure can be closely controlled without requiring the compressor to start/stop or load/unload. Reciprocating compressors are designed as two-step (start/stop or load/unload), three-step (0%, 50%, 100%) or five-step (0%, 25%, 50%, 75%,

100%) control. These control schemes generally exhibit an almost direct relationship between motor power consumption and loaded capacity.

c) Centrifugal compressor control

Similar to inlet valve modulation on displacement compressors, a control scheme applied to centrifugal compressors also throttles the inlet either via a butterfly valve or inlet guide vanes. When used on centrifugal compressors, more efficient results are obtained, particularly with the use of inlet guide vanes, which direct the air in the same direction as the impeller inlet. The amount of capacity reduction is limited by the potential for surge and minimum throttling capacity.

Centrifugal compressors are dynamic machines and behave efficiently on part load. Output is normally reduced by modulation to 70% of the design flow. For installations where the demand is sometimes less than this, machines with automatic dual control systems should be installed to avoid wasting energy due to the blowing off of pressurized air at part loads.

Inlet guide vanes are preferable to butterfly valve inlet throttles, because they improve the part load efficiency and turndown range, particularly at off-design inlet conditions. VSD's are unsuitable for centrifugal compressors unless specifically designed for the purpose.

15.1.9 Multiple compressor control

By definition, system controls control the actions of the multiple individual compressors that supply air to the system. Prior to the introduction of automatic system controls, compressor systems were set by a method known as cascading set points. Individual compressor operating pressure set points were established to either add or subtract compressor capacity to meet system demand. The additive nature of this strategy results in large control ranges.

The objective of an effective, automatic system, control strategy is to match system demand with compressors operated at or near their maximum efficiency levels. This can be accomplished in a number of ways, depending on fluctuations in demand, available storage, and the characteristics of the equipment supplying and treating the compressed air.

Sequencers are, as the name implies, devices used to regulate systems by sequencing or staging individual compressor capacity to meet system demand. Sequencers are referred to as single master control units because all compressor, operating decisions are made and directed from the master unit. Sequencers control compressor systems by taking individual compressor capacity on and off-line in response to monitored system pressure (demand).

The control system typically offers a higher efficiency because the control range around the system target pressure is tighter. This tighter range allows for a reduction in average system pressure.

Again, caution needs to be taken when lowering average system header pressure because large, sudden changes in demand can cause the pressure to drop below minimum requirements, leading to improper functioning of equipment. With careful matching of system controls and storage capacity, these problems can be avoided.

Various forms of automatic sequencing control exist for optimizing the operation of multiple installations and equalizing the wear through rotation of the sequence. Microprocessor-based systems have much more accurate pressure control than pressure switch or air governor controls and avoid large pressure differentials and energy waste. They can take into account lower pressure requirements during non-productive hours and adjust accordingly and can also control system isolation valves. Some multiple machine control systems work with a combination of pressure and demand signals to ensure that only the correct machines are on-line at any one time.

Network controls offer the latest in system control. It is important that these controllers be used to shut down any compressors running unnecessarily. They also allow the operating compressors to function in a more efficient mode. Controllers used in networks are combination controllers. They provide individual compressor control as well as system control functions. The term multi-master refers to the system control capability within each individual compressor controller. These individual controllers are linked or networked together, thereby sharing all operating information and status.

One of the networked controllers is designated as the leader. Because these controllers share information, the compressor operating decisions with respect to changing air demand can be made more quickly and accurately. The effect is a tight pressure control range, which allows a further reduction in the air system target pressure.

Although, initial costs for system controls are often high, these controls are becoming more common because of the resulting reductions in operating costs. Control systems can be built into building management systems along with compressor condition monitoring, automatic operation of zone isolation valves, compressor electric motor input readings and departmental air demand metering from remote outstations.

15.1.10 Sizing

Compressors should be sized as closely as possible to the duty. It is not economical to run any machine for long periods at low loads, due to electric motor inefficiencies. For new installations with multiple compressors, it is worthwhile considering installation of a selection of unit sizes, so those compressors operating close to full output can meet the demand. Care should be taken to ensure that the overall system efficiency is improved, taking into account the lower generating efficiencies of some smaller compressors.

15.1.11 Compressor scheduling

Another common malpractice is to generate compressed air at times when it is not needed. In many cases there is no need for compressed air at all during non-production hours, but compressors are often not switched off.

15.1.12 Heat recovery

As much as 80–93% of the electrical energy used by an industrial air compressor is converted into heat. The heat is low grade and usually wasted, but in many cases, it can be recovered. A properly designed heat recovery unit can recover anywhere from 50–90% of this available thermal energy and put it to useful work heating air or water.

Heat is given off by the compressors themselves, by intercoolers on multi-stage compressors (which improve their efficiency) and by aftercoolers. Compressors can be air or water-cooled. On water-cooled compressors heat is normally removed from the compression cylinders by water jackets. Hot water at around 50°C can be collected from a piston compressor and used for a variety of purposes, including increasing the temperature of boiler feed water, process water or domestic hot water. Warm air can be ducted from air-cooled compressors, particularly packaged rotary machines, and can be used for duties such as space heating and air curtains.

a) Heating air with air-cooled compressors

Air-cooled packaged rotary screw compressors are very amenable to heat recovery for space heating or other hot air uses. Ambient atmospheric air is heated by passing it across the system's after-cooler and lubricant cooler, where it extracts heat from both the compressed air and the lubricant that is used to lubricate and cool the compressor. Since packaged compressors are typically enclosed in cabinets and already include heat exchangers and fans, the only system modifications needed are the addition of ducting and another fan to handle the duct loading and to eliminate any backpressure on the compressor cooling fan.

These heat recovery systems can be modulated with a simple thermostatically controlled hinged vent. When heating is not required - such as in

Table 15.2   Heat recovery available from air cooled rotary screws compressors at full load.

Capacity (I/s)	Nominal Motor Power (kW)	Warm Air Flow (I/s)	Heat Available (kWh/h)
40	15	450	12
60	22	810	18
159	55	1,600	45
314	110	3,700	89
450	160	5,600	130
858	200	8,900	162
725	250	8,900	203

the summer months - the hot air can be ducted outside the building. The vent can also be thermostatically regulated to provide a constant temperature for a heated area.

Hot air can be used for space heating, industrial drying, preheating aspirated air for oil burners, or any other application requiring warm air. As a rule of thumb, approximately 15 kWh/hour of energy is available for each 3m³/min of capacity (at full load). Air temperatures of 17 to 22°C above the cooling air inlet temperature can be obtained. Recovery efficiencies of 80-90% are common.

If the air supply for the compressor is not from outside, you should be careful not to draw in heated air because this will reduce the compressor efficiency. During the summer months, any hot air should be ducted to atmosphere, otherwise it will be dissipated to the surrounding area and could subsequently be drawn back into the compressor, again reducing efficiency.

b) Heating water with air-cooled compressors

Using a heat exchanger, it is also possible to extract waste heat from the lubricant coolers found in packaged water-cooled reciprocating or rotary screw compressors and produce hot water. Depending on design, heat exchangers can produce non-potable (grey) or potable water.

When hot water is not required, the lubricant is muted to the standard lubricant cooler. Hot water can be used in central heating or boiler systems, industrial cleaning processes, plating operations, heat pumps, laundries, or any other application where hot water is required. Heat exchangers also offer an opportunity to produce hot air and hot water and allow the operator some ability to vary the hot air/hot water ratio.

c) Heat recovery with water-cooled compressors

Heat recovery for space heating is not as common with water-cooled compressors because an extra stage of heat exchange is required, and the temperature of the available heat is lower. However, since many water-cooled compressors are quite large, heat recovery for space heating can be an attractive opportunity. Recovery efficiencies of 50-60% are typical.

When calculating energy savings and payback periods for heat recovery units, it is important to compare heat recovery with the current source of energy for generating thermal energy, which may be a low-price fossil fuel such as coal.

d) Use of hot compressed air for process duties

Some process applications, such as spool valves in a glass factory or drop forging hammers, benefit from hot compressed air. Hot compressed air is not often used because of safety concerns, since there is a risk of compressor oil carry-over spontaneously igniting if the discharge temperature is too high.

If hot compressed air is to be used, all the air pipe work should be lagged to prevent cooling and an over-sized condensate recovery system should be fitted to take care of the additional condensate, which will form. An after-cooler will not be required. Using hot air is especially worth considering if the air is compressed near to the point of usage and the pipe runs (and hence the heat and pressure loss) are therefore small. The volumetric increase achieved by using hot air will save up to 25% of the energy used on the duty, provided the air is kept hot up to the usage point.

15.1.13 Maintenance

Like all electro-mechanical equipment, industrial compressed air systems require periodic maintenance to operate at peak efficiency and Minimize unscheduled downtime. Inadequate maintenance can have a significant impact on energy consumption via lower compression efficiency, air leakage, or pressure variability. It can also lead to high operating temperatures, poor moisture control, and excessive contamination. Most problems are minor and can be connected by simple adjustments, cleaning, part replacement, or the elimination of adverse conditions. Compressed air system maintenance is similar to that performed on cars: filters and fluids are replaced; cooling water is inspected, belts are adjusted, and leaks are identified and repaired.

All equipment in the compressed air system should be maintained in accordance with manufacturers' specifications. Manufacturers provide inspection, maintenance and service schedules that should be followed. In many cases, it makes sense from efficiency and economic standpoints to maintain equipment more frequently than the intervals recommended by manufacturers, which are primarily designed to protect equipment.

One way to tell if a system is being maintained well and is operating properly is to periodically benchmark the system by tracking power, pressure and flow. If power use at a given pressure and flow rate goes up, the system's efficiency is degrading. This benchmarking will also let you know if the compressor is operating at full capacity, and if the capacity is decreasing over time. On new systems, specifications should be recorded when the system is first set up and operated properly.

Maintenance issues for specific system components are discussed below.

15.1.14 Compressor package

The main areas of the compressor package in need of maintenance are the compressor, heat exchanger surfaces, air lubricant separator, lubricant, lubricant filter, and air inlet filter. The compressor and inter-cooling surfaces need to be kept clean and foul free. If they are dirty, compressor efficiency will be adversely affected. Fans and water pumps should also be inspected to ensure that they are operating at peak performance.

The air lubricant separator in a lubricant-cooled rotary screw compressor generally starts with a 0.1 – 0.2 bar differential pressure drop at full-load when new. Maintenance manuals usually suggest changing them when there is about a 0.7 bar pressure drop across the separator. In many cases it may make sense to make an earlier separator replacement, especially if electricity prices are high.

The compressor lubricant and lubricant filter need to be changed per manufacturer's specification. Lubricant can become corrosive and degrade both the equipment and system efficiency. For lubricant-injected rotary compressors, the lubricant serves to lubricate bearings, gears, and intermeshing rotor surfaces. The lubricant also acts as a seal and removes most of the heat of compression. Only a lubricant meeting the manufacturer's specifications should be used.

Inlet filters and inlet piping also need to be kept clean. A dirty filter can reduce compressor capacity and efficiency. Filters should be maintained at least per manufacturer's specifications, taking into account the level of contaminants in the facility's air.

a) Compressor drives

If the electric motor driving a compressor is not properly maintained, it will not only consume more energy, but also be apt to fail before its expected lifetime. The two most important aspects of motor maintenance are lubrication and cleaning.

b) Lubrication

Too much lubrication can be just as harmful as too little and is a major cause of premature motor failure. Motors should be lubricated per the manufacturer's specification, which can be anywhere from every 2 months to every 18 months, depending on annual hours of operation and motor speed.

On motors with bearing grease fittings, the first step in lubrication is to clean the grease fitting and remove the drain plug. High quality new grease should be added, and the motor should be run for about an hour before the drain plug is replaced. This allows excess grease to be purged from the motor without dripping on the windings and damaging them.

c) Cleaning

Since motors need to dissipate heat, it is important to keep all of the air passages clean and free of obstruction. For enclosed motors, it is vital that cooling fins are kept free of debris. Poor motor cooling can increase motor temperature and winding resistance, which shortens motor life and increases energy consumption.

d) Belts

Motor v-belt drives also require periodic maintenance. Tight belts can lead to excessive bearing wear, and loose belts can slip and waste energy. Under normal operation, belts stretch and wear and, therefore, require adjustment. A good rule-of thumb is to examine and adjust belts after every 400 hours of operation.

e) General

Compressors run for many hours, often in appalling conditions. Equating the example 30 m³/min compressor to a car, it would cover 113,000 kilometers per annum at an average speed of 50 km/h. Some compressors run the equivalent of 400,000 kilometers per annum on this basis. Good maintenance is therefore essential.

Piston compressors, particularly the oil-free type, suffer the most in efficiency terms from lack of maintenance. The efficiency of rotary vane and screw machines does not deteriorate so rapidly; however, there is a finite life for such compressors. As a guide, these types of machine must receive major maintenance after 25,000 hours of life to maintain good efficiency.

Oil-free toothed rotor and screw machines perform well for periods of up to 40,000 hours, after which there is a slow fall off in efficiency due to gradually increasing internal clearances. These types of machines then need major refurbishment to maintain efficiency.

Centrifugal compressors, having few moving parts and comparatively large 'as built' clearances, will maintain their efficiency over longer periods. The inlet air filters, cooling water system and the intercoolers must be rigorously maintained, or efficiency will fall off rapidly.

It is a false economy to ignore maintenance on any type of compressor. It is recommended that manufacturers, or their accredited agents, are used for service work and that genuine spare parts, to the original design, are used. An apparently cheaper component, such as an incorrectly designed replacement discharge valve, costs more in the long term due to the detrimental effect that it has on the compressor efficiency.

15.1.15 Supply side energy efficiency measures

- Operate compressors efficiently

- Maintain compressors as per manufacturers recommendation or based on predictive or reliability centered maintenance system

- Control multiple compressors with a sequencer or a centralized master network controller (in a system with 3 or more compressors, a control system is feasible)

- Avoid running more than one compressor at partial load

- Run all compressors as baseload, with only one compressor running as a trim or load following compressor

- Ensure the trim compressor has the most efficient part load control

- Correctly size the trim compressor to avoid control-gap issues

- If all the compressors are fixed speed, trim with the smallest compressor

- If one or more compressor has variable speed or modulating control, trim with the largest compressor

- Size the min-max range of the VSD compressor to be larger than the baseload compressor capacity

- Ensure the trim compressor is the first compressor to switch on, and the last compressor to switch off

- Supply average demand from generating capacity. Supply peak demand from storage

- Reduce pressure drop at the compressors' intake (e.g. check inlet filter pressure drop)

- Decrease temperature at the compressors' intake
- Duct heat of compression out of the compressor room
- Is possible, duct intake air from a lower temperature area
- Ensure the system pressure is at its lowest possible pressure to still support productive demand
- For each 1 bar supply pressure reduction, 6% power are saved on displacement compressors
- Ensure that at a minimum all compressors have dual control to prevent a compressor running unloaded at 25–30% of full load power during no production, e.g. over a weekend
- Set up a targeting and monitoring program. This will help 'benchmark' consumption and indicate future irregularities.

15.2 Distribution and Treatment

The main factors that affect energy consumption in the distribution are:

- Pressure losses due to inadequate pipe sizing;
- Water condensing in the lines, causing damage to components and also reducing pipe cross-sectional areas which leads to additional pressure losses;
- Air leakage from pipework and end-using equipment, due to poor maintenance and in many cases permanently open condensate drain valves.

A typical compressed air system is outlined in the figure below. The following sections refer to this diagram, describing the main design criteria and components.

15.2.1 Distribution main

Generally, a ring main is the most effective method of supplying compressed air to a point of use. The main advantages of this type of network are that:

- Velocity to any one point is reduced, since air can converge from two directions, thereby reducing pressure drop over the system;
- Automatic zone valves can be fitted to isolate areas operating different working patterns;

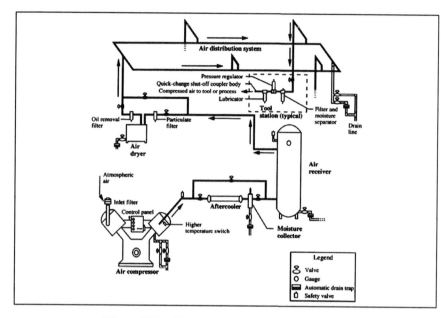

Figure 15.4   Compressed air system components.

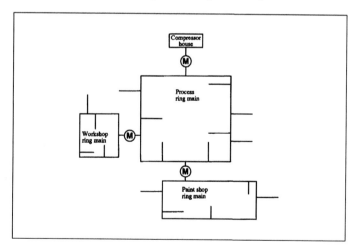

Figure 15.5   Preferred distribution line layout.

• Alteration or extension of the distribution system is made easy.

Ideally a ring main should be placed around each building and a single branch point should feed the main, enabling each area of the network to be metered by a single meter. An example of such a network is given in Figure 15.5.

Regarding the acceptable air velocities, the 5/10/15 m/s rule applies. The air velocities should be less than:

- 5 m/s in the compressor room

- 10 m/s in the main distribution header

- 15 m/s in the take-off points from the header to the end-users

These values will ensure flow is sufficiently low to prevent an excessive pressure drop. For a reference, the nomographs outlined in Figure 15.6 and Figure 15.7 are a useful guide to sizing piping. The distribution system should be designed to cause no more than 0.15 bar pressure drop (excluding treatment) at peak demand at the point of use.

When sizing ring mains, it is advisable to err on the high side as future demand may increase. The consequence of under-sizing is very significant

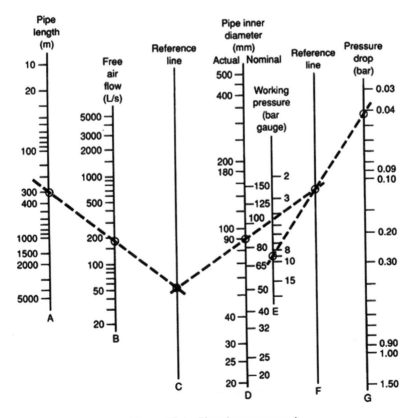

Figure 15.6 Pipe sizes nomograph.

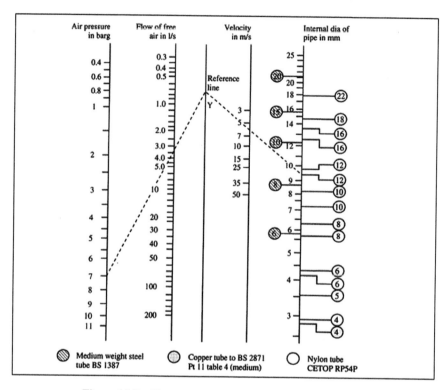

Figure 15.7   Pipe carrying capacities at varying velocities.

in energy efficiency terms because air velocity will be excessive leading to high-pressure drops and nonseparation of condensed water. Table 15.3 shows the power wasted for different pipe diameters with a flow rate of 30 m³/min at 7 bar pressure.

Much energy can be wasted during distribution by having to generate overpressure to overcome incorrect pipe, valve and other air-line component sizing which cause high flow velocities and pressure drops. All systems should be designed to Minimize pressure drops.

It is worthwhile obtaining a flow/pressure profile of the distribution network to establish where the bottlenecks occur and how they can be overcome. In conjunction with establishing the correct pipe diameters for the flow, a check on the pressure drops caused by the major valves and fittings should be made. The table below gives the equivalent pipe length for these components at the relative nominal pipe diameter. The equivalent lengths should be added to the actual pipe length to be used, and the total length should then be used with the nomograph shown in Figure 15.8 for finalizing the pipe diameter.

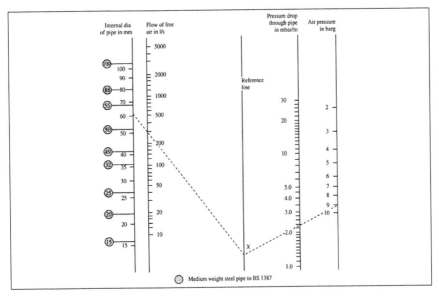

Figure 15.8 Pressure drop in steel pipes.

Table 15.3 Distribution line power wastage (30 m3/min).

Pipe Nominal Bore (mm)	Pressure Drop per 100 m (bar)	Equivalent Power Lost (kW)
50	2.6	18
65	0.9	5
80	0.2	0.8
100	0.1	0.4

It is important that site integration of air compressors is considered at the planning and design stages to get the maximum benefit of using packaged compressors with integrated heat recovery systems. These packaged systems generally use rotary screw compressors, which have the additional benefit of operating with low noise.

When there is a choice between using a central installation or smaller compressors nearer to the points of end use, the choice will largely depend on:

• the physical layout of the factory;

• the position of off-takes,

• the compressor operating hours.

Smaller compressors are generally less efficient than larger ones, and this must be taken into account when justifying decentralization. Where practicable, air

Table 15.4   Pressure loss through steel fittings.

Item	Equivalent Pipe lenghts in meters									
	Inner Pipe Diameter (mm)									
	15	20	25	40	50	80	100	125	150	200
Gate valve Fully open	0.1	0.2	0.3	0.5	0.6	1.0	1.3	1.6	1.9	2.6
Gate valve Half Closed		32	5	8	10	16	20	30	40	
Diaphragm valve Fully open	0.6	1.0	1.3	2.5	3	4.5	6	8	10	
Angle valve Fully open	1.5	2.6	4	6	7	12	13	18	22	30
Globe valve Fully open	2.7	4.8	7.5	12	15	24	30	38	45	60
Ball valve (full bore) Fully open	0.5	0.2	0.2	0.4	0.3	0.4	0.3	0.5	0.6	0.6
Ball valve (red. bore) Fully open	3.4	4.9	2.4	2.2	5	2.6	4.1	3.3	12.1	22.3
Swing check valve Fully open		1.3	2.0	3.2	4	6.4	8	10	12	16
Bend R = 2d	0.1	0.2	0.3	0.5	0.6	1.0	1.2	1.5	1.8	2.4
Bend R = d	0.2	0.3	0.4	0.6	0.8	1.3	1.6	2	2.4	3.2
Mitre bend 90°	0.6	1.0	1.5	2.4	3	4.8	6	7.5	9	12
Run of tee	0.6	0.3	0.5	0.8	1.0	1.6	2	2.5	3	4
Side outlet tee		1.0	1.5	2.4	3	4.8	6	7.5	9	12
Reducer		0.3	0.5	0.7	1.0	2	25	3.1	3.6	4.8

compressors should be sited near to points of large air demand and, if possible, near to heat demands, if recovery is an option, to reduce pipe runs and also capital and running costs.

15.2.2 Condensate drain traps

Condensate drain traps are fitted on water separators, aftercoolers, dryers and receiver tanks to remove unwanted condensate out of the compressed air system.

Automatic timer drain traps are very common, and commonly responsible for a huge, compressed air loss. In fact, it is not uncommon for these timed electronic trap types to be the largest area of compressed air waste in a plant. These traps work on a timer setting, and either do not stay open long enough to remove the entrained condensate or stays open too long wasting expensive compressed air. Timed electronic traps should always be replaced.

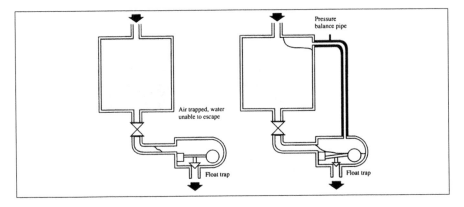

Figure 15.9 Air binding of water traps.

Reliable electronic level sensing condensate traps are available that ensure water is regularly drained away. They are more expensive but usually pays for themselves well within one year.

Manual traps left open account for a substantial percentage of total wastage. They can, however, be quite compressed air efficient if personnel have the discipline to drain these at least twice each day.

The ball float type of drain trap is also common because it gives a positive shut off, opening only if water is present and closing immediately the water has cleared. These traps are also zero air loss drain traps, but they require very regular maintenance and cleaning. If there is a possibility of large quantities of water at the trap, then air binding can take place and a balance pipe must be fitted. With this arrangement, the water will flow freely into the trap, displacing air, which then passes through the balance pipe and into the main system.

All drain traps require occasional maintenance, to remove any build-up of oils or emulsions, which may be present in the condensate. If oil or emulsion build-up is heavy, consideration should be given to using drain trays, which have a blast action discharge.

15.2.3 Air quality

Air needs are defined by the air quality, quantity and pressure required by the end uses in the plant. Assessing needs carefully will ensure that a compressed air system is configured properly.

As illustrated in the following table, compressed air quality ranges from plant air to breathing air. Industrial applications typically use one of the first

Table 15.5 Air quality classifications.

Plant Air	Instrument Air	Process Air	Breathing Air
Air tools, air-actuated valves, general plant air	Laboraties, paint spraying, powder coating, climate control	Food and pharmaceutical process air, electronics	Hospital air systems, diving tank refill stations, respirators for cleaning and/or grit blasting

three air quality levels. The quality is determined by the dryness and contaminant level required by the end-uses, and is accomplished with filtering and drying equipment. The higher the quality, the more the air costs to produce. Higher quality air usually requires additional equipment, which not only increases initial capital investment, but also makes the overall system more expensive to operate in terms of energy consumption and maintenance costs.

Air treatment is often required to provide compressed air of the quality required at the point of use. This avoids product contamination, product spoilage and poor control of, or damage to, air-using equipment. Treatment needs energy in terms of additional generation pressure, and possibly additional compressed air or electrical demand depending on the type of treatment used.

Compressing air concentrates the contaminants per unit of volume of air delivered at pressure. Compressed air can be contaminated by water vapor; condensate; particulate matter (either airborne or pipe-scale); oil in vapor or liquid state (either inhaled by the compressor from the atmosphere or added during compression); and microbes. The amount of treatment will depend on the users' needs.

The desired air quality in terms of dirt water, oil and microbial burden is achieved by treatment after compression. The higher the quality specified, the greater the energy consumed by the treatment system, and the higher the additional generation pressure needed to overcome losses during treatment. Table 15.6 gives the ISO8573 recommendations on air quality classes.

Treatment systems range from a simple aftercooler, which is neatly always supplied with the compressor package, through to filters and refrigerated-, sorption-, deliquescent-, and desiccant dryers. There are many variations of each system; some are more energy efficient than others.

The requirement for high quality compressed air is increasing as production methods become more sophisticated. A general breakdown of recommended standards for different manufacturing applications is included Table 15.7. This table is intended for guidance only; in practice there are very many other combinations needed.

Table 15.6 Air quality classifications ISO/DIS 8573.1.

Quality Class	Dirt Particle size (micron)	Dirt Concentration (mg/rn3)	Water Pressure dew point (°C(ppm vol) at 7bar)	Oil (including vapour (mg/m3)
1	0.1	0.1	−70(0.3)	0.01
2	1	1	−40(16)	0.1
3	5	5	−20(128)	1
4	15	8	+3(940)	5
5	40	10	+7(1240)	25
6	-	-	+10(1500)	N/A
7	-	-	No spec	N/A

Table 15.7 General recommended standards for air purity.

Application classes	Typical Quality Classes Oil	Dirt	Water
Air agitation	3		2
Air bearings	2	2	
Air gauging	2	3	3
Air motors	4	4 – 1	5
Brick and glass machines	4		
Cleaning of machine parts	4	4	4
Construction	4	5	5
Conveying, granular products	3	4	3
Conveying powder products	2	3	2
Fluidics, power circuits	4	4	4
Fluidics, sensors	2	2 – 1	2
Foundry machines	4	4	5
Food and beverges	2	3	1
Hand operated air tools	4	5 – 4	5 – 4
Machine tools	4	3	5
Mining	4	5	5
Micro-electronics manufacture	1	1	1
Packaging and textile machines	4	3	3
Photographic film processing	1	1	1
Pneumatic cylinders	3	3	5
Process control instruments	2	2	3
Paint spraying	3	3	3
Sand blasting	–	3	3
Welding machines	4	4	5
General workshop air	4	4	5

There is a very wide range of requirements for air quality. It is important to install the right equipment, and equally important to keep the energy requirements within reason. Every effort should be made to avoid unnecessary levels of treatment.

Many plants need only part of the air treated to very high quality. In these cases, treating all the generated air to the minimum acceptable level and improving the quality to the desired level close to the usage points can achieve excellent savings.

15.2.4 Condensate

Ambient air typically contains 12.5g of water for every 1 m³ of free saturated air at 15°C. If a compressor produces air at 30 m³/min, the compressed air produced each hour will contain 22.5 l of water. Provided the free air is maintained at about 15°C, the water will remain as vapor: however, if the air is cooled or compressed the water will be condensed. The temperature at which water condenses is known as the dew point.

The rise in air temperature in the compressor generally prevents condensation, but when the air passes though the after-cooler a large amount of water condenses. Typically, the air temperature following the after-cooler will be around 35°C and water content will have been reduced. Water will, however, still be present as vapor and if the air temperature falls there will be further water condensation.

The figure below shows the amount of water removal required for differing end temperatures. To remove significantly more water from the compressed air than can be achieved by aftercooling, a dryer is necessary. Conventional refrigerated air dryers typically take the air from the compressor after-cooler at a maximum temperature of 35°C.

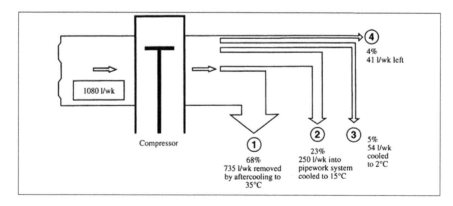

Figure 15.10   Drying.

15.2.5 Distribution piping

For undried compressed air, system problems may occur through water condensation in the distribution network. It is good practice to remove as much
of this water as possible. Condensation typically occurs where the air main
travels outside the buildings and is therefore subject to temperatures below
those in the compressor house.

The accumulation of condensed water and scale in the system can lead
to pressure drop. To prevent this occurring, the air mains should slope to
strategically located drain legs equipped with automatically operated drain
valves (avoiding air wastage, which frequently occurs with manually operated drain valves).

Building layout will dictate the best position for drain points, but in
general the main should be installed with a fall of not less than 1 m in 100 m
of ring main pipe-work in the direction of air flow. The recommended distance between drain points is approximately 30 m.

Any branch line should be taken off the top of the main to prevent any
water in the main pipe from running into it. In addition, the bottom of a falling branch line pipe should be drained.

15.2.6 Desiccant dryers

For a water quality class of 1 to 3, heated or heatless twin tower desiccant
dryers with special desiccant and drying cycles are employed. This type of
dryer consumes a lot of energy, requiring up to 15% purge air for desiccant
regeneration (or even more if the desiccant vessel bed is not full).

The example 30 m^3/min demand, when supplying 1.1.1 quality air,
could cost approximately 21% per annum more due to the treatment devices
than if it were simply delivering after-cooled air. As the requirement for air
quality becomes less intense than 1.1.1, the energy requirement reduces.
When supplying air of 2.2.1 quality, energy would cost approximately 15%
more than delivering after-cooled air if it used a lower specification desiccant
dryer with pre- and after-filters performing at 40°C pressure dewpoint.

15.2.7 Heat of compression dryers

Air of 2:3:1 quality can be provided with a heat of compression dryer. A very
small motor slowly rotates a drum, which is impregnated with the drying
medium. Compressed air is fed through a sealed segment of the drum and
dried within a range of −15°C to −40°C, depending on the compressor load.
The drying medium in the part of the drum not being used to dry the air is

regenerated by hot air taken directly from before the compressor after-cooler, i.e. by the waste heat of compression. The cost to provide 2:3:1 quality air by this method, is approximately 3% more than delivering after-cooled air.

15.2.8 Deliquescent (Absorption) dryers

Deliquescent dryers operate by passing the compressed air over soluble material, such as salt, which dissolves as it absorbs moisture. Their main advantages are that they do not consume any energy other than that required to overcome the pressure drop within the dryer (0.1 to 0.4 bar) and they do not lose any air volume. The dryers are not, however, regenerative and deliquescent material needs to be replaced periodically, incurring both labor and material costs. Deliquescent dryers are the least expensive dryer and are very energy efficient but can only produce dew points about 6 – 10 °C below the inlet temperature. Consequently, these dryers have fallen out of favor and are not that common anymore. They are also called "dewpoint suppression dryers".

15.2.9 Refrigeration dryers

Compressed air water quality of 3°C dewpoint and above can be provided by refrigerated dryer, which are the most common dryer found. The overwhelming majority of industrial applications only require these type of water levels which can reliably be supplied by refrigerated dryers. In climates where the dewpoint produced is above winter ambient temperatures, water taken outside the buildings will condense. It is recommended that a condensate trap be fitted to the system where it enters the next building to prevent problems.

Refrigerated dryers can also be cycling or non-cycling part load performance control, which refers to the technology used to operate the dryer at partial load requirements. Cycling style refrigerated dryers start and stop the refrigeration compressor, and uses a thermal mass to cool down the compressed air rather than directly from the refrigerated cycle, and are the more efficient option if loads of less than 50% of its flow capacity are encountered. Non-cycling style refrigerated dryers do not start/stop, and use a hot gas bypass to bypass the refrigerant at part load conditions, and provide stable dewpoints.

15.2.10 Dryer installation

Dryers should be installed in well-ventilated areas. For continuous processes, all filters should be duplexed with changeover valves for ease of maintenance.

A dryer by-pass should also be installed for emergency maintenance; this must be locked off during normal running to prevent accidental operation, which would contaminate the dry air main.

With all dryers, particularly desiccant types, the dew point should be checked regularly. Many will be operating well below specification, and yet the energy consumed will be continuing at the same rate as that needed for design dew-point performance.

15.2.11 Dryer sizing

It is extremely important that driers are adequately sized, not according to the manufacturers' indicated nameplate capacity, but according to job-site conditions. For proper application of refrigerated air dryers, the dryer performance must be adjusted to account for the worst-case operating condition expected at the actual job site condition in which the dryer is expected to function. The worst case is defined as follows:

- The highest compressed air inlet temperature to the air dryer,

- the lowest compressed air inlet pressure to the air dryer, and

- the highest ambient air temperature at the cooling airflow intake to the refrigeration condenser.

Air dryer manufacturers provide correction factors that are applied to an air dryers' catalogue performance airflow capacity rating (in accordance with ISO 7183). For proper air dryer selection, the actual airflow requirement (m³/m) is divided by the proper correction factors for the actual job site operating condition.

To determine the maximum airflow rate available for an existing air dryer at a given job site condition, the existing dryer's catalogue performance

Table 15.8 Example of typical air dryer performance correction factors.

Inlet Air Temperature	Correction Factor	Inlet Air Pressure	Correction Factor	Ambient Air Temperature	Correction Factor
30°C	1.21 →	6 bar →	0.96 ┐	20°C	1.06
35°C	1.00	6.5 bar	0.98	25°C	1.00
40°C →	0.84 ┘	7 bar	1.00 ┘	30°C →	0.94
45°C	0.70	8 bar	1.03	35°C	0.88
50°C	0.59	9 bar	1.06	40°C	0.82

Note: These correction factors are typical. Always refer to the manufacturer's published performance data.

rating is multiplied by the appropriate correction factors based on the existing job site condition.

15.2.12 Filters

Filtration can be one of the most neglected parts of a compressed air system, however paying attention to this is crucial when optimizing a compressed air system. Various filters of different specifications for almost any end user requirement are available.

Oil removal filters (microfilters), water removal filters, dust (particle) removal filters and activated carbon vapor absorber unit may be needed. Filters cause pressure drops in compressed air systems. To save energy, it is recommended that only the minimum filtration requirement be met.

Filters should be adequately sized for the duty; if the filter connections are considerably smaller than correctly sized pipework, they will cause pressure drops. It is better to pay more for filters with correctly sized flanges, and avoid pressure drop and energy wastage.

Fouling causes an increase in the pressure drop across all filter elements, leading to a higher generation pressure and additional energy use. It is important to keep pressure drops to a minimum. All filters should be fitted with differential pressure gauges, which should be calibrated regularly.

15.2.13 Storage

Air receivers provide a supply buffer to meet high volume intermittent (short-term) demand spikes, which can occur faster than the compressors can respond, or can exceed the compressor generating capacity. They also serve to assist the dryer in removing liquids, and a receiver tank after treatment is a good location for a pressure signal to control compressors from. It also reduced the cycling frequency of load/unload compressors.

A "wet" receiver will be located before the dryer, and a "dry" receiver after the dryer (although they are essentially the same piece of equipment). If a high-volume intermittent demand occasion pulls the entire system pressure down by more than 0.3 bar, a receiver tank close to this demand is required. Storage can be used to control these demand events in the system by controlling both the amount of pressure drop and the rate of decay. Storage can be used to protect critical pressure applications from other events in the system.

Storage is used to control the rate of pressure drop in demand while supporting the speed of transmission response from supply. Many systems have a compressor operating in modulation to support demand events, and sometimes strategic storage solutions can allow for this compressor to be turned off. Storage can also help systems ride through compressor failure or short energy outages.

The only component in a compressed air system where "more is better" is storage capacity. Storage volume in a system has multiple benefits:

- It increases load/unloading cycling time, enabling compressors to properly separate oil from the compressed air and improves the cycling energy efficiency

- it facilitates condensate take-out,

- it supplies air to high intermittent demand events with a lesser impact and a lesser fluctuation on the system pressure, and

- it provides a system pressure buffer during a supply side event i.e. failure of a compressor.

15.2.14 System isolation

Sometimes it is necessary to keep parts of a distribution network pressurized when other parts do not require compressed air. In these cases, the compressed air system in the idle plant should be isolated from the active plant. For example, an assembly department should be isolated during non-productive hours to prevent wastage due to leakage or misuse. Manually or electronically operated zone isolation valves can be installed in the distribution network to shut off at properly arranged times.

15.2.15 Distribution and treatment energy efficiency measures

- Engineer storage volume to supply high volume intermittent demand events, to reduce load/unload compressor cycling, to facilitate condensate takeout, and to buffer the system pressure when a supply event occurs e.g. a compressor trips

- Valve off equipment when not in use

- Only use dry air when and where necessary.

- Minimize pressure drops in the distribution system by reducing air velocity to acceptable levels

- Only dry and filter to the required level – over-drying and over-filtering increases energy cost

- Dry and filter as close to the point of use as possible

- When implementing a change in the system, consider that anything that is changed in a compressed air system will influence something else

15.3 Demand Side

Compressed air use should be constantly monitored and re-evaluated. Investigating where and how compressed air is used around site will reveal the areas in which major savings can be achieved.

It is vitally important that each use is investigated in detail to establish whether:

- it needs to be operated by compressed air at all;

- the supply pressure is greater than necessary;

- there is adequate facility for isolating the supply line when it is not in use.

Commonplace examples of misuse are using compressed air for cleaning, cooling, or drying duties. Alternatives exist for cleaning benches or drying product, and cooling duties can generally be carried out using high pressure fans or a lower pressure blower. Typical overall efficiency when compressed air is used is around 10%. So, the air used should be of minimum quantity, pressure and duration.

15.3.1 Leakages

Although compressed air leaks often go unnoticed because they are invisible and usually masked by plant noise, they are a frequent and expensive defect in compressed air systems, resulting in loss of air capacity and increased energy consumption. It is not practical to maintain compressed air systems completely leak free, but as a rule of thumb, leakage should not exceed 10% of compressor capacity.

However, it is common in industrial systems for leakage to account for 30% of the rated compressor capacity. A leakage rate as high as 77% and 86% respectively have been measured by the author. Leakage is not only a direct source of wasted energy but is also an indirect contributor to operating costs. As leaks increase, system pressure drops, air tools function less efficiently and production is affected. Often the only solution is to increase generation pressure to compensate for the losses. Increased running time can also lead to additional maintenance requirements and increased unscheduled downtime. Leaks can lead to adding unnecessary compressor capacity.

While leakage can come from any part of the system, the most common problem areas are:

- Couplings, hoses, tubes, and fittings,

- Open condensate traps and shut-off valves,

- Pipe joints, disconnects, and thread sealant,

- Leaking pressure regulators,

- Air cooling lines left open permanently,

- Air-using equipment left in operation when not needed.

Table 15.9 shows an estimate of compressed air leaks for the operating conditions shown. The data is based on a sharp-edged orifice with a flow coefficient of 0.61. Leakage and cost could be increased by as much as 60% for a well-rounded hole (flow coefficient = 0.97).

a) Testing for air leaks (compressor with load/unload control)

This test consists of timing the "load" and "unload" cycle of the air compressor as it supplies only the air lost through leakage in the distribution system, *i.e.* with all users of compressed air shut off. When switched on, the compressor brings up the air pressure to the maximum set point and then unloads.

With no air leakage the pressure would remain constant and the compressor would remain in the unloaded mode. Air leakage would cause the pressure to drop and when the minimum set point is reached, the compressor would then switch to the load mode. The compressor would cycle between the load and unload modes as required to maintain air pressure.

b) Simplified air leakage test

- **Step 1:** Determine the Free Air Delivery (FAD) supply (Q) of your compressed air generation (m³/min).

- **Step 2:** During a time when equipment is connected but not being used on the compressed air system, turn on the compressor and allow it to come up to full pressure.

- **Step 3:** Record the time (t) until the compressor starts again (loads).

- **Step 4:** Record the time (T) until the compressor stops (unloads).

Table 15.9 Discharge of air through an orifice.

Gauge pressure before orifice, bar	Diameter of Orifice, mm (note: calculated flow rate assumes orifice coefficient of 0.61)											
	1	2	3	4	5	6	7	8	9	10	15	20
4	0.03	0.11	0.25	0.45	0.70	1.01	1.38	1.80	2.28	2.82	6.34	11.28
4.5	0.03	0.12	0.28	0.50	0.78	1.12	1.52	1.98	2.51	3.10	6.98	12.40
5	0.03	0.14	0.30	0.54	0.85	1.22	1.66	2.16	2.74	3.38	7.61	13.53
5.5	0.04	0.15	0.33	0.59	0.92	1.32	1.79	2.34	2.97	3.66	8.24	14.65
6	0.04	0.16	0.35	0.63	0.99	1.42	1.93	2.52	3.19	3.94	8.87	15.78
6.5	0.04	0.17	0.38	0.68	1.06	1.52	2.07	2.70	3.42	4.23	9.51	16.90
7	0.05	0.18	0.41	0.72	1.13	1.62	2.21	2.88	3.65	4.51	10.14	18.03
7.5	0.05	0.19	0.43	0.77	1.20	1.72	2.35	3.06	3.88	4.79	10.77	19.15
8	0.05	0.20	0.46	0.81	1.27	1.82	2.48	3.24	4.11	5.07	11.40	20.27
8.5	0.05	0.21	0.48	0.86	1.34	1.93	2.62	3.42	4.33	5.35	12.04	21.40
9	0.06	0.23	0.51	0.90	1.41	2.03	2.76	3.60	4.56	5.63	12.67	22.52
9.5	0.06	0.24	0.53	0.95	1.48	2.13	2.90	3.78	4.79	5.91	13.30	23.65
10	0.06	0.25	0.56	0.99	1.55	2.23	3.03	3.96	5.02	6.19	13.94	24.77

- **Step 5:** Repeat the measurements at least four times.
- **Step 6:** Average the t and T cycles.
- **Step 7:** Calculate the leakage:

$$Leakage\ rate \left(m^3 /\mathrm{min}\right) = \frac{Q \times T}{T + t}$$

c) Savings and payback calculations

After determining the leakage using the above rate, the cost of these leaks can be calculated:

Leakage Cost ($/Yr.) = Leakage rate (m³/min) × System Specific Power (kW/m³/min) × Operating Time (hrs/yr.) × Energy Cost ($/kWh)

Where:
- Leakage rate: Calculated using above test

- System Specific Power: Measured system specific power (as designed, normally about 6–7 kW/m³/min, dependent on compressor type)

- Operating Time: Operating hours per year

- Energy Cost: Consumption and demand aggregate charges

This calculation will show the annual cost of the leaks. While it would not be possible to eliminate 100% of the leakage, the magnitude of the cost as calculated here will give you some indication of the level of repairs which can be justified on a payback calculation.

Worked Example
<u>Given:</u>
- Q (average air delivery capacity over a year)   = 23.6 m³/min

- kW (average power over a year   = 175.3 kW

- Operating time   = 4 022 hrs/yr.

- Average electricity cost   = $0.15/kWh

Measured:

	T (on time)	t (time between starts)
	30	180
	32	178
	33	188
	30	182
Avg.	31.25 sec.	182 sec.

$$Leakage\,rate\left(m^3/min\right) = \frac{Q \times T}{T + t}$$

$$Leakage\,rate\left(m^3/min\right) = \frac{23.6 \times 31.25}{31.25 + 182}$$

$$= 3.458 \text{ m}^3/\text{min}$$

Energy Loss Due to Leakage = $(3.458) \times (175.3/23.6) \times 4{,}022$ hrs/yr.
= 103,320 kWh/yr.

\$ Lost Due to Leakage = \$0.15/kWh $\times$ 103,320 kWh/yr.
= \$15,498/yr.

d) Testing for air leaks (compressor with modular control)

This air leakage test is suitable for displacement compressors having inlet valve modulation, variable displacement, or variable speed drive control. The test must also be conducted during plant shutdown and with all air users isolated from the air supply system.

This test is coined a "receiver pump up test". Measurements are taken at a receiver tank when the compressor is isolated from the air distribution system, i.e. with the inlet to the receiver tank is closed. Pump up the receiver tank to operating pressure (P1), and then close the isolating valve. Record the time (T) for pressure to drop to a lower pressure (P2), approximately half of P1. The volume of all receiver tanks and the approximate air mains volume downstream of the receiver isolating valve should also be known.

The leakage volume can then be calculated:

Where:

V_{system} = System volume [m³/min]
P1 = Initial pressure of system [bar$_g$]
P2 = Final pressure of system [bar$_g$]
T = Time for pressure decline [minutes]
$P_{ambient}$ = Atmospheric pressure = 1.013 bar at sea level

e) Managing leaks

The first step in tackling leaks is to recognize the costs involved and make a commitment to a plant-wide awareness program. Regular, continuous attention to the compressed air system coupled with proper maintenance will lead to effective progress in minimizing leaks.

Having established the size of the problem, a realistic target for leakage rate of at least 10% should be set. No-load tests should then be carried out regularly, approximately every two to three months, with inspections when necessary during shutdown conditions.

Managing leakages is not a once off project but requires continuous and aggressive management to keep leaks consistently below the targeted 10%. A good leak prevention program will include the following components: identification (including tagging), tracking, repair, verification, and employee involvement. All facilities with compressed air systems should establish an aggressive leak program. A crosscutting energy management team involving decision-making representatives from production should be formed.

A leak prevention program should be part of an overall program aimed at improving the performance of compressed air systems. Once the leaks are found and repaired, the system should be re-evaluated.

Having established the size of the leakage problem, an aggressive campaign of leak reduction should take place. Targets should be set, and careful monitoring of results conducted. This work will involve inspections during silent hours checking for pipe work and tool leaks, and checking hoses and couplings for air tightness.

f) Leak detection

During shutdown of the whole plant, the detection of larger leaks within the compressed air system is simple, as they are audible. Once the compressor is started the exact leak positions should be marked with tags. In addition, checking joints and unions with soapy water is recommended to identify the smaller leaks, which invariably develop with time. An organized approach is required to obtain good results.

An Ultrasonic Leak Detector is a more effective leak detection method as it can detect leaks against a background of other equipment noise. The detectors work by picking up the very high frequency sound emitted by a leak, inaudible to the human ear. They are simple to use and do not pick up frequencies emitted by the mechanical actions of machines. These portable units consist of directional microphones, amplifiers, and audio filters, and usually have either visual indicators or earphones to detect leaks.

g) Fixing leaks

Once leaks have been detected they should be repaired as soon as possible. Simply tightening components and shutting off valves, which have been left open, can repair most leaks. One method of motivating people to fix leaks is to offer a reward for the person who finds the most leaks (the motivation chosen should not inspire people to make leaks though!).

Leaks occur most often at joints and connections. Stopping leaks can be as simple as tightening a connection or as complex as replacing faulty equipment such as couplings, fittings, pipe sections, hoses, joints, drains, and traps. In many cases leaks are caused by bad or improperly applied thread sealant. Select high quality fittings, disconnects, hose, tubing, and install them properly with appropriate thread sealant. Non-operating equipment can be an additional source of leaks. Equipment no longer in use should be isolated with a valve in the distribution system.

Another way to reduce leaks is to lower the demand air pressure of the system. The lower the pressure differential across an orifice or leak, the lower the rate of flow, so reduced system pressure will result in reduced leakage rates. Stabilizing the system header pressure at its lowest practical range will Minimize the leakage (as well as Minimize compressor load and thus electrical demand). Where a system cannot be shut down to test for leaks this method is recommended. Once leaks have been repaired, the compressor control system should be re-evaluated to realize the total savings potential.

15.3.2 Inappropriate use

Compressed air is the most expensive form of energy available in a plant. It is also clean, readily available, and simple-to-use. As a result, it is often chosen for applications in which other energy sources are more economical. Users should always consider more cost-effective forms of power before considering compressed air.

Many operations can be accomplished more economically using alternative energy sources. For example, plants should:

- Use air conditioning or fans to cool electrical cabinets instead of compressed air vortex tubes.

- Apply a vacuum system instead of making a vacuum using compressed air Venturi methods that flow high-pressure air past an orifice.

- Use blowers instead of compressed air to provide cooling, aspirating, agitating, mixing, or to inflate packaging.

- Use brushes, blowers, or vacuum systems instead of compressed air to clean parts or remove debris.

- Use blowers, electric actuators, or hydraulics instead of compressed air blasts to move parts.

- Use low-pressure air instead of high pressure compressed air for blow-guns and air lances.

- Use efficient electric motors for tools or actuators where safe and appropriate (electric tools may have less precise torque control, shorter lives, and lack the safety of compressed air powered tools).

- Use dedicated high-pressure blowers rather than compressed air for air knives. On conveyors, these can be automatically switched off if the product stops passing beneath the knife.

- Improper uses of compressed air are also unregulated end-uses and supply air to abandoned equipment.

15.3.3 System operating pressure

The system operating pressure are commonly set in excess of that required by the processes to ensure that surplus safety margin is built in to avoid production complaints.

Air piping losses are caused by excessive air velocities that cause a reduction in delivered pressure which can be excessive if the distribution piping is inadequate. To provide the required end-use pressure, distribution losses are then commonly compensated by increasing the system pressure at the compressor. Thus, improved piping designs will reduce power requirements.

15.3.4 Artificial demand

Artificial Demand is the increased compressed air flow consumed by a compressed air system when the applied demand side pressure is increased above the lowest optimum pressure necessary to support productive air use. All unregulated compressed air use and unregulated leakages contribute to the system's total artificial demand.

Applying increased air pressure (bar) to an orifice increases the flow rate (m³/min) of compressed air through the orifice. An 8 mm diameter orifice with a 0.61 coefficient and 7 bar applied upstream, will pass 2.88 m³/min of compressed air flow.

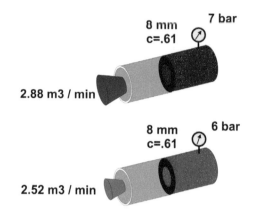

Figure 15.11   Artificial demand at increased pressure.

Suppose instead of 7 bar, the upstream pressure is controlled to be 6 bar. The same 8 mm diameter hole would only pass 2.52 m³/min of compressed air. That is about 12% less air demand with 1.0 bar less pressure applied to the system.

A pressure regulator is used to limit maximum end-of-use pressure and is placed in the distribution system just prior to the tool. If a tool operates without a regulator, it uses full system pressure. This results in increased system air demand and energy use since the tool is using air at this higher pressure. High-pressure levels can also increase equipment wear, resulting in higher maintenance costs, and shorter tool life.

15.3.5 Perceived high pressure demands

Care must be taken in identifying critical or high-pressure end users which may bottleneck the pressure in the system and cause the entire system to operate at an elevated pressure. The actual required pressure at these users should be investigated. As is often the case, when measuring the pressure at these users, it is found that the perceived pressure and the actual pressure received is not the same and that such users can operate at much lower pressures than originally anticipated.

For example, at a steelworks plant, measurements found an average air demand of 300 m³/min at 7 barg. After investigation, it was established that only 120 m³/min were being used appropriately at 7 barg, 120 m³/min were used at 3 bar and 60 m³/min were used for non-compressed air duties such as water-jetting and bearing cooling.

15.3.6 High volume intermittent demand events

High volume intermittent demand events consume a large airflow rate for relatively short periods of time. The demand event is followed by a longer period of relatively low air use. These events are characterized with high peak airflow requirements and relatively low average air demand.

High volume intermittent demand events erratically affect the system pressure profile. They also create peak airflow requirements that are not characterized by average air demand.

Frequently, the entire system responds to High Volume Intermittent Demand Events. The effect of rapid airflow changes impacts the system pressure profile. In addition, compressor control signals, system supply pressure, distribution pressure gradient, and use point pressure are all briefly affected.

High volume intermittent demand events often initiate a compressor start-up. Considering that 15 to 20 seconds or more may pass for a compressor to start-up and begin delivering air to the system, a short duration event may be over before the compressor is online. The compressor response is ineffective and wastes energy. The air demand is better supported with the application of air from storage.

One common operational remedy is to increase overall system pressure. Excessive system operating pressure under normal operation to support the intermittent pressure drawdown to maintain an acceptable valley pressure can waste energy.

15.3.7 Demand side energy efficiency measures

- All flow pushed into a compressed air system will be consumed by artificial demand

- For each 1 bar system pressure reduction, the flow lost to artificial demand is reduced by 6 to 12%

- Operational actions are by far the most cost-effective opportunities in these systems

- Manage leaks to 10%

- If leaks are not managed, they will increase by 5% per year

- Ensure that the end-use is appropriate

- Avoid cooling, cleaning, blowing, or drying with pressurized compressed air, and consider an alternative energy source e.g. a blower or fan

- Consider an alternative source of energy with a more efficiency energy conversion than pneumatic energy

- Use electrically powered devices instead of pneumatic powered devices

- Use properly engineered nozzles or air knives where appropriate

15.4 Compressed Air Systems Assessments

This section outlines a strategy for identifying opportunities, including some auditing techniques that can easily be implemented. Ideally, before any actions are taken to improve a compressed air system, an assessment (also referred to as an audit) should be carried out to determine the annual costs of the current system.

If metering is installed, this will provide an enormous amount of information to help find the best solutions. Without meters, the energy consumption of each compressor will have to be estimated from the size of the motor, its average load (or its on/off times) and the number of hours it operates. The total energy costs can be calculated by adding the information for all the compressors.

Compressed air system users should consider using an independent auditor to examine their compressed air system. Experts exist that specialize in compressed air system audits. An informed consumer should be aware that the quality and comprehensiveness of audits could vary. Independent auditors should provide recommendations, which are systems-neutral and commercially impartial. Independent auditors should neither specify nor recommend any particular manufacturer's products.

Having calculated the annual costs and established a baseline against which improvements can be measured, an audit of the complete compressed air system should be carried out. A comprehensive compressed air system audit should include an examination of both air supply and usage and the interaction between the supply and demand.

Auditors typically measure the output of a compressed air system, calculate energy consumption in kilowatt-hours, and determine the annual cost of operating the system. The auditor may also measure total air losses due to leaks and locate those that are significant. All components of the compressed air system are inspected individually, and problem areas are identified. Losses and poor performance due to system leaks, inappropriate misuse, and total system dynamics are calculated, and a written report with a recommended course of action is provided.

It is best to start with the end users, because any improvements here may well influence the air distribution network (i.e., redundant pipe work and reduction in pressure losses) and compressor demand. It is also normally the area where the greatest savings can be achieved.

15.4.1 Leakage assessment

The first priority is to assess the site leakage rate, as this is often one of the greatest wastages. To do this, a leakage test must be carried out. From the results, the total percentage air lost, and the annual costs of leakage can be calculated. Following this a leakage survey should be carried out and all leaks identified on a site drawing, as well as by tagging. The auditor should recommend a leak management program.

15.4.2 End users assessment

After the leakage appraisal, it is essential to look at each significant compressed air user in detail. The major tasks that need to be carried out are to:

- Estimate the volume of major plant items, from either plant ratings or calculations, and note the number of hours they are operational, to help produce a breakdown of air usage and assist in deciding whether distribution lines are adequately sized;

- In some cases, recommendations such as specifying equipment that operates at a lower pressure will be made. An auditor may also recommend replacing existing compressed air-powered equipment with equipment that uses a source of energy other than compressed air.

- Compare the actual operating pressure with the design pressure and, if appropriate, fit a reducing valve (if the overall distribution line pressure cannot be reduced).

- Local storage and other modifications may be recommended.

- Investigate other methods of operation not involving the use of compressed air.

15.4.3 Distribution assessment

The distribution network should be surveyed, and drawings obtained. The main things to look out for are:

- Zoning arrangements to isolate areas on different working patterns;

- Adequate pipe sizing and drainage: a pressure profile across the mains would be useful to identify large pressure losses;

- Elimination of redundant pipework or shortening of supply lines.

15.4.4 Air treatment assessment

The following program should be carried out:

- The auditor typically examines the compressed air applications and determines the appropriate level of air treatment required for proper operation of the equipment. Actual air quality levels are then measured. If the air is not being treated enough, alternative treatment strategies are recommended. If the air is being over-treated (an indication of energy being wasted), recommendations are made to modify the system. In some cases, only certain end-use equipment requires highly treated air, and the auditor may recommend a system that, allows for different treatment levels at different points in the system.

- The total air-drying capacity required should be calculated during the end user audit. If more air than necessary is being dried, the possibility of having two distribution systems, a wet and a dry, should be considered. Consideration should also be given to treating the higher quality air at the point of use.

- All drainage traps should be checked to ensure that they are neither leaking nor air binding.

15.4.5 Compressor room assessment

Having established the lowest possible demand profile for compressed air, it is necessary to ensure that the demand is serviced in the most efficient way possible. To do this it is necessary to carry out the following steps:

- Record the electricity consumption of the compressors over a week by installing portable recording power meter on the supply cables.

- Have an air flow meter installed, record the actual air demand over the week.

- Record the pressure at identified critical point throughout the network to develop a pressure profile in order to identify areas of excessive pressure loss or pressure gradient.

- From the electricity and airflow recordings, calculate an air generation efficiency.

- Investigate the load profiles of each compressor with a view to deciding whether the optimum size machines are running at any one time.

- Consider better methods of compressor control, such as predictive switching or rotational sequencing depending on the compressor load profiles.

- The location of the air intakes into the compressors should be checked to ensure that they are not supplying warm, wet or dusty air.

System audits are designed to identify system inefficiencies. If a system is found poorly designed, in unsatisfactory operating condition or in need of substantial retrofit, a more detailed analysis of the system may be recommended.

A comprehensive evaluation may also include extensive measurements and analysis of supply and demand interactions. A financial evaluation should be performed, including current and proposed costs after retrofits are taken.

15.4.6 Demand profile

The required capacity for a compressed air system can be determined by summing the requirements of the tools and process operations (considering load factors) at the site. The demand requirement is not the sum of the maximum requirements for each tool and process, but the sum of the average air consumption of each. High short-term demands should be met by air stored in an air receiver.

Systems may have more than one air receiver. Strategically locating air receivers near sources of high demand can also be effective. In most cases, a thorough evaluation of system demand may result in a control strategy that will meet system demand with reduced overall compressor capacity.

Oversized air compressors are extremely inefficient because most systems use more energy per unit volume of air produced when operating a.t part-load. In many cases it makes sense to use multiple, smaller compressors with sequencing controls to allow for efficient operation at times when demand is less than peak.

If a system is properly designed and maintained but is still experiencing capacity problems, an alternative to adding another compressor is to re-examine the use of compressed air for certain applications. For some tasks, blowers or electric tools may be more effective or appropriate.

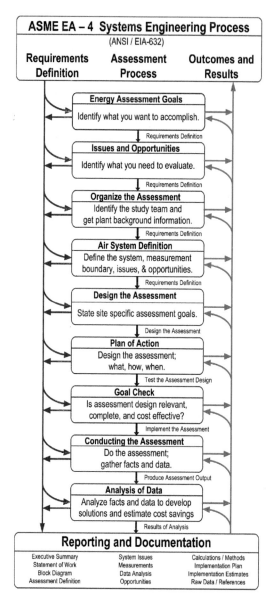

Figure 15.12 Systems engineering process for compressed air systems assessments.

Another key to properly designing and operating a compressed air system is assessing the plant's compressed air demand profile, that is, its requirements over a period of time. The variation in demand for air over time is a major consideration in system design. Plants with wide variations in air demand need a system that operates efficiently under partload. Multiple

compressors with sequencing controls may provide more economical operation in such a case. Plants with a flatter load profile can use simpler control
strategies.

15.4.7 Pressure profile

Different tools and process operations require different pressures. Pneumatic
tool manufacturers rate tools for specific pressures, and the process engineers
should specify process operation pressure requirements. Required pressure
levels must take into account system losses from dryers, separators, filters,
and piping. As mentioned before, a rule of thumb is that every 1.0 bar increase
in operating pressure requires an additional 6% in operating energy costs.

Energy can be saved in most multi-compressor installations by improving the pressure control system. The majority of systems have two basic
shortcomings:

- Pressures are maintained at a higher level than is needed by the end
  users; and

- Generation pressures are set too high and not varied according to demand.

The consequence of both failings is demonstrated in the figure below, which
represents a typical cascade control system.

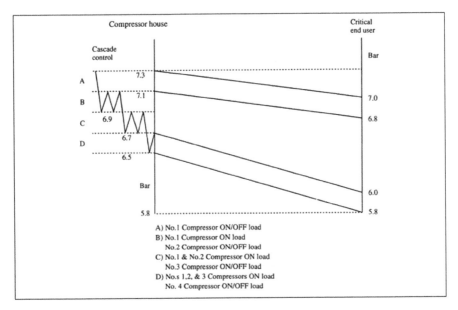

Figure 15.13 Cascade pressure control typical situation.

Usually, the minimum pressure needed by the most critical piece of machinery sets the lowest acceptable pressure at the compressor house. To ensure that this pressure is achieved at the critical point, the pressure at the compressor house (i.e. the control pressure) will need to be set to 0.7 bar above the value required, to overcome line pressure losses on the distribution network.

This includes occasions when the airflow rate is highest and hence the distribution losses are greatest. For example, if 5.8 barg is required, the control pressure will need to be 6.5 barg. This control pressure compensation is shown above by the lower two lines. The left-hand axis shows the cascade switching of the compressors and it represents a typical cascade pressure control system.

At maximum flow rates all four compressors will be operating, as designated by region D. As the air usage falls, the pressure in the lines at the compressor house will rise and one compressor will unload. If usage falls further, the pressure moves into region C where another compressor unloads, up to region A where only one compressor is providing the load. Due to the nature of the pressure switches, the minimum control bands are 0.2 bar for each compressor leading to a very wide overall control band (0.8 bar).

The consequence of a wide control band is that, except at maximum air usage, the end user and compressor control pressures will always be up to 10% higher than those actually required. This has two negative effects: firstly, it takes 6% more electricity to generate the air for every 1 bar greater pressure and secondly, the usage (and wastage) of air in most applications is directly proportional to its pressure, causing waste to artificial demand, which is a loss of 6–12% for every 1 bar greater pressure.

To keep generation costs to a minimum:

- Pressure control should be based on the pressure at the most sensitive/ critical pieces of machinery;

- Compressor sequencing should be based on as narrow a pressure band as possible to always achieve the minimum generation pressure.

Chapter 16

Large Scale Cooling and Industrial Refrigeration Systems

Albert Williams

Institute of Energy Professionals Africa, South Africa

Industrial Chilled water and Refrigeration (CR) systems refer to systems in industry that are responsible for comfort cooling, process cooling, and refrigeration. The refrigeration process transfers the heat energy from or to the products, processes, or the environment. Energy in form of electricity or heat is used to power mechanical equipment designed to transfer heat from a colder, low-energy level to a warmer, high-energy level.

There are two basic types of refrigerating systems, which will be dealt with in the chapter: *Vapor compression*, which is most commonly used, and *Absorption* which has the ability to use relatively low grade heat such as low pressure steam or solar energy to produce a cooling effect. The energy input into the refrigeration systems must be carefully managed to minimize cost, especially in the larger systems encountered in industrial and commercial facilities. Numerous opportunities exist for improving energy management and reducing operating cost.

Refrigeration deals with the transfer of heat from a low temperature level at the heat source to a high temperature level at the heat sink. The second law of thermodynamics states that heat cannot flow from a body of low temperature to another body at higher temperature unless work is being done to supply energy to the system. All conventional refrigeration cycles require that power be introduced into the refrigeration system to compress gas or vapor from a low suction pressure to a high condensing pressure creating a temperature lift.

16.1 Refrigerants

Refrigeration systems using vapor depend on the fact that a vaporizing liquid requires relatively large amounts of heat and that the temperature at which vaporization and condensation take place depends upon pressure. By regulating the vaporization and condensation pressures, refrigerant temperatures can be controlled for useful cooling and heating.

16.1.1 Desirable refrigerant characteristics

The refrigerants for industrial, commercial and institutional refrigeration and heat pump systems are selected to provide the best refrigeration effect at a reasonable cost. The following characteristics are desirable:

- Non-flammable to reduce fire hazard.

- Non-toxic to reduce potential health hazards.

- Large heat of evaporation to minimize equipment size and refrigerant quantity.

- Low specific volume in the vapor phase to minimize compressor size, critical for reciprocating and screw type compressors.

- Low liquid phase specific heat to minimize the heat required when subcooling the liquid below the condensing temperature

- High heat transfer coefficient.

- *Non-stratospheric ozone destroying properties.*

16.2 Vapor Compression Refrigeration Cycle

A CR system is a subsidiary of thermodynamics, heat transfer and refrigeration. An overview of a simplified CR system can be seen in Figure 16.1.

The basic refrigeration cycle, as illustrated in Figure 16.1, entails four steps:

- **Step 1 - Evaporator**
  A cool, low pressure liquid refrigerant is brought in contact with the heat source, the medium to be cooled. The refrigerant, being at low pressure, absorbs heat from the medium being cooled and boils, producing low pressure vapor at the saturation conditions. The heat exchanger used for this process is called the Evaporator.

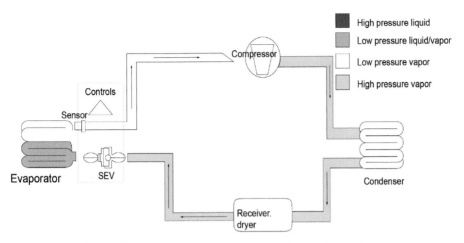

Figure 16.1 Vapor compression refrigeration cycle overview.

- **Step 2 - Compressor**
  The addition of the shaft work by the compressor raises the pressure of the refrigerant vapor. Increasing the gas pressure raises the boiling and condensing temperatures of the refrigerant. Once the refrigerant gas has been sufficiently compressed, its boiling point temperature is above the temperature of the heat sink, which is the higher temperature medium. The equipment doing the work is the compressor.

- **Step 3 - Condenser**
  The high pressure refrigerant gas, now carrying the heat energy absorbed at the evaporator and the work energy from the compressor, is pumped to a second heat exchanger called the Condenser. Because the refrigerant's condensing temperature is higher than that of the heat sink, heat transfer takes place, condensing the refrigerant from high pressure vapor to a high pressure saturated liquid. The heat source has been cooled by pumping the heat energy to the heat sink.

- **Step 4 - Throttling**
  The condensed liquid is returned to the beginning of the next cycle. Its pressure must be reduced to prevent the high pressure liquid from entering the low pressure evaporator and to reduce the boiling temperature of the refrigerant to below the temperature of the heat source. A throttling device such as valve, orifice plate or capillary is generally used for this purpose.

16.2.1 Coefficient of performance

Coefficient of performance (COP) is a measure of the amount of input energy compared to the amount of output energy. It is expressed as follows:

$$COP = \frac{Power\,output}{Power\,input}$$

COP is another measurement of energy efficiency: the higher the COP number, the more efficient the system is. COP has no magnitude; therefore, it is dimensionless. This is because the input power and the output power are both measured in watts.

Look at an example of an electrical heater where all the input energy is converted into heat when it enters the system. In this case, all the energy is used and not wasted. The power input, which is electricity, is equal to the power output, which is heat. Therefore, the COP is equal to one. The COP can be used in any system, not just cooling and heating systems.

If the example of a heat pump is used, it uses power to move heat from one place to another. When cooling occurs, the air conditioner moves the heat from the space or room that is being cooled to another space, which is usually outside. A heat pump works on the same principle, but it transfers heat from the outside to the space or room being heated inside, for example, an office room.

The efficiency of the refrigeration system is measured by the COP. The theoretical or Carnot Cycle efficiency of refrigeration can be written as:

$$COP = \frac{Tc}{Th - Tc}$$

Where:

COP = Coefficient of performance

Tc = Cold temperature

Th = Hot temperature

From the previous equation, the following can be deduced: As the difference between hot and cold temperatures increases, the COP becomes lower. When the difference decreases, the COP becomes higher. Therefore, a CR system is more efficient when the required cooling temperature is as close as possible to the temperature outside. When there is a huge difference in the temperatures, it causes the CR system to pull more power.

Example of how to calculate **COP**$_{Carnot}$

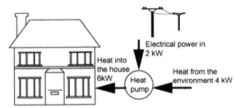

Figure 16.2 Example of COP for a heat pump in a heating system.

What is the energy efficiency of an CR system that is cooling a process to 20°C if the outside temperature is 36°C?

Solution

$$COP = \frac{Tc}{Th - Tc}$$

$$COP = \frac{20 + 273,15}{(36 + 273,15) - (20 + 273,15)}$$

$$COP = \frac{193,15}{16}$$

$$COP = 18.32$$

When you look at Figure 16.2, you will see that the heat pump takes power from the environment. The environment is outside, and the heat pump uses electric power to move energy from the outside to the space where it is needed, namely, inside. More energy is transferred into the building than electricity is used.

The $COP_{practical}$ of this system is 3. This is obtained using the following formula:

$$COP_{practical} = \frac{\text{heat into the building}}{\text{power supplied to the compressor motor}}$$

$$COP = \frac{6W}{2W}$$

$$COP = 3$$

The same principle applies for a CR system, but it works in the opposite direction. A CR system transfers the air from the area inside to the outside world. In Figure 16.3, the reverse happens where 2 kW of power is required to move 4 kW of power into the building, and a condenser dissipates 6 kW of

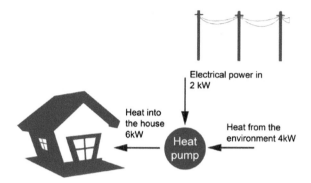

Figure 16.3   COP example of a CR system.

power into the environment. The CR system is using more than the electricity consumed.

The COP in this case is 2.

$$COP = \frac{\text{heat from environment}}{\text{input electrical power}}$$

$$COP = \frac{4}{2}$$

$$COP = 2$$

16.2.2 Practical considerations for vapor compression refrigeration systems

Refrigeration and heat pump cycles are more complex than the theoretical vapor compression cycles would indicate. Practical limitations such as equipment size, system pressure and design temperatures at the evaporator and condenser reduce the effectiveness of the actual system. Some of the limitations are as follows:

a) Heat transfer

Operating temperatures in actual cycles are established to suit the temperature required at the cool medium and the temperature acceptable for the heat sink. The practical temperature gradient required to transfer heat from one liquid to another through the heat exchanger is in the range of 5 to 8°C. This means that the refrigerant entering the evaporator should be 5 to 8°C colder than the desired medium temperature. The saturation temperature at the condenser should be 5 to 8°C above the temperature of the heat rejection medium. This causes an increase in the work required to produce the refrigerating effect because the temperature difference has increased.

b) Hot gas by-pass

Hot gas by-pass is a method of placing an artificial heat load on the refrigeration system to produce stable suction pressure and temperatures, when the refrigeration load is very low. The heat load is produced by passing hot gas from the compressor discharge to the evaporator inlet or the compressor suction. While permitting stable compressor operation at low load, *hot gas by-pass wastes energy*.

The total refrigeration load on a compressor with hot gas bypass will be equal to the actual load plus the amount of hot gas by-pass. Typically, hot gas by-pass on a reciprocating machine is 25% of the nominal refrigeration capacity for a 4-cylinder unit, 33% for 6-cylinder unit, and 37.5% for an 8-cylinder unit. For centrifugal equipment, by-pass varies with the load and impeller characteristics.

16.3 Absorption Cycle

Absorption refrigeration cycle is similar to the vapor compression cycle. It has an evaporator, a condenser and an expansion valve, but the compressor is substituted by an absorber and a generator as shown in Figure 16.4. Thus the mechanical compressor is replaced by the heat from a steam boiler to produce the necessary pressure differential between evaporator and condenser.

In the absorption cycle, the purely mechanical compression process is substituted by a chemical process activated by the steam or high temperature hot water.

A brief description of the absorption cycle is as follows:

*   **Step 1 – Absorber**
    After expansion in the evaporator, the refrigerant is absorbed by a low temperature absorbent fluid in the absorber.

*   **Step 2 – Generator**
    This solution is pumped to the generator where heat is supplied to drive the off the refrigerant (water) as gas.

*   **Step 3 – Expansion**
    The refrigerant is then condensed in the condenser and flows to the evaporator through the expansion valve for expansion.

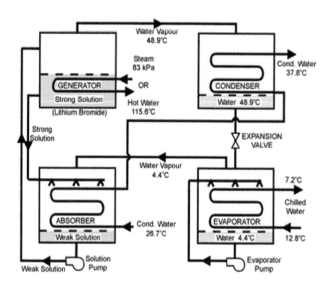

Figure 16.4 Absorption cycle overview.

Early absorption machines used ammonia as the refrigerant, as it is readily soluble in water. Modern machines also use water as the refrigerant and lithium bromide as the absorbent. Absorption refrigeration machines are simple. They operate without vibration, need little electric power, but require cheap steam and abundant cooling water. Their thermal efficiencies are very low with single-stage COP at about 0.8 and two-stage system COP at about 1.2. (In comparison, vapor compression systems operate with COPs ranging from 3 to 10).

16.4 Refrigeration System Components

The following major components are required in vapor compression refrigeration system.

16.4.1 Refrigerant compressors

Both displacement and dynamic compressors are commonly used in CR systems:

- ***Displacement*** machines increase the refrigerant pressure by reducing the volume of the compression chamber. This is done by applying shaft work to the mechanism. This category includes reciprocating, rotary (vaned), and screw (helical rotary) compressors.

- *Dynamic* machines increase refrigerant pressure through a continuous exchange of angular momentum between a rotating mechanical element and the fluid being compressed. Centrifugal and turbo compressors are in this category.

Displacement and dynamic refrigeration compressors are classified as hermetic, semi-hermetic or open:

- *Hermetic* compressors, including motor and drive, are sealed in a welded casing to contain the refrigerant and lubricating oil. They are available only in small sizes, are reasonably dependable and low in cost, but impractical to service.

- *Semi-hermetic* compressors are similar to the hermetic type, but the motor and compressor are in fabricated enclosure with bolted sections or access panels to facilitate servicing.

- *Open* compressors are characterised by an external drive shaft that extends through a seal in the compressor housing.

16.4.2 Evaporators

Evaporators commonly used in process cooling and air-conditioning systems fall into two categories:

- Direct expansion (DX) coils - primarily used for cooling air or other gas streams.

- Liquid coolers (shell and tube water chillers) - primarily used for producing chilled water, glycol, or brine for process cooling or air-conditioning.

a) DX coils

Direct expansion (DX) *coils* consist of a series of tubes through which refrigerant flows. The tubes are arranged into a number of parallel circuits fed from a single expansion valve. The hot refrigerant vapor is collected in the outlet (suction) gas header. The tubes are finned to increase the heat transfer rate from the medium to be cooled, generally air, to the boiling refrigerant.

DX coils are used only in positive displacement compressor systems because dynamic machine pressure-ratios are too low for proper coil operation. DX coils are subdivided into two types, flooded and dry.

With a *flooded* coil, a float valve maintains a preset liquid level in the coil, keeping the evaporator coil nearly full of liquid refrigerant. This full

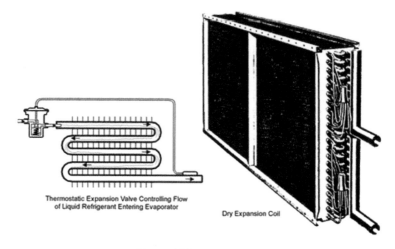

Thermostatic Expansion Valve Controlling Flow
of Liquid Refrigerant Entering Evaporator

Dry Expansion Coil

Figure 16.5   Evaporators.

contact of the liquid with the tube walls ensures a high rate of heat transfer. However, because of the large quantities of refrigerant required, flooded type evaporators are often impractical.

Dry coils contain little liquid refrigerant, reducing the cost of the refrigerant charge. A metering device, called a thermal expansion (TX) valve, regulates the amount of liquid that enters the coil in order to maintain a predetermined amount of superheat in the refrigerant at the coil outlet. A dry expansion coil contains mostly liquid at the inlet and only superheat vapor at the outlet, after having absorbed heat from the medium to be cooled.

b) Liquid coolers

Shell and tube heat exchangers are used to cool liquids, which can be used as a secondary refrigerant, or to cool the final product directly. These exchangers are referred to as chillers or liquid coolers. Applications include:

*   Chilling water for air-conditioning coils

*   Chilling milk after the pasteurization process

*   Chilling water in a drinking fountain

*   Process cooling

Liquid coolers are subdivided into two categories:

*   In a dry cooler, the liquid refrigerant is contained within tubes, and water or brine circulates through the shell of the cooler (evaporator).

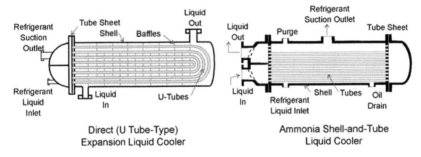

Figure 16.6   Liquid coolers.

- In a flooded cooler the water or brine circulates through the tubes. Usually, the tubes are finned to increase the heat transfer rate and reduce the evaporator size.

Dry type coolers are used in air-conditioning and refrigeration systems under 615 kW cooling, because the refrigerant charge is smaller, and the risk of equipment damage from freezing is less. Flooded coolers are more efficient on larger systems.

16.4.3 Throttling devices

A throttling device in a vapor compression system maintains the pressure differential between the high pressure (condenser) side and the low pressure (evaporator) side. The device regulates the flow of liquid refrigerant to the evaporator to match the equipment and load characteristics.

- A constant pressure expansion valve maintains a constant load on the compressor, regardless of the load on the evaporator, by metering the liquid refrigerant flow into the evaporator, based on suction pressure.

- The thermostatic expansion valve, the most widely used control device, automatically meters the flow of liquid refrigerant to the evaporator at a rate that matches system capacity to actual load. Connection of several DX evaporators in parallel using only one compressor is possible when each evaporator is provided with individual control. The valve senses the pressure and the temperature of the refrigerant leaving the evaporator and regulates the liquid refrigerant flow into the coil. Temperature is sensed at the coil outlet and pressure at the coil inlet.

- Float valves are used for metering refrigerant flow to a flooded liquid cooler. A low-side float valve is located on the low pressure side of the

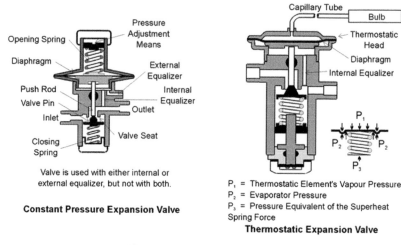

Figure 16.7   Expansion valves.

throttling device. A high-side float valve is located on the high pressure side of the throttling device. Liquid refrigerant is admitted by the float valve to the evaporator shell, at the same rate at which it is removed by the compressor. In some systems, the float operates an electrical switch that controls a solenoid valve. The solenoid valve periodically admits liquid refrigerant to the evaporator, allowing the liquid level to fluctuate within preset limits.

16.4.4 Condensers

Condensers are generally shell and tube type heat exchangers with refrigerant flow through the shell and coolant flow through the tubes. The lower portion of the shell acts as a liquid receiver. Where the lower tube sections are submerged in the refrigerant, the exchanger also acts as a subcooler to Minimize flash gas in the throttling process.

Other configurations are air-cooled coils, and evaporative condensers where water is sprayed over the coil. Auxiliary receivers and coolers are often used with these arrangements. Fans increase air flow over the coils and thus increase the heat transfer rate.

a) Water-cooled condensers

The following points must be examined if water-cooled condensers are being considered.

•   A supply of cooling water for heat rejection is required.

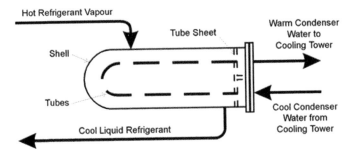

Figure 16.8 Shell and tube type heat exchanger.

- Where an inexpensive cooling water supply is not available, a cooling tower may prove practical.
- Auxiliary pumps and piping for recirculation of cooling water are required.
- Water treatment is required in water recirculation systems.
- Space requirements.
- Maintenance problems.
- Freeze protection for winter operation.

b) Air-cooled condensers

Air-cooled condensers use outside air as the cooling medium. Fans draw air past the refrigerant coil and the latent heat of the refrigerant is removed as sensible heat by the air stream. Air-cooled condensers are characterized by:

- Low installation costs.
- Low maintenance requirements.
- No water requirements. (Freezing, scaling, corrosion, water piping, circulating pumps and water treatment are eliminated).
- Outdoor installation is standard.
- Higher power requirements per kW cooling than evaporative or water-cooled condensers.
- Operating difficulties caused by increased condensing capacity and lower loads when operating at low ambient temperatures.
- Possible noise problems because of the high air volumes required for removing condenser heat.
- Multiple units are required in large systems.

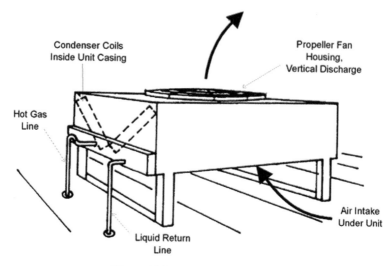

Figure 16.9 Air-cooled condenser.

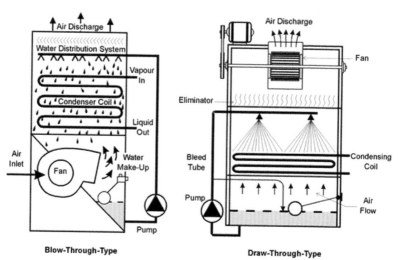

Figure 16.10 Evaporative condenser.

c) Evaporative condensers

In an evaporative condenser a water spray is directed over a refrigerant coil. The water absorbs heat from the refrigerant vapor in the coil causing the refrigerant vapor to condense. A fan draws air over the coil to remove saturated water vapor and heat. Water is added to make up for losses owing to evaporation, drift and blowdown. In winter, evaporative condensers may be operated without water. In this case, they act as air-cooled condensers.

Evaporative condensers incorporate characteristics of both air-cooled and water-cooled condensers:

- For a given capacity, less circulating water is required than for a water-cooled condenser with a cooling tower.

- Piping sizes are smaller and overall lengths are shorter.

- System pumps are smaller.

- Indoor locations are possible.

- Water treatment is required.

- Large capacity units are available.

- Space requirements are less than for air-cooled condensers, or shell and tube condensers when a cooling tower is used.

16.4.5 Heat rejection equipment

Common methods of rejecting heat are:

- Air-cooling.

- Water-cooling

- Evaporative cooling

a) Air-cooling equipment

General discussion of air-cooled equipment is included in the "Condensers" section of this chapter.

b) Water-cooling

A *water-cooled* system requires a clean and inexpensive source of cool water. Lake or river water may be practical only if both water treatment (required for prevention of scale buildup and corrosion protection) and filtration requirements are minimal. Municipal by-laws often limit the amount of potable water used for once-through, direct cooling, or refrigeration systems. Cooling towers and closed circuit evaporative coolers are used for rejecting heat when natural or municipal water sources are impractical.

c) Evaporative cooling

In a *cooling tower*, water is sprayed into an airstream. The latent heat of vaporization is removed when a fraction of the water evaporates. The cooled

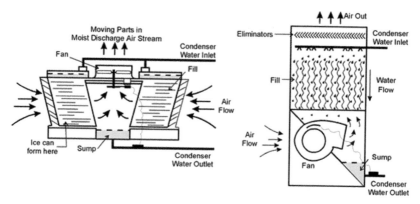

Figure 16.11   Water cooled system.

water is then reused. A cooling tower limits the amount of make-up water to that required to offset water loss caused by *evaporation, drift,* and *blowdown.* Water treatment is required to prevent algae growth and scale buildup. Blowdown is required to remove minerals and water treatment chemicals which are concentrated by the evaporation of the water.

Cooling tower performance is limited by the wet bulb temperature. At wet bulb temperatures close to the dry bulb temperature the air is close to saturation and has less ability to evaporate water. For refrigeration systems, it is usually impractical to lower the condenser water temperature to within 4°C of the ambient wet bulb temperature (i.e. an *approach* temperature of less than 4°C).

Closed circuit *evaporative coolers* use evaporation of water as the prime method of heat removal. Construction is similar to evaporative condensers, but the fluid being cooled is an intermediate heat transfer fluid, typically water or water-glycol solution. The cooled fluid is circulated to a shell and tube condenser to remove heat from the refrigeration system.

d) Other cooling systems
Other heat rejection methods are gaining acceptance.

- *Well water* that is adequate in capacity and quality may be used for condensing purposes. Heat pump applications make it possible to extract heat from an *aquifer* for winter heating, and reject heat to the aquifer during the cooling season. In this case, the aquifer acts as the heat source, and the heat sink. Special permits for using ground water are required in many countries.

- *Ground source* heat pumps use the earth as the heat sink or heat source. Installation costs tend to be high owing to the extensive coil area, and excavation required. Maintenance is costly. A careful balance between heat added to, or removed from the soil must be maintained so that unit cooling capacity is not jeopardized. Using the ground coil as a condenser for rejecting heat limits the cooling performance by drying the soil in the vicinity of the coil.

16.5 Industrial Refrigeration Applications in Food Industry

In the food processing industry, the food freezing step varies depending on food type and desired final product. Some fruits and berries are frozen almost immediately upon harvesting, while other foods are processed before freezing. Selected foods such as fried fish are frozen first, thawed for processing and then refrozen. Take cognizance of:

- The time-temperature profile of the freezing process is important due to its impact on frozen food quality.

- Slow freezing encourages large ice crystal formation whereas fast freezing favors formation of large number of small crystals.

- Large crystal formation leads to severe textural damage, caused by the 9% volume difference between liquid water and ice, of those products such as fruits and vegetables whose cell walls and membranes provide structural network. This damage is less important in processed foods.

- For optimum frozen food quality, the fastest possible freezing rate is normally preferred, although economic considerations also play a role in the selection of the appropriate food freezing process.

There are four primary classes of food freezing methods, defined as follows:

16.5.1 Still air or blast freezing

Still air freezing, the least efficient freezing method, is used mainly for food storage. Air blast freezing uses the movement of cold air, typically -10 to −40°C around the food to increase the freezing rate. Air blast freezing is the most widely practiced freezing method in commercial food processing facilities.

16.5.2 Cryogenic freezing

With cryogenic freezing an inert, low boiling liquefied gas is used in direct contact with the food. This freezing method is employed in small food

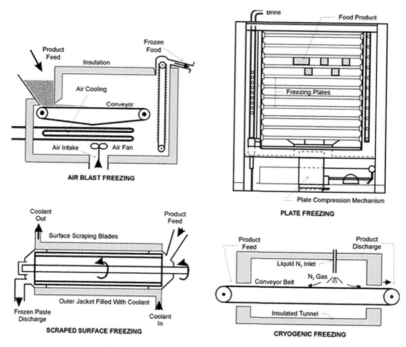

Figure 16.12   Four food freezing methods.

processing installations and for high value foods such as shrimps etc. Primary freezing agents include nitrogen and carbon dioxide. The main advantages of this freezing method are the extremely fast freezing rate and low cost of equipment installation. The main disadvantage is the high overall processing cost resulting from the expensive freezing agents.

16.5.3 Plate freezing

With plate freezing foods are frozen on metal plates that are internally cooled by liquid coolant. The heat transfer is by conduction. This type of freezing is used for rectangular packages of vegetable products, ice cream cartons and blocks of fish. With plate freezing, heat transfer is improved by having the cooled metal plates in direct contact with the food.

16.5.4 Scraped surface freezing

With scraped surface freezing unpackaged goods such as fruit, juices and ice cream are frozen on the inside surface of a barrel, which is cooled by liquid coolant. The frozen food is continuously scraped off mechanically. The scraped surface freezing is a very effective freezing method for unpackaged goods, since heat transfer is very high.

16.6 Energy Efficiency Ratios

The performance of a CR system can be expressed as the Energy Efficiency Ratio (EER) or Seasonal Energy Efficiency Ratio (SEER), based on certain test standards. EER is the measure of instantaneous energy efficiency, the ratio of the rate of heat removed from a cooled space by the equipment to the rate of electricity consumption in a steady operation, with the units Btu/Wh.

$$EER = \frac{\text{output cooling energy} (BTU)}{\text{electrical input energy} (\text{watt hour})}$$

Example of how to calculate EER
A CR system of 4 ton cooling capacity and has a power of 3,58 kW. What is the energy efficiency ratio?

$$EER = \frac{output\ cooling\ energy (BTU)}{electrical\ input\ energy (watt\ hour)}$$

Solution

$$EER = \frac{output\ cooling\ energy (BTU)}{electrical\ input\ energy (watt\ hour)}$$

$$EER = \frac{4 \times 12\,000}{3,58 \times 1000}$$

$$EER = 13,4$$

The 4 t is multiplied by 12 000; this conversion factor converts tons of cooling to BTU/h.

The EER can be specified at some temperature difference (this is the temperature difference between the inside and the outside space). Table 16.1 shows the changes with these temperature differences as well as the conditions that EER is usually given under.

To convert EER to COP, you need to convert the units used, that is, 1 BTU is equal to 1 055 J. The BTU energy and the electrical input energy is

Table 16.1   Temperature difference and EER conditions.

	Dry bulb temperature (°C)	Wet bulb temperature (°C)	Relative humidity (%)	Dew point (°C)
Outside temperature	3	24	40	19
Inside temperature	27	19	51	16

converted to joules. Electrical energy, which is measured in Wh, is converted into joules through the following conversion:

1 Wh is equal to 3 600 Ws or 3 600 J; so, to find COP using EER, the equation shown below is used.

$$COP = \frac{Output\ energy}{Input\ energy} = EER$$

$$1\,BTU \ / \ Wh = 1\ 055\,J$$

$$EER = \frac{1\ 055\,J}{3\ 600\,J}$$

$$= 0,293$$

SEER is the ratio of the total amount of heat removed by the equipment during a normal cooling season to the total amount of electricity consumed, with the units Btu/Wh. The relationship EER = 3.412 COP_r can thus be derived.

For CR systems, the EER and SEER ratings are commonly used. Many CR systems have a SEER rating of between 13 and 21, which correspond to COP values of between 3.8 and 6.2. The EER or COP decreases with decreasing temperature requirement, with the effect that it is not economical to refrigerate at a lower temperature than required, and important aspect to determine during an energy audit.

The efficiency of CR systems differs through the day due to the variation in ambient temperature, with the hottest part of the day resulting in the highest COP. It also varies with the actual load on the equipment. The metric, Integrated Energy Efficiency Ratio (IEER) is used to determine the cooling EER rating based upon the weighted average of efficiencies at various loading levels. The formula is as follows:

IEER = (0.02*A) + (0.617*B) + (0.238*C) + (0.125*D)

Where:

A = EER at 100% net capacity at AHRI standard condition (35°C)
B = EER at 75% net capacity and reduced ambient (27.5°C)

C = EER at 50% net capacity and reduced ambient (20°C)
D = EER at 25% net capacity and reduced ambient (18.3°C)

16.7 Sensible and Latent Heat

You have already learned some basic information on sensible and latent heat in a previous section. In this section, it focuses more on its application in CR systems. In a CR system, the air is conditioned or changed. The conditioning of the air in the CR system is dependent on two factors: sensible heat and latent heat. Both latent and sensible heat are types of energy that are released into the atmosphere. Latent heat occurs when there is a change in phase between a gas, solid and liquid, while sensible heat is related to a change in temperature of a gas or object with no change in phase. When speaking about CR systems, latent heat refers to the moisture in the air and sensible heat refers to the temperature. You cannot sense latent heat, since it is energy that is given off when, for example, a gas changes to a liquid, but you can sense sensible heat because it refers to the temperature of something.

Therefore, in a CR system, sensible heat is responsible for changing the temperature without influencing the pressure and volume. Latent heat, on the other hand, is responsible for humidifying and dehumidifying in the CR system.

Figure 16.13 shows the difference between the sensible and latent heat. It shows that the sensible heat increases in a uniform manner with temperature while the latent heat increases without an increase in temperature.

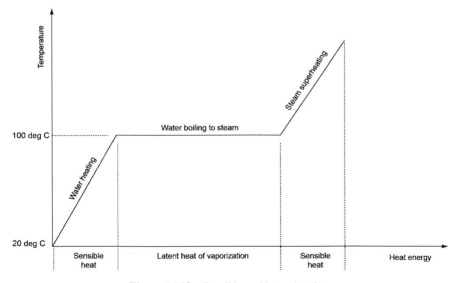

Figure 16.13 Sensible and latent heating.

16.7.1 Sensible heat

The sensible heat is part of the heat exchange by a thermodynamic system that changes the temperature without any effect on variables such as volume and pressure. This is the type of heat that can be felt, or "sensed". Sensible heat is only described by its temperature.

Sensible heat and temperature are interrelated: if there is an increase in temperature, the sensible heat content will also increase. If an increase is on the sensible heat content, it does not mean the substance that is heated will also abide by the same increase. Some substances will increase at their own rate while others may follow the rate of the sensible heat. The characteristics of substances are definitely different and that is why the equation representing the specific heat and temperature has a constant in it for specific heat capacity. The equation to calculate the sensible heat is as follows:

$$Q_{sensible} = mC_p\Delta T$$

$Q_{sensible}$ represents the sensible heat, the body mass of the product, C_p the specific heat capacity of the product and ΔT the change in temperature. The general rule of thumb is that if there is a sudden increase in heat, that gain is accompanied by a change in either volume or pressure of the substance. This is evident with water when it is heated for both sensible and latent heat.

16.7.2 Latent heat

The latent heat, as shown in Figure 16.13, takes place when temperature is constant. Latent heat occurs when energy is released or absorbed by a thermodynamic system. However, the energy is only released or absorbed during a constant temperature process like when a substance goes through a phase transition. For example, heat energy is released when ice melts or when water boils (when a phase change occurs). When, for example, ice melts, the water molecules lose their strength during the phase change from a solid to a liquid. This molecule breakage requires some sort of energy to make sure that the process becomes a success. This energy is the latent heat.

Therefore, latent heat takes place as a result of sensible heat. The sensible heat changes the temperature while the latent heat absorbs or releases it. For example, ice will start to melt because of a change in sensible heat, but the actual phase change releases energy. However, the temperature of the product under latent heat does not change even if sensible heat is imposed on it. Because the latent heat is a form of energy, it is only increased when specific heat is increased, but the actual temperature of the product or object under latent heat will remain constant. The ice melting example can help to explain this. The energy used to break the ice's molecules is conserved until nothing can be done after the molecules are apart.

The temperature on the melting ice only starts to change once the ice has melted into liquid. The only change that takes place when the ice is exposed to excess heat is in sensible heat. The latent heat, because it cannot be felt, can be noticed by trying to reverse the process of melting the ice. The sudden change of temperature to as low as 0°C cannot transform melted ice back to its former self. It will take time before all the energy (latent heat) is removed from the liquid before it gets frozen.

Overall, the heat energy is conserved regardless of the phase change that is taking place. This means that in the CR system, the heat used by the chiller can never be lost due to either latent or sensible heat. The excess heat used by sensible heat is absorbed by the latent heat to be used at a later stage or when needed. For example, if cool air is required an hour after the setpoint has been reached, the heat energy in the latent heat will be released resulting in the required air being produced. This helps to Minimize the costs on energy as extra energy is not required to change the condition of the air to cool the area/process.

16.8 Energy Efficiency Measures for CR Systems

The possible cost saving opportunities in a CR system includes properly sizing equipment and designing equipment for the energy efficiency within the facility. The cost saving opportunities are realized mostly at the design stages of the CR system in most industrial facilities. The inclusion of components like dampers, supply and exhaust fans, filters, humidifiers, dehumidifiers, heating and cooling coils, ducts, and various sensors plays a significant role in achieving cost savings on the CR system. However, these components must work optimally for energy and cost saving to take place. Table 16.2 provides measures to ensure that your CR system runs optimally, which will provide you with opportunities to save costs.

Moreover, energy monitoring and control systems must be put in place to ensure that the energy consumption of the CR system is detected and recorded. This will help to reduce the time necessary to spot the defects and address them accordingly. These systems play a bigger role in managing and optimizing the CR system to make sure that energy consumption is within specified limits. The control during non-operational hours may be adjusted via floating temperature control to potentially save considerable energy.

Table 16.2 Optimal operation of a CR system which leads to cost saving opportunities.

Measurement	Target value (potential)	Potential retrofit action
Leakage in ducts	A reduction in air handler flow with 10%	Sealing of ducts using aeroseal or tape or mastic
Insulation on ducts	R6 and R8 types of insulation to be applied for all ducts including outside conditioned space	Insulation is added to ducts
Air flow at the registers	It must be similar to the one in approved manuals	Registers to be replaced, dampers opened/closed, and the system flow resistance reduced by straightening out the existing ducts or replacing them with new straight ones.
Air handler flow	Cooling should be achieved with less than 12 Nm^3/min/t for dry climate and less than 10 Nm^3/min/t for humid climate. Heating should be maintained at approximately 0.0000203 m^3/J.	The filters must be replaced, and the duct restrictions fixed. The fan must be replaced with a highly efficient one with speed control unit. The extra return must be added in the return restricted systems.
Filter condition	It will be clean and adhere to the set-out standards	It must be replaced with the standard filters with the OEM recommended sizes.
Thermostat setting	For comfort cooling, heating should be in the region of approximately 20°C and cooling in region of 25°C	Thermostats rise in summer and in winter subsides. This will create a balance between these two seasons for better distribution among others.
Spot ventilation	An appropriate source that is capable of 0,07 Nm^3/min/W rating can be used.	Fans with higher efficiency unit or cleaning of both ducts and fan is an appropriate action.
CR system lifespan	Determine the exact lifespan of the system	Periodic cleaning and maintenance are required and the system should be considered for replacement if the lifespan has exceeded 20 years.

Table 16.3 Energy management opportunities in CR systems.

Step	Actions
Determine the need	• Document real heating/cooling system load requirements. • Separate fuel energy used for required heating/cooling. • Determine design and ultimate requirements for use of the system • Revise the load on the system as it will change as new energy management systems are used.
Match the need	• Ensure the process/comfort temperature is not significantly greater than the highest requirement. • Operate at the minimum possible temperature. • Reduce flows/temperatures to match ultimate requirements for use of system. • Eliminate inappropriate use of cooling, e.g. cooling and heating systems that are 'fighting' against each other.
Maximize efficiency	• Minimize air infiltration / exfiltration where applicable • Ensure tight seal in industrial refrigeration applications • Ensure insulation is up to standard.
Optimize supply	• Minimize solar gains when cooling and maximize them when heating. • Use solar heating technology for space or water heating, especially combined with improved insulation • Optimize chiller control

The use of reflective equipment on buildings, especially the roofing, can also help to save costs. In summer, for example, energy and costs can be saved because the heat required to stabilize temperatures can be harnessed from the sun. The ventilation systems like low-emittance windows can be used because they regulate the amount of heat energy transmitted into the building. This helps in an increase in insulation ability.

List of Abbreviations

Abbreviations	Definition
AC	Alternating current
AC	Air conditioning
ACE	Air change effectiveness
Ah	Amp-hours
AMOC	Atlantic Meridional Overturning Circulation
Amp	Ampere
ASD	Adjustable speed drive
ASHRAE	American Society of Heating, Refrigeration and Air-Conditioning Engineers
ASME	American Society of Mechanical Engineers
BAS	Building automated systems
BEA	Building energy audit
BEP™	Certified Business Energy Professional
BMS	Building management systems
BTU	British thermal unit
C	Coulomb
CAP™	Certified Carbon Auditing Professional
CASO	Compressed Air System Optimization
CEA™	Certified Energy Auditor
CEM®	Certified Energy Manager
CENELEC	Comité Européen de Normalisation Électrotechnique
CFC	Chlorofluorocarbons
CIEP™	Certified Industrial Energy Professional
CLEP™	Certified Lighting Efficiency Professional
clo	A unit to measure the insulation of material
CMVP®	Certified Measurement and Verification Professional
CO_2	Carbon dioxide
COP	Coefficient of performance
COP	Conference of Parties
CPR	Cardiopulmonary Resuscitation
REP™	Certified Renewable Energy Professional
CSIR	Council of Scientific and Industrial Research

CU	Coefficient of utilisation
dBAeq	Equivalent A-weighted decibels
DBT	Dry bulb temperature
DC	Direct current
DDC	Direct digital control
DDT	Dichlorodiphenyltrichloroethane
DIN	Deutsches Institut für Normung
DSM	Direct system monitoring
EEC	Energy efficiency calculator
EMO	Energy management opportunities
FSAT	Fan system assessment tool
GFA	Gross floor area
GHG	Greenhouse gases
GIZ	Deutsche Gesellschaft für Internationale Zusammenarbeit
GJ	Gigajoules
HCFC	Hydrochlorofluorocarbon
HFC	Hydrofluorocarbon
HRSG	Heat recovery steam generator
HVAC	Heating, ventilation and air conditioning
HWR	Heating water return
Hz	Hertz
IAQ	Indoor air quality
IEA	International Energy Agency
IEC	International Electro-technical Commission
ISO	International Organisation for Standardisation
ITP	Industrial technologies program
J	Joules
kg	Kilogram
kg/m²	Kilogram per meter square
km	Kilometer
kPa(g)	Kilopascal gauge
kVa	Kilovolt-ampere
kW	Kilowatt
kW	Kilowatts
kWh	Kilowatt-hour
kWh/m²	Kilowatt hour per square meter
L	Litres
L/s	Litres per second
l/s/m²	Litres per second per square meter floor area
l/s/p	Litres per second per person

LCC	Life cycle cost
LPG	Liquefied petroleum gas
LTMS	Long-term mitigation scenarios
m	Meter
m²	Meter squared
mm	Millimeter
MSO	Motor System Optimization
mv²	Kinetic energy
MVA	Mega volt ampere
N	Newton
N.m	Newton meter
NEMA	National electrical manufacturers association
Nm³/min	Normal cubic meters per minute
NPSH	Net positive suction head
ODS	Ozone-Depleting Substances
OHSA	Occupational Health and Safety Act
P	Power
p/MW	Per megawatt
Pa	Pascal
PC	Personal computer
PF	Power factor
PMV	Predicted mean vote
POP	Persistent Organic Pollutants
PoU	Point of use
PPE	Personal Protective Equipment
PPM	Part per million
PSAT	Pump system assessment tool
PSO	Pump System Optimization
PV	Photovoltaic
PVC	Polyvinyl chloride
QSE	Quality of a service
RCA	Recycled concrete aggregate
RH	Relative humidity
RMS	Root mean square
RPM	Revolutions per minute
RTD	Resistance temperature detectors
S	Second
SCADA	Supervisory Control and Data Acquisition
SEU	Significant Energy Uses
SHW	Service hot water

SSAT	Steam system assessment tool
SSO	Steam System Optimization
SSST	Steam system scoping tool
T	Ton
TB	Tuberculosis
TOU	Time-of-use
TVOC	Total volatile organic compounds
UA	Unoccupied area
UNFCCC	United Nations Convention on Climate Change
USB	Universal serial bus
VA	Volt-ampere
VA/m²	Volt ampere per square meter
VDE	Verband der Elektrotechnik
VFD	Variable frequency drive
W	Watts
W/m²	Watts per square meter
WBT	Wet bulb temperature
Wh	Watt-hour
WHMIS	Workplace hazardous material information system
WHRB	Waste heat recovery boiler
WWF	World Wildlife Fund

Definitions

Words	Definition
Abrasions	Damage to the body caused by scraping the skin
Accountability	When an organisation or individual is obligated to account for its activities
Acoustic	Related to sound
Actuator	A type of motor that is responsible for moving or controlling a mechanism or system.
Adhesive	Any substance applied to the surfaces of materials that binds them together.
Airborne contaminants	Impurities; any material associated with a chemical, a pharmaceutical preparation, or an infectious agent that is carried by air.
Ambient air pressure	On an object is the pressure of the surrounding medium, such as a gas or liquid, which comes into contact with the object.
Amenable	Easily controlled.
Angular velocity	The rotational speed of an object about an axis
Annual	On a yearly basis
Armature	A component or device used in motors and generators to connect the magnet poles
Asynchronous	Not taking place at the same time
Atom	The smallest bit of ordinary matter
Atrium	A large open space located within a building
Auxiliary equipment	Equipment not directly used in system; offline equipment
Aviation	Aircraft engineering
Backfill	To refill an excavated hole with the material dug out of it
Baffle	A construction which is used to reduce the flow of fluid and transfer heat.
Barometric	An instrument used in the study of atmosphere to measure the pressure that relates to the atmosphere of the earth.

Baseline   A standard basis used for comparing or controlling measurements.

Benchmark   An objective reference point that things will be compared to

Best practice   A technique or, in this case, operating methodology that has been proven to reliably lead to a desired result

Boiler feedwater Treated water used as feed to a boiler to produce steam

Boost   This is a dc-dc power converter with the input voltage greater than the input voltage

Buck   A type of converter that steps down the voltage and steps up the current

Buck-boost   A type of equipment used to make adjustments to alternating current equipment

Building condition surveys A method that will let you understand the general condition of a building, including all building defects.

Building envelope A building envelope is the physical separator between a conditioned and unconditioned area of a building including the resistance to air, water, heat, light and noise transfer

Calibrate   To match or compare the readings collected with the standard ones.

Capacitance   The amount of charge that can be stored

Capture velocity The minimum average air speed necessary to draw air through a filter and effectively remove contaminants in the air stream

Caulking   The processes and material (also called sealant) to seal joints or seams in various structures and some types of piping

Cavitation   Pumps and pumping systems play a huge role in commercial, industrial and most municipality fraternity

Cavity walls   Consist of two 'skins' separated by a hollow space (cavity). The skins are commonly masonry such as brick or concrete block

Circulatory   To move in circle

Cladding   A covering or coating on a structure or material

Climate   The generally prevailing weather conditions of an area including, temperature, air pressure, humidity, precipitation, sunshine, cloudiness, and winds, throughout the year, averaged over a series of years

Cogeneration system	A system that creates both electricity and useful heat at the same time. It is also called combined heat and power
Commission	To bring something (newly produced) into working condition
Commutator	A device that reverses the direction of the current
Comprehensive	Including or dealing with all or nearly all elements or aspects of something
Condensate	A liquid formed when gas cools down and turns into its liquid phase
Condenser	A piece of equipment that removes heat from vapors or a vapor/liquid mixture resulting in the condensation of the product. The cooling medium is generally water.
Conduction	The flow of heat between two materials of different temperatures that are in direct physical contact
Conductor	A material that allows an electric current to pass through
Confined	(of a space) restricted in area or volume; cramped
Contaminants	Something that get into a substance, and makes that substance unsuitable for use
Control devices	Adjusts the controlled value to comply with the set point value.
Convective	The transfer of heat by means of air currents
Corrosion	Damage caused to metal because of a chemical reaction
Crank	A device that causes a rotary action; it is made up of a handle attached at right angles to the shaft
Current	Flow of electrons in a material
Dalton's law of partial pressure	Determines the individual pressures of each gas in a mixture of gases
Damper	A device that deadens, restrains, or depresses
Data loggers	Devices used to record measurements over a certain period of time and create a profile of that particular parameter that is being measured
Dbaeq	An expression of the relative loudness of sounds in air as perceived by the human ear. In the a-weighted system, the decibel values of sounds at low frequencies are reduced, compared with unweighted decibels, in which no correction is made for audio frequency.
Deaerator	A device that is widely used for the removal of oxygen and other dissolved gases from the feedwater to the steam-generating boiler

Deferring	Putting off for a later time
Degradation	Lowering the quality or state of something
Dehumidifies	Controlled reduction of water vapor from the air
Demand response	Any measure taken to reduce the demand
Destratify	To form or place in layers
Diffuse radiation	The sunlight that has been scattered by molecules and particles in the atmosphere but that has still made it down to the surface of the earth
Diffuser	A duct that widens an airflow and slows it down
Displacement power factor	The power factor due to the phase shift between voltage and current at the fundamental line frequency
Distilled water	Water which is pure and most of the impurities are removed through a process called distillation
Distortion	The number of fluctuations the current will have before it reaches the end user
Distributed system	Two or more systems connected together
Domestic hot water	Water used, in any type of building, for domestic purposes, principally drinking, food preparation, sanitation and personal hygiene
Dry bulb temperature	Temperature of the air as measured by a standard thermometer
Economies of scale	The cost advantage that arises with increased output of a product
Economizer operations	Operations of devices intended to reduce energy consumption
Economizers	A piece of mechanical equipment that preserves heat to use it for other purposes like preheating the fluid.
Electrical pylon	Used to transport electricity
Electromagnet	A type of magnet in which the magnetic field is produced by an electric current
Electromagnetic radiation	A type of energy that is produced by a disturbance in electrical or magnetic waves
Electron	A subatomic particle with a negative elementary electric charge.
Element	A substance that is made totally from one type of atom
Emission	The release of substances (like greenhouse gases e.g. Co_2) into the atmosphere
Emissivity	The ratio of the energy radiated from a material's surface to that radiated from a blackbody at the same temperature and wavelength and under the same conditions

Emit	Produce and discharge (something, especially gas or radiation)
Energy	The capacity for doing work; having several forms that may be transformed from one to another, such as thermal (heat), mechanical (work), electrical or chemical
Energy audit	A survey, inspection or analysis of energy consumption to see how energy can be conserved in a building, process or system
Energy security	In countries with economies based on exported oil and gas, the larger concern is security of demand, a demand with little changes
Energy sub-metering	The measurement and billing of energy consumption for individual suites in a multiunit building or provide separate meters on all major uses in the building, including chillers, car parks, air-handling fans, lifts and common area light and power
Energy surge	A sudden increase in electricity
Energyplus	The name of a weather data program
Enthalpy	The sum of sensible and latent heat of an air-moisture mixture relative to the sensible plus latent heat at 0°C at standard atmospheric pressure
Ergonomic	A type of science that makes use of the correct equipment design in the workplace, this is used to maximize productivity in the workplace
Excited	An action caused by an electrical current, creating a magnetic field
Exfiltration	Uncontrolled outward air leakage from inside a building, including leakage through cracks and interstices around windows and doors and through any other exterior partition or penetration
Explosion	A violent release of energy which is caused by chemical, nuclear or mechanical energy
Exposure	When unprotected, and there is a risk of being in contact with danger
Extinguish	Put out
Extrapolate	To estimate (the value of a variable) outside the observed range.
Facades	The main front of a building, that faces onto a street or open space
Farad	The unit of capacitance and has the symbol f
Fatality	Death, not from natural causes

Feasibility	Can be easily done
Fenestration	The arrangement of windows in a building
Flammable	Burns easily
Flow rate	The amount (volume or mass) of substance that passes per unit time
Flue	Duct, pipe, or opening in a chimney for conveying exhaust gases from a fireplace, furnace, water heater, boiler, or generator to the outdoors
Forced air drafts	Using a flow of air or air forced through a pipe or system of pipes by fans or blowers
Formaldehyde	A naturally occurring organic compound with the formula CH_2O
Fossil fuel	A natural fuel such as coal or gas, formed in the geological past from the remains of living organisms
Free electrons	A negatively charged particle that is not attached to any atom
Full-rated load input power	The input power of the machine when the load is as stipulated on the nameplate
Glaze	Windows, doors or other transparent elements including their frames (such as glass bricks or glazed doors) located in the building
Green buildings	Buildings that are environmentally responsible and resource-efficient throughout, from siting to design, construction, operation, maintenance, renovation and deconstruction.
Green star rating system	A tool used to assess the environmental impact of a project's design, site and construction according to a number of categories.
Greenhouse gas emissions	Gases that can absorb the solar radiation and trap it in the earth's atmosphere. These gases include carbon dioxide, water vapor, methane, nitrous oxide and others
Gross floor area	Floor area of heated or cooled spaces, excluding non-habitable cellars and unheated spaces, including the floor area on all stories if more than one
Harmonic distortion	The degree to which a waveform would deviate from the fundamental waveform
Harmonics	Any of a series of periodic waves whose frequencies are integral multiples of a fundamental frequency

Head	The maximum height the pump can deliver or move the liquid upwards
Heart defibrillator	A device that uses electricity to control irregular heartbeats and prevent heart attacks
Heat exchanger	A device used to transfer heat from one medium to another, where the mediums are not in direct contact with each other
Holes	This refers to the absence of electrons on an atom.
Homogenous	Of the same kind; alike.
Humidification	The artificial regulation of humidity in home environments, industrial environments and health care applications such as artificial respiration.
Humidity	A measure of the moisture content of air
Hybrid	A thing made by combining two different elements.
Hygiene	Practicing cleanliness to maintain good health
Hypotenuse	The longest side of a right-angled triangle
Hypotenuse of the triangle	The longest side of a triangle
Ignition	Starting a fire, or causing something to burn
Illumination	A light that is directed into a space and shines onto something.
Immobilize	To prevent someone/something from moving
Implications	Consequences
Impulse steam turbine	Types of turbines consisting of fixed nozzles which are used to increase the velocity of the high-pressure steam.
Incandescent lighting	This is the least efficient type of a lighting system and it is mostly found in residential areas
Incentive	Reward that serves as a motivational device for a desired action
Incentive schemes	A formal scheme used to promote or encourage specific actions or behavior by a specific group of people during a defined period of time.
Incident radiation	The radiation (solar energy) hitting a specific surface
Incremental	Added or gained
Inductance	When a wire resists the flow of electric current
Inductive reactive current	The effect a current has in a circuit and this causes the current to lag the voltage
Industrial competitiveness	Different industries competing with one another relating to the supply and demand of the same product. In this case competing in terms of energy efficiency mechanisms.

Inert gases	Types of gases that do not react chemically under any conditions
Inertia	The refusal of an object to any change in its state of motion.
Infiltration	The entry of outside air into a building, which is similar to ventilation except that the entry of air with infiltration is unintentional or uncontrolled.
Inflammation	This is a reaction to injury or infection where that part of the body gets red, hot, swollen and often painful
Infrared gun	Devices used to determine surface temperature using the heat radiated from that particular equipment.
Inhale	To breath in
Inrush current	Immediate or instant current that is drawn by an electric device when it is switched or turned on.
Insulation	Materials that prevent or slow down the movement of heat.
Insulator	A substance that does not easily allow heat to pass through it
Integer	A whole number
Interrelated	To relate or connect to each other
Isolating	Separating
Kelvin	The units used to measure temperature
Kinetic energy	The energy something possesses because of its movement
Laminar	Something that takes place along constant streamlines, without turbulence.
Latent heat	The change in heat content that occurs with a change in phase and without change in temperature
Latent heat of fusion	The amount of heat produced to change a solid into a liquid with no change in temperature
Latent heat of vaporization	The input energy required to change the state from liquid to vapor at constant temperature
Ligaments	A type of fibrous tissue that holds bones or cartilage together
Linear load	A load is considered non-linear if its usage changes with the applied voltage
Load shedding	When there is not enough electricity to meet the demand and it is necessary to interrupt electricity supply in certain areas
Lubricated	When machinery is greased with oil to prevent or reduce friction

Magnetising flux	This is the amount of magnetic field passing through a surface
Magnitude	Amount of something
Maintain	To keep something in a good condition by making repairs
Mandatory	Change to required or needed.
Masonry	The building of structures from individual units laid in and bound together by mortar; the term masonry can also refer to the units themselves
Mastic	Any of the various pasty materials used as protective coatings or cements
Matter	A substance that occupies space
Media	Substances, like air, through which a force acts or an effect is produced
Metabolic rate	The speed at which your body uses up energy
Methane	An odorless gas but highly flammable
Migrant workers	A worker that moves from place to place to find work
Mitigation	Reducing the severity, seriousness, of something
Modulation	The process of adding information to a steady electronic signal
Molar	Relating to one mole of a substance
Motor pole	The number of electromagnetic windings that a motor has.
Motor speed	The speed measured at the shaft of the motor.
Multiples	A multiple is a product of any quantity and an integer
Network analyzers	An instrument that measures the network parameters of electrical networks
Neutral	When an atom has an equal number of protons and electrons
Night-setback	Changing the temperature to a lower setting on your heating system at night
Nonlinear load	This is when the usage does not change with the applied voltage
Non-revenue water	Water that has been produced and is "lost" before it reaches the customer
Noxious effluent control	Control flow of poisonous fluids
Objective	Based on fact, not on opinion (the opposite of subjective)
Occupancy applications	Applications or control systems used to determine whether there are people in a particular space or not.

Occupancy sensor	A device that detects the presence or absence of people within an area and causes lighting, equipment or appliances to be regulated accordingly.
Orbital	The path of an electron around the atom's nucleus
Orientation	The wind direction that a building's windows face (like north or south)
Overhaul	To dismantle equipment in order to repair it thoroughly
Parameters	A numerical or other measurable factor forming one of a set that defines a system or sets the conditions of its operation.
Partial pressure	In a gas mixture, each gas
Peak energy demand reduction	The building should reduce its peak electrical demand load.
Per capita	Per person
Photons	An elementary particle, the minimum amount of light and all other forms of electromagnetic radiation
Photovoltaic	This is a method that is used to convert solar energy into direct current using photovoltaic cells
Photovoltaic shingles	Solar panels or solar modules designed to look like and function as conventional slate.
Plane	A two-dimensional flat surface.
Pneumatic	Powered by compressed air
Point of end-use	Point where a product is used for the ultimate application for which it has been designed
Portable	A smaller version of something which can be easily carried around
Potential	Might happen, but has not happened yet
Potential difference	The work done when one unit charge is moved from one point to another
Power factor	This is the ratio of the real power that is used to do work and the apparent power that is supplied to the electricity grid
Prefix	A letter or a group of letters that represents a word with some of its meaning
Preliminary	Prior to or preparing for the main matter, action, or business
Pressure differential	Pressure difference that exists between two points
Process effluent	An outflowing of water or gas from a process or system.

Proton	A positively charged subatomic particle found in the nucleus of every atom
Psychrometric	A field interested in the thermal and physical properties of gas-vapor mixtures
Quantitative	Describing something relating to a type of information or data that is based on quantities obtained, using a quantifiable measurement process
Quotient	The answer obtained when dividing two numbers
Radiant energy	Energy that can travel through space or an energy of electromagnetic waves
Radiation	The transfer of heat through matter or space by means of electromagnetic waves
Reaction steam turbine	Types of turbines consisting of shaped rotor blade nozzles to create a reaction which causes the turbine shaft to rotate.
Real time	The actual time during which a process takes place, or an event occurs
Reciprocal	A number that when multiplied by a given number gives one as a product.(r = 1/u)
Rectifier	An electric device that converts alternating current into direct current
Regulations	A rule, which is maintained by an authority
Relative humidity	The amount of water vapor in the air compared to the actual amount of water vapor that the air can hold at a specific temperature and pressure
Relay	An electrical device, typically incorporating an electromagnet, which is activated by a current or signal in one circuit to open or close another circuit
Replenish	To fill again
Repulsion/repel	The force with which two things (charges) want to move away from each other
Retrofit	Install or fit (a device or system, for example) for use in or on an existing structure, especially an older dwelling
Reverse cycle heat pumps	A special heat pump that can draw heat from the outdoor air and circulate it into your home during winter and in the summer, it reverses the process and draws heat from the inside air and releases it outdoors
Rotor	The moving component of an electromagnetic system in an electric motor

R-value	A measure of the capacity of a material to resist heat transfer. The r-value is the reciprocal of the conductivity of a material (u-value). The larger the r-value of a material, the greater its insulating properties
Sankey diagrams	Type of flow diagrams in which the width of the arrow is shown proportionally to the flow quantity used to visualise energy or material or cost transfers between processes.
Saturate	To absorb more liquid until it can no longer be absorbed
Scalar	A quantity that has magnitude but no direction
Sensible heat	Energy that jostles molecules and atoms in substances such as water. The more movement, the hotter the substance becomes. Sensible energy gets its name from the fact that we can sense it, by touching the substance directly or indirectly with a thermometer of some type. It is the heat absorbed or released when a substance undergoes a change in temperature
Set point	A set point is the desired value for the controlled variable
Simulation calculation	This is a calculation used to analyze the thermal energy in a building using several factors
Sine wave	A waveform that has an oscillating (back and forth) motion
Sinusoidal	A sine wave or mathematical curve that repeats in the same back and forth movements
Slip	The difference between the motor speed and synchronous speed.
Smart technology	The simpler and easier ways of doing traditional things in a more effective and productive manner. For example, sending a text message rather than a letter through the post office to someone on urgent matters.
Smother	Cover something so that no air can get to it
Solar water heating	The conversion of sunlight into renewable energy for water heating using a solar thermal collector.
Solvents	A substance that dissolves a solute to form a solution, these are found in items such as hairsprays, paints, etc.
Specific heat capacity	The quantity of heat required to change the temperature of one unit weight of a material by one degree
Stagger demand	Demand to place or arrange in alternating or overlapping positions or time periods to prevent confusion or congestion
Stator	Stationary part of the rotary system in an engine

Steam system model	A plan created to use a steam system efficiently.
Step size	The uniform position used to determine the spacing between readings.
Strenuous	Requiring a lot of effort
Stroboscopic effect	The appearance of light in a slow, cyclical manner or stationery.
Subjective	Based on opinion, not on fact (the opposite of objective)
Sub-metering	The installation of metering devices to measure actual energy consumption additionally to the primary utility energy meter
Superficial	Only on the surface, does not go below the skin
Superheater	A piece of equipment that is used to dry the wet steam for use in steam engines or other processes
Sustainable development	Development that meets the needs of the present without compromising the ability of future generations to meet their own needs (according the un)
Synchronous	To exist or take place at the same time
Synchronous speed	The rated speed of the motor
System head curve	The relationship between the total head and the pump discharge
Systems approach	An approach used to analyze something as being a system and consisting of a set of parts related to one another.
Tensile strength	The resistance of a material against breaking under tension
Thermal	Relating to heat and temperature
Thermal comfort	When you are happy with the temperature of your environment.
Thermal energy	The energy developed through the use of heat energy; it is generated and measured by heat
Thermal envelope	Some form of insulation layer that controls heat flow out the building, is part of a building envelope but may be in a different location such as in a ceiling
Thermal layer/ envelope	The part of a building envelope that controls heat within the building.
Thermal processes	It refers to the process that takes place when a substance changes from one state to another; the steps or path between the initial and final thermodynamic states

Thermocouple	A thermoelectric device for measuring temperature, consisting of two wires of different metals connected at two points, a voltage being developed between the two junctions in proportion to the temperature difference
Thermodynamics	The study of physics that focuses on heat and energy relations to energy and work.
Thermometer	An instrument used to measure the temperature and indicate it.
Thermostat	A device, as in a home heating system a refrigerator, or an air conditioner, that automatically responds to temperature changes and activates switches controlling the equipment
Thermostatic	Of or relating to a thermostat
Three phase active power	The power of the three-phase motor.
Thyristor	A solid-state semi-conductor with alternating layers of n and p-type material; it is used as a bistable switch
Transients	Refers to short mismatches on the voltage, current or frequency.
Unitary	Relating to a unit or units
Unity	It refers to the power factor of 1,0 which is obtained when current and voltage are in phase
U-value	The overall heat transfer coefficient that describes how well a building element conducts heat or the rate of transfer of heat (in watts) through one square meter of a structure divided by the difference in temperature across the structure
Va/m²	Volt ampere per square meter
Vaporize	When a liquid changes into a gas due to higher temperatures
Variable speed drive	Equipment used to control the speed of machinery
Vector sum	The result of the addition of two or more vectors
Vectors	This is a quantity that has both magnitude and direction
Veneer	A non-load bearing layer of masonry on the exterior of an enclosure
Vgb	The name for another (unknown) power supply utility
Vital signs	Are measurements of the body's basic functions, the four basic vital signs are pulse rate, breathing rate, body temperature and blood pressure

Voltage optimization	This is a term given when there is a controlled reduction in the voltage received by the consumer in order to reduce energy use and power demand
Volumetric pricing	Pricing strategy that allows discounts for bulk purchases
Waste heat recovery	The process of recovering waste heat (heat not used by a certain process) and using it elsewhere
Water use inventory	A list showing estimated water use or consumption
Wick	A strip of porous material up which liquid fuel is drawn by capillary action to the flame in a candle, lamp, or lighter
Wind washing	Cold air passing through insulation
Windings	Wires or conductors that are wound around an object to form a coil
Zero-referenced	The object that it is being referenced against is equal to zero

Resources

The following resources were used in writing this manual.

- BEAT Course
- http://www.usgbc.org/redirect.php?DocumentID=3340
- http://www.socomec.com/files/live/sites/systemsite/files/DOCUMENTATION/UPS_hors_cata/power_quality_audit/doc_109043.pdf
- Krarti, M. 2010. Energy Audit of building systems: An engineering approach. CRS Press. USA. Second edt.
- https://chemengineering.wikispaces.com/Pressure
- http://www.chm.davidson.edu/VCE/Calorimetry/HeatCapacity.html
- http://blog.khymos.org/2007/02/
- https://en.wikipedia.org/wiki/Convection
- http://www.engineeringtoolbox.com/radiation-heat-transfer-d_431.html
- http://energy.gov/energysaver/articles/types-insulation
- https://www.nrcan.gc.ca/sites/www.nrcan.gc.ca/files/oee/pdf/publications/infosource/pub/cipec/energy-audit-manual-and-tool.pdf
- http://vitalsigns.ced.berkeley.edu/res/downloads/rp/hvac/hvac-sml_opt.pdf
- http://greenlivingideas.com/2014/09/26/the-basics-of-hvac/
- http://www.nwu.ac.za/faculty-engineering-energy-saving-home-water-heating-systems
- http://yourenergysavings.gov.au/energy/hot-water/gas-hot-water
- https://www.gbcsa.org.za/green-star-rating-tools/existing-buildings-performance-pilot/
- http://hdimagelib.com/green+building+design
- http://www.buildingscience.com/documents/digests/bsd-013-rain-control-in-buildings

- http://evstudio.com/top-ten-ways-to-reduce-energy-demand-in-a-net-zero-building/
- http://www.cs.berkeley.edu/~culler/cs294-f09/m197content.pdf
- Wikipedia, the different types of hazards in the workplace.
- http://www.slideshare.net/whitecardonlineau/fire-hazards-on-construction-sites-14949588
- http://www.hse.gov.uk/risk/identify-the-hazards.htm
- http://www.slideshare.net/speak2vinod/fire-hazards-in-a-building
- http://www.wikihow.com/Calculate-Joules
- http://physicsnet.co.uk/gcse-physics/energy-transfers-efficiency/
- http://www.solarchoice.net.au/blog/power-and-energy/
- http://www.tc.umn.edu/~dama0023/solar.html
- https://www.hoecoop.org/?q=node/319
- http://timberdesign.co.za/energy-efficiency-understanding-the-new-building-regulations-in-south-africa/
- https://en.wikipedia.org/wiki/Power_factor
- http://engineering.electrical-equipment.org/forum/general-discussion/is-power-factor-correction-that-important
- http://ecmweb.com/content/harmonic-current-and-voltage-distortion
- https://en.wikipedia.org/wiki/Distortion#Harmonic_distortion
- http://legendpower.com/product-info/terms-and-faq/what-are-resistive-loads/
- http://portal.fke.utm.my/energy/electricity-tariff/load-factor/
- GIZ resources
- http://energy.gov/sites/prod/files/2013/11/f5/53827-2.pdf
- www.shutterstock.com
- Occupational Health and Safety Act, 1993 Environmental Regulations for Workplaces, 1987
- http://apps1.eere.energy.gov/buildings/publications/pdfs/building_america/26467.pdf
- http://simplemotor.com/calculations/
- http://webbooks.net/freestuff/motor_selection.pdf
- http://www.unido.org//fileadmin/user_media/Publications/Research_and_statistics/Branch_publications/Research_and_Policy/Files/

Working_Papers/2011/WP112011%20Energy%20Efficiency%20in%20Electric%20Motor%20Systems.pdf?CFID=70390&CFTOKEN=13999318

- http://ecmweb.com/motors/motor-efficiency-power-factor-and-load
- http://www.nrcan.gc.ca/energy/products/reference/15297
- http://www.saskpower.com/wp-content/uploads/electric_motors_efficiency_guide.pdf
- http://www.electricneutron.com/electric-motor/motor-loads-calculation/
- CEA Tenchologies Inc. (2007). *Electrical Motors Reference Guide.*
- Currie, J., & Wilson, I. D. *The Efficient Modelling of Steam Utility Systems.* Auckland: AUT University.
- Patel, P. (2013). Energy saving by modification in HVAC as a cost saving opportunity for industries. *International Journal of Pharmaceutical Sciences and Research* , 3348-3354.
- Occupational Health and Safety Act, 1993 Environmental Regulations for Workplaces, 1987
- http://energy.gov/sites/prod/files/2014/02/f8/Motor%20Energy%20Savings%20Potential%20Report%202013-12-4.pdf
- http://electrical-engineering-portal.com/8-energy-efficiency-improvement-opportunities-in-electric-motors
- http://www.academia.edu/2169234/Applications_of_variable_speed_drive_VSD_in_electrical_motors_energy_savings
- http://www.globalspec.com/learnmore/motion_controls/motors/ac_motors
- http://electrical-engineering-portal.com/4-motor-designs-identified-in-nema-mg1
- http://energy.gov/sites/prod/files/2014/04/f15/amo_motors_handbook_web.pdf
- http://www.pge.com/includes/docs/pdfs/mybusiness/energysavingsrebates/incentivesbyindustry/agriculture/industrial_guidebook.pdf
- http://www.easa.com/MaintainingMotorEfficiency
- http://www.plantengineering.com/single-article/consideration-when-deciding-to-repair-nema-premium-motors/70c9f37073c-da83307342c3b4e49a3ba.html
- http://www.easa.com/sites/files/resource_library_public/EASA_AEMT_RewindStudy_1203-0115.pdf

- http://www.engihub.com/
- http://www.ced.berkeley.edu/courses/fa10/arch244/?p=1481
- http://www.world-nuclear.org/info/Current-and-Future-Generation/Cooling-Power-Plants/
- http://ietd.iipnetwork.org/content/fan-systems
- http://www.eskom.co.za/sites/idm/Documents/124538_Fans_Brochure.pdf
- https://en.wikipedia.org/wiki/Dust_collector
- http://www.nmbtc.com/fans/white-papers/fan_efficiency_important_selection_criteria/
- http://www.pumpfundamentals.com/
- Improving Pumping System Performance – a Sourcebook for Industry (1999)
- Pump Life Cycle Costs – A Guide to LCC Analysis for Pumping Systems (2001)
- Variable Speed Pumping – A Guide to Successful Applications (2004)
- http://energy.gov/sites/prod/files/2014/05/f16/pumplcc_1001.pdf
- http://knowmechanical.blogspot.com/
- http://cdn.intechopen.com/pdfs-wm/40201.pdf
- https://www.compressedairchallenge.org/library/factsheets/fact-sheet04.pdf
- http://us.kaeser.com/Images/Kaeser%20Leaks%20White%20Paper%20-%20web-tcm9-327154.pdf
- https://www.dep.state.pa.us/dep/deputate/pollprev/techservices/paiof/PDF/Compressed%20Air%20System%20Leaks.pdf
- http://www.brighthubengineering.com/hvac/39508-daltons-law-of-partial-pressure-applied-to-air/
- http://www.soloheatinginstallations.co.uk/heat_recovery.htm
- http://forum.downsizer.net/Efficient_kettle_usage__about84023.html&sid=54ef84e9438b2484a4f27193b125e567
- https://hsiehy3.wordpress.com/2011/04/12/psychrometric-charts/

- Taranto, T., Perry, W., McKane, A., Industrial Systems Optimization – Expert Training Manual, Module 4 Compressed Air Systems, U.S. Department of Energy Office of Energy Efficiency and Renewable Energy, April 2012, United Nations Industrial Development Organisation
- The Introduction to The Energy Solutions Training Program © Energy Training Foundation
- The Core Training Program produced by the SADC Industrial Energy Management Project (SIEMP)

Index

About the Author

Albert E. Williams is an energy engineer who has instructed more than 150 training courses on Energy Management, Energy Auditing, Compressed Air-, and Pump-Systems. Since 2006, he has conducted in excess of 220 energy audits, and has traveled and worked in over 40 countries. He is an instructor and contributing developer of various energy training courses, including the internationally certified CIEP™, CEM®, and CEA™. Albert has won multiple international energy engineering awards and serves on the Global Guidance Committee of the Association of Energy Engineers. He is currently internationally certified as CEM®, CEA™, CIEP™, CMVP®, CAP™, REP™, BEP™, CLEP™, CASO-, PSO-, SSO-, and MSO-Expert.